CRETE

Cadogan Books plc
London House, Parkgate Road,
London SW11 4NQ, UK

Distributed in the USA by
The Globe Pequot Press
6 Business Park Road, PO Box 833, Old Saybrook,
Connecticut 06475–0833

Book and cover design by Animage
Cover illustrations by Mary Stubberfield
Illustration on p.175 by F. G. Newton
Maps © Cadogan Guides, drawn by Map Creation Ltd

Series editors: Rachel Fielding and Vicki Ingle
Editing: Linda McQueen
Proofreading: Fiona Clarkson Webb
Indexing: Judith Wardman
Production: Rupert Wheeler Book Production Services

ISBN 1–86011–030–4
A catalogue record for this book is available from the British Library

*The author and publishers have made every effort to ensure the accuracy of
the information in the book at the time of going to press. However, they
cannot accept any responsibility for any loss, injury or inconvenience
resulting from the use of information contained in this guide.*

Output by Bookworm Ltd.,
Manchester. Printed and bound
in the UK by Redwood Books Ltd
on Challenger Cartridge.

CHANIA

About the Author

Dana Facaros and Michael Pauls live in France with their children Jackson and Lily. Dana's Greek father comes from the Dodecanese island of Ikaría, and her golfing mother once shot four holes-in-one in a single year.

Acknowledgements

Thanks to all the countless people who took the time to talk about Crete, especially Jeannette Maraki of the *Kriti News*, Micheli and Despina of Chamezi, and Helen Zachariou. At Cadogan, a special thanks to Linda for her dedication and Kicca for her expertise.

Please Help Us Keep this Guide Up to Date

Every effort has been made to ensure the accuracy of the information in this book at the time of going to press. However, practical details such as opening hours, travel information, standards in hotels and restaurants and, in particular, prices are liable to change. We would be delighted to receive any comments concerning existing entries or omissions. Significant contributions will be acknowledged in the next edition, and authors of the best letters will receive a copy of the Cadogan Guide of their choice.

Contents

Introduction

Column of the Levant,
My Crete, beautiful island,
Your soil is made of gold,
Your each stone a diamond.

traditional Cretan *mantináde*

Golden, diamond Crete is an enchanted isle, one of the last ones anywhere. Other Greeks, with a mixture of envy and awe, call it the *Megalonisos*, the 'big island', a place apart, remote and mysterious: the home of King Minos and his dark labyrinth, of snow-capped mountains blinding in the sun and of memory older than history, of bulls and double axes and indomitable resistance fighters who believed in Freedom or Death and yellow clouds of butterflies in jagged ravines and El Greco and shepherds improvising verses and Zeus of the thunderbolts and bare-breasted goddesses wearing scarlet lipstick, lemon groves and Zorba and Kazantzákis and wild thyme honey and Ariadne spinning on her dancing floor made by Daedalus: Crete is anything but ordinary.

Back in 1942, Henry Miller wrote, 'Crete is a cradle, an instrument, a vibrating test tube in which a volcanic experiment has been performed.' The greatest of these volcanic experiments was ancient Greek culture. Its gods and oldest myths were born with the Minoans, the first civilization on European soil, which burst into bloom like the first rapture of spring and created art shot through with an ecstatic beauty that can take your breath away even after 3500 years. A century ago the Minoans were a secret outside the boundaries of myth, and their discovery has gone a long way in explaining the essential Cretan difference. Having created so much, so early, the big island withdrew into its own world, familiar yet different, Greece in a magnifying glass, a disproportionate enchantment: the colours are richer, the mountains taller, the sun bigger, the drink stronger, the music and dances faster, tempers quicker, laughter easier, perfumes more intense. Imagination is clothed in tangible, sensuous form, then melts into myths and archetypes that tease our deepest dreams.

A Little Geography

Crete on the map is an odd, horned, wasp-waisted creature that seems to scoot along the 35th parallel; midway between Europe, Africa and Asia, the south coast of Crete is only 320km from Egypt and further south than the Mediterranean coasts of Morocco and Algeria. It is Greece's largest island, and the fifth largest in the Mediterranean after Sicily, Sardinia, Cyprus and Corsica, roughly 260km long, and an average of 50km wide (160 by 30 miles). These rather limp numbers are ground into nonsense, however, by Crete's tremendous mountain ranges, especially the White Mountains (Lefká Óri) and the Idean Mountains (Psilorítis), both topping 2400m (8000ft), covered with snow until June and making any journey from A to B an adventure. Crete simply wouldn't be Crete without this tremendous spine: the mountains are responsible for its extraordinary beauty, its diverse climates, its free independent spirit and resistance to heavy-handed invaders, be they Dorian, Roman, Venetian, Turkish or Nazi, and its tendency towards mysticism (peaks and caves—3000 of them—were the first shrines, even before the Minoans). In many cases the same peaks and caves have churches on or in them to this day.

Just under half a million people call Crete home, and they speak with many distinct accents and dialects. There are enough local ones that a shepherd from Sfakiá in the west often cannot understand his counterpart from Sitía in the east; across Crete, linguists have found four different pronunciations of the sound *sti*, perhaps a last echo of the Achaeans, Dorians, Pelasgians and Eteocretans described by Homer in the *Odyssey*. It's also a matter of pride: not only do Cretans like to emphasize the things that set them apart from other Greeks, but what sets them apart from other Cretans.

Unlike most Greek islands, Crete rarely looks to the sea, but turns inward, self-absorbed and nearly self-sufficient. The island has in effect only three seasons: the grey, rainy one, from November to the end of February; an exuberant spring, when nearly all of its 1500 kinds of flowers seem to bloom at once; and a dry hot summer of harvests—the Mediterranean winter, if you will. Vineyards, olive and citrus groves cover the coastal plains and hillside terraces of the north. Cereals, potatoes, pears, apples, walnuts and chestnuts come from the well-watered mountain plains, especially up around Lassíthi. Acres of plastic greenhouses blanket the south coast, providing no advantage to the landscape but bushels of winter vegetables and fruit for the rest of Greece, including bananas, avocados and pineapples. Sheep, goats and cattle provide protein and a variety of cheeses. Aromatic and pharmaceutical plants are an important source of income, and in the past so much honey was exported that the island's Venetian name, Candy, became synonymous with sweets.

Crete's hot climate and bountiful beaches make it a major package holiday destination from early spring until the end of October; there were 2,380,000 charter flight arrivals in 1994: 1.5 billion drachmas (around $450 million) added to the economy through tourism. After the Acropolis, Knossós receives more visitors than any site in Greece. Much of this business, however, is concentrated on the northeast coast, and is easy enough to escape from by foot, motor-bike or car—or by coming out of season, in early spring.

A Guide to the Guide

The three mighty mountain ranges of Crete neatly divide the island into four sections. These have become modern Crete's political divisions and are used for reference in this book, by province (*nomós* in Greek). Contrary to most guides to Crete, which start in Herákleon and bounce around, the desciptions in this book run from west to east, not only for consistency's sake but also because the west is the best place to start.

The White Mountains define the westernmost *nomós* of **Chaniá**, with the elegant city of Chaniá, a string of sandy beaches and a series of spectacular keen-edged gorges cutting their way through the mountain fastness to the Libyan sea; the Gorge of Samariá, the longest in Europe, is only the most famous. Generally speaking, this province is the best for wildflowers and wildlife and traditional villages in the mountains and others by the sea, with a few tavernas that have rooms, ideal for travellers put off by mass tourism; even the largest resort, Paleochóra, is hardly overwhelming.

Between the White Mountains and Psilorítis (Mount Ida) is the rugged *nomós* of **Réthymnon**, with the delightful little minaret-studded city of Réthymnon, more long north coast beaches, famous monasteries and caves, the Amári valley and other traditional villages on the slopes of Mt Ida, with their frescoed Byzantine churches, and the laid-back resort of Ag. Galíni in the south.

Between Psilorítis and the Lassíthi Mountains lies the *nomós* of **Herákleon**, home of the grey, sprawling, unavoidable capital of Crete, its superb archaeology museum and Knossós. The *nomós* also contains the biggest concentration of major Minoan sites at Mália, Phaistós, Ag. Triáda and Archánes, the Dorian-Roman city of Górtyn, and the cave-lined beach of Mátala. There's more superb scenery, especially around the Diktean mountain villages and Zarós. Just east of Herákleon, the excellent sandy beaches are densely lined with package resorts, great if you want to meet lots of foreigners and disco the night away.

East of the Lassíthi (or Diktean) Mountains is the *nomós* of **Lassíthi**, the hottest and driest province, where spring comes earlier and the south coast is lined with plastic tunnels. Cosmpolitan Ag. Nikólaos is the provincial capital, set among the spectacular cliffs around the Gulf of Mirábelo and fancypants resorts on the road to Eloúnda. Consider Sitía to the east as a genteel alternative to Ag. Nikólaos. The lofty Lassíthi plateau with its Diktean cave, the frescoed church of Kéra Panagía at Kritsá, the Dorian city of Lato, and Palm Beach at Vaï are favourite excursions. There are innumerable minor Minoan sites, and a pair of major ones, the Palace of Zákros and Gourniá.

A Note on Pronunciation

There is no general agreement within Greece on a standard method of transliterating the Greek alphabet into Roman letters. This means that you will constantly come across many variations in the spellings of place names and words, in books, on maps and on road signs. When transcribing, we have used D for the Greek *delta* (Δ), which you may see elsewhere as DH or TH; CH for *chi* (X), which is pronounced like the 'ch' in 'loch' and which you may see written as H, e.g. in Chaniá; F for *fi* (Φ), which you may see as PH; and G for the Greek *gamma* (Γ), which sounds more like a guttural GH verging on a Y, e.g. with '*agios*', pronounced more like '*ayios*'. Exceptions are made where there is a common English variant, e.g. Phaistós not Festos.

Stressing the right syllable is essential to the correct pronunciation of Greek; in this book the stressed letter of each word or name is accented with an acute (´) accent.

Travel

By Air

There are no direct scheduled flights to Crete from the UK or North America, but in summer there is a stream of direct charter flights from at least seven UK airports to Herákleon, and to a far lesser extent to Chaniá. Coming from outside Europe, your best hope for a bargain is a discount flight to London, and from there a last-minute charter flight to Crete at a bucket shop. Another alternative is flying to Athens, from where connections to Crete are easy and frequent. **Olympic** has five to six flights daily from Athens to Herákleon, and three to Chaniá, as well as several flights weekly to Herákleon and Chaniá from Thessaloníki and Rhodes. **Kríti Air**, a new private airline, has additional flights between Athens and Chaniá and Herákleon, which usually underprice Olympic.

Scheduled Flights

Scheduled flights are more expensive than charters but offer the advantage of letting you book well in advance and staying longer than permitted on a charter. There are direct flights to Athens from London, Manchester and Belfast: **Olympic**, **Virgin** and **British Airways** are the main carriers. Superpex flights offer substantially reduced fares, with flights from London ranging from £190 low season to £280 high season. They must, however, be paid for instantly and are not refundable or flexible. Normal flight prices range from £212 return midweek in low season to £298 weekends in high; a night flight can save your money.

From North America there's an ever-changing number of airlines serving Athens; if you use **Olympic Airways** you may get a cheap ongoing flight to Crete included in the deal. American economy fares range from $900 New York–Athens in low season to $1300 high season.

Olympic Airways:	London ✆ (0171) 409 3400/493 3965.
	New York ✆ (212) 838 3600.
	Herákleon: ✆ (081) 223 400/229 191.
British Airways:	London ✆ (0181) 897 4000.
Virgin Atlantic:	London ✆ (01293) 747747; rec. info. ✆ (01293) 511581.
Delta:	New York ✆ (800) 241 4141/(800) 221 1212.
KLM:	Montreal ✆ (514) 933 1314.
TWA:	New York ✆ (800) 892 4141; ✆ (212) 290 2141.
	London ✆ (0171) 439 0707.

Bona-fide students under 26 are sometimes eligible for discounts, especially with Olympic Airways who currently offer 25% discount to ISIC card holders on all connecting flights from Athens to the islands, even when booked from London: **Trailfinders**, 42–50 Earls Court Road W8 6FT, ✆ (0171) 937 5400; **STA Travel**, 86 Old Brompton Road, London SW7 or 117 Euston Road, London NW1, ✆ (0171) 937 9962; and **Campus Travel**, 52 Grosvenor Gardens, London SW1, ✆ (0171) 730 8111, can get you some of the best current deals. Returning from Crete, it is advisable to confirm your return flight a few days prior to departure.

Charter Flights

'The air and sky are free,' Daedalus told son Icarus as he planned his escape from Crete on those ill-fated wings. They aren't any more, but you can fly for less if you look around. Charter flights to Crete are big business and swoop down from nearly every northern European capital, including Prague and Warsaw: from the UK and Ireland in the summer there are departures for Herákleon from Gatwick, Luton, Manchester, Newcastle, Glasgow, Belfast, Dublin and the Midlands. Check the travel sections in your weekend newspapers for likely deals. In the **UK**, 'bucket shops' specialize in spare charter tickets, or try the consolidators, firms like Avro who offer flight-only deals, often at the last minute and very cheap. They all advertise widely: browse through *Time Out*, the *Evening Standard* or the Sunday papers. **Americans** and **Canadians** with more time than money may find the cheapest way of getting to Crete is to take a trans-Atlantic economy flight to London and from there to buy a bucket shop ticket to Athens or Crete, although this may be tricky in July or August. UK charters run from May to mid October but some firms feature early specials in March and April depending on when Greek Easter falls, usually from Gatwick and Manchester.

Charter flight tickets have fixed outward and return dates and are governed by several rules as the Greek Civil Aviation Authority sees them as concessions, like rail saver tickets, and imposes similar restrictions. Tickets are valid for a minimum of three days and a maximum of six weeks and must be accompanied by an accommodation voucher stating the name and address of the hotel, youth hostel villa or campsite, even if it's mythical. Although a formality, every so often there is a crackdown aimed at what the Greeks consider undesirables flouting the law.

Student/youth charters are exempt from the voucher system and can also be sold as one-way tickets. If you're under 26 or a full-time student under 32 with an **International Student Identity Card** to prove it, you can stay longer. If you're not a student but under 26, STA Travel offers a **Go 25** card, a subsitute for the ISIC. Even if you intend to stay longer than four weeks or travel to other countries, using just half a charter ticket may be cheaper than a scheduled flight, so shop around. Sometimes last-minute package deals, especially in spring and autumn, can be even cheaper than flights if you are prepared to drop everything and jet off. If you are going it alone and travelling light some companies sell courier seats cheap. Your stay is restricted to 10–14 days and you can only take 10kg of hand baggage. The new Greek departure tax is added on to all ticket prices. The good news is that you can now fly 'open jaws' into one Greek airport and out of another. Not all tour operators offer this option, so check before you buy your ticket.

discounts and special deals

Avro plc, ✆ (0181) 715 1999/1910; (0161) 489 2989; (01293) 567916; (0141) 303 0303. Flights from Gatwick, Manchester, Glasgow, Luton, Cardiff, Newcastle and Birmingham.

Owners Abroad Travel Ltd, ✆ (01293) 554400; (0161) 742 2277; (0121) 666 6688. Flights from Gatwick, Manchester, Birmingham.

Meridian Travel, ✆ (0171) 493 4312/0641. Athens charters from Gatwick and Manchester.

Aleco's Tours, ✆ (0171) 267 2092. Olympic Airways consolidator.

Island Wandering, ✆ (01580) 860733. Reasonable schedules to Athens, Olympic island packages and 'open jaws' routes. Uses Olympic Airways flights.

Joe Walsh Tours, ✆ (01) 678 9555. Budget fares from Dublin.

Campus Travel, London, ✆ (0171) 730 3402; Leeds, ✆ (0113) 246 1155; Bradford, ✆ (01274) 383261; Bristol, ✆ (0117) 929 2494; Manchester, ✆ (0161) 274 3105; Edinburgh, ✆ (0131) 668 3303; Oxford, ✆ (01865) 242067; Cambridge, ✆ (01223) 324283. Runs own student/youth charters to Athens in summer.

STA Travel, London, ✆ (0171) 937 9921; Bristol, ✆ (0117) 929 4399; Leeds, ✆ (0113) 244 9212; Manchester, ✆ (0161) 834 0668; Oxford, ✆ (01865) 792800; Cambridge, ✆ (01223) 66966. Has special youth/student deals and 'open jaws' tickets.

USIT, branches include: Dublin, ✆ (01) 677 8117; Cork, ✆ (021) 270 900; Belfast, ✆ (01232) 324 073. Student/youth fares from Eire and Northern Ireland.

Flights from Athens to Crete

Flights from Athens to Crete can be booked in advance through **Olympic Airways**, 11 Conduit Street, London W1R 0LS, ✆ (0171) 493 3965. North Americans who do not have a local Olympic Airways office can call toll-free ✆ (800) 223 1226 for information. There's a special price deal but to be assured of a seat, especially in the summer, you should book your ticket as far in advance as possible. In the past few years Olympic Airways have been offering **island-to-**

island flights in season, a pleasant innovation that may preclude the need to go to Athens; routes between Crete and Rhodes, Crete and Santoríni and Crete and Mýkonos seem fairly well-established. It's also possible to get a scheduled 'open jaws' ticket to Athens and on to any permutation of islands, but you have to return home from Athens. At the time of writing the **prices** of one-way flights from Athens to Crete range between 11,000 and 16,000dr.

Olympic Airways (Athens)

6 Óthonos, ✆ 926 9111 (Int. and Dom.).

96 Leofóros Syngroú, ✆ 926 7251/4.

East Airport, ✆ 969 9703 (Int.).

West Airport, ✆ 936 9111 (Int. and Dom.).

children and pregnancy

Free child places on package holidays and discount air fares for tiny travellers vary from company to company: get a good travel agent, trawl through the brochures and read all the small print. The big package operators, like Thomson, geared to family holidays, offer a wide range of child discounts and seasonal savers with in-resort amusements, kiddie clubs and baby-sitting for the very young as well as deals for children under twelve in hotels and teenagers up to seventeen in self-catering accommodation.

On some UK charter flights infants under two travel free on a full fare-paying adult's lap, while on others you may be charged £15–£20 for the baby, usually 10% of the adult fare. Children from two to twelve cost 25%–65%, and over twelve you'll have to fork out the full fare. On **Olympic** scheduled flights you'll have to pay 67% of the adult fare for children aged two to twelve, 10% for infants under two. Children go for half the full fare on all Greek domestic flights. By law children aged two and over travelling on British registered airlines must occupy a seat and have a full baggage allowance. Babies under six months must travel on your lap with a lap strap, as must infants up to two unless there's a vacant seat. They don't have a baggage allowance but you can take a pushchair for free. Otherwise infants can travel in a car seat with a safety harness as long as it can be secured facing forward in the aircraft seat. Watch out for birthdays; if your toddler has crossed the magic two-year-old age barrier by the return journey you'll have to pay for another seat. As most airlines won't let single mothers travel with two infants, it may be the answer to have one on the lap and the other in the car seat if you are travelling alone. Explain the position to the airline when you book in case they are adamant about the one child per adult rule or turn you away at the check-in. **Britannia Airways** is especially child-friendly, offering free colouring book and crayons, video cartoons, junior radio show, special children's meals and drinks and nappy-changing facilities.

If you're pregnant, think before you fly. Greek hospitals and maternity services are basic to say the least, so make sure your insurance covers repatriation. Most airlines will carry women up to 34 weeks of pregnancy—Olympic even later—but you will have to provide a doctor's certificate after 28 weeks to prove you are fit and well enough to fly. Again check when you book.

By Rail

There are three daily trains from London to Athens, the *Athenai Express*, the *Acropolis Express* and the *Hellas Express*, all of which take about three days. And a hot, crowded, stuffy three days too. Given the current situation in the former Yugoslavia it is advisable to double-check on trains from Britain to Greece with British Rail International, © (0171) 834 2345.

The alternative and pleasant though slightly costlier route is to go through Italy, either to Ancona or further south to Brindisi, and take the ferry over to Corfu and Pátras. British people under the age of 26 can travel on **Interail** passes, good for a month's rail travel in Europe—which gets you there and back at a reasonable price. Interail passes are also available to British residents over 26 for either 15 days or a month.

Americans and Canadians can buy two-month **Eurail** and **Youth Eurail** passes before leaving home. However, they're a bad bargain if you're only going to Greece, which has a limited rail service. For men over 65 and women over 60, the **Rail Europ** senior card saves up to 50% on rail fares in Greece and several other European countries, and 30% on most sea crossings. It costs £5 and can be purchased at any British Rail Travel Centre by holders of a British Rail card.

By Bus

Taking a bus from London to Athens is a possible alternative if you're afraid to fly—prices are usually about the same as a standby flight. But with 2½ days (or more) on the road and Adriatic ferry, adventures are practically included in the ticket price. **Eurolines**, 52 Grosvenor Gardens, Victoria, London SW1W 0AU, © (0171) 730 8235, offers 3-day journeys from London to Athens which cost around £218 return if you're over 26; there's a £12 saving if you're under 26. Departures from London are on Friday mornings in July, August and September only. **Olympic Bus Ltd**, 70 Brunswick Centre, London WC1 1AE, © (0171) 837 9141, offers 2½-day journeys from London to Athens via Brussels and Italy for a mere £50 one-way, or £100 return, departing London on Friday evenings. A daily bus runs from Thessaloníki to Piraeus/Athens, then boards the ferry to Crete, and takes you directly to Crete. And vice versa. In Chaniá, call © (0821) 23 052; in Herákleon, © (081) 245 020; in Thessaloníki, © (031) 512 122.

From Italy

The only lines that sail direct to Crete from Italy are **Minoan Lines** and **Adriatica** (*see* below). Otherwise, there are daily ferry services from Ancona, Bari, Brindisi, Otranto and Venice to Pátras, most of which call into Corfu the next morning. Passengers are usually allowed a free indefinite stopover in Corfu before continuing to Igoumenítsa or Pátras, but make sure it is noted on your ticket. If you plan to sail in the summer, make reservations in advance, especially if you bring a car (most travel agents can do this for you). Students and young people can get a discount of up to 20%, and you can often cut a similar percentage off the price if you buy a return ticket. The quality of service among the different lines varies; some ships are spanking clean and are plushly furnished—one at least has a laser disco—while others have been in service so long that they creak. However, the sullen demeanour of the crews seems to be uniform.

ferries

Ports	Frequency	Company
Ancona–Corfu–Pátras	6 times a week	Strinzis Lines 26 Aktí Possidónos Piraeus, ✆ 412 9815
Ancona–Corfu–Igoumenítsa–Pátras–Trieste	2/4 times a week	ANEK Lines 54 Amalías Avenue Athens, ✆ 323 3481
Ancona–Igoumenítsa–Corfu–Pátras ´	5 times a week	Minoan Lines 2 Vass. Konstantinoú Athens, ✆ 751 2356
Ancona–Igoumenítsa–Pátras	2 times a week	Marlines 38 Aktí Possidónos Piraeus, ✆ 411 0777 and 422 4950
Brindisi–Corfu–Igoumenítsa–Pátras	3 times a week	Hellenic Mediterranean Lines 28 Amalías Avenue Athens, ✆ 323 6333
Bari–Corfu–Kefaloniá–Igoumenítsa–Pátras	Daily	Ventouris Ferries 26 Amalías Avenue Athens, ✆ 324 0276

Bari–Igoumenítsa	Daily	Arkadia Lines 215 Kifissiás Avenue Athens, ✆ 612 3402
Brindisi–Corfu–Igoumenítsa –Pátras	Daily	Fragline 5a Réthymnou Street Athens, ✆ 822 1285
	Daily	Adriatica 85 Aktí Miaoúli 18538 Piraeus, ✆ 429 1397
	Daily	Hellenic Mediterranean Lines (see above)
Brindisi–Pátras	Daily	Vergina Ferries 274 Alkiviádou Street Piraeus, ✆ 453 1882
	4 times a week	European Seaways 86 Fílonos Street 18536 Piraeus ✆ 429 3903
Brindisi–Kefaloniá–Pátras	Daily in summer	Hellenic Mediterranean Lines (see above)
Brindisi–Corfu	Daily in summer	Marlines (see above)
Venice–Bari–Piraeus–Herákleon– Alexandria	Once a week March–Jan	Adriatica (see above)
Ancona—Kefaloniá–Pátras– Herákleon—Çeşme (Turkey)	Once a week	Minoan Lines (see above)

From Piraeus and Other Greek Ports

Driving from London to Athens at a normal pace takes around 3½ days. Don't even consider driving down unless you are planning to spend a few weeks, and if that's the case the smaller the better, both for squeezing it on to the ferry, and for negotiating the sometimes very narrow village roads.

The people of Crete own the large clean and comfortable ships—among the finest in Greece—that sail nightly from Piraeus to Herákleon and Chaniá, and most nights to Réthymnon, Ag. Nikólaos and Sitía, The 12-hour journey through the night, in a cabin, or on a warm night out on deck, can be quite pleasant besides reminding you that Crete, after all, is an island. In Piraeus, central agents for Crete are **ANEK,** 32 Akti Possidónos ✆ 411 8611, 📠 411 4188 and **Minoan Lines,** 28 Akti Possidónos, ✆ 463 5241 (both for Chaniá and Herákleon); **Rethymniaki,** 2 Akti Possidónos, ✆ 417 7787, 📠 417 8980 (for Réthymnon); and **Nomicos,** 120 Karaískou, ✆ 429 6740, 📠 429 6858 (for Ag. Nikólaos and Sitía).

You can also sail to Herákleon from other Greek ports: daily by ferry or fast catamaran from Santoríni, and frequent connections to Mýkonos, Andros, Náxos, Páros, Tínos, Ios, Sýros, Rhodes, Pátras, and Thessaloníki. Other connections are possible via Crete's smaller ports. From Kastélli ferries sail twice a week to Kýthera and Gýthion, Neápolis and Monemvassía in the Peloponnese. Ag. Nikólaos and Sitía have twice-weekly connection with Kássos, Kárpathos, Rhodes and Mílos.

When purchasing tickets, try to buy them from a shipping line's central agency. Other agencies may tell you that the boat is full, when in truth they've merely sold all the tickets allotted them by the central agency. To get unbiased, non-partisan answers to sailing schedule questions, telephone the port authority (they don't often speak English, however, so you may have to get a Greek to help); phone numbers are included in the 'Getting Around' sections in the text.

On the big Piraeus–Crete ferries the cabins are air-conditioned, but on summer nights sleeping out can be an inexpensive and pleasant alternative, especially if you have a sleeping bag; it can get chillier than you think. It's worth getting on board at least an hour early to claim some quiet deck space.

You'd do well always to keep your ticket with you, at least until the crew enacts its 'ticket control', a comedy routine necessitated by the fact that Greeks don't always check tickets when passengers board. Instead, after one or two pleas on the ship's loudspeaker system for passengers without tickets to purchase them forthwith, you suddenly find all the doors on the boat locked or guarded by bored but obdurate sailors, while officers rove about the decks checking tickets.

Prices, though no longer cheap, are still reasonable, and begin at around 5200dr for a deck class ticket. Children under the age of four travel free, and between four and 10 for half-fare. Over 10 they are charged the full fare. A small car will cost around 18,000dr. In the summer it is wise to buy tickets in advance, to guarantee a place and because they can cost 20% more when bought on board. Refunds are rarely given unless the boat itself never arrives, stuck in Piraeus for tax delinquencies. Boats will arrive late or divert their course for innumerable reasons, so if you have to catch a flight home allow for the eccentricities of the system and leave a day early to be safe.

Entry Formalities

All **European Union** members can stay indefinitely from 1995 on. The only reason you would need special permission to stay would be for working or if complicated banking procedures were involved requiring proof of residence; contact the Aliens Bureau: 173 Leof. Alexandrás, 115 22 Athens, ☏ 790 57211. The formalities for **non-EU tourists** entering Greece are very simple. American, Australian and Canadian citizens can stay for up to 3 months in Greece on presentation of a valid passport. South Africans are permitted 2 months.

Getting Around

By Bus

The domestic bus service (ΚΤΕΛ) in Crete is efficient, regular, recently computerized and still relatively cheap. If there's a bus station or ticket booth, you purchase your ticket before boarding; if not, the conductor will sell you one on board. There are never enough seats in the summer, nor is it customary to queue, although if you have a ticket with a seat number you can claim your rights (note that the numbers are on the back of each seat, not on the seat in front; this has led to unseemly international squabbles). Buses are rarely crowded early in the morning.

By Car

Although the buses are fine for basic travel to Crete's larger towns and best-known sites, many others can only be reached by your own transport, be it shoe-leather, motorbike or car. There are so many rent-a-car companies on Crete that it's hard not to fall over them. Many are family-run, and many are ripe rip-offs: read the small print with care and, if it's off season, don't be shy about negiotiating. Arriving at a car hire agent's with a handful of brochures from the competition has been known to strengthen one's bargaining position. If you pay in cash it doesn't hurt to ask for a discount; **Duke of Crete** is one company with branches across the island that usually gives 15%.

Crete has a terrifying accident rate, and not all the fatalities get the little roadside shrines you see because many who die are foreigners. Most of the mishaps happen along the road east of Herákleon, especially when the Old and New roads merge in the middle of resorts like Gouvés (where 50 people, mostly pedestrians, have been killed in the last five years). Traffic regulations and signalling comply with standard practice on the European continent (i.e. driving on the right) and most signs have their Roman equivalents (if you can read them through the bullet holes, that is— Cretan hunters like to use them for target practice). Crossroads and low visibility in the mountains are probably the greatest hazards. Where there are no right-of-way signs at a crossroads, give priority to traffic coming from the right, and always beep your horn on blind corners. If you're exploring, you may want to take a spare container of petrol along, as petrol stations can be scarce on the ground and only open during shop hours. There is a speed limit of 50km per hour (30mph) in inhabited areas; other speed limits are indicated by signposts in kilometres.

By Motorbike or Moped

Motorbikes and the even more popular mopeds are ideal for getting around Crete in the summer. It almost never rains, parking is easy and what could be more pleasant than a gentle thyme-scented breeze freshening your journey over the mountains? Motorbikes (Greeks call them *papákia*, 'little ducks', supposedly for the noise they make) are inexpensive to hire, and include third party coverage in most cases. For larger motorbikes (and you'll need one if you want to get up Crete's mighty mountains) you may be asked to show a driver's licence. The down-sides: not a few hospital beds in Crete are occupied every summer by careless tourists, and the noise in the villages drives everyone (at least everyone not astride one) buggy. By law, helmets are required at all times; in practice the only ones you'll see are worn about the elbow, which judging by the daredevil way they pilot their machines is where many young Greeks keep their brains.

By Bicycle

Cycling has not caught on in mountainous Crete, either as a sport or as a means of transport, though you can usually hire an old bike in most major resorts; one place in Chaniá hires out mountain bikes (*see* p.88) and a tour company in Réthymnon (p.136) runs excursions that take you and the bike to the top of the mountains so you only have to cruise downhill. If you're a serious cyclist, planes carry bicycles for a small fee, and Greek boats generally take them along for nothing.

Special-interest Holidays

Holidays based around a special interest are an increasingly popular way to visit Crete. Your National Greek Tourist Office (for addresses, *see* p.34) may have additional listings.

From the UK

British Museum Tours, 46 Bloomsbury Street, London WC1B 3QQ, ✆ (0171) 323 8895. Archaeological guided tours.

Filoxenia, Sourdock Hill, Barkisland, Halifax HX4 0AG, ✆ (01422) 371796. Guided archaeological tours in Western Crete; spring nature-watch tours and walking in ancient Crete.

Simply Crete, Chiswick Gate, 598–608 Chiswick High Road, London W4 5RT, ✆ (0181) 994 4462. Walks off the beaten track, spring flowers, watercolour holidays.

Artscape, Suite 4, Hamlet Court Business Centre, 18 Hamlet Court Road, Westcliff on Sea, Essex SS0 7LX, ✆ (01702) 435990. Painting courses in Western Crete appealing to golden girls and more mature professional women.

Pure Crete, 79 George Street, Croydon, Surrey CR0 1LP, ✆ (0181) 760 0879. Wildflower and painting holidays.

Waymark Holidays, 44 Windsor Road, Slough SL1 2EJ, ✆ (01753) 516477. Guided hiking groups in the gorges and spring and autumn breaks.

Peregrine Holidays, 40–41 South Parade, Summertown, Oxford OX2 7JP, ✆ (01865) 511642. Natural history and walking tours.

Norfolk and Suffolk Wildlife Holidays, Dudwick House, Buxton, Norwich NR10 5HX, ✆ (01603) 278296. Join members of the Norfolk and Suffolk Wildlife Trust on botany and birdwatching trips.

Ramblers Holidays, Box 43, Welwyn Garden City, Hertfordshire AL8 6PQ, ✆ (01707) 331133. Walking tours with an emphasis on archaeology and wildflowers.

From the USA

Archeological Tours, 271 Madison Ave, New York, NY 10016, ✆ (212) 986 3054. Tours of the Minoan and other sites with special guest lecturers.

Classic Adventures, P.O. Box 153, Hamlin, NY 14464, ✆ (716) 964 8488, toll free (800) 777 8090. Walking and cycling tours of Crete; their guide is also an archaeology expert.

Cloud Tours, 645 Fifth Avenue, New York, NY 10022, ✆ (212) 753 6104, toll free (800) 223 7880, ✉ (212) 980 6941. Scuba-diving tours, honeymoon tours.

Practical A–Z

Children

Greece is one of the best Mediterranean countries to bring a child, as children are not barely tolerated as they are in more 'sophisticated' holiday resorts, but generally enjoyed and encouraged. Depending on their age, they go free or receive discounts on ships and buses. You can also save on hotel bills by bringing sleeping bags for the children. However, if they're babies, don't count on Crete's pharmacies stocking your baby's brand of milk powder or baby foods—they may have some, but it's safest to bring your own supply. Disposable nappies, especially Pampers, are widely available.

Travelling with a baby is like having a special passport. Greeks adore them, so don't be too surprised if your infant is passed round like a parcel. Greek children usually have an afternoon nap (as do their parents) so it's quite normal for Greeks to eat *en famille* into the wee hours of the night. The attitude to children is very different to the British one of being seen but not heard—Greek children are spoiled rotten. Finding a babysitter is never a problem. If you're renting holiday accommodation on Crete, **Kid-Equip** hires out baby and toddler equipment for your stay (contact Tracey James, © (0897) 41 381).

Superstitions are still given more credit than you might expect; even in the most cosmopolitan of households you'll see babies with amulets pinned to their clothes or wearing blue beads to ward off the evil eye before their baptism. Beware of commenting on a Greek child's intelligence, beauty or whatever, as this may call down the jealous interest of the old gods. The response in the old days was to spit in the admired child's face, but these days, superstitious grannies will say the ritual 'phtew-phtew-phtew', as if spitting, to protect the child from harm.

Climate and When to Go

Crete manages to squeeze in three different climates: a typical Mediterraean in the north, hot and dry in the south, and cool and temperate up in the mountains in the middle. In general, the ideal time to visit is towards the end of April; when you'll avoid the worst crowds; the Libyan Sea is usually warm enough for bathing, the wild flowers are glorious and the higher mountains are still capped with snow. Note that the Gorge of Samariá doesn't open until 1 May, when its torrent recedes sufficiently for safe passage. The first rains usually begin at the end of September, fall their hardest in November and December, and practically come to halt by May. October is another good month, with many perfect days and a lingering warm sea. In summer, especially in August, the *meltémi* winds from the Aegean tend to whip northern Crete head-on for several days at a stretch, making for slightly cooler temperatures and frothing seas. The south wind from Africa, the *notos,* is said to make the sap rise in the spring, both in trees and men.

Average Monthly Temperatures in °Celsius

J	F	M	A	M	J	J	A	S	O	N	D
12.3	12.5	13.8	16.8	20.4	24.4	26.4	26.4	23.0	20.3	17.2	14

Average Monthly Sea Temperatures in °Celsius

J	F	M	A	M	J	J	A	S	O	N	D
15.2	15.4	16	18.7	20.6	24	25.9	25.6	23	22.4	19	16

Events and Cultural Attractions

Every church has its *panegýri*, or saints' day festival, celebrated with various degrees of enthusiasm. Most of the best ones are up in the interior villages; along the coast, events are organized with tourists in mind, although the Cretans attend them as well. There are local listings in the main text; main annual events, including some of the bigger *panegýria*, are listed below. Note that festival dates for saints' days vary over a period of several given days, or even weeks, due to the Greek liturgical calendar's calculations for Easter; check these locally. It is also important to remember that the main partying happens the night *before* the saint's day.

April

Good Friday, big fair at Voukouliés (Chaniá).

Easter, Ag. Nikólaos. Resurrection service, burning of effigy of Judas and other celebrations; also at Toploú monastery and Chersónisos.

23rd: St George's Day, at Asigonía. Shepherds bring cattle to be blessed in the church, and fresh milk is distributed to all, followed by a huge feast. Also in Plakiás.

May

Constantine and Helen's Day, Nochia (Kíssamos). Religious service and feast of seafood, cheese and wine, with traditional songs (*tavlas*) and dances.

Last Sunday: Virgin of Thymianis, Chóra Sfakíon.

June

Klidónas Day, Chaniá. Traditional feast celebrating the old custom of water-divining for a husband, with amusing songs and ethnic dances.

Tomato Day. Age-old Cretan festival in the village of Plátanos near Kíssamos.

Apricot Festival, Achlade (Réthymnon).

July

Lato Festival. Artistic events in Ag. Nikólaos and the ancient city of Lato.

Kyrvia Festival. Festivities in Ierápetra celebrating one of the town's ancient names.

Kritsá Festival. More culture in the village of Kritsá near Ag. Nikólaos, Crete.

Kornaria Festival, Sitía. Wide range of cultural events in the birthplace of 15th-century Cretan poet Kornáros.

Crete International Festival, Chaniá. Greek and foreign dance troupes, exhibitions and local celebrations.

Homage to Cretans Abroad. Evenings of traditional Cretan music and song, athletics games and folk art exhibitions at Kastélli-Kíssamou.

Gavalchori Folk Festival with festivities organized by the local Folk Art Museum in the Cretan village.

17th: Ag. Marína, at Ag. Pelagía and Ag. Marína.

Wine Festival in Skepasti (Réthymnon).

Last ten days: Réthymnon Wine Festival.

July and August: Lato Cultural Festival with handicrafts exhibits, Ag. Nikólaos; also the **Kyrvia**, Ierápetra—cultural events and exhibitions.

26th: Ag. Paraskévi, Kalýves and Phalassarná (Chaniá).

27th: Ag. Panteleimon, Kaló Chório (Lassíthi), Phouní (Chaniá), Árvi (Herákleon)

August

Irákleio Festival, Herákleon. Cultural events organized by the city.

First 10 days: Musical August, Paleochóra.

6th: Transfiguration, Eloúnda and Georgioúpolis.

Renaissance Fair. Wide range of cultural events in Réthymnon.

10th–15th: the Anogeia, competitions in Cretan song, dance and *lýra* at Anógia. Also, **Grape Festival**, at Epano (Herákleon).

10th–25th: Cultural events, dances and fish evenings at Tymbáki.

15th: Assumption of the Virgin Mary, the biggest *panegýri* of them all at Palaíkastro, Neápoli, Koxáre, Ierápetra, Chrysoskalítissa Monastery, Kolimbári, Theríssos, Archánes, Veneráto, Mochós, Kali Liménes, Koudoúma Monastery.

Sultanina Grape Festival, Sitía.

26th: St John's Day, in Balí.

September

14th: Timios Stavros, Alikianós (Chaniá). Wine, music and song.

15th: Ag. Nikitas, Frangokástello.

First Sunday after the 20th: Chestnut Festival at Élos. Merry-making and old songs, and sweets made from chestnuts offered to visitors.

24th: Panagia Myrtidiotissa, Spiliá (Chaniá). One of the largest *panegýria* in Crete, with plenty of food, wine, singing and dancing.

End of month: Raisin Festival, Peramá.

October

7th: St John the Hermit, Gouvernétou (Akrotíri). Day-long feast including improvized singing.

Fish evening, Gourniá. Free fish dinners and wine.

November

Tsikoudiá Festival, Voukoliés, in Kíssamos, where you can taste the local *tsikoudiá*, slightly less powerful than rocket fuel.

30th: Ag. Andreas, Malaxa (Chaniá). A Cretan pot-luck lunch after the church service.

December

6th: Ag. Nikoláos, in Pánormos.

14th: Ag. Barbara, Herákleon.

Food and Drink

> *'...well, you just fill yourself up with more heaps of luscious food, which doesn't all turn into dung. There's something which stays, something that's saved and turns into good humour, dancing, singing, wrangling even—that's what I call Resurrection'.*

Níkos Kazantzákis, *Zorba the Greek*

As Zorba himself says, true eating in Crete is more than an intake of calories, but it is not anything like the religious gourmet epiphanies you expect from the culinary temples of Italy or France. Rather, on Crete, dining is not an end but a means, the always good excuse to get together with as many family members and friends as can squeeze around the table; a meal out is not the prelude to an evening out, it *is* the evening out. Because of the intense heat in summer, Greek families tend to eat a late lunch at home followed by their siesta or *mesiméri*. Housewives spend all morning cooking but in the evening, especially at weekends, everyone will head out of doors, working up an appetite and meeting friends during the *vólta* or ritual stroll to see and be seen, before choosing a taverna. Greeks eat late, rarely before 10pm, and meals can go on into the small hours, often increasingly boisterous, punctuated with fiery discussions, maybe bursts of song or dance, if there's sufficient *kéfi* or 'soul' in the air. Across Crete you'll find large, mostly outdoor country tavernas called '*Kentro Kritiko*' which offer live Cretan music, dancing and singing, and sometimes exuberant pistol shots in the air.

Although food is not the prime consideration, the poor reputation Greece has acquired in the kitchen comes from the growing pangs of tourism: too much, too fast, and too many people who never should have opened restaurants geared up to mass-produce the ubiquitous village salad with a sliver of feta, sad reheated moussaká, kebabs, livid pink taramosaláta and more kebabs, or strange hybrid dishes to appeal to Germans, Brits and Scandinavians who want food from back home. Instead of being welcomed into the kitchens to choose your meal, garish photoboards are springing up outside tavernas to show off what's on the menu McDonald's-style. *Wiener Schnitzel*, fish and chips, pizza, *smorgasbord*, 'English breakfast' are all on offer along with that other delicacy, 'amboorgass'. Add cold tough chops, barbecued chicken, a few stuffed vine leaves and expensive fish and those out to make a fast buck have compounded the misguided view that all Greek food is unimaginative, largely inedible and best fed to the cats.

For every taverna that's sold out you can find the real thing if you are prepared to look, ask, and go that extra mile. It's worth it; proper Greek food, prepared from recipes handed down from mother to daughter and making the best of what's in season, is delicious. Vegetables like butter beans, green beans or okra stewed in rich tomato and olive oil sauces; veal in egg and lemon; *briáms* of aubergines and courgettes; spicy sausages; beetroot with hot garlic *skordaliá* dip; stuffed, lightly battered courgette flowers; octopus *stifádo*; beef stew with baby onions, and whitebait so fresh they're almost wriggling—such delicacies are their own reward.Through poverty and resourcefulness Greek cooks have always gathered food for free—fresh young greens from the hills, wild asparagus, sea urchins, snails, fish, fruit and nuts. In many villages in Crete women still make their own cheeses and cook for their families on tiny gas rings or wood-burning ovens outside the house, relying on the local baker to roast their meat or bake their big trays of biscuits.

One criticism levelled at Greek food by tourists is that it's stone-cold. It usually is, and that's because Greek eating habits differ from ours. They think tepid food is better for the digestion than hot. The climate calls for cool food, too, although in winter you can find plenty of hot stews and casseroles. Nor is the essential laid-back lingering over meals possible for anyone overly concerned about hot food. A second criticism is that Greek cuisine is 'swimming in grease'. Food without olive oil is unthinkable to Greeks. They think it aids digestion—it certainly has laxative qualities—and think we're crazy boiling our vegetables until sodden, destroying all the vitamins. They hate waterlogged food. Many recipes call for the rich, oily tomato sauce which is a staple for ragouts and vegetable dishes known as *latherá*, so it's difficult to avoid. If you don't like olive oil you can ask for things *chorís láthi*, without oil, or stick to grills and roasts from the barbecue or rotisserie. Look for grills to order, *tis óras*, delicious free-range chickens, lamb or fish scattered with local herbs.

Eating habits are changing, though, as modern Western ways get a grip. Fast food is becoming popular and increasingly cosmpolitan in Crete's four capitals: *souvláki*, gyros and Greek burger joints, pizzerias, gelaterias, and stands catering to European sweet teeth with doughnuts (ΝΤΟΝΥΤΣ), croissants and crèpes offer solace to the homesick, impecunious, and teenaged.

Eating Out

So how can you find a good place to eat? The main rule applies here as elsewhere: look for locals. Greek families, workmen, fishermen aren't going to throw away hard-earned cash on tourist food. The back-street taverna may look grotty with plastic tablecloths held down by elastic, hard wooden chairs, and plates and cutlery that don't match, but you can bet that the cooks know what's what and you'll have a meal to remember for a fraction of tourist-trap prices. A second rule: the best eateries are almost never in the obvious places. Rarely do they enjoy good views or depend on the passing trade; many favourites are a few miles out of town, buried in the country or some unlikely suburb.

Greek eating places are divided into five categories by the police, who fix the prices. **Tavernas** and ***estiatória*** (restaurants) are found everywhere and the differences between them tend to get a bit blurred. But you'll generally find the *estiatório* has a wider menu, is a bit more upmarket and serves the kind of food you'll find in Greek homes. Tavernas are like family-run bistros and can range from shacks on the beach to barn-like affairs providing music and entertainment in the evening. There may not be a menu as such. The waiter will reel off what's on or you can go and have a look for yourself. Often choice depends on what fate has produced. Mine host may have a dish of the day, lobster or a special fish (if by any chance this happens to be a 'silver snapper', jump for it and damn the expense).

Wherever you eat, a typical meal will be bread, a selection of communal starters, salads and main courses, and unless you specify or stagger your order, everything will come at you in one fell swoop. In the more touristy areas there's been a move to introduce courses, Euro-style, and some restaurants even serve sweets and coffee, something unheard of in the past, when it was customary to move on to the *kafeneíon* or *zacharoplasteío* for coffee, brandy and a gooey cake or pudding. Another recent trend are lighter meals that consist entirely of **mezédes**—a wide variety of well prepared starters or hors-d'œuvres, salads or small portions, served with a basket of bread. The most typical of these *mezédes* are *taramosaláta* (fish roe paste), *tzatzíki* (cucumber, yoghurt and garlic dip), *melizanosaláta* (aubergine dip), *saganáki* (fried cheese with lemon), *choriatíki*, the famous Greek village salad with tomatoes, onions, cucumbers, green peppers, olives and feta cheese, and the rarer *achinosaláta*, a paste made from sea-urchin ovaries. The menu often includes big trays of different filo pastry pies; maybe green beans, okra or butter beans in sauce or fried courgettes and aubergines. For your main course, you can usually choose between a few oven dishes like *pastítsio*, moussaká or stuffed vegetables or meat grilled while you wait, *tis óras*, which nearly always means chops (*brizóles*), lamb cutlets (*paidhákia*), meatballs (*keftédes* or *tsousoukákia*) or sausages (*loukanika*).

Tavernas catering especially to red-blooded **meat eaters** are called *psistariá*, or grills, offering fresh meat of all kinds, kebabs, home-made sausages, chicken, lamb, pork or *kokorétsi*, a kind of lamb's offal doner kebab, spit-roast over charcoal. Some have electric rotisseries, others hand-cranked *soúvla*. At the seaside you'll find the **fish tavernas**, *psarotavérnes*, specializing in all kinds of seafood from freshly fried calamari, shrimps, giant prawns, to red mullet, swordfish, bream and sardines. Fish is very expensive in Greece, which seems crazy—blame cut-throat overfishing in the Mediterranean—but you can get some cheapies like huge dishes of fresh white-bait (*marídes*), cuttlefish stew (*soupiá*), small shrimps (*garídes*), sometimes cooked in feta cheese, and fish soups like *psarósoupa* or spicy *kakávia*, a meal in themselves with hunks of fresh bread and a bottle of wine. When eating fish soup it's customary to remove the fish, put it on a plate, drink the broth then tuck into the fish. Each type of fish has its own price, and portions are priced by weight.

The *estiatório* is generally open all day and is particularly busy at lunchtime, with a wide range of dishes simmering away in the kitchen. As well as all the vegetable dishes in oil, *latherá*, in giant pots there will be fricassees and ragouts like *stifádo* and *kokinistó*, maybe veal *youvétsi* with tear-drop pasta, lamb roast in paper bags, fish with special sauces, liver, as well as the usual pies and starters. In Crete you may still find a **mayerikó**, a cooking stall where you take your food from the stove by the plateful, *miá merítha*, rather than pick and mix from different pots.

Cretan specialities

Cretan agriculture is dizzying in its variety and richness. Nearly every kind of fruit, from apples to bananas to oranges, grows on the big island, and the plastic farms along the west and south coast may not be very aesthetic but provide many of

Greece's winter vegetables from November on. The large markets at Herákleon and Chaniá have heaving counters of produce and herbs grown on the island (many prettily packaged to make inexpensive gifts, although be aware that what looks at first like an incredibly good deal in saffron is usually merely a decent buy in turmeric). Cretan mountain honey has had a deservedly high reputation since antiquity: the ultimate snack, served in many *kafeneía*, is thick homemade sheep's milk yoghurt sweetened with wild thyme honey.

As the island's honeymoon with tourism matures in the 1990s, there has been an amazing renaissance of traditional Cretan cuisine; rather than clobber visitors with yet more *Wiener Schnitzel* and chips, new restaurants offer a selection of Cretan dishes on their menus. Herbs and spices (the usual Greek dill, mint, oregano, thyme and cinnamon, but also basil, coriander and caraway seeds, long abandoned in the cuisine of the mainland), and local cheeses, many aged in caves in baskets, are two essential ingredients. The best known Cretan cheese, *myzíthra*, is a soft white ewe's milk cheese sold in bags, similar to fresh ricotta. It comes either sweet, a favourite ingredient for Cretan pastries, or lightly salted, made into savoury cheese pies or served on rusks with tomatoes (*dákos*). Other Cretan cheeses are hard yellow *graviéra,* a fresh white whey cheese called *anthótiro* or dried (*anthótiro xeró*), which is sometimes served fried as a *mezéde*. *Ladótiro* is a cheese cured in olive oil; *stáka* a rich white cheese, often baked in a cheese pie or served fried as a hot, creamy dip. Omelettes contain a variety of cheeses, but if you're really hungry order a *sfougáto*, a Cretan omelette stuffed with fried potatoes.

The Cretans do delicious things with lamb, as in a *toúrta* or *kriotópita* , where tit-bits are baked with four kinds of cheese in pastry topped with sesame seeds. Other classics are lamb baked in a tangy yoghurt and egg and lemon sauce, lamb sausages (*spilogáradiyna*), served with a creamy sauce called *áfogalo,* and *arní kleftíko,* 'bandits' lamb', the meat, vegetables and often a bit of cheese, baked in paper (to conceal the aroma and the bandits' whereabouts).

The local love of yoghurt and its widespread use in cooking is perhaps the most obvious Turkish influence in the Cretan kitchen. Rabbit baked with yoghurt, or suckling pig baked in yogurt, lemon, thyme and oregano are delicious. Kid and game dishes, traditional Cretan staples, are stewed in orange and quince juice or served with a rice pilaf. Two types of snails live on the island, either with large dark or small grey shells, and the Cretans eat far more of them than most Greeks, served as a *mezéde* or a ragout, or cooked with rice, tomatoes, garlic and cinnamon. Pies are popular: the Cretans picked up the word '*calzone*' from the Venetians and bake mini spinach pies called *kalitsoúnia*. *Souchilia* are veal pies, often served as a starter. Cretan onion pies are taste treats, but even more popular are *bourékia*, pastries filled with *myzíthra* and courgettes, a recipe left behind by the Turks. One of the most exotic of Cretan dishes is *kephalgraviéra*: a dish made with *graviéra* cheese, tomatoes, aubergines, and artichokes stuffed with minced meat flavoured with bay and nutmeg.

Crete has a sweet tooth, and again everything tends to be baked into a pastry. Two favourites are *amygadalópitta* or almond pie, and *myzithropitákia*, baked with sweet *myzíthra* cheese and served with honey. *Kaltzoúni* are little tarts, made with cheese, honey and cinammon; *mamoúlia* are even more decadent, made of walnuts, honey and *rakí*. A *xerotígana* is a sweet pancake, filled with honey and nuts. At Christmas, look for *melomakárona*, little cakes made with walnuts, cinammon, oranges and cloves and dipped in a honey syrup. At Easter, look for *kalichouniá*, olive oil pastries made from *myzíthra* cheese; for the recipe, *see* pp.224–5. Other favourite Greek sweets drenched in honey such as *baklavá* and *loukoumádes* (little round fritters, served warm) often taste better in Crete than elsewhere, and there seems to be a widespread weakness for *bougátsia*, soft rectangular custard pies in a flaky pastry, ideally served warm.

vegetarians

Of all the people in the EU, the Greeks eat the most meat per capita, but they also eat more cheese per head than anybody, even the French. Basically they just eat a lot, which means (at least in theory, if not always in practice) that there are plenty of dishes for vegetarians, especially from the range of *mezédes:* dips and salads made from a wide range of pulses, and fresh vegetables—artichokes, green beans, aubergines, okra, beetroot leaves, spinach-style greens with lemon, and in some places *cápari*, pickled caper plant which looks like prunings from a rose bush but tastes delicious. There are delicate cheese and spinach pies in flaky filo pastry; peppers and tomatoes stuffed with rice; deep-fried courgettes; *dolmádes*, sometimes using cabbage leaves instead of vines; and *oftés patátes*, potatoes roasted in their jackets. Pasta and pizzas and omelettes are reliable stand-bys; **chorís kréas** means '**without meat**'. One positive sign is that many places, especially the newer ones, now make a point of having a vegetarian dish or two on their menu every day.

etiquette

For many people, dining with Greeks can come as a shock, especially if you've grown up with the idea of each diner having his or her own 'space'. Communal eating with forks and fingers is the norm; starters especially are always shared. In country tavernas it's quite acceptable to pitch into someone else's plate with your fork or offer choice morsels to your neighbour. Men enjoy feeding women guests tit-bits like baby birds, so don't be surprised if you suddenly get a prawn or a chunk of watermelon thrust at you while your table-mates keep pinching your chips. Greeks eat fish heads with gusto, pick up chicken, gnaw at bones.

Side-plates are rare in many tavernas; just plonk your chunk of bread by your plate but again, don't expect that to mean it's your private property. You pour wine for

each other—always guests first—and drink constant toasts, glasses chinking—
steen yámass, good health to us, *steen yássoo* or *yássas*, good health to you or, in
Crete, *Avíva* or *Áspro Páto*—bottoms up. On no account bring your glass down on
another person's (unless your intentions for the evening are entirely dishonourable). If a man does it to your glass, it's best to say 'Cheers' and act dumb,
unless you want to take him up on it.

Greeks find the sight of a person eating alone—especially a female—a piteous spec-
tacle, so you may well be asked to join a table. In Crete's mountain villages it's still
a question of honour to make *xenoí*—the name for guests and strangers are one
and the same—feel welcome. Most tavernas cram people in, joining up tables,
adding chairs to Last Supper proportions, so you won't feel lonely for long. Unless
you expressly want to be on your own, or have a romantic table for two, sharing is
common and it's easy to get chatting to fellow travellers and holidaymakers if you
need some company. Sociability is all if you eat with Greeks and there's no
Western nit-picking over who's had what. You share the food, drink, company and
the bill, *to logariasmó*, although hosts will seldom let foreign guests part with a
drachma. Unless you've agreed to go Dutch or are determined to stand your
corner, the idea of women paying is anathema to them.

prices

A menu, or *katálogos*, will have two-tier prices, with and without tax; you pay the
highest. Prices are fixed according to category and there can be seasonal fluctua-
tions like at Easter. If you suspect you're being ripped off, the system makes it
easier to complain. Menus usually come in Greek and English, or German, sometimes Italian or Scandinavian languages in big international resorts (the English is
often hand-scrawled and full of howlers like Fresh Crap and Lamp Chops—
everyone has their favourite after a while). An average taverna meal—if you don't
order a major fish—usually runs at around 2000–3000dr a head with house wine.
Prices at restaurants or blatantly touristy places tend to be a bit higher, and remote
spots can be just as costly because of extra transport prices. In the 'Eating Out' sections of this book, any price given is per person with house wine.

cafés

In small villages, cafés or **kafeneíons** double as social clubs, frequented almost
exclusively by men, who discuss the latest news and play cards or backgammon.
They serve tiny cups of Greek coffee (*café hellinikó*), with its distinctive finely
ground sludge on the bottom guaranteed to make the novice gag. There are 40 different ways to make this, boiled to a foam with various degrees of sugar, although
glykó (sweet), *métrio* (medium) and *skéto* (no sugar) are the basic orders. It is
always served with a glass of water. Instant coffee (nearly always Nescafé) has by
popular tourist demand become available everywhere, though Greeks prefer it iced
(*frappé*) with or without sugar and milk. Soft drinks, beer, ouzo (the national, clear

anise-flavoured aperitif which many dilute with water) and raki round out the average café fare. Brandy, or Metaxá (the Greeks know it by the most popular brand name), is usually a late-night treat. The more stars on the label (from three to seven), the higher the price and, in theory at least, the better the quality. As the Greeks look askance at drunkenness, alcohol is traditionally served with a little plate of snacks called *mezés*—grilled octopus, nuts, cheese, tomatoes and so on, but now that the world's going to hell in a handcart they don't always come without asking (and paying). Enough people miss them that *mezapolions*, or bars specializing in the little snacks, have begun to sprout up in the cities, alongside new *ouzeries*, or traditional Greek dens of demon ouzo. In tourist haunts, attempts at milkshakes, fruit juices, cocktails and even cappuccinos are available. If drinking tap water makes you nervous, Crete bottles its own natural mineral water: ETANAP from the White Mountains and Zaros (both still and carbonated) from Psilorítis.

bars

The influx of tourists has resulted in the growth of trendy bars, usually playing the latest hit records and serving fancy cocktails as well as standard drinks. These establishments come to life late, after everyone has spent the day on the beach and the earlier part of the evening in a taverna. They used to stay alive much later, but in 1994, amid huge protest, the Greek Government decreed a closing hour for bars (2am weekdays, 3am on weekends), claiming that the nation was nodding off at work after a night on the tiles. In general bars aren't cheap, sometimes outrageously dear by Greek standards, and it can be disconcerting to realize that you have paid the same for your Harvey Wallbanger as you paid for your entire meal half an hour before in the taverna next door. Cocktails have now risen to beyond the 1000dr mark in most bars, but before you complain remember that the measures are triples by British standards. If in doubt stick to beer, ouzo, wine and Metaxá (Metaxá and Coke, if you can stomach it, is generally about half the price of the better-known Bacardi and Coke). You may have difficulty in finding beer, as the profit margin is so small that many bars stop serving it in the peak season, thus obliging you to plump for the higher-priced drinks. Another unfortunate practice in resorts is the doctoring of bottles, whereby some bar owners buy cheaper versions of spirits and use them to refill brand-name bottles. The only way to be sure is to see the new bottle being opened in front of you.

Wine

Crete is not only one of Greece's biggest wine producers, but was first off the mark; in Vathýpetro near Archánes you can see the oldest known wine press in Europe, where some 4000 years ago the Minoans made their favourite plonk. The best wines from Crete are labelled *Kritikós Topikós Oénos,* the equivalent of a *vin de pays*, made with indigenous grape varieties. Chief of these appellations is Pezá, the region south of Knossós, the only place in the world where *vilana* grapes grow, producing a fresh white thirst-quenching wine that is best drunk young. The slightly spicy red wines from Archánes (part of the Pezá appellation) are a blend of low acid, low tannin *kotsífali* (usually about 80%) and tannin-rich black *mandelará* grapes, the latter one of Greece's most ancient varieties. Top Pezá producers include Minoikos, both red (in Greek 'black' or *mavro*) and white (and both costly, in the 2500dr range in a *káva*, or wine shop) and Ktima Lyraki; less expensive but worthy labels include Minos Palace, Logado and Xerolithia. Boutari, one of Greece's biggest wine companies, owns a piece of Pezá, where it is investing heavily in improving *vilana* rootstock and has just begun experimenting with a new grape variety, grenache rouge that bodes well. Crete's second appellation area is Sitía, which chiefly produces strong dry white wines from *liátiko* grapes; Myrto, one of Sitía's better labels, comes in red, white and rosé, all around 11.5%. The vinters of Western Crete around Chaniá and Kastélli-Kíssamou may lack an appellation but produce good ordinary wines (the white has a distinct sherry tinge) and Ostria, a fortified (20%) red wine drunk chilled as an aperitif.

The **house wines** of Crete, red (actually it's usually quite brownish), rosé and white, are often good bargains—*krasí varelísio* or *krasi chéma*, *krasí* meaning 'wine', *varelísio*, 'from the barrel'; *chéma*, 'loose'. The customary way of serving these is in small, copper-anodized jugs, in various metric measures (500cl and 250cl being the most common; a standard wine bottle holds 750cl).

Although Crete in the past never had much use for **retsina**, Greece's best known (and, incidentally, cheapest) wine, the Chaniá co-operative and EKABH in Pezá have started to produce it by popular demand from Hellenophile tourists who have acquired a taste for it. Retsina dates from the time when Greeks stored their wine in untreated pine casks. Many people can be put off by the pungent odour and sharp taste of some bottled varieties; retsina is best appreciated direct from the taverna barrel (*retsína varelísio*). Retsina is admirably suited to Greek food, and after a while you may find non-resinated wines a rather bland alternative. Traditionally it is served in small tumblers, and etiquette requires that they are never filled to the brim or drained empty; you keep topping up your colleagues' glasses, as best you can.

rakí

Rakí (or *tsikoudiá*), an *eau-de-vie* distilled from grape skins and seeds in a hundred mountain stills, is Crete's firewater, its moonshine, the quintessence and its pure hot-blooded soul. Unlike sweetish, anise-flavoured ouzo, a shot of *rakí, a sfyráki*, is always as clear as water and should never be diluted, and never refused; like the bread and salt in the Middle Ages, it is synonymous with hospitality, whether offered in a village *kafeneíon* or a monastery. In early October, old-fashioned stills in communal huts, usually hidden in the mountains, come to life with a huge stoking fire, a blast of steam, and a continuous party of barbecued meats and song, fuelled by fresh still-warm *rakí*: if you get an invitation to see how it's done, it's not to be missed (getting home could be a problem, though). Off the beaten track, *rakí* is often sold in plastic two-litre Coke bottles. If you're buying it in properly taxed glass bottles to take home, Roka Tsikoudia is one of best. Whatever you do, don't light up a cigarette immediately after a snort!

Health

The word for doctor is *iatrós*, and any local you ask can tell you where to find the nearest one. Their offices tend to be open from 9 to 1 and from 5 to 7. Crete's four capitals all have hospitals which are open all day, and usually have an outpatient clinic, open in the mornings—first come, first served and inexpensive. British travellers are often urged to carry a Form E111, available from DSS offices (apply well in advance on a form CM1 from post offices), which admit them to the most basic IKA (Greek NHS) hospitals for treatment; but this doesn't cover medicines or nursing care, which still have to be paid for. In any case, the E111 seems to be looked on with total disregard and incomprehension. As private doctors and hospital stays can be very expensive, you should take out a travel insurance policy, then claim your money back on return. General practitioners' fees are usually reasonable.

Most doctors pride themselves on their English, as do the pharmacists (found in the *farmakeío*), whose advice on minor ailments is good, although their medicine is not particularly cheap. If you forgot to bring your own condoms and are caught short, they are widely available from *farmakeía* and even kiosks, with lusty brand names such as 'Squirrel' or 'Rabbit'. If you can't see them on display, the word *kapótes* (condom) gets results. You can also get the Pill (*chápi antisiliptikó*), morning-after Pill and HRT over the pharmacy counter without a prescription. Be sure to take your old packet to show them the brand you use.

If you have a serious injury or illness, consider leaving Crete for treatment back home if you are well enough to travel, because the best hospitals even in Athens lag many years behind northern Europe or the USA in their methods of care and treatment. It's quite common for families to bring food in for the patient. Make sure your holiday insurance has adequate repatriation cover.

For a health emergency, dial © **166**; for police, © **100**.

Money

The word for **bank** in Greek is *trápeza*, derived from the word *trapézi*, or table, used back in the days of money-changers. Normal banking hours are 8–2, 8–1 on Fri, closed on Saturdays and Sundays. Better still, **post offices** will exchange cash, traveller's cheques and Eurocheques; they also charge less commission than banks, and the queues are usually shorter. The numbers of 24-hour **automatic cash tellers** are growing in the cities and large resorts.

Credit cards can be used to withdraw cash at banks; put your account into credit before going abroad, and this will often be the cheapest way to transfer money. The Commercial Bank of Greece will allow you to withdraw money by Visa, and the National Bank of Greece will exchange on Access (MasterCard). Money can also be withdrawn from some automatic tellers (24 hours daily) using either credit cards or **bank cards** such as Eurocheque cards, Cirrus and Plus cards in the cities and the bigger tourist resorts.

Eurocheques are accepted in banks and post offices.

Traveller's cheques are always useful even though commission rates are less for cash. The major brands of traveller's cheques (Thomas Cook and American Express) are accepted in all banks, post offices and most travel offices; take your passport as ID, and shop around for commission rates.

The Greek drachma is circulated in coins of 100, 50, 20, 10, 5, 2 and 1 drachma and in notes of 100, 500, 1000 and 5000 drachma. Shops will always round up (or down) to the nearest 5dr.

Museums and Sites

All significant archaeological sites and museums have regular admission hours. Nearly all are closed on Mondays, and open other weekdays from 8 or 9 to around 2, while outdoor sites tend to stay open later, until 4 or 5pm or even sunset. Hours tend to be shorter in winter. As a rule, plan to visit cultural sites in the mornings. Entrance fees are still reasonable: count on 500–800dr in most cases; exceptions are Knossós (1500dr), Phaistós (1200dr) and the Herákleon Archaeology Museum (1500dr). Students with a valid ID card and senior citizens often get a discount on admission fees; on Sundays admission is generally free. If you're visiting a church or monastery, it's good manners to dress decently. In the old days this used to mean no shorts or sleeveless tops, but these days all they tend to require is any kind of shirt at all and something bigger than your bathing suit on down below.

Music and Dancing

Cretans have had music and dance in their souls since Ariadne tripped across her dancing floor at Knossós. In this century they count among Greece's best known composers and musicians, among them Ioánnis Markopoúlos, whose haunting music is based on traditional instruments and songs, Ioánnis Xenakis, who is just the opposite, a friend of Le Corbusier who composes on computers in Paris, and big Míkis Theodorákis, most famous as the composer of the *Zorba the Greek* film theme, but best known in Greece for his long collaboration with deep-voiced Maria Farandoúri and his settings to modern Greek poetry.

You can hear all kinds of Greek music on Crete, from big popular bouzoúki tunes in the big nightclubs outside of Herákleon and Chaniá, venues for Greece's most popular singers (don't arrive too early—they tend to play records or washed-out muzak until midnight—and bring lots of money). Small bars, especially in Chaniá ,play everything from *rembétika* (derived from the hashish dens of Asia Minor) to Anatolian music and Greek jazz. A phenomenon of recent years are packaged 'Greek Nights', where tourists are brought in by coach to be entertained with live music; even some discotheques in the resorts have bouzoúki or Greek nights.

But what Cretans like most of all is Cretan music, played on two instruments, both introduced by the medieval Venetians: the lute and the three-stringed *viola da braccio*, renamed the *laoúto* and *lýra* by the Cretans. The *lýra*, set on the knee, is played on only the outer two strings, while the centre one serves as a kind of continual drone; sometimes the bow has 'hawkbells' (*gerakokoundoúna*) on the end for the player to emphasize the rhythm; it is the virtuoso star of the performance, capable of playing a wide range of moods, to the slow and brooding to lightning-fast improvization. In the old days a *lýra* would be carved by the lyrist himself, ideally out of ivy wood or black mulberry. The *lýra* is invariably accompanied by the deeper pitched *laoúto*, traditionally picked with an eagle's quill. The *laoúto* generally introduces the song, setting the rhythm and dominant mode, then provides a kind of harmonic rhythm throughout. In the last few years, however, the solo *laoúto* has enjoyed a modest renaissance for accompanying ballads and love songs. Occasionally other instruments—the guitar, violin, bouzoúki and a small drum— may join in. Selíno, the region in the far southwest, is the only place on Crete where the clarinet is popular. Goatskin bagpipes (*askómantra*) have pretty much vanished, as has the large thunder-*lýra* and the large *laoúto*, or *outi*.

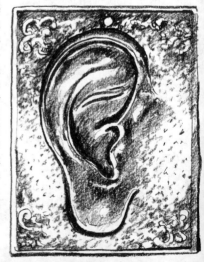

Cretan dances, fuelled by shots of *rakí*, are among the most vigorous and ancient in Greece. The favourite pan-Cretan dances are the *pentozáli*, a furious, machine-gun-fire five step dance and the *pedektó*, a general term for a dance that requires energetic jumping and stamping and every last drop of adrenalin; the dancers hold hands, the elbows bent, while a good leader, 'always dark, handsome and 20 years old', performs astonishing leaps that prove at least some white men—the heirs of the bull-leaping Minoans—can jump. Among the other distinct, regional dances you might see at a village *panegýri* (saint's day festival) or wedding are *chaniotikos*, *ortses*, *malevyzyitikos*, *siteiakos*; a *siganos* is characterized by its slow movements. Ioánnis Kondylákis' 19th-century *Patouchas*, a comic novel set in a Cretan village, describes a typical party:

> *The sound of feet echoed together so loudly one thought the ground was shaking. There were moments when the lyre positively barked... Then the dancers seemed to grow into giants whose heads almost touched the ceiling. The daggers shook in the belts of the young men, and breasts of the female dancers trembled and throbbed under the silk bodices. In the meantime couplets cross back and forth like arrows with the fast pace of the dance...*

These couplets are 15-syllable syncopated *mantinádes*. The name is again Venetian, although the tradition and form of improvising verses goes back long before Homer; songs predating *mantinádes*, *rizitika*, or 'songs from the roots' are still sung in the mountains of Safkiá. A *mantináde* can be humorous and witty, erotic, melancholy, or patriotic—Greek ethnologists have come up with over 200 thematic classifications, including a recent batch inspired by the Battle of Crete. Cretan song contests test not only the ability to come up with appropriate impromptu verses, but to come up with the *mot juste* from the vast *mantináde* repertoire. The all-time favourite source is the 17th-century epic poem, the *Erotókritos*, composed in *mantinádes* in Cretan dialect by Vicénzo Kornáros (*see* p.235); some old shepherds can recite huge sections off the tops of their heads and it's recently been introduced to a whole new generation of Greeks in a popular recording by Níkos Xiloúris, Chistodoúlos Chalaris and Tánia Tsanakioú. In Crete today you'll see posters everywhere, advertizing performances of current idols, often at 'Cretan centres', *Kentro Kritiko*—big tavernas that feature live Cretan music for Cretans, which are much more fun than organized 'Greek Night' excursions; one name to watch out for is the young lyrist and *mantináde* singer Manólis Alexákis.

National Holidays

Note that most businesses and shops close down for the afternoon before and the morning after a religious holiday. If a national holiday falls on a Sunday, the following Monday is observed. The Orthodox Easter is generally a week or so after the Roman Easter.

1 January	New Year's Day	*Protochroniá*; also *Ag. Vassílios* (Greek Father Christmas)
6 January	Epiphany	*Ta Fórce/ Epifánia*

February–March	'Clean Monday' (precedes Shrove Tuesday, and follows a three-week carnival)	*Katharí Deftéra*
25 March	Greek Independence Day	*Ethniki Giorti/ Evangelismós*
late March–April	Good Friday	*Megáli Paraskeví*
	Easter Sunday	*Páscha*
	Easter Monday	*Theftéra tou Páscha*
May	Labour Day	*Protomayá*
15 August	Assumption of the Virgin	*Koímisis tis Theotókou*
28 October	'*Ochí*' Day (in celebration of Metaxás' 'no' to Mussolini)	
25 December	Christmas Day	*Christoúyena*
26 December	Gathering of the Virgin	*Sináxi Theotókou*

In Greece, Easter is the big national holiday, the equivalent of Christmas and New Year in northern climes and the time of year when far-flung relatives return to Greece to see their families back home; it's a good time of year to visit for atmosphere, with fireworks and feasting and shooting rifles at the moon. After the priest has intoned: '*O Christós Anésti!*'—Christ has risen!—families walk home with lighted candles, mark the sign of the cross on the doorpost, and tuck into a special meal of *magirítsa* (lamb innards) soup. On Easter Sunday the Paschal lamb is spit-roasted and music and dancing goes on day and night. After Easter and May 1, spring (*ánixi*—the opening) has offically come; everyone goes into the country to picnic and weave wreaths of flowers, and the tourist season officially begins.

Packing

Even in the height of summer, evenings can be chilly in Crete, especially when the *meltémi* wind is blowing. Always bring at least one warm sweater and a pair of long trousers. Those who venture off the beaten track into the thorns and rocks should bring sturdy and comfortable shoes—trainers (sneakers) are good, but for walking down the gorges (Samariá is only the most famous) serious trekking footgear is in order. Cover the ankles if you really like wilderness, where scorpions and harmful snakes can be a problem. Plastic swimming shoes are recommended for rocky beaches, where there are often sea urchins; you can easily buy them near any beach if you don't want to carry them around with you.

Summer travellers following whim rather than a predetermined programme should bring a sleeping bag, as lodgings of any sort are often full to capacity. Serious sleeping-baggers should also bring a Karrimat or similar insulating layer to cushion them from the gravelly Greek ground. Torches are very handy for moonless nights, caves, Byzantine frescoed churches and rural villages.

On the pharmaceutical side, seasickness pills, insect bite remedies, tablets for stomach upsets and aspirin will deal with most difficulties encountered. Women's sanitary towels and sometimes Tampax are sold from general stores, but in remote areas you'll need to seek out the *farmakeío*; if there's no pharmacy, you've had it. Soap, washing powder, a clothes line and especially a towel are necessary for those staying in class C hotels or lower. Most important of all, buy a universal-fitting sink plug if you like sinks full of water; Greek sinks rarely have working ones. A knife is a good idea for picnics and *panegýria*, where you are often given a slab of goat meat with only a spoon or fork to eat it with. A photo of the family and home is always appreciated by new friends.

Unless you completely isolate yourself you can buy whatever you forgot to bring in the cities or big resort towns. Toilet paper and anti-mosquito defence weapons are the two most popular purchases on arrival. Let common sense and the maxim 'bring as little as possible and never more than you can carry' dictate your packing; work on the theory that, however much money and clothing you think you need, halve the clothing and double the money.

Photography

Crete lends herself freely to beautiful photography, but a fee is charged at archaeological sites and museums. For a movie camera of any kind, including camcorders, you are encouraged to buy a ticket for the camera (1000dr on archaeology sites, 600dr in museums); with a tripod you pay per photograph at sites, but cameras (especially tripod-mounted ones) are not allowed in museums, for no particular reason other than the museum maintaining a monopoly on its own (usually dull) picture stock. 35mm film, both print and slide, can be found in many shops, though it tends to be expensive and the range of film speeds limited (100 ASA and 64 ASA are easily available though if you take slides). Disposable and underwater cameras are on sale in larger resorts. One-hour developing services now exist everywhere, though again this costs more than at home.

The light in the summer is often stronger than it seems and is the most common cause of ruined photographs; opting for slow film (100 ASA or less) will help. Cretans usually love to have their pictures taken, and although it's more polite to ask first, you should just go ahead and take the photo if you don't want them to rush off to beautify themselves and strike a pose. Avoid taking pictures (well, who would want to anyway?) of the aircraft, military installations and barracks, communications systems on mountain tops, and Army look-out posts. The 'Photography Forbidden' sign shows a camera with a cross through it and speaks for itself.

If you bring an expensive camera to Greece, it never hurts to insure it. Above all, never leave it alone 'for just a few minutes'. Although Greeks themselves very rarely steal anything, other tourists are not so honest.

Post Offices

Signs for post offices (*tachidromío*) as well as postboxes (*grammatokivótio*) are bright yellow and easy to find. Many post office employees speak English. Stamps can also be bought at kiosks and in some tourist shops, although they charge a small commission. Stamps are *grammatósima*. Postcards can take up to three weeks to arrive at their destinations, or only a week if you're lucky; letters sent abroad are faster, taking just over a week, depending on the route. If you're really in a hurry you can send letters express for extra cost.

If you do not have an address, mail can be sent to you poste restante to any post office in Crete, and can be picked up with proof of identity. After one month all unretrieved letters are returned to sender. If someone has sent you a parcel, you will receive a notice of its arrival, and you must go to the post office to collect it. You will have to pay a handling fee of 650dr, and customs charges and duties should the parcel contain dutiable articles. 'Fragile' stickers attract scant attention. In small villages, mail is not delivered to the house but to the village centre, either a café or bakery. If you want to mail a package, any shop selling paper items will wrap it for a small fee.

Sports

watersports

Naturally these predominate. All popular beaches these days hire out pedal boats and windsurf boards; some have paragliding, banana boards and jet skis. Large resort hotels can usually get you on a pair of waterskis. **Nudism** is forbidden by law in Crete, except in designated areas. In practice, however, many people shed all in isolated coves, at the far ends of beaches, or ideally on beaches accessible only by private boat. On the other hand, topless sunbathing is now legal on the majority of popular beaches away from settlements, but do exercise discretion. It isn't worth wounding local sensibilities, no matter how prudish other people's attitudes may seem. You could be arrested on the spot and end up with three days in jail or a stiff fine. Canoodling on public beaches in broad daylight can also offend.

Freelance diving is strictly forbidden, to keep divers from snatching any antiquities and to protect marine life. However, snorkelling is fine, and several resorts now have scuba-diving school. Even if you already have a diving certificate, you have to go out with their boats.

Resort areas have tennis courts, nearly every village has a basketball net, and at the time of writing the National Tourist Organization of Greece is helping to fund four golf courses in Crete, one for each *nomós*. You can watch Herákleon's first division Ofi take their licks in the Greek football league, or even ski down Psilorítis (above Anógia) with a little ski lift to take you back up again, but by far the most popular activities in Crete are walking and climbing. If you plan on doing some serious trekking bring your sturdy boots and hat, and pick up a Harms-Verlag Crete Map, based on the Greek army's ordnance surveys, with paths well marked. An increasing number of local walking guides are on sale on Crete, or pick up Sunflower Books' *Landscapes of Western Crete* and *Landscapes of Eastern Crete* by Jonnie Godfry and Elizabeth Karsalake. Also see special interest holidays (pp.11–12). Local mountain climbing organizations (EOS) in Herákleon (53 Dikeosínis, ✆ 227 609), Chaniá (90 Tzanakáki, ✆ 24 647) and Réthymnon (12 Dimokratías, ✆ 22 655) are good sources of information if you're venturing into the White Mountains or Psilorítis, or on the new E4 path that crosses all of Crete.

Telephones

The Organismós Telefikoinonía Elládos, or **OTE**, has offices in the larger towns, which tend to be the easiest places to make international calls, especially if you want to call collect (reverse charges), send a telegram or send a fax. Otherwise you can dial abroad direct (for Great Britain dial 0044 and for the USA 001 before the area code) from any kiosk (*períptero*), or from travel agents with a metered phone. A 3-minute call to the UK will cost about 750dr, to the US 1600dr. Payphones have been replaced with cardphones. Phonecards are sold at *períptera* for 1000dr for 100 units or *monádes*. To defeat the beeps, whirrs and buzzes you often get instead of a connection, wait for the series of six clicks after the area code is dialled before proceeding.

Toilets

Greek plumbing has improved in the past few years, and in the newer hotels you can flush everything away as merrily as you do at home, at least as often as your conscience lets you in a country strapped for water. Tavernas, *kafeneíons* and sweet shops almost always have facilities (it's good manners to buy something before you excuse yourself); there are often public pay toilets in strategic area of the towns.

In older pensions and tavernas, the plumbing often makes up in inventiveness for what it lacks in efficiency. Do not tempt fate by disobeying the little notices 'the papers they please to throw in the basket'—or it's bound to lead to trouble. Also, a second flush in immediate succession will gurgle and burp instead of swallow.

Many places in Crete have only a ceramic hole. Women who confront this for the first time should take care not to wet their feet: squat about halfway and lean back as far as you can. Always have paper of some sort handy.

If you stay in a private room or pension you may have to have the electric water heater turned on for about 20 minutes before you take a shower, so if you were promised hot water but it fails to appear, ask. In most smaller pensions, water is heated by a solar panel on the roof, so the best time to take a shower is in the late afternoon, or the early evening (before other residents use up the finite supply of hot water). In larger hotels there is often hot water in the mornings and evenings, but not in the afternoons. Actually 'cold' showers in the summer aren't all that bad, because the tap water itself is generally lukewarm, especially after noon. A good many showers are of the hand-held variety and are designed so that you soak the floor and your towel.

Tourist Information

The National Tourist Organization of Greece (in Greek **EOT**) have offices in each of Crete's four 'capitals' as well as in your home country. If they can't answer your questions about Crete, at least they can refer you to someone who can.

Australia

51–57 Pitt Street, Sydney, NSW 2000, ℭ 241 1663/4, ✉ 235 2174.

Canada

1300 Bay Street, Toronto, Ontario, ℭ (416) 968 2220, ✉ 968 6533.

1233 De La Montagne, Montreal, Quebec, ℭ (514) 871 1535,
✉ 871 1498.

Great Britain

4 Conduit Street, London W1R 0DJ, ℭ (0171) 734 5997, ✉ 287 1369.

USA

Head Office: Olympic Tower, 645 Fifth Avenue, 5th Floor, New York, NY 10022, ℭ (212) 421 5777, ✉ 826 6940.

168 N. Michigan Avenue, Chicago, Illinois. 60601, ℭ (312) 782 1084,
✉ 782 1091.

611 West Sixth Street, Suite 2198, LA, Calif. 90017, ℭ (213) 626 6696,
✉ 489 9744.

The consumers' rights **Tourist Assistance Programme** (1 Milatou and Ag. Titou, Herákleon, ℭ (081) 240 666) has recently been set up with European Commission funding to help visitors who have been mistreated, misled or ripped off by hotels, travel agents, or any other tourist-orientated business. They can also put you into contact with a bilingual lawyer if things have really got out of hand.

Hotels

All hotels in Crete are divided into six categories: luxury, A, B, C, D and E. This grading system bears little relationship to the quality of service; it's more to do with how the building is constructed, size of bedrooms, etc. If the hotel has a marble-clad bathroom it gets a higher rating. For this reason, some D and C class hotels can be better than Bs. Pensions, some without restaurants, are a confusing subdivision in Greek hotel classifications, especially as many call themselves hotels. They are family-run and more modest (an A class pension is roughly equivalent to a C or D class hotel and is priced accordingly).

prices

Prices are set and strictly controlled by the tourist police. Off season you can generally get a discount, sometimes as much as 40%. In the summer season prices can be increased by up to 20%. Other charges include an 8% government tax, a 4.5% community bed tax, a 12% stamp tax, an optional 10% surcharge for stays of only one or two days, an air-conditioning surcharge, as well as a 20% surcharge for an extra bed. All these prices are listed on the door of every room and authorized and checked at regular intervals. If your hotelier fails to abide by the posted prices, or if you have any other reason to believe all is not on the level, take your complaint to the tourist police.

1996 hotel rates (drachma) for mid–high season (1 May–30 Sept)

	Lux	A	B	C	D
Single room with bath	9000–30,000	6700–15,000	6700–10,000	4500–8000	2700–5000
Double room with bath	13,100–35,000	9900–17,000	5700–14,000	4600–10,000	4000–6000

Prices for E hotels are about 20% less than D rates.

During the summer, hotels with restaurants may require guests to take their meals in the hotel, either full pension or half pension, and there is no refund for an uneaten dinner. Twelve noon is the official check-out time. Most Luxury and class A, if not B, hotels situated far from the town or port supply buses or cars to pick up guests. Hotels down to class B all have private bathrooms. In C most do. In D you will usually find a hot shower down the hall, and in E forget it: in these hotels neither towel nor soap is supplied, although the bedding is clean.

The importance of reserving a room in advance, especially during July and August, cannot be over-emphasized. Reservations can be made through the individual hotel or through the Hellenic Chamber of Hotels, 24 Stadíou St, 105 61 Athens, © (01) 323 5485 (from Athens: between 8 and 2), @ (01) 322 5449.

In the 'Where to Stay' sections of this book, accommodation is listed according to the following price categories:

luxury	28,000 to astronomical
expensive	12,000–28,000
moderate	6000–12,000
inexpensive	4000–6000

Please note that prices quoted are for double rooms and are approximate.

Rooms (domátia) in Private Homes

These are for the most part cheaper than hotels and are sometimes more pleasant. On the whole, Cretan houses aren't much in comparison to other European homes mainly because people spend so little time inside them; but they are clean, and the owner will often go out of his or her way to assure maximum comfort for the guest. Staying in someone's house can also offer rare insights into Greek domestic taste, which ranges from a near-Japanese simplicity to a clutter of bulging plastic cat pictures that squeak when you touch them; lamps shaped like ships, made entirely of macaroni; tapestries of dogs shooting pool; and flocked sofas covered in heavy plastic that only the Patriarch of the Orthodox Church is allowed to sit on. Increasingly, however, rooms to rent to tourists are built in a separate annexe and tend to be rather characterless concrete barracks, though some of the newer ones are nicer than hotels. While room prices are generally fixed in the summer (the going rate in high season is now 4000dr) out of season they are always negotiable with a little finesse, even in June.

Prices depend a lot on fashion. Speaking some Greek is the biggest asset in bargaining, although not strictly necessary. Claiming to be a poor student is generally effective. Always remember, however, that you are staying in someone's home, and do not waste more water or electricity than you need. The owner will generally give you a bowl to wash your clothes in, and there is always a clothes line.

Youth Hostels

Some of these are official and require a membership card from the Association of Youth Hostels, or alternatively an International Membership Card (about 2600dr) from the Greek Association of Youth Hostels, 4 Dragatsaníou Street, Athens, © 323 4107; other hostels are informal, have no irksome regulations, and admit anyone. Most charge extra for a shower, sometimes for sheets. Expect to pay 1200–2000dr a night, depending on the quality of facilities and services offered.

The climate of summertime Crete is perfect for sleeping out of doors. In July and August you only need a sleeping bag to spend a pleasant night on a remote beach, cooled by the sea breezes that also keep the mosquito menace at bay. Unauthorized camping is illegal, although each village enforces the ban as it sees fit. Some couldn't care less if you put up a tent at the edge of their beach; in others the police may pull up your tent pegs and fine you. All you can do is ask around to see what other campers or friendly locals advise. Naturally, the more remote the beach, the less likely you are to be disturbed. If a policeman does come by and asks you to move, you had best do so; be diplomatic. Many beaches have privately operated camping grounds—each seems to have at least one. These are reasonably priced, though some have only minimal facilities.

There are three main reasons behind the camping law: one is that the beaches have no sanitation facilities for crowds of campers; secondly, forest fires are a real hazard in summer; and thirdly, the law was enacted to displace gypsy camps, and is still used for this purpose. If the police are in some places lackadaisical about enforcing the camping regulations, they come down hard on anyone lighting any kind of fire in a forest, and may very well put you in jail for two months; every year forest fires damage huge swathes of land.

Camping prices are not fixed by law but these are the approximate guidelines.

Typical camping rates (per day during high season)

Adult	800–900dr
Child (4–12)	400–500dr
Caravan	1000dr
Small tent	650dr
Large tent	900dr
Car	500dr
Electricity	500dr

Renting a House, Apartment or Villa

On Crete you can rent houses, apartments or villas, generally for two weeks, or a month or more at a time. Although you may be able to find something on the spot in a mountain village, don't count on finding anything in a city or coastal resort in the summer without going through a rental agent or holiday company; see also listings in the weekly *Kriti News*, available at most newsstands. Facilities normally include a refrigerator, hot water, plates and utensils, etc. Generally, the longer you stay the more economical it becomes. Things to check for are leaking roofs, damp, water supply (the house may have a well) and a supply of lamps if there is no electricity.

By and large you won't find the specialist brochures at your travel agent, as many are small operations belonging to the **Association of Independent Tour Operators** who tend to advertize in the quality Sunday papers or else depend on word-of-mouth recommendations from clients. Your Greek National Tourist Organization (*see* p.34) has a list of tour operators. The specialist companies listed below offer packages with hand-picked accommodation ranging from villas and small hotels to restored village houses and unusual ethnic gems, designed for visitors who want to avoid the concrete jungles of mass tourism. Many of the operators listed here offer 'loosely packaged' holidays that will appeal to free spirits and independently minded travellers.

From the UK

The Best of Greece, 23–24 Marger St, London, W1N 8LE, ℂ (0171) 255 2320. Deluxe accommodation arranged in the finest hotels and select villas.

Catherine Secker (Crete), 102A Burnt Ash Lane, Bromley, Kent BR1 4DD, ℂ (0181) 460 8022. Home-run business with the personal touch featuring luxury villas with swimming pools on the Akrotíri Peninsula near Chaniá. Catherine Secker offers all mod cons in quiet beachside villages with everything from hairdryers to highchairs and toyboxes. Removal of noisy dogs and cockerels guaranteed.

First Choice Greece, First Choice House, London Road, Crawley, West Sussex RH10 2GX, ℂ (0161) 745 7000. Villas and apartments.

Filoxenia Ltd, Sourdock Hill, Barkisland, Halifax, West Yorkshire HX4 0AG, ℂ (01422) 371796. Not so much tailor-made as haute couture holidays. Suzi Stembridge and family have scoured Crete for unusual holiday places. Houses, villas, tavernas, pensions, fly-drive and special interest tours. Also **Opus 23** for travellers with disabilities.

Island Wandering, 51A London Road, Hurst Green, Sussex TN19 7QP, ℂ (01580) 860733, ✉ (01580) 860282. Fly–drive holidays on Crete. Charters from most UK airports plus scheduled Athens flights.

Inspirations, Victoria House, Victoria Road, Horley, Surrey RH6, ℂ (01293) 822 244. Villas in Plakiás and other Crete locations.

Kosmar Villa Holidays plc, 358 Bowes Road, Arnos Grove, London N11 1AN, ℂ (0181) 368 6833. Self-catering villas, studios and apartments in Chaniá, Paleochóra and in the Ag. Nikólaos area. Two-centre holidays, flights from Glasgow and Newcastle and family savers.

Manos Holidays, 168–172 Old Street, London EC1V 9BP, ✆ (0171) 216 8000. Good value holidays to the major resorts and two-centres. Friendly approach, ideal for children, low-season specials and singles deals.

Pure Crete, 79 George Street, Croydon, Surrey CR0 1LP, ✆ (0181) 760 0879. Houses and farms on Crete.

Simply Crete, ✆ (01810) 994 4462, Greek-English family-run concern with an excellent reputation, offering country cottages, villas with pools, apartments and small family run hotels; multi-centre 'Island Wandering' scheme.

Travel Club of Upminster, Station Road, Upminster, Essex RM14 2TT, ✆ (04022) 25 000. Quality apartments and hotel bookings.

From the USA/Canada

Crown Peters, 33–36 Broadway, Astoria, New York, NY 11106, ✆ (718) 932 7800. Arranges accommodation for independent travellers in Crete.

Trianena Poseidon Tours International, 72 Hutchison St, Montreal, Québec H3N 1ZL, ✆ (800) 361 0374. Upmarket villa holidays.

Women Travellers

Crete is fine for women travellers but foreign women travelling alone can be viewed as an oddity. Be prepared for a fusillade of questions, Greeks tend to do everything in groups or pairs and can't understand people, especially women, who want to go solo. Yet on the whole they refrain from annoying women as other Mediterranean men are known to do, while remaining friendly and easy to meet; all Greek men from sixteen to sixty like to chat up foreign women, but extreme coercion and violence such as rape is rare. A recent rape case west of Chaniá was resolved as they always have been: the woman's family had two of the three rapists killed and the third is sure to be shot down the minute he shows his face in public.

Kamáki means harpoon in Greek, and it's what the Greeks call those Romeos who roar about on motorbikes, hang out in the bars and cafés, and hunt in pairs or packs. Their aim is to collect as many women as possible, notching up points for different nationalities. There are highly professional *kamákis* in the big resorts, gigolos who live off women tourists, gathering as many foreign hearts plus gold chains and parting gifts as they can; they winter all over the world with members of their harem. Other Greeks look down on them, and consider them dishonourable.

Many young Greek women are beginning to travel alone—that blonde with the rucksack could just as well be Greek as Swedish nowadays—but this is no indication that traditional values are disappearing. Although many women in the larger towns now have jobs, old marriage customs still exert a strong influence. 'Poverty and nakedness are nothing, provided you have a good wife,' is an old Cretan saying. Not a few old Cretan customs relate to young women guessing who they might marry: the *kledonas*, or looking into the water to see the face of a future husband, or the custom of the beans. On New Year's Eve at midnight, they take three beans: one natural, one shelled, one peeled. With eyes closed a girl chooses a bean: the natural one means a young husband, a shelled one means a widower, and a peeled one means a poor man.

Weddings are sometimes less a union of love than the closing of a lengthily negotiated business deal. A young man, generally in his late twenties or early thirties, will spot a likely girl on the promenade (the *vólta*) or will hear about her through the grapevine; many men who work abroad will come back to their villages specifically to find a wife. He will then approach the father to discover the girl's dowry—low wages and high housing costs demand that it contain some sort of living quarters from the woman's father, often added on top of the family house. If both parties are satisfied, the young man is officially introduced to the daughter, who can be as young as 16 in the villages. If they get along well together, the marriage date is set. The woman who never marries and has no children is sincerely pitied in Greece. The inordinate number of Greek widows (and not all wear the traditional black) is due to the average 10- to 20-year age difference between husband and wife.

Working in Crete

If you run out of money in Crete, you may just be able to find a temporary job, ranging from polishing cucumbers to laying cement or working in a bar or restaurant in a resort (although with the influx of impecunious Albanians these are becoming harder to find, and wages are even lower than usual). The local *kafeneíon* is a good place to enquire. With the universal interest in learning English these days, you may land a job as English teacher at a *frontistírion* or private school, although these usually demand a university degree or TEFL (teaching English as a foreign language) certificate. Teachers have been known to survive merely on under-the-table private lessons, although you need to live in one of Crete's cities and have a certain amount of chutzpah to get by. EU citizens can often find jobs as greeters/co-ordinators with travel offices that deal with package tour companies, but start looking in early spring or you'll need to be incredibly lucky.

Mythology

> *...[the Cretans] declare that most of the gods proceeded from Crete to many parts of the inhabited world, conferring benefits upon the race of men and sharing among each of them the benefits of their own discoveries.*
>
> Diodorus Siculus

Roman mythographers and modern scholars alike have always puzzled over the complex web of tales that involve Crete. These interlaced legends lie at the very core of Greek mythology's history and meaning, and they provide any number of fascinating hints about life and religion in the time of the Minoans. In their strange, indirect way they can tell us many things the scholars of archaeology alone would never find out.

Ever since the fuzzy sciences were invented, psychologists, anthropologists, sociologists and worse have had a high time smelting down Greek mythology in their various forges, generating a modicum of good glittering gold along with impressive heaps of slag. There is more in the old myths than can be explained by any of their more modern mythologies; storytelling is one of the basic ways mind works, conveying a wealth of meaning on many different levels and transcending the limitations of simplistic rational thinking. Between the lines of the myths, we can read a tremendous amount of information about the hidden corners of Greek history and religion and their ultimate sources.

Myths have no author—not even Homer. Wherever the seed of a story comes from, it is polished and refined by each generation. Long before any of these stories were written down, innumerable poets in the oral tradition added bits on, and meaningfully deleted or repressed others, until the story as a whole became truly the product of the Greek people.

The most important stories often serve to chronicle, in their fashion, important changes in culture and religious conceptions, especially those stories that explain how something 'came to be': how a city was founded, or where the gods came from, or why a particular religious ritual or dance was performed. Because so much of Classical Greek religion found its beginnings with the Minoans, a thousand years and more before the Parthenon was built, it is no surprise that the important tales so often find their way back to Crete.

If there is an underlying conflict, a recurring theme in Greek myth, it is the oldest battle in the world—the one between men and women, on earth and reflected in the heavens. In the 'Greek dark age', the northern invaders brought down their patriarchal warrior society and male, all-powerful sky god and imposed it on older societies, such as that of the Cretans, which were ultimately matriarchal and conserved strong traces of the original many-faceted 'great goddess', worshipped under a hundred names across the western world.

The Rise and Fall of Zeus

It is only natural that caves figure so prominently in the myths that involve Crete; cave sanctuaries were among the most important sites for Minoan religion before the building of the temples, and a Cretan cave was the birthplace of the ruler of the gods himself. But to begin at the beginning of time, we have Uranus (Sky), son of Mother Earth and Chaos. Uranus was father of the Cyclopes and the Titans. The latter rebelled against his tyrannical ways, goaded on by Mother Earth and led by the youngest Titan, Cronos (Time). They crept up on their father while he was sleeping and castrated him with a stone sickle.

The dying Uranus cursed Cronos, declaring that one of his own sons would do him the same treat, so as a preventative measure Cronos swallowed every baby his wife Rhea, daughter of the Earth, presented to him. After this had happened five times (to Hestia, Demeter, Hera, Hades and Poseidon) Rhea determined on a different fate for her sixth child, Zeus. When he was born she smuggled him to Crete and gave Cronos a stone instead, which the old fellow duly swallowed. Mother Earth hid the baby in the Diktean cave and set young Cretan warriors called the Kouretes (*kouroi*) to guard him; they were ordered to shout and dance and beat their shields to drown out the baby's cries.

In the cave, Zeus was nursed by the goat-nymph Amaltheia, whose single horn was the horn of plenty, or cornucopia; her son Pan was his foster brother. According to one account, though, Zeus had a golden cradle that was hung in a tree, so that Cronos could not find him on earth or in heaven. When Zeus came of age, his mother Rhea slipped Cronos a Mickey Finn that not only laid him out, but made him vomit up the swallowed siblings. Zeus then led them in a 10-year war against Cronos and the Titans in which the new Olympians were finally victorious. The Battle of the Gods and Titans was a favourite subject for Classical temple sculpture. It meant the founding of a new cosmic order, that of the reasonable, humanized gods of Olympos.

In Classical times, Cretans took visitors to see the birthplace of Zeus in the Diktean cave; centuries later they would be doing it with northern European tourists of the

Romantic era, rediscovering the ancient world and its myths. Even stranger, though, Cretans of the old days liked to show their guests the *grave* of Zeus, on Mount Júktas near Knossós. Such heresy helped considerably in giving the Cretans their ancient reputation as liars, but behind the curious fancy of the greatest of the gods actually dying lies an important insight into the roots of Greek religion.

A similar theme is explored in the first great work of anthropology, Sir James George Frazer's *The Golden Bough*: the 'sacred king', the symbolic consort of the great goddess for a fixed period of time, who in the earliest stages of religion was fated to be supplanted and killed by a son or a rival. Remember that Zeus himself overthrew and killed his own father. In a less direct way, mythology records Zeus' worries about suffering the same fate through his dalliance with women or goddesses who the oracles declared were destined to bear a son greater than him. One such was Metis. Zeus couldn't resist, and after he had his way with her he avoided danger by simply swallowing her (unnecessary in any case, since the only offspring was the girl later born from Zeus' head—Athene). For the same reason Zeus had to give up the nereid or sea-nymph Thetis; marrying a mortal, she became the mother of Achilles.

Behind all those reasonable, human gods of Olympos stand ancient, shadowy figures, transcendent goddesses and the males who were their children, their lovers and finally their victims. Before Zeus fought his way to the top he was, like almost all the other gods, a *daimon* of the year. The *kouroi* were young warriors and, as a hymn records, Zeus was 'the greatest *kouros*'. In ancient Crete, they would have danced and clashed their shields at a ritual, perhaps where one of their number 'became' the god himself, or the god's representative as sacred king. Now—there's no way to put it gracefully—a sacred king's business is to give his life for the luck of the year and the crops. Like Jesus or John Barleycorn, he, as *daimon* of the year, must die.

Some anthropologists trace the beginnings of change in the old religion to men's discovery of the facts of paternity—that they too had something to do with life and growth and keeping the world going. Whatever, somehow the boys figured out that this brand of religion was giving them a bum deal, and they became increasingly intolerant of the domination of goddesses and priestesses. At one stage, the sacred king's reign on Crete was extended to a longer astronomical cycle, the eight-year agreement of lunar and solar months, the 'marriage of sun and moon' (*see* below). And later, when the men were more in control of things, a substitute was found for the sacrifice of the king. These may have been human sacrifices; evidence from Cretan digs hints at this. By the more civilized time of the palaces, it was the animal associated with the sacred kings that was sacrificed—the bull. In the ocean of Greek myth, the closer you look at the history of any important god—Zeus, Dionysos,

Poseidon or whoever—the more you come to realize they are essentially all the same being, and that the shadows they cast all have horns.

So the Cretans were right about Zeus' demise, even though it was heresy to the Classical Greeks, who had begun to imagine deity as something perfect and eternal. They ensured that the Cretans kept their reputation as liars all through Antiquity. The clever Cretans, however, turned this reputation into a means for torturing the brains of Classical philosophers, and all of us since, with the simplest, neatest logical paradox of all time:

> *Epimenides the Cretan says: 'All Cretans are liars.'*

Europa and her Children

So Zeus started out as a fertility god, and throughout his career as an Olympian he certainly did his best to fertilize anything in a skirt that he could get his hands on. Once his attentions fell on a girl named Europa, a cowherd near Tyre (in Phoenicia, now Lebanon). One day, while she was grazing her herd near the seashore, Zeus turned himself into a a beautiful white bull and insinuated himself among them. Europa, struck by his gentleness, began to play with him, but when she climbed on his back for a ride the bull immediately thundered off into the sea and did not stop until he reached Górtyn, in Crete. There, Zeus changed himself from a bull to an eagle (god knows why) and ravished poor Europa; the result was three fine boys named Minos, Rhadamanthys and Sarpedon.

What may originally have been an image of a priestess leading a bull off to the sacrifice was turned into this pretty story by later mythographers. Or not a priestess, but the Middle Eastern moon goddess Astarte, who in art was often pictured riding the bull-god El. This myth is telling us how something important in Cretan religion came from the East. Basically, this girl Europa, who gave her name to an entire continent, *is* Astarte; like the sacred kings, the great goddess is visible behind a hundred different names around the Mediterranean. In Classical times Zeus was worshipped at Górtyn as 'Zeus Asterion'—a telling example of how the male Olympian gods took over the names of their female predecessors, just as they gradually took over their rites and functions.

Although it is generally recognized that Aegean culture, including the Minoans, Mycenaeans and Cycladic peoples, was an original and independent growth, elements of Aegean religion may well have been adopted from the East. Relations and cross-influences between the Minoans and the Egyptians and Anatolian peoples is a subject that has still not been fully explored.

King Minos and the Birth of the Minotaur

The three brothers were adopted by King Asterius (there's that name again) of Crete. By some accounts, they began to quarrel over the love of a beautiful boy named Miletus, who escaped them all and founded the famous city that bore his name on the coast of Asia Minor. Their quarrel continued when they succeeded to the Cretan throne after Asterius' death. Minos claimed primacy for himself, and justified his arrogance by stating that he was the favourite of the gods and that they would grant him anything he asked. To prove it, he made preparations for a sacrifice to Poseidon and prayed for a bull to emerge from the sea as a sign. Poseidon delivered—a beautiful white bull, no less—and Minos liked it so much that he decided to keep it for himself instead of sending it to the sacrifice.

Now, for the Greeks, a sacrifice was always part religious rite and part barbecue. Gods were content with the fat and bones, and the aroma, while the celebrants took care of the rest of the animal (much tastier, when you think about it, than communion wafers). No doubt Minos's brothers were even more cross with him after missing out on the expected feast. But he was acclaimed king, and chased the unhappy Sarpedon off to Cilicia in Asia Minor (where he became king of the Milyans). More significantly, though, Minos had also incurred the wrath of Poseidon, and this ill-tempered deity found a truly novel way of getting his revenge. He caused Minos' new bride Pasiphaë to acquire an unnatural but extremely fervent passion for this white bull. At first the poor girl didn't know what to do, but fortunately she was able to take her problem to the master problem-solver of the age, Daedalus, who had been exiled from his native Athens for the murder of his apprentice and rival Talos, and washed up at Crete. Daedalus agreed to help her, and constructed a wooden cow large enough for Pasiphaë to fit inside, with wheels under the hooves and a trap door in just the right place. They rolled it out to the pasture where the white bull was grazing, and Pasiphaë climbed in. The wooden cow must have been quite skilfully made and more than a little attractive, as before long Pasiphaë found herself in the family way. The result, if you have not already guessed it, was the Minotaur: the body of a man with a bull's head.

What Pasiphaë thought of her new baby is not recorded, but Minos was beside himself. In the dream time of mythology, as in any other age, appearances counted for everything, and the king's first thought was making sure the neighbours didn't find out. Daedalus came in handy once again. He built the famous Labyrinth under the king's palace at Knossós to hold the monster and conceal him.

The kingdom of Minos prospered, ruling the seas and exacting tributes from across the Mediterranean. A son of Minos, Androgeus, once visited Athens to compete in the Athenian games, and won the prize in every sport. Either out of jealousy or because he suspected Androgeus of aiding some Athenians who were in revolt, King Aegeus of Athens had him ambushed on his way to some funeral games in Thebes and Androgeus died in the battle. In revenge, Minos ordered the Athenians to send seven youths and seven maidens to Crete every ninth year, and sent them into the Labyrinth to be devoured by the Minotaur.

Theseus and Ariadne

The Athenians had twice sent their consignment (chosen by lot) to Minos, and on the third occasion Theseus, the hero of Athens, decided to take his place among the 14 victims to see if he could end the humiliating tribute. Like the Minotaur he was soon to meet, this Theseus had an interesting conception; his mother Aethra had slept in the same night with King Aegeus and with Poseidon. This happened in Troezen, across the Saronic Gulf from Athens. Aegeus abandoned mother and child, as Greek heroes were wont to do, and went back to Athens, leaving his sword and sandals under a heavy stone altar of Zeus. If when the boy grew up he proved strong enough to lift the altar and recover them, he would be welcome at Aegeus' court. When the time came, Theseus managed this easily and set off for Athens, dispatching various monsters and miscreants along the way, sometimes with a club and sometimes with his bare hands—among his other accomplishments Theseus was the inventor of wrestling and knew all the good holds.

Arriving in Athens, Theseus immediately had some trouble with a wicked stepmother—none other than the famous sorceress Medea, who had taken refuge with Aegeus. Medea, being a sorceress, knew who Theseus really was; Aegeus didn't. She had convinced the king to let her poison the stranger as a spy, but Aegeus noticed the serpents (Erechtheid royal symbols) carved on Theseus's sword—the one Aegeus had left him—and knocked the cup from his hands just in time.

When Theseus was setting out for Crete with the tribute ship, Aegeus gave him a black sail and a white one, and bade the sailors hoist the white one if Theseus was victorious, and the black one if he had been killed by the Minotaur. There are several different versions of what Theseus actually did in Crete. The original travel writer, Pausanias, wrote in the 2nd century AD that in the Theseion, a temple still standing in Athens today, there was a famous painting of Theseus emerging from the sea, holding a ring and a crown. The story goes that Minos doubted that Theseus was really a son of Poseidon and, to make him prove it, the king threw his ring into the sea and demanded that the hero bring it back to him. Theseus swam down to the bottom and found it, with the aid of dolphins and the nereids, who took him to their palace and gave him a golden crown with rubies shaped like roses that had belonged to Thetis.

Minos's daughter Ariadne had a look at Theseus and fell in love straight away. She promised to help him deal with the Minotaur if he would carry her off with him. She asked Daedalus for a little something to help Theseus find his way through the Labyrinth, and the old magician came up with something no more complicated than a ball of string (although by one account it was a magic ball of string that threaded the maze by itself). Ariadne gave it to Theseus; unwinding the thread as he went, he made his way into the Labyrinth, slew the Minotaur with his bare hands, and used the thread to retrace his steps. With the princess's help, he next freed his 13 companions. They made their way to the Greek ship and sailed off. Minos's fleet soon appeared in pursuit, but when night fell the Athenians were able to slip safely away.

They landed first on the island of Náxos, and here the story takes a strange turn. Theseus left Ariadne on Náxos, and none of the poets and mythographers could ever explain why. Her laments when she awoke to find herself alone make a touching scene in the poetry of Ovid and others, and the abandonment was a common subject for Classical painting. As a consolation prize, she got the god Dionysos, who arrived on Náxos shortly afterwards with his ivy-crowned satyrs and maenads, and the cymbals and drums playing, and carried Ariadne away on his ship. Divine retribution, perhaps, caught up with Theseus while his ship was approaching Athens. He hoisted the wrong sail, the black one; his father took it to mean Theseus had been killed and he threw himself from the cliffs into the sea.

What Was That All About?

Could the story of Theseus in Crete be a distant echo of a Mycenaean raid on Knossós, or the capture and sacking of the city that historians have speculated about? Athens too was a Mycenaean city, the only one to survive intact through the post-Mycenaean dark age; it may have participated in a revolt against Minoan overlordship. Plutarch records a version altogether different from the common one recounted above: no Minotaur and fairy-tale motifs, but a simple naval invasion in which Theseus lands while Minos is away, kills his son Deucalion, and marries Ariadne to create an alliance between Crete and Athens.

In mythology, it is often the seemingly inconsequential details that provide the biggest clues. The story of Theseus and the Minotaur is set at the time of the key event in Minoan religious life—the festival that took place every eight years, when Athens had to send its tribute of youths and maidens to Crete. Another myth records that, every eight years, Minos conferred with his father Zeus. There is an astronomical period, known in Classical times and undoubtedly to the Minoans too, of this length. More precisely, it is 99 lunar months, the period when lunar and solar months coincide, the 'marriage of sun and moon'. This would once have been the extent of Minos's—the sacred king's—reign; by the height of Minoan civilization the great festival would have been commemorated by some important sacrifice, replacing what had been the death of the king himself. The famous 'bull vaulting' pictured on the Knossós fresco (in the Archaeology Museum, Herákleon), and on so many other works, has a male figure, ceremonially dyed red, representing the sun while he passes through the crescent horns of the bull.

Most writers on Crete assume automatically that the courtyard at the centre of the palace at Knossós was the site of the bull vaulting. No one has ever stopped to wonder how they got the bulls inside. The bull vaulting may indeed have been performed at this festival, but the real purpose of the courtyard is clear enough:

> *...a dancing floor like that which once in the wide*
> *spaces of Knossos*
> *Daedalus built for Ariadne of the lovely tresses...*

Iliad, Book XVIII

The ancient 'Labyrinth', meaning the 'house of the double axe', was probably called after the complex, spiralling dance that was performed in its courtyard, the heart of the ritual that accompanied the sacred marriage every eight years. The famous Phaistós Disc (in the Archaeology Museum, Herákleon) seems to be a very sacred object; if it is ever deciphered, its spiralling hieroglyphic inscription may have more to say about this.

The crown that Theseus brought up from the sea and gave to Ariadne was later placed by Zeus in the heavens, and you can see it there today—*Corona Borealis*, the Northern Crown. The handle of the Big Dipper points towards it, and it is close enough to the pole to be visible most of the year. Interestingly, the Celts associated this circlet of stars with Arianhrod, a version of the great goddess who, in her worship as in her name, seems to have much in common with Ariadne. Only here the constellation was not a crown but a castle, Arianhrod's seven-towered silver castle where Celtic warriors went after their deaths.

Although it isn't mentioned in most versions of the tale, the Minotaur had a name, Asterius, which besides its associations with Astarte can be translated as the 'starry way'—interestingly, the same as the original king of Crete who adopted Minos. All this brings up the very intriguing question of astronomical connections with Minoan religion and myth. Besides Ariadne's crown, on a summer night you can go out and see Amaltheia, Zeus' goat-nymph nursemaid, with her cornucopia marked in stars—none other than Capricorn. As for the white bull, it turns up later in mythology breathing fire and devastating the countryside. Capturing it was the seventh of Heracles' Twelve Labours. He brought it into Greece, where it was later killed by Theseus. The Greeks said it was the Taurus of the zodiac.

Why did Theseus jilt Ariadne? Some accounts say he had another girl, but the most coherent version of the myth is that Dionysos cast a spell over Theseus while he slept on Náxos that made him forget; this would fit in with a common fairy-tale motif. In terms of religion, the abandonment makes perfect sense. Ariadne, like her mother Pasiphaë, is only another mask for the ancient Cretan great goddess—certainly someone the Classical Athenians, worshippers of Olympian Zeus, would rather not have around. Not just the helpful maiden of a fairy-tale, the real Ariadne was the mistress of the Labyrinth, the goddess of the double axe—even in Classical times she survived as an orgiastic goddess who had once demanded human sacrifice, worshipped in many places around Greece and as far afield as the Crimea.

If Theseus and the Athenians had no use for her, she was more than welcome in the cult of Dionysos—a throwback to the old religion, with its maenads, mountain revels and tearing of raw flesh.

The End of Minos

Minos was furious when he discovered the part Daedalus had played in the business, and threw the inventor and his young son Icarus into the Labyrinth. Although they managed to find their way out, escape from Crete was impossible, as Minos controlled the seas. But Daedalus, never at a loss, decided that what they couldn't accomplish by sea they would do by air. He fashioned wings of feathers and wax for himself and Icarus, and on the first fine day they flew towards Asia Minor. All went well until an exhilarated Icarus disobeyed his father's command not to fly too close to the sun. The wax in his wings melted, and he plunged and drowned off the island that took his name, Ikaría.

Minos heard of Daedalus' escape and pursued him all over the Mediterranean, hoping to trap the wily inventor by offering a great reward to whoever could pass a thread through a spiralling nautilus shell. Finally, at Heracleía Minoa in Sicily, Minos gave the shell to King Cocalus and he brought it back threaded—Daedalus was indeed there, and had performed the task by tying the thread to an ant. At once Minos demanded that the king turn Daedalus over to him. The king hedged, and instead invited Minos to stay at his palace. Cocalus' daughters were dismayed at the thought of losing the man who had made so many enchanting mechanical toys for them, and while Minos was in his bath they put a pipe through the ceiling and poured boiling water through it, scalding him to death. Zeus then sent him down to Hades to judge the dead, a task he shared with his brother Rhadamanthys and his enemy Aeacus.

Talos and Daedalus

> His name was Talus, made of yron mould,
> Immovable, resistless, without end;
> Who in his hand an yron flale did hould,
> With which he thresht out falshood, and did truth unfould.

The Faerie Queene, Book V, canto I

It took considerable poetic licence to convert Talos, the Bronze Man of Crete, into the iron companion of Spenser's Sir Artegall, who in the fifth book of *The Faerie Queene* wanders the world bashing miscreants with his 'yron flale', all in the name of Justice. In Spenser's hallucinatory verse it is hard to imagine Talos as anything more than a kind of sinister motorized dustbin, or maybe a Dalek. The original Talos, though, is even stranger. Some accounts say he had a single vein, running from his head to his heel, and that he 'ran around the coasts of Crete three times a day', guarding the land; whenever enemies appeared, Talos would sink their ships by casting great boulders at them. If any enemy happened to land, Talos would hop into a fire until he was red-hot, then seize the invader and burn him alive in his firey metal embrace, laughing like thunder. When Jason and the Argonauts sailed by, Medea cast a hypnotic spell over him, and pulled the pin from his heel, draining away his immortal *ichor*, or blood. After death he was transformed into a partridge.

It is generally agreed that Talos was Daedalus' nephew, and both (like Theseus) were members of the Erechtheid royal house of Athens (descended from Erechtheus, the first Athenian king, who was half man and half serpent). One mythological account has Talos as the nephew of Daedalus and the father of Hephaestus, the smith god. According to Apollodorus, Talos was Daedalus' apprentice, a clever boy who invented the compass for drawing circles, the potter's wheel and the saw, this last from observing the bones of a fish. His talent made Daedalus tremendously jealous. The master finally murdered his pupil, and escaped or was exiled to Crete.

Somehow it is all tied together—everything in mythology that has to do with making things, with the male mysteries of crafts and metallurgy that aided men in gaining their eventual religious and cultural supremacy. In the Bronze Age Aegean, the smith's art was something veiled by magic and secrecy, conducted in the *andreion*, or 'men's house', the centre of these new mysteries. One of the things a master-of-all-trades such as Daedalus would be involved with, naturally, was casting in bronze. The Minoans were skilled at this and, like other peoples around the Mediterranean, they used what is called the *cire-perdue*, or 'lost wax' method. A wax model of the desired result is made, and then the mould is formed around it. Then the mould is heated, the wax melts and pours out through a hole left in the bottom—through the heel, for a figurine or idol— and the wax is replaced by molten bronze. Now think of our bronze man Talos, with his 'single vein', and his relation Hephaestus with his lame foot (any number of smith gods from different cultures have the same curious feature, not to mention Achilles' heel, or Oedipus' lameness). Curiously, in myth all this is connected to partridges, perhaps for the hobbling way they walk. This bird may have been a kind of totem animal of the smiths.

Like Zeus, Poseidon and many other gods with a greater standing in Classical times, Talos began as a year *daimon*, and Daedalus probably did too. But the enduring importance of these two is their works, a reminder of how ancient Crete with its advanced culture must have truly seemed a land of sorcerers to its simpler Greek neighbours. Talos had other duties, more concerned with affairs of state. It is said that he carried the laws of Minos around Crete on bronze tablets to instruct the people. His three daily circuits around the island may recall a system of signal beacons that really guard the coast. In this curious figure, the functions of artisan, magician, soldier and lawgiver are combined. The great goddess may still have ruled Crete's heart and soul, but men with their imposing works were becoming ever more insistent on a share of recognition and power.

Demeter

And I am come from Crete across the wide sea-water wave

Homeric hymn to Demeter

The familiar tale of Demeter and her daughter, how Persephone was abducted and taken to the underworld by Hades, has more to do with Sicily than Crete (Lake Pergusa, where it happened, is not far from Heracleia Minoa), but Demeter like her brother Zeus was a Cretan, and another aspect of the great goddess. The sacred myths the Minoans knew are lost to us, but it has been established that their goddesses Diktynna and Britomartis correspond neatly to Demeter and Persephone.

One story tells how at a wedding feast Demeter was seized with a sudden passion for a Titan named Iasion. He couldn't wait either, and the two of them sneaked out together and made love in the open air, in the furrow of a 'thrice-ploughed field'. As Jane Harrison wrote, this is 'one of the lovely earth-born myths that crop up now and again in Homer, telling of an older, simpler world, of gods who had only half-emerged from the natural things they are, real earth-born flesh and blood creatures, not the splendid phantoms of an imagined Olympic pageant.'

The gods of Olympos, those late, pale creations of a sophisticated, literary age, whose temples were by Classical times little more than glorified museums, never really had much to do with genuine religion. But though the Greeks were never as pious a people as, say, the Romans, the religious impulse definitely existed among them, evidenced in the Orphic and Dionysian cults and especially in the worship of Demeter. Here, we have something ancient and conservative, relics of the old matriarchal religion that survived and prospered in men's (and especially women's) hearts despite the coming of the Olympians and the patriarchal, warrior-based society they represented. Wherever you visit sites of the Greek world, from Sicily to Syria, you will find vast numbers of little plaques and figurines on display in the museums—*ex votos*, or thank offerings, left in Demeter's temples by the common people. No other gods or goddesses commanded such popular devotion.

The most important rites involving Demeter were the Mysteries, as practised at Eleusis, near Athens, at Samothrace, Thrace and elsewhere. These initiation rituals, popular until their extinction at the hands of Christianity, were kept so closely secret that that scholars today still puzzle endlessly over what went on in the mystery caves. One thing that seems sure is that the Mysteries originated in Crete, and indeed may have been a direct survival of the religion of the Minoans. Diodorus

Siculus, that excellent 1st century BC historian who is responsible for much of what we know about the curiosities of the Classical world, mentions that the rites other people kept secret were in Crete completely open and available to all. This in a way is what the story of Demeter and Iasion illustrates. It is likely that the climax of the mysteries (and of the old Cretan religion) included a sexual union between the sacred king (or the initiate) and a priestess representing the goddess.

Minoan Religion

Beyond what can be inferred from myth, extremely little is known for sure about Minoan beliefs and practices. Lacking definitive texts, writers on the subject are forced into ingenious interpretations based on the evidence of paintings, seals, bronzes and such. But what if the figure apparently engaged in a religious rite really represented a character in a popular legend, a scene from everyday secular life, or a flight of the artist's fancy? Nearly everyone emphasizes that the the Minoans were a god-ridden people whose every move was determined by rituals and priestesses. This is only because the scholars themselves have chosen to interpret the evidence this way; imagining religious associations is always the easiest way out.

Most of the Minoan texts so far deciphered have been simple temple records, but at least they tell us the names of some of the gods. Often even these are only aspects (additional or alternative titles) of single deities: *Potnia*, for example, the most common name of the great goddess, means 'Lady', and is often used in conjunction with other names, such as *Atana*—the origin of the Greeks' Athena. Zeus' mother Rhea and his wife Hera seem to have originated as similar titles of the Lady. One extremely ancient and important aspect of the goddess is her role as the mountaintop 'mistress of the wild things', the way she is most frequently pictured in art, between two griffins, lions or other animals. She resembles the later divine huntress Artemis, and her common name, Britomartis, gives away the connnection. But these divinities hate being pinned down to a single identity, and one form always seems to shade into the next, as in the aforementioned equation of Britomartis and Diktynna with Persephone and Demeter. Sometimes seals and gems show a male 'master of the wild things', a consort of the goddess or a later male substitution for the original. Zeus doesn't appear at all under his common Greek name, but the male *daimon* of the year is called the greatest *kouros* or *Velchanos*. Other male gods, or perhaps aspects of a single male god, are mentioned: *Poteidan* (Poseidon), who seems to have been the most important, and also *Palaiwon* and *Enualios*, the forerunners of the Greek Apollo and Ares.

'Temple', incidentally, is a word that comes easily to us but one probably completely foreign to the religious practices of the Minoans. Even the Classical Greeks did not build proper temples until a rather late date, the 8th century BC. Before these the Greeks had only sanctuaries, sites for the most important rite: the sacrifice. This was probably true for the Minoans too. Their sanctuaries would have included an altar and perhaps a sacred tree or grove of trees. Oak and olive trees seem to have been especially revered. Similar enclosed shrines are very common on Minoan seals; occasionally, in place of a tree there will be a sacred pillar, perhaps like those decorated with double-axes, on the Ag. Triáda sarcophagus. The goddess as 'mistress of the wild things' was worshipped in shrines on the sacred mountains. These, along with the caves, such as the Diktean cave, were the most important religious sites in early Minoan times, and gradually gave way to the urban temples as Minoan society grew more opulent and complex.

Four striking symbols, repeated over and over in Minoan art, may be keys to understanding Minoan culture. First and most importantly, the double axe. Plenty of them, small ritual gold or bronze models with no practical use, have been unearthed, and they appear frequently in art, sometimes placed between the bull's horns or atop a pillar. They are commonly associated with the Cretan goddess or goddesses; the double axe is the *labrys*, in Greek, after which the Labyrinth was named. Bulls and bulls' horns are equally common, from those that appear on seal rings to the architectural versions that decorated the cornices of Knossós. A third symbol is the sacral knot, a looped strip of cloth with its fringed ends extending downwards. These commonly occur on female figures, but the Minoans left us with no real hints as to their significance. The fourth is the shield, a figure-eight shape reminiscent of the double axe in its symmetry. These are the shields that the *kouroi* clashed in their dance at the birth (and death) of Zeus. Real ones would have been made, not surprisingly, out of the hides of bulls.

Looking at Minoan art or trying to figure out the puzzle of their culture, it's only natural to ask sometimes 'What were these people on?' The answers are wine, obviously, as in the later cult of Dionysos, but also opium. Statuettes of goddesses with crowns of opium poppy heads have been discovered, and the common decorative motif usually called a 'rosette' is probably the top of a poppy head as well. This, perhaps, explains a lot, but nevertheless there is still so very much about the Minoans that we may never understand. If the Minoans did in plain sight what were Mysteries for others, why should their ways remain so mysterious to us? Contemplating other ancient cultures, we find it hard to resist the tendency to put their rulers, gods and celebrants into our shoes, and make them think and act as we would. With the Minoans this never seems to work; they are simply too *different*, and therein lies their special fascination. They remind us that this world of ours is a wide and a strange one, capable of more surprises and more delights than we know.

History

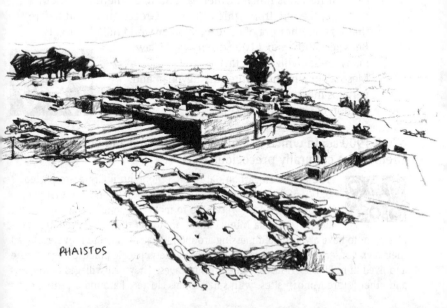

PHAISTOS

The mysterious legends and above all the matchless art of Minoan Crete exert a special fascination. Poetically, we know the island first from Homer:

> *One of the great islands of the world in midsea, in the winedark sea, is Krete: spacious and rich and populous, with ninety cities and a mingling of tongues. Akhaians there are found, along with Kretan hillmen of the old stock, and Kydonians, Dorians in three blood-lines, Pelasgians—and one among their ninety towns is Knossós. Here lived King Minos whom great Zeus received every ninth year in private council.*

> Odyssey, book XIX, translated by Robert Fitzgerald)

Myths hinted obscurely at an age when Crete had been much more important than it was in Homer's time, but it was not until 1900 with the discoveries of Arthur Evans that Europe's first great civilization rose up again from historical oblivion. We learned in school to think of everything before the Dark Ages as 'Classical Antiquity', and everything before that as 'Prehistory', but a score of astounding archaeological discoveries over the last century have cast our horizons much further back in time. There was another dark age, the one from which Classical Greece grew, and before that was another era of culture, another world full of marvels.

Between 2000 and 1100 BC, this world saw many great civilizations thrive: the Mesopotamian, the Hittite, the Egyptian and, perhaps most marvellous of all, the Aegean civilization of Crete and Mycenae.

6200–1900 BC: In which a dinner of bread, wine and olives helps the Cretans to a culturally precocious start

The first radiocarbon dates for settlement in Crete are placed at 6200–5800 BC. It may come as a surprise to imagine that people at that early date were able to make the long sea voyage (most likely from Asia Minor) necessary to get there, but Neolithic peoples seem to have always liked messing around in boats. On Crete they developed their own conservative, long-lasting Neolithic society; people practised agriculture and lived in mud-brick houses, sometimes in caves. They built villages at Knossós and other future Minoan sites, with small rooms clustered around a central open area, presaging the floor-plans of the famous palaces. They worshipped goddesses in the depths of caves and on top of mountains—the future peak sanctuaries of the Minoans.

Until recently, it was believed that Minoan civilization, like every other early European civilization, appeared as a result of learning new techniques and ideas from the Middle East. But as the archaeological record fills out, it becomes increasingly clear that growth and development were original and independent: the Aegean area is one of the true cradles of culture. The evidence is also accumulating that the civilization of Minoan Crete was not a radical break with the past or a sudden dramatic blossoming of culture. Continuity was an ever-present feature of Minoan culture, change gradual and evolutionary. Most of the main centres of Neolithic Crete, unfortunately, were the same locations as those used at the height of the palace culture—the palace builders changed the landscape around Knossós and elsewhere to fit their new creations, effectively destroying any record of what had gone before.

Long before the palaces, though, before 2000 BC, Cretans practised metallurgy, built imposing buildings (like the one recently discovered at Vassilíki), and produced excellent ceramics and jewellery, exporting them around the eastern Mediterranean. The population grew steadily throughout the 3rd Millenium, implying a relatively peaceful life and continual improvements in technology. The skill of bronze casting was imported from the Balkans or the Middle East, resulting in better tools and weapons, but the great advances of the late Neolithic Aegean area were agricultural: the development of the essential Greek way of life, depending on the triad of an early form of wheat, the olive and the grape. All three of these can easily be stored, and olives and grapes require little labour. These three blessings of nature made greater surpluses and more leisure possible—a perfect diet for any Neolithic people looking for cultural advancement.

You'll note, by the way, that this word 'Neolithic' is supposed to mean 'late Stone Age'; in many places, Neolithic people were already working bronze—shouldn't they be in the Bronze Age? This is an indication of the disarray archaeology is in these days, caused by new discoveries from all over the world and the refinement of radiocarbon-dating techniques. Quite simply, terms such as 'Bronze Age' and 'Copper Age', or really any classifications by tool use, have become totally meaningless—you'll still see them often enough in books and museums, but they can be safely disregarded. The past is getting more complicated all the time.

An alternative way to come to terms with it is to call the latter half of this period the **Pre-Palatial period** (2600–1900 BC), according to Professor Níkos Pláton's useful revision of Evans' original chronology. This is the age when Minoan culture really took off, as evidenced by the first monumental *tholos* tombs (as at Archánes), the building of sanctuaries at the highest points of settlements, and the apparent beginning of a ruling or priestly (or priestessly) class, who dwelt in palaces (or temples) with red-plastered walls. Trade contacts were established and expanded in Egypt, the Cyclades and the Middle East. The Minoan taste for refinement shines through at the end of the period, in exquisite work in gold, semi-precious stones and miniature sealstones, some bearing the first signs of writing in ideograms. It is interesting to note that Crete in this era was already exporting, not importing, high-quality finished goods. More Cretan items are found in Egypt and the Middle East than items from those places in Crete. The island may not have produced great monuments like the pyramids and ziggurats, but in many other ways it may already have been the most advanced culture around.

1900–1700 BC: The Caphtorites found an empire, and build great palaces without telling anyone whom they were for

 When Arthur Evans began excavating Knossós, he found a completely unknown culture and was forced to give it a name: he labelled it 'Minoan' after the legendary King Minos. And everyone will probably go on calling them Minoans, even though ancient records have finally provided the people of old Crete with a name of their own: the Egyptians called the Cretans the *Keftiu*, and they appear in Syrian inscriptions as the *Caphtorites*, under which name they also appear in the Old Testament. 'Minos', incidentally, denotes a title, rather than a single individual, taken from the Egyptian *menes*, a royal title taken from the name of the founder of the contemporary reigning dynasty. Cretan kings, though, were probably religious figureheads with little political power (*see* **Mythology**).

It is about 1900 BC that these Caphtorites begin to make a name for themselves. Pláton's **Old Palace period** (Evans' Middle Minoan: 1900–1700 BC) saw a hitherto unheard-of concentration of wealth and power in Crete. Built over the sites of their simpler predecessors, the 'palaces' of Knossós, Mália, Phaistós and Zákro appear. Some argue that these buildings are really temples, or even the shrines of a cult of the dead. We may never know their purpose, and it is likely that the reality would not make a perfect fit with our conceptions of a 'palace' or 'temple'. They may well have been a little of both. The rulers at Knossós may have been kings or queens or chiefs, colleges of priestesses or priests, or there may even have been citizen democracies like the later Greek city-states—the evidence gives so few clues that no idea can be completely discounted.

Whatever, 'palaces' seems as good a word as any for the great building complexes; they were kitted out with the first known plumbing and lavishly decorated with frescoes and stylized sacred 'horns of consecration'. The vast storehouses on the lower levels at Knossós and (on a lesser scale) the other palaces hint at a role as 'centres of redistribution': in other words, treasuries. Goods collected in taxation could be stored at the palaces and later redistributed among the needy, exchanged for profit or used to finance foreign adventures or public works. Some imaginative writers have seen the Minoan system as primitive communism, others as royal tyranny; again, we know little about the truth of the arrangement. Certainly the palaces were the economic centres of Cretan life, and in this period the new cities of Crete grew up around them. Most of the workshops so far discovered cluster around the palaces, along with large, well-constructed residences.

Both towns and palaces were unfortified, suggesting political unity on the island, or at least close cooperation among various city-states, and supporting the references in myth to a thalassocracy, or sea empire; no walls were needed thanks to the Minoans' powerful fleet. Their ships traded extensively with Cyprus, Egypt and the Greek islands; Egypt in particular seems to have had a strong influence on Cretan religion and culture. Minoan colonies have also been found at Kéa, Mílos and Kýthera. There was a system of writing in ideograms, most famously on the undeciphered Phaistós disc in the Herákleon museum. Roads paved with flagstones crossed the island, and the first large irrigation projects were dug. Art reached new heights in stonecarving, fresco painting and pottery. In 1700 BC a huge earthquake ripped across the eastern Mediterranean and devastated the buildings, but this did not mean the end of Minoan culture, or even a serious setback. The best was yet to come.

1700–1100 BC: A great civilization reaches its height—and we still don't really know what was going on in it

Forced to start afresh, the Minoans rebuilt better than ever during the **New Palace period** (1700–1450 BC). The palace complexes were rebuilt in the same style: a warren of rooms illuminated by light wells, overlooking a central court where religious ceremonies took place. To build the new palaces with more 'give' in case of earthquakes, wooden beams and columns (the distinctive reversed cedar trunks, thin at the bottom and wide at the top) were combined with stone. Workshops and vast storerooms were clustered around the palaces, the contents of the latter recorded on clay tablets in a writing system known as Linear A. Fancy villas were built outside the palaces, most famously at Ag. Triáda, and scattered throughout the countryside were farms, with pottery kilns, wine presses and looms. Densely populated towns have been excavated at Gourniá, Móchlos, Palaíkastro, Zákros and Pseíra island. Some of the houses show traces of frescoes like those in the palaces—one of many clues that prosperity was widespread, not limited to the élite in the palaces. Burials at this time became more elaborate, their paraphernalia more monumental, more various; many people were interred in painted clay sarcophagi, or *larnaxes*, these possibly an Egyptian influence. Impressive port facilities were built, especially along the north and east coasts, and shields, daggers, swords and helmets have been discovered, although land defences have never been found.

If the Cretans themselves had little need for weapons or town walls, their nation was throwing a big shadow across the Aegean and perhaps beyond. New trade counters were established on Santoríni, Rhodes, Skópelos, and on the mainland of Greece and Asia Minor; script similar to Linear A has been found as far west as Panarea, an island off the north coast of Sicily. Miletus, the very ancient city that was long the metropolis of western Asia Minor, seems to have been of Cretan foundation. Nearby peoples, the Lycians and Carians, had strong ties to Crete, as did the more distant Pulesati—the Philistines of the Old Testament. Greek myths are filled with echoes of Minoan colonization, or settlement, or conquest, or whatever it was—remember, for example, the story of Minos' brother Sarpedon going off to become king of Cilicia. Place names also give clues. Gaza, for one, an important religious centre in Classical times, was originally called Minoa, and there is a Heracleia Minoa on the southern coast of Sicily, near the place where Minos, searching for Daedalus, is said to have met his end.

One thing that's certain is that this Cretan empire did not include Mycenaean Greece. Until about 1550 BC the mainland Greeks had little culture to speak of, but from then on we see an impressive flowering of the arts, heavily influenced by Crete. The Mycenaean city-states grew rapidly in wealth and power, and one intriguing interpretation of the admittedly scanty evidence on Crete has the 17th century BC as a period of invasions, in which Greeks from the mainland conquered the island and headed a synthetic, Greek-run society that managed to maintain its prosperity and cultural brilliance. As we will see, this is just what most historians assume to have happened later, in 1450. Some day, perhaps, more written sources will appear, and be deciphered, to clear all this up.

One of the biggest and longest-running arguments about ancient Crete centres on just what happened to bring the great Middle Minoan period to an end. Until recently, the consensus was that the great eruption of Santoríni, c. 1450, with its subsequent tidal waves and earthquakes, left Crete in ruins—in some places along the north coast a 20cm layer of *tefra* (volcanic ash) has been found. This is the time when Knossós and the other palaces were destroyed. Unfortunately, refinement in carbon dating now figures the eruption to have taken place about a half-century earlier. Another theory has invaders from Mycenaean Greece putting the torch to the palaces and gaining control of the country. But, as always in Minoan affairs, theories are cheap and conclusive evidence completely lacking.

The end of the palaces marks the beginning of the **Late Minoan** or **Post-Palace period** (1450–1100 BC). Many scholars now believe that Mycenaean infiltration was much more gradual, and that for a long period the Mycenaeans co-existed peacefully side by side with the Minoans. Since we know nothing of the states or the politics of the time, this too is only speculation; the destruction of the palaces could as easily have been the result of civil strife or even revolution. What is certain is that cultural and political supremacy in the Aegean area now passed to the Greek mainland, to Mycenae and the other city-states of the Peloponnese. Of the Cretan palaces, only Knossós was rebuilt; interestingly, the only important new part of the palace from this period was the so-called 'throne room', perhaps implying a royal ruler and a more centralized state. The Knossós palace burned once and for all in *c.* 1380 BC. In other places, such as Ag. Triáda, typical Mycenaean palaces, or *megarons*, have been found. Linear B became the dominant script (in Mycenaean Greek, replacing the undeciphered native language written in Linear A), and the free natural decoration of Cretan art became ever more conventional and stylized, as it always was in Mycenae. The island maintained its great fleet, and according to Homer it was able to contribute 90 ships to the Trojan War.

The really big troubles began around 1200, a time of upheavals all around the Mediterranean world (the usual date given for the fall of Troy is 1180 BC). The Egyptians were plagued by a host of invaders that included the 'Ahhiwasha'— Homer's Achaeans—who were Greeks, of course. Confusingly enough, the archaeologists record that about the same time the Achaeans' Mycenaean civiliza-tion itself was destroyed. The champion hoodlums among the Greeks seem to have been the Dorians, a people with few manners but plenty of advanced iron weapons who came down from Epirus in northwestern Greece to conquer the Peloponnese about 1200. Crete was spared for another century, but the Dorians conquered it too about 1100.

1100–67 BC: A long period of conservative rule, under which Crete declines to participate in Greece's Classical Age

 The coming of the Dorians brought a cultural dark age to the whole Greek world. On Crete the Minoans lived on as a subject people, though some, known as the Eteocretans, or true Cretans, took to the hills, especially south of Sitía. Their art grew weird and misshapen as they declined; in Praisós they left mysterious inscrip-tions in the Greek alphabet still waiting to be translated. Other Cretans were treated according to the amount of resistance they had offered the Dorians; those who fought the most were divided among the conquerors as slaves. Burials of this period begin to show a sharp difference between a small class of wealthy aristocrats and the impoverished masses—rather like the divisions of feudal society in western Europe during the later Dark Age.

For almost a thousand years the Cretan cities were governed as rigidly aristocratic republics, where the small class of Dorian landholders elected ruling committees called *kosmoi*. As in Sparta, another Dorian land, the population was divided into three rigid castes: the free citizens (mostly the descendants of the Dorian warriors); the *perioeci*, free people with no political rights, including artisans, merchants and seamen; and slaves, who might belong either to private individuals or to the state.

By 900 BC Crete was divided, like the Greek mainland, into autonomous city-states: a hundred, according to ancient writers. The Minoan goddess was dragooned into the patriarchal Greek pantheon—Atana became Athena, Brito-martis became Artemis, her son and consort Welchanos became Zeus, father of the gods. The 8th century brought a period of rapid cultural and economic advance throughout the Greek world and, at least in the beginning, Crete seems to have shared fully in it. New towns were founded (Lato, Dreros, Aptera, Polyrrenia) far from traditional Minoan centres, nearly all perched high over the sea and bristling with walls, with views down to their harbours. Overcrowded Greek towns were sending out colonies across the Mediterranean, and the Cretans with their maritime tradition at first seem to have been in the forefront. Doric Crete was also one of the art centres of Greece in the Archaic period (650–550 BC).

Something—there isn't enough evidence to guess exactly what—happened about 600 BC; after that date the number and quality of finds drops off drastically. Herodotus and other writers hint at civil wars on the island, but the crucial factor in Crete's new decline was probably the expansion of Ionian influence in the Mediterranean. Athens and Miletus and the other Ionian cities were elbowing out Cretan manufactures and trade. Crete would have been hindered by its reactionary Doric constitution, which discouraged expansion and trade; as a kind of political Sparta, trying to play the cultural and economic role of an Athens, Crete could never have gone very far.

The rest of the Greek world was entering its Classical Age. During this period Crete sat out on the margins of history, its cities wasting their energies in countless petty wars against each other. Many Cretans fled their increasingly impoverished island for a soldier's life; Cretan mercenaries are frequently mentioned, from the Peloponnesian Wars to the campaigns of Alexander the Great and Julius Caesar. Spartan influence remained strong on Crete until about 250 BC, when much of the island became a protectorate of the Ptolemies, the Greek rulers of Egypt. Other towns fell under the sway of other Hellenistic states, such as Macedonia or the Seleucid Empire (both, like Ptolemaic Egypt, fragments of Alexander's short-lived empire). Still, warfare between the towns continued unabated, often reaching frightful excesses such as the total destruction of Lyttos by Knossós in 220 BC.

Not long after that event, an unusual attempt at unification was made under a pan-Cretan council called the *koinon,* in which all the cities were to have equal rights. The *koinon* is not well documented, but it does not seem to have had much effect on the prevailing fratricidal anarchy. Some of the towns with fleets turned to piracy in this period and this brought in the Aegean's biggest maritime power, Rhodes, which built up a sphere of influence in the east of the island.

A menace much greater than Rhodes was already looming from the west. Fresh from its final victory over Carthage in the Punic Wars, the incredibly strange (from a Greek point of view) and bellicose Roman Republic was proceeding to its easy conquest of the Greek East. Górtyn, then the strongest Cretan city, was the early centre of pro-Roman sentiment (though that city was briefly embarrassed when Hannibal took refuge there for a short time on his escape from the Romans). Knossós, Górtyn's arch enemy, logically became the leader of anti-Roman opposition. Pirates were still active in Cretan ports, causing Rome to plan the conquest of the island in 74 BC. The job was entrusted to a senator named Marcus Antonius—father of the more famous Mark Antony, no less. Unfortunately for him, the Cretans gave his fleet a sound whipping before it ever landed any troops, earning Marcus Antonius the derisive title of 'the Cretan'. Unfortunately for Crete, this only served to make the Romans thoroughly angry. They succeeded in landing a huge force in 69 and, despite the wholehearted resistance of a finally united island, the legions wiped out all resistance within two years.

---

67 BC–AD 1204: Thirteen rather nondescript centuries, decorated by dour Romans, piratical Arabs and perfumed Byzantines

Under Roman rule the centre of power on the island moved south to Górtyn on the fertile Mesará plain, which was made capital of the province of Crete and Cyrene (Libya). Knossós, wrecked in the conquest, was refounded as a Roman colony, called *Colonia Julia Nobilis* and settled largely by Italians from Capua.

With peace established, the population on Crete grew to some 300,000. The Romans, always more respectful towards the Greeks than their other subject peoples, left Crete and its institutions alone for the most part. The *koinon* continued to function and towns still minted their own coins and ran their own affairs. Wealth and trade increased, and important public works appeared all over the island. Christianity came to the island early, when St Paul appointed one of his Greek disciples, Titus, to found the first church at Górtyn in 58 AD; this suggests the island had a sizeable Jewish community. Christian Crete especially prospered after the founding of Constantinople in *c.* 330, when rich basilicas were constructed across the island, most importantly at Knossós, Chersónisos, Górtyn, Líssos, Sýia, Ítanos and Kainoúrios.

In the first centuries of the eastern, Byzantine empire, Crete continued as a provincial backwater. The chroniclers of this period mention only a few minor disasters:

two terrible earthquakes that levelled most of Górtyn in the 6th century, a plague or two, and a raid by Slavic pirates in 623. This last unusual occurrence presaged Byzantine weakness and greater troubles to come. The Muslim Arabs, expanding in every direction in the first generations after Mohammed, first raided the Cretan coast in 656. Their attacks on the island continued, and the Arabs finally took control of the entire island in 824, taking advantage of the confusion caused by an anti-Byzantine revolt. The new conquerors, however, had not come from nearby Egypt or Sicily. They came from, of all places, Spain. After some civil strife in the Caliphate of Andalusia, the losing faction under Abu Hafs 'Umar fled to the East in 40 ships. After briefly occupying Alexandria, they turned their attentions to Crete as a safe refuge for themselves.

One lasting feature of their stay was the building of the first castle at Herákleon, called *al-Khandaq* ('the ditch'), or Candia, a name which grew to mean all of Crete in the Middle Ages (and eventually became synonymous with the sweet honey and nuts it exported, hence 'candy'). The century of the Arab Emirate of Crete is also remembered in some village names, such as Sarkenos and Aposalemis (Abu Salim), but the occupation was too short to effect substantial changes (or many religious conversions), nor did the Arab rulers achieve much in either culture or commerce. What they were good at, following the old Cretan tradition, was piracy. Cretan fleets ravaged the Greek islands, and even sacked Thessalonika and Mount Athos.

In 961 Byzantine general and future emperor Nikephóros Phokás reconquered Crete, with massacres and looting that put the pirates' best efforts to shame, and sent the pirates' treasure back to Constantinople. The victorious Greek soldiers were among the first new colonists given tracts of land, in an attempt at repopulation; Emperor Alexius I Comnenus later sent his own son and other young Byzantine aristocrats to Crete as a ruling class of landowning *archons*, one that continued to dominate Cretan life for centuries.

1204–1669: In which the Lion of St Mark plants his heavy paw on the island, and keeps it there for 400 years

 To a land power in any age, Crete is of little importance; this is why the Muslims, who never understood the importance of the sea, made little effort to keep it. To a state whose future lay in controlling the trade routes of the eastern Mediterranean, however, Crete meant everything. And just such a state was growing up at this time: a true thalassocracy King Minos would have appreciated—the Republic of Venice.

Venice engineered the conquest of Constantinople in the Fourth Crusade in 1204. In the division of the spoils, Crete was awarded to one of the Frankish barons, Boniface of Montferrat. Having no use for the island, he sold it cheap to the

Venetians who, after a brief tussle with arch rival Genoa, occupied the entire island in 1210. Venice did everything she could to hold on to Crete, as the key to her interests in the East, and kept the island until 1669.

The first two centuries of rule by the Most Serene Republic proved neither serene nor republican. The Venetians high-handedly imposed their model of government; the island was even divided into six *sestieri* like Venice itself, and ruled by its own doge, or *duca*, based in Herákleon. Laws attempted to diminish the influence of the Orthodox Church and replaced the Orthodox hierarchy with a Catholic one. This, along with eternal high taxes for defence and forced Cretan labour on Venetian galleys, caused over a dozen serious revolts, often led by the *archons*, the old Byzantine nobles. Nearly every time they won important concessions from the Venetians until, by the 15th century, the Greek Orthodox population and Venetian Catholics (some 10,000) lived in reasonable harmony—except of course for the majority, the *villani*, or serfs, who in addition to working long hours for their lords were compelled to build the immense walls around the cities, even though they were not allowed to live inside them.

Cretan–Venetian relations were cemented with the fall of Constantinople in 1453, when the Venetians were keen to keep the Greeks on their side. In accordance with Greece's age-old tradition of absorbing the invader, many Venetians were hellenized, spoke Greek better than Italian and converted to Orthodoxy. As a refuge for scholars and painters from Constantinople and mainland Greece, Crete became the centre of Greek culture and the key point of contact between the East and the Italian Renaissance. In the 15th and 16th centuries Cretans were prominent among the large community of learned Greeks in Venice, giving the Renaissance a big push by reprinting and translating countless classical works previously unknown or inaccessible in the West. Crete produced, among other artists, Doménikos Theotokópoulos, who moved to Venice and later Spain, where he became known as El Greco. Creto-Venetian schools and academies, architecture, theatre, literature, song and romantic epic poetry blossomed, culminating in the dialect epic poem *Erotókritos* by Vicénzo Kornáros.

The fall of Constantinople, and the end of the Byzantine Empire, only replaced Venice's old, decrepit Christian enemy with a young, ambitious and formidably strong Muslim foe: the Ottoman Turks. By 1500 they had a fleet to match that of Venice, designed to gain control of the eastern Mediterranean and perhaps areas beyond. Crete once again found itself living in interesting times.

Although pirate raids, especially by such famous nasties as Barbarossa and his successor Dragut (both Greek by birth), were a constant menace in the 1500s, the tremendous coastal fortifications the Venetians had forced the Cretans to pay for finally proved their worth. The island held out until 1571, when the Battle of

Lepanto put an end to the first great wave of Ottoman expansion and ushered in a long period of relative tranquillity. Even so, Crete was left in isolation as the only important bastion of Christian Europe in the East. By the 17th century Venice was suffering its long economic and military decline, and it was clear that the Turks would be back as soon as they felt strong enough to try.

In 1645, Sultan Ibrahim declared war on the Knights of Malta after the privateering knights supposedly captured his wife and son as they sailed to Mecca. There is no evidence that such a thing actually happened—it may have been just a pretext to start hostilities—but the sultan accused the Venetians on Crete of aiding the pirates, and sent a fleet of 450 ships after them. They stopped in Kýthera to purchase coffee and sugar, and the Venetian commander there sent word to his counterpart in Chaniá to allow the fleet safe passage. On 12 June, the sultan's ships turned their guns on the city, which fell after a siege of two months. Réthymnon shared its fate a year later. The Turks turned their attentions to the capital soon after, but Herákleon, with the strongest fortifications of any city in the eastern Mediterranean, proved a tougher nut to crack. For years the siege dragged on, proving a major embarrassment for the Turks. In 1666 the sultan had his commander beheaded, replacing him with the extremely capable Grand Vezir Ahmet Köprülü.

Now the battle recommenced in earnest. The European powers, finally realizing the seriousness of the struggle, sent help. The Spaniards sent food, ships and money, and troops came from Italy, France, and even some of the German states. It proved too little and too late, and the western commanders often made things worse by quarrelling among themselves. After 21 years of siege, one of the longest in history, Herákleon fell in September 1669. The Venetians negotiated a liberal surrender: they were allowed to leave in peace, and the entire population of the city with them. Venice continued to keep a few coastal strongholds, tiny islet pin-pricks in the Ottomans' side, refuges for rebellious Cretans, always hoping to recapture the island. In 1692 a Venetian force unsuccessfully attempted to take Chaniá. This proved to be the last gasp. The remaining three Venetian toeholds, Spinalónga, Néa Soúda and Gramvoúsa, were handed over by treaty in 1715.

1669–1898: In which the Cretans come under Turkish rule—a marriage made in heaven

 As the Greeks tell it, the period of Ottoman rule was one long night of indescribable cruelty and oppression. But as always in this part of the world, their version is best taken with a large pinch of salt. Certainly, after the ravages of the long war, Crete was depopulated and its towns in ruins. The Ottomans piled on more misery with taxes perhaps even worse than Venice's had been, and quartered large numbers of janissaries on the island—

probably to get them far away from Istanbul. The janissaries, once the finest fighting force in the world, had by this time degenerated into a lawless and dangerous band only interested in enriching themselves. Their outrages against the population became legendary, and civilian governors could do little against them.

The Turks did expel the Italian Catholics and restore the Orthodox Church to primacy, but almost from the beginning their occupation was marked by huge numbers of Cretans converting to Islam, often entire villages at a time—the higher taxes levied against infidels had more than a little to do with this. Turkish settlers were also encouraged, and by the late 18th century nearly half the island's population was Muslim.

The Turks attempted to restore Crete's towns and trade, though in a time of general economic decline throughout the region the odds were hardly in their favour. Herákleon in particular recovered very slowly, and travellers of the time report Crete looking sad and impoverished. Still, in the 1700s things began to pick up. Crete exported grain around the eastern Mediterranean and as far as France, while manufacture in the towns began to grow again, especially soap-making, a new use for the island's excellent olive oil.

One small corner of Crete was not included in the regular Turkish system. This was Sfakiá, the wild mountainous region on the southern coast. After the Turkish conquest, the sultan donated this region to the holy cities of Mecca and Medina, and imposed a religious tithe on the Sfakians in place of the usual taxes. It wasn't the most generous of gifts; Sfakiá was nearly inaccessible by land, with a long tradition of mountaineer independence, and no ruler ever found it easy to squeeze much cash out of it. In the 18th century, the Sfakians began to build boats and go into the shipping trade—a phenomenon familiar on islands such as Chíos, and the beginning of modern Greece's important shipping interests.

Sfakiá's tradition of freedom, its isolation and the progressive outlook fostered by trade made it the natural focus for a century of revolts—more than 400 of them—until Crete finally gained its independence. From the beginning of Ottoman rule, mountain bandits called the *hayins* (similar to the *klephts* on the mainland) made life difficult for the Ottoman government, but the first organized revolt did not come until 1770. The Daskaloyánnis Rebellion, which began in Sfakiá, was brutally repressed the following year when help promised by the Russians—fellow Orthodoxes and the Turks' worst enemy—never materialized.

The next big outbreak came in 1821. While the rest of Greece was fighting for its independence, the Cretan revolt began once again in Sfakiá and spread across the island. The Cretans formed a general assembly and an army and held most of the island, but the tide turned against them with the arrival of an Egyptian army led by Mehmet Ali. The Egyptians subdued the last rebels in 1824, but then the next year the revolt started up again. By now the pattern was becoming familiar: the Cretans would liberate all of the countryside, while the Turks (or Egyptians) would wait inside the still-formidable Venetian walls of the towns for help to arrive. When it did, a few villages would be burned, the rebels would surrender, and next year the whole cycle could start again. By 1830 the Cretans were actually close to victory, but their fight was betrayed, as Cretans like to put it, by the new thalassocracy in the neighbourhood, Britain, which opposed Greece gaining control of Crete and forced a diplomatic solution under which Mehmet Ali would rule the island. British warships subsequently forced the surrender of the last rebel strongholds on the coast.

Egyptian rule lasted only a decade, but it proved a surprisingly liberal and beneficial regime, under which some long-needed roads and other public works were begun. It was certainly not good enough for the Cretans, who had their minds set on union with newly independent Greece. The disruptions caused by endless revolts, and the ferocity of the Christians, had caused many Muslim Cretans to emigrate by this time, and their numbers declined to less than a quarter of the population—even many of these still thought of themselves as Greeks first.

The revolts continued, especially after military embarrassments in Syria forced Egypt to give Crete back to the Turks in 1840. The Cretans gained a charter and an elected assembly from the increasingly weak Ottoman state, but this only served to fuel their campaign for freedom. A revolt in 1866 witnessed a dramatic event. When Turkish troops were on the point of taking a rebel stronghold, the monastery at Arkádi, the revolutionaries ignited the large store of munitions inside, killing themselves, many of the Turks—and most of the 600 women and children who had taken refuge inside. This bizarre act of revolutionary bravery caught Europe's attention, and even gained much sympathy for the rebels' cause. It was clear that the 'Cretan Question' would finally have to be faced.

Another major revolt, in 1878, secured the Cretans the right to a Christian governor. In 1898, Greece declared war on Turkey, and asked the Great Powers for aid. Britain did little, in spite of searing accounts of atrocities sent home by Arthur Evans, but finally the Turks made the fatal mistake of killing the British consul and 14 British soldiers in Herákleon. As British, French, Russian and Italian troops subdued sections of the island, Prince George of Greece was appointed High Commissioner of an 'autonomous' Crete; the Powers, for their own reasons, were still not ready to permit union with Greece.

1898–present: The Nazis come for a Mediterranean holiday and find both the accommodation and the service deplorable

Independent Crete is a curiosity perhaps known only to philatelists. The most important effect of the brief but well-timed period of independence was that Crete kept all the Minoan finds from the excavations of Evans and the others, instead of seeing them shanghaied off to the National Museum in Athens. At the start, the islanders worked in earnest to create all the institutions of an independent state. Prince George proved to be a repressive autocrat, and his high-handed actions resulted in the Revolution of Thérisso in 1905, led by his Justice Minister, Elefthérios Venizélos of Chaniá. Now Crete was fully independent. A large majority, though, still favoured *enosis*, union with Greece, and everyone knew this would be only a matter of time despite British opposition. Crete had become the hot political issue in Greece itself. In 1909 Venizélos was appointed Prime Minister of Greece, a position that enabled him to secure Crete's union with Greece after the Balkan War of 1913.

Venizélos continued to be the dominant figure in Greece's political life well into the 1920s. Crete's history from this point follows that of the nation as a whole. The island was affected by the ghoulish 'exchange of populations' agreed by the Turkish and Greek governments in 1923 after Greece's failed invasion of Turkey. The remaining 30,000 Cretan Muslims were robbed of their property and forced from their homes, their places taken by a nearly equal number of Greek refugees from Asia Minor—part of the nearly two million Greeks who had suffered the same fate.

When the Nazis overran Greece, the government in Athens took refuge on Crete (23 April 1943), the last bit of free Greek territory, defended by 30,000 British, New Zealand and Australian troops hastily transferred from the mainland. Crete's own battalions were trapped near the Albanian frontier; the only Greek soldiers on the island were cadets and untrained recruits. But then again, no one suspected what Goering and General Student, his second-in-command of the Luftwaffe, had in store—although some writers now say that the British command were well aware of what was happening, but didn't think Crete was worth the risk of betraying the fact that they had just cracked the Germans' secret code. After a week of bomb raids, Nazi paratroopers launched the world's first successful invasion by air on 20 May 1941. The Allied and Greek forces, along with hundreds of poorly armed men, women and children, put up such stubborn resistance for 10 days that the Germans were forced to expend the cream of their forces to subdue the island—at the cost of 170 aircraft, 4000 specially trained paratroopers, and the decimation of their 7th airborne division.

The Battle of Crete proved, if nothing else, the folly of attack by parachutists alone, and as Churchill wrote in *The Grand Alliance*:

> *The German losses of their highest class fighting men removed a formidable air and parachute weapon from all further part in immediate events in the Middle East. Goering gained only a Pyrrhic victory in Crete, for the forces he expended there might easily have given him Cyprus, Iraq,*

Syria and even perhaps Persia. These troops were the very kind needed to overrun large wavering regions, where no serious resistance would have been encountered. He was foolish to cast away such almost measureless opportunities and irreplaceable forces in a mortal struggle, often hand-to-hand, with the warriors of the British Empire.

In spite of brutal German reprisals, the Cretan resistance to the occupation, aided by British and ANZAC agents in the mountains and based in Egypt, was legendary. Resistance culminated in the sheer audacity of Major Patrick Leigh Fermor and Captain Billy Moss's daring abduction of General Kreipe, the German commander of Crete, from Herákleon in 1943. As a massive manhunt combed the island, Kreipe was relayed across the mountains and put on a submarine to Egypt from Rodákino on the southwest coast, earning a final, grudging comment from the General: 'I am beginning to wonder who is occupying the island—us or the English.'

Because of its Venizélan, republican traditions, Crete was spared the civil wars between left- and right-wing factions that divided most of Greece in the years after the war; communist-dominated militias simply were not as popular or as well-organized as in the north of the country. Just the same, Crete usually leans to the left in elections, and it has always been one of the strongholds of PASOK (Papandréou's Pan-Hellenic Socialist Movement, with its rising green sun symbol)—despite the fact that Constantine Mitsotákis, leader of the Néa Demokratikí opposition, is a scion of one of Crete's most influential families.

Crete today, or forty whacks with the double axe

You, pilgrims of modern times, guard yourselves from the songs of Cretan sirens and their false allures.

Pausanius, 2nd century AD

 Homer spoke of several 'Cretes', and the same is true at the end of the 20th century. Two predominate: the Crete of the villages and the Crete of the sirens and coast. The first one is doing relatively well. European agricultural subsidies that make the old family olive groves and vineyards a viable alternative to waiting tables in Mália have something to do with it; even sons of immigrants have begun to return to the land for the first time. New paved roads have replaced mule tracks and Japanese pick-up trucks have replaced the mules. Older men still cut a dash in their baggy breeches or *vráche*, their black shirts and waistcoats, their high jackboots and unusual black-fringed doiley-like kerchiefs, or *tsalvária,* which the Turks forced the Cretans to wear as a sign of their state of servitude, but which, even after the law was rescinded, the Cretans continued to wear to show their defiance. Young men still have a tendency to wear black, even if the young women are beginning to refuse to wrap themselves up in a cocoon of black scarves and shawls. Even many younger Cretans are taking an active role in preserving their culture, and pour disdain on 'the long-trousered men' who have exploited the coast.

To be fair, the other Crete really wasn't asked, back in 1960s during the Fascist reign of Papadopoulous, whether or not it would like to be the guinea pig for Greece's new vocation in mass tourism, but there's no turning back the clock in the near future. The lovely beaches along the north coast have been raped by toad-stool strips of jerry-built hotels, shops, restaurants and discos, veritable Euro-compounds most often run by Athenians or foreigners, where bars advertise daily video showings of *The Beverly Hillbillies* (or the Dutch, or German, or Finnish equivalents), the latest football scores, baked beans and permanently sozzled happy hours. The money was good, at least in the beginning, and much easier to make than olive oil. Cement mixers went hell for leather to fill every seaside spot on the north coast with a few columns and a floor, the minimum to call it a building, even if 'abusive' (without a permit). They know no politician will touch them; the problem is far too widespread and involves far too much money and influence.

This has happened in numberless other sunny places, but it seems even more tragic on Crete than elsewhere, perhaps because it has resisted so many other enemies for so long. More has been lost in the past 30 years than in the 243 under the Turks. But now the double axe of paradox is striking Crete's developers back on the rebound and they seem genuinely puzzled as to why. Tourist numbers are down, the drachma is up; Greece is no longer cheap in relation to other currencies. But perhaps most of all many travellers have begun to ask for more than a plot of sunny sand for their holidays. How Crete goes about trying to compete in the evolving cut-throat world of Mediterranean tourism is one of its biggest challenges.

There have been a few tentative moves in the right direction. High-rise hotels have been banned. Old houses and villas in the villages are being restored rather than bulldozed. Funds from the Orthodox patriarchy and EU are slowly seeping in to restore some (20 so far) of the island's 850 frescoed churches and monasteries before they fall over. Cretan cuisine and wines are enjoying new prestige in the restaurants; Cretan music and dancing is alive and well. Environmentalists have pushed issues such as garbage disposal, clean seas, water conservation, alternative power sources and wildlife and forest preservation to the fore. Even the rights of domestic animals get a mention now and then—if mostly from British residents. Old crafts (weaving and lacemaking, pottery, basketweaving, jewellery), have yet to die out and in some places are being revived, such as by the women at Gaval-ochóri who are bringing silkmaking back from the brink of extinction. The revival of interest in natural remedies has led to a new interest in cultivating the island's magical herbs.

Nor have the Cretans lost their pluck. A couple of years ago, an old man was asked: 'Grandfather, if you could relive your life, what would you do?' and he replied, unhesitatingly, in the old Cretan spirit: 'The same thing, and worse!'

Cretan Art

MINOAN BELL GODDESS

Minoan art is the one thing that sets Crete's ancient civilization apart from every other, a vibrant, flowing art, one far closer to modern tastes than the stiff, hieratic figures of Middle Eastern cultures or even the self-consciously perfect art of Classical Greece. The Minoan frescoes and vases were a revelation when Sir Arthur Evans' men reconstructed them from the fragments of Knossós, and, even though we know more about their meanings and contexts today, they remain a revelation still.

Other lands show us imposing monarchs, mysterious figures of gods and demons, vast funeral pomps and such; compared to these the Minoans often seem to have dropped in from another planet. Not only is their art entirely free from the political propaganda and state-worship that plagued so many other cultures, but even those works that are obviously religious seem to be more human, less threatening and shadowy. Most astounding of all is that many Minoan works have little or nothing to do with affairs of church and state; they are some of the western world's first examples of art for art's sake, born of a sense of delight so strong that it catches our fancy too, despite all the centuries that separate us from the enigmatic people who created it.

Pre-Palatial Period (2600–1900 BC)

Pottery was already well established in Neolithic times, and the first works of the Minoans were simple, graceful vessels decorated with simple linear patterns painted in red or incised in the clay. Several distinct styles have been identified, notably  the mottled red and black Vasilikí ware, which possibly was intended to imitate stone. Stone vases (from marble, serpentine, alabaster and 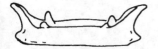 simpler stone) were always a Minoan luxury speciality. The techniques were learned from the Egyptians, and as early as 2500 BC they appeared on the island, more for decoration than for practical use.

Interestingly, ceramic ship models were also common in this age, suggesting that Cretans believed in an after-death passage similar to that of the Egyptians.

From fragments that survive, we can often deduce what the archaeological record leaves out—in this case, that the Early Minoans had a good deal of gold and silver ware. Most of it would have been melted down and re-used in later ages, but we can guess at its use and status from the large number of ceramic imitations of gold and silver vessels. Metals were also used in jewellery and for ornamental swords and daggers, though these rarely reached the level of sophistication seen in the era of the palaces.

Minoans always liked to wear rings, usually big oval ones; about 2300 BC the first seal rings appeared, for 'signing' documents inscribed on clay tablets; some apparently also served as magic talismans. The tiny, intricately carved designs on these rings have yielded a wealth of information on Minoan culture and religion—even though that information is never as precise as we would like it to be. Other arts are even less helpful in this distant age. Only fragments of Pre-Palatial buildings remain, but there is evidence that in these a simple kind of wall painting was practised, a forerunner of artistic triumphs to come.

Old and New Palace Periods (1900–1450 BC)

The best-known and most appealing creations of Minoan art are of course the frescoes, mainly from the palace of Knossós, created for the most part between 1700 and 1450 BC (others just as accomplished have been discovered on Santoríni, and can be seen in the National Museum in Athens). They have been enthusiastically called 'the world's first naturalistic art', although a close look at some of the paintings from contemporary Egypt, and the even older frescoes from the city of Mari in Syria, will show that the Cretans weren't alone; in fact much of the style and subject matter derived from Egyptian sources. Just the same, the paintings of the Minoans, both men and women, were wonderfully sensual and full of life, as were the delightful depictions of flowers and marine life. They portrayed themselves with wasp waists and long black curls, the men clad in codpieces and loincloths, the women with eyes blackened with kohl and lips painted red, clad in their famous bodices that exposed the breast, flounced skirts decorated with complex patterns, and exotic hats. You may notice that Minoan boys are red, girls are white. This is a convention taken over from Egyptian art, though it is quite possible that men in the religious ceremonies would dye themselves (and the women may have done themselves up with powdered alabaster).

Fresco of tribute-bearers from the Corridor of the Procession, Knossós, 15th century BC

Although the frescoes often seem to be a consciously élitist form of art—scenes with human figures mostly dealt with the court or palace religious ceremonies—frescoes were by no means limited to the palaces; other fragments have been discovered in villas and houses around Crete. None of these works is a true fresco, because they were painted on dried, not freshly applied plaster. If the Minoans had known the later technique their works might have been in better shape today—though, considering that literally nothing of Classical Greek painting has survived, they weren't doing too badly. Many artists must have done their own plastering, since in some of the frescoes figures were cleverly moulded in the plaster before painting to create a relief effect. Mycenaean Greece learned its art from Crete, but towards the end of the Middle Minoan period influences from the younger art of the mainland are recognizable in the slightly stiffer, more formal approach.

Like fresco painting, pottery reached its height in the Middle Minoan period. The great technical advance was the introduction of the potter's wheel, allowing artists to make ever more perfect forms. They decorated them in the same free, vivid style as the frescoes; for the first time figurative motifs appeared, mostly the Cretans' favourite floral themes and scenes of marine life. The thinner, more precisely made black and white 'Kamares

Kamares ware jug, from Phaistós, MMIIb

Kamares ware amphora, from Knossós, MMIII

ware', popular throughout the Palace periods, is considered by many the height of this art. Most of the finest Minoan vases were found in the palaces; plain folk apparently had to get by

Barbotine designs

with much simpler stuff. Minoans were also capable of making special numbers such as the giant *pithoi* in the palace store rooms; too big to be done on a potter's wheel (or even moved), they were formed to perfection by hand.

Another style of vase was the textured Barbotine ware, which first appeared in Middle Minoan I and became gradually more elaborate up to and including Middle Minoan III. Arthur Evans' theory about this pottery was that it was influenced by marine surfaces such as barnacles, prickles, spines and scales as well as wave motions.

Barbotine ware jug, southern Crete, MMIIb

An interesting set of faïence plaques in the shape of houses, discovered at Knossós, gives away the basics of Minoan architecture: mud-brick walls, perhaps plastered or stuccoed, interlaced with long squared beams to create a pleasing effect. Good stone was largely limited to the important parts of the palaces, and these are of course the greatest monuments Crete has to show. The obvious and most unusual architectural feature is the total disregard for any kind of monumental planning and symmetry, and this is another of the key Minoan puzzles. Other contemporary cultures built shrines and palaces that by their imposing forms would magnify the status of their gods and rulers. The Minoans never seem to have felt this urge. Similarly, no great monuments or inscriptions proclaim the glory of Minoan kings or goddesses; there is not even any large-scale sculpture from this time. Were the Minoans somehow spared the political and religious neuroses of their neighbours, or is there a different, as yet unsuspected explanation?

It may be that the lost upper storeys would have helped make architectural sense of the rambling piles at the palace sites. Nevertheless, there is a pattern common in all of them. Each was built around a rectangular central court, curiously orientated slightly east of north, and had a monumental entrance facing it on the western side. Upper storeys and entrances were supported by wooden columns, tapering at the bottom and brightly painted. The northern part of the palaces commonly held banqueting rooms and kitchens, while the western parts contained the major shrines, and near to them rooms used for record-keeping and storage.

Jewellery too reached its apogee in the Palace periods, with original, intricate work that has rarely been equalled since. Two new techniques helped the artists achieve

it: filigree and granulation, in which thin golden wire and grains of gold were used to create fine detail. Jewellery using beads of semi-precious stones was also common, and Minoans continued to make seals in a number of forms: round, prismatic (three-sided), oval, almond-shaped, or even discs with pierced centres meant to be worn on a chain. In the early days most seals had been made of common steatite, but at the height of the New Palace period we find them in carnelian, jasper, rock crystal, amethyst, agate and other semi-precious stones.

As far as we know, sculpture, either as large statues or reliefs, was never popular in Crete. This is surprising, seeing the skilful care Minoan stonemasons took in cutting blocks for the palaces and the virtuosity of their stone vases. Of the small figurines, there were bronzes, but most items were ceramic; some objects, including the famous 'snake goddess' from Knossós, were made of ivory—easily obtainable from the east, where people were busy driving the Syrian elephant to extinction. Bronze-working began about 1600 BC, with the introduction of *cire-perdue* casting (*see* p.51). Cretans liked to leave the surfaces of their bronze figurines rough (like Rodin), and they saved their wonted precision for their fine daggers and swords—the man's status symbol of choice. Most Minoan daggers, and even the swords, inlaid with fine gold, silver and niello work, were strictly ornamental. Such items made up a large part of Crete's luxury export trade.

Post Palatial Period (1450–1100 BC)

It's always fascinating watching art deteriorate—as if weary of perfection, sated with imagery, a culture turns on the one hand to the strange and exotic, and on the other to shopworn, standardized versions of the old favourites just to keep up tradition. The Minoans after 1450 seem to have maintained their prosperity in spite of difficult times (and perhaps foreign rule), but the vision that had animated the earlier stages of their culture seems to have vanished.

In pottery, this period was marked by an increasing stylization and stiffness, as if the wonderful spontaneous flow of earlier times had somehow drained away. The Late

Minoan II period has been called 'baroque', an art straining for the ornate and grandiose. Also, it is easy to see how many designs became standardized and lifeless when turned out in number. In the Late Minoan III there was an increasing tendency towards abstract designs, and the few figurative scenes often seem primitive and cartoon-like. One novelty is the quantity of *larnaxes*, small terracotta chests for burials; although they go back to the Pre-Palatial period, they only became common in the Late Minoan period (earlier ones may have been made of wood, which had become scarce). The most fascinating *larnaxes* were painted with religious scenes such as the famous Ag. Triáda sarcophagus (*see* p.170).

Perhaps the most characteristic works of this period are the strange, bell-shaped terracotta goddesses, usually with arms uplifted. As primitive as these seem, it should be remembered that they represent a more 'popular' art (they are sometimes called 'household goddesses'). There were still craftsmen in Crete capable of making fine, classically styled jewellery, bronzes and ivories, and weapons. Often these were still made for export; many Cretan artists seem to have emigrated over to the mainland and kept up their traditions there. Seal rings of various types were still made, and surprisingly these were often even more naturalistic than in earlier times.

After the Minoans

In the 12th century Minoan art was already in serious decline, and with the coming of the warrior Dorians, who had no interest in such decadent fancies, it nearly disappeared altogether. The small amount of items discovered were often imported, or showed a simple, almost barbaric style, much like the 'household goddesses' mentioned above. The depths of Greece's Dark Age are referred to in art as the **Proto-Geometric period** (1100– 900 BC), from the simple, non-figurative decoration of pottery.

Art from the recovering **Geometric period** (900–700 BC) shows Eastern influences; works in bronze are especially fine, and Crete for a short time was one of the artistic centres of the Aegean. Towards the end of the period the first bronze statuettes by Daedalos (not to be confused with the inventor of myth) and his school appeared, with their characteristic wide eyes, thick hair and parted legs. The actual existence of this Daedalos is doubted by many, but legend credits him with the invention of making statues in

Abstract & Geometric-style stirrup jar, LM, Kato Zakros

marble and hammered bronze. At the end of this period Crete was once more in serious decline, spending its energy on building good strong walls rather than golden jewellery and pretty pots, and in the centuries that followed the island had little to contribute to Greece's golden age.

Byzantine and Venetian Periods

Time, earthquakes, and pirates have wiped clean much of what followed in the **Roman** and the **First Byzantine period** (330 BC–AD 824), leaving only a few tit-bits to show that if Crete didn't hold high the torch of culture at least it muddled through with a 40-watt bulb: a few statues, mosaic floors, aqueducts and huge cisterns, and remains of simple three-naved basilicas. The 7th-century cathedral of Ag. Títos at Górtyn provides eloquent witness that the Cretans had completely forgotten how to build on a monumental scale.

The art purge of the **Iconoclastic period** (726–843) and Saracen interlude (824–961) ensured that Crete was well behind the rest of Eastern Christendom as the Macedonian style of fresco (named after the Macedonian emperors) slowly infiltrated the Greek provinces. The old Roman basilica plan was jettisoned in favour of what became the classic Byzantine style: a central Greek-cross plan crowned by a dome, elongated in front by a vestibule (narthex) and outer porch (exonarthex) and at the back by a choir and three apses.

In Crete these began to appear in the island's **Second Byzantine period** (961–1210), but only a few Macedonian frescoes survive (most notably at Myrioké-fala and Kéra Panagía in Kritsá). The Venetians' arrival coincided with the second golden age of Byzantine art under the Comnene emperors (13th–14th centuries). As in Italy, this period marked a renewed interest in antique models: the stiff, elongated hieratic figures with staring eyes were given more naturalistic proportions in graceful, rhythmic compositions. It also produced some fine painting: the 14th-century frescoes in the aforementioned Kéra Panagía at Kritsá offer a neat comparison. By this time the itinerant artists—only a few left their names behind—had already been influenced by the Italian artists the Venetians brought over to decorate their own, long-gone Catholic churches; the 14th was the century of plague; Last Judgements were especially popular. The arrival of artists from Constantinople in the late 15th century and the artistic cross-fertilization with Venice as the relaxation developed over time into the Cretan school of Byzantine painting.

What never changed was the intent of Byzantine art, which is worth a small digression because 15th-century Western sacred art went off in an entirely different direction—so much so that everything before is disparagingly labelled 'primitive' in most art books.

One of the most obvious differences is the strict iconography of Byzantine painting: if you know the code you can instantly identify each saint by the cut of his beard or his or her attribute. Their appeal to the viewer, even when the figures were given more naturalistic proportions, is equally purely symbolic; a Byzantine Christ on the Cross, the Virgin *Panagía*, the 'all-holy', angels, saints and martyrs never make a play for the heartstrings, but reside on a purely spiritual and intellectual plane, miles away from Western art invented in the Renaissance 'based on horror, physical charm, infant-worship and easy weeping' as Patrick Leigh Fermor put it. Icons and Byzantine frescoes never ask the viewer to relive vicariously the passion of Christ or coo over Baby Jesus (who, born as 'the man of wisdom', is always symbolically depicted as a pint-sized adult, never as a rosy-cheeked *bambino*). Byzantine angels never lift their draperies to reveal a little leg; the remote, wide-eyed *Panagía* has none of the luscious charms of the Madonna. They are never supposed to stray from their remote otherworldliness.

And yet, in 16th- and 17th-century Venetian Crete they do wander a bit, especially in the works of Michális Damaskinós, whose finest paintings (you can hardly call them icons) are in Ag. Ekateína in Herákleon. They offer the Byzantine equivalent of Renaissance painting in Italy, a not entirely comfortable synthesis;. The one genuinely original artist Crete produced, Doménikos Theotokópoulos (El Greco; *see* pp.149–51) didn't synthesize at all but picked up the most extreme, late 16th-century thread of Italian Mannerist painting, moved to Toledo and took it to the edge of pure spirit in a way no other Byzantine painter had ever imagined.

By 1669, when Crete fell to the Turks, the Venetians had given it fine architectural souvenirs: impressive fortifications and gates, lighthouses, fountains, arsenals, public buildings, town houses and country manors. The island had an incredible one thousand active monasteries, of which only a few dozen still house a handful of monks or nuns, and no two are alike. Many have façades and gates inspired by the Venetians (Moní Arkádi is the finest example), and although over half are completely ruined they represent a large proportion of Crete's reputed 800 more-or-less-intact frescoed churches. Nor did figurative art completely perish under Crete's Muslim rulers: see Ioánnis Kornáros' magnificent icon *Great is the Lord* (1770) with its cast of thousands, at Moní Toploú. Most of Crete's meagre Turkish heritage is concentrated in a few small mosques, fountains, and houses in Réthymnon and Chaniá, and in the Herákleon historical museum, where you can see much of the finest moveable art produced in Crete in the last 2000 years.

Nomós Chaniá

GORGE OF
SAMARIA

To my mind, this Cretan countryside resembled good prose, carefully ordered, sober, free from superfluous ornament, powerful and restrained. But between the severe lines one could discern an unexpected sensitiveness and tenderness; in the sheltered hollows the lemon and orange trees perfumed the air, and from the vastness of the sea emanated an inexhaustible poetry.

Kazantzákis, *Zorba the Greek*

Unless you have only a few days and want to concentrate on the high shrines of Minoan culture around Herákleon, consider easing yourself gently into this complex island by starting with its westernmost *nomós* or province. Chaniá, urbane and lively and easily the most elegant of the four provincial capitals, forms an ideal introduction to Crete; its *nomós* has the fewest tourists but the most beautiful landscapes. Beaches in the province, perhaps because they were developed later than the sprawl around Herákleon, are mostly innocent of dense cacophonous strips of bars, pubs, fast food places, discos and car hire shops. The three 'heads' of Crete, dotted with sandy coves and venerable monasteries and coastal islets, add interest to the north coast. The far west, beyond the busy little port town of Kastélli-Kíssamou, is fringed with gorgeous beaches, from Phalassarná to the lagoon of Elafonísi, a tropical beauty only a 15-minute drive from deep chestnut forests.

Just behind the plain of Chaniá rise the stunning White Mountains, the Lefká Óri, which hit the sky at 2451m at Mount Pachnés and are sliced down the middle by one of Crete's five-star attractions, the Gorge of Samariá, the classic day walk that emerges by the Libyan sea. But it's only the most famous track: the whole lofty central-south region of the *nomós* provides excellent hiking. Geology helps support western Cretans' feelings of superiority; their half of the island is rising thanks to the movement of Africa's tectonic plate, while the east end is slowly sinking. In 1500 years Mt Pachnés should stand an inch taller than current height champ, Mount Ida; mountain-climbers from Chaniá make a point of adding a stone each time they scale Pachnés to encourage Nature along.

A few small towns on the Libyan coast have grown into modest resorts; Paleochóra is the largest but still comfortable, while Loutró, on a smaller scale, owes a good deal of its charm to the fact that it's only accessible by sea. Once fierce Chóra Sfakíon, the blazing centre of Cretan resistance, has mellowed to the point that it looks like any other Greek island port, while just east of it, under a haunted Venetian castle, stretches the delicious beach of Frangokástello. Some people never get any further.

Nomós Chaniá

20km
10 miles

N

To Piraeus

AKROTIRI

Bouvernetou Monastery
Ag. Triada

Profitis Ilias

Stavros

Kourakies
Aroni

Souda

Nea Souda

CHANIA

Mournies

Malaxa

Neo Chorio
Fre

Aptera

Kalyves
Almirida
Vamos

Kefalas

DRAPANON

Kokkino Chora

Georgioupolis

Lake Kournas

Alikampos

Askyfou

Asfendos

Asigonia

Rodakino

RETHYMNON

NOMOS RETHYMNON

Frangokastello

Vryssis

White Mountains

Mt. Pachnes
(2451m / 8045ft)

Ag. Ioannis

Anopolis Chora
Stakion

Loutro

Libyan Sea

Ag. Theodoroi

Platanias

Ag. Marina
Galatas

Fournes

Meskla
Therisso

Lakki
Sourva

Omalos

Gorge of Samaria

Ag. Roumeli

Prassa

Alikianos

Sougia

Lissos
Eyros

Paleochora

To Gavdos

Menias (Diktyna)

Ag. Ioannis Gionas

SPILDA RODOPOU

Afrata

Moni Gonias Monastery
Kolimbari

Maleme

Tavronitis

Rodopos

Kastelli Kissamou

Agriagramvousa

Gramvousa

Phalassarna

Platanos

Polyrenia

Sfinari

Kambos

Kouneni

Elos

Topolia

Kakodiki

Kandanos

Temenia

Chrysoskalitissa Monastery

Elafonisi

85

Chaniá

With the ghostly forms of the snow-capped White Mountains hovering over its rooflines and palm trees, Chaniá (XANIA) is a seductive town and an exceedingly old one, its urban fabric like a wall encrusted with circus posters, peeling here and there to reveal its depths. Venetian, Turkish and neoclassical monuments line its streets and waterfront. Unfortunately, many were lost forever in bombing raids during the Battle of Crete; fortunately, perhaps, the war-scarred ruins stood neglected for so many decades that they're now incorporated as unique garden settings for bars and restaurants. The lovely inner and outer Venetian harbours become magnets in the evening, where unwinding over a drink can easily become addictive.

The ancient historian Diodoros Sikelus wrote that Chaniá was founded by Minos and that it was one of the three great cities of Crete. Buildings in the Kastélli quarter go back to 2200 BC, and archaeologists are pretty sure that the Minoan palace and town, KY-DO-NI-JA, referred to on a Linear B tablet found at Knossós, lie hidden under the modern town. Kydonia was so important that for a time its name referred to all of Crete. In modern Greek, *kydónia* means quince, a fruit loved by the Minoans: the word (like 'hyacinth', 'labyrinth', and 'sandal') may have come from the ancient Minoan language.

Quince Town survived the rest of Cretan history to get a mention in Homer, to know glory days in the Hellenistic and Roman periods, then to decline so far between the 10th and 13th centuries that it was better known as 'Rubbish City'. Revived under the Venetians, who Italianized its name into La Canea, it was so splendid by the 1500s that its was nicknamed the 'Venice of the East'. Made Crete's capital by the Ottomans in 1850, Chaniá became the island's cosmopolitan window on the outside world, with consulates and embassies; it prospered as the fief of statesman Elefthérios Venizélos. Although it lost its capital status to arch-rival Herákleon in 1971, Chaniá remains Crete's second city (pop. 60,000); one of its more recent contributions to national life was former Néa Demokrátiki Prime Minister Konstantínos Mitzotákis, elected in 1990 when Greece got fed up with the scandals and false promises of Papandréou and PASOK, only to be thumpingly voted out in 1993 for trying to make Greece bite the bullet.

Chaniá © (0821–)   ### Getting There and Around

Chaniá's **airport** is on the Akrotíri peninsula, © 63 264 or 63 219. The Olympic Airways office is at 88 Stratigoú Tzanakáki, © 58 005; buses run from here to coincide with Olympic flights. **Ferry** tickets from Soúda to Piraeus are available from ANEK (daily at 8pm), on Venizélou, in the market square © 23 636 or 25 656, and from Minoan (three times a

Chaniá

200 metres
200 yards

N

Lighthouse

Venetian Harbour

San Salvatore
Firkas Tower
AKTI ENOSEOS
EPIMENIDOU

Swimming Pool
Naval Museum
Mosque of the Janissaries
Kastélli
AKTI KOUNTOURIOTOU
THEOTOKOPOULOU
ATKI KANARI
APOSTOLIDOU
To Nea Chora

Renieri Gate
Minoan Ruins
TOMBASI
ATKI TOMBASI
ARCHOLEON
KALERGON
Venetian Arsenal
Ag. Irini
AKTI MIAOULI
MINOOS
KIPROU

Topanás
PIREOS
ZAMBELIOU
THNON
KANEVARO
SIFAKA
DASKALOGIANNI
San Rocco
Plateía 1821
VOURDOUBA
Splántza
Ag. Nikolaos
MELIDONI
Ag. Anargyri
KALISSOU
KOUMI
N. EPISKOPOU

PATR. MEL. NIKIOU
Plateía Syntrivani
KARAOLI-DIMITRIOU
Archaeological Museum
Cathedral
HADZIMIKHALI DALIANI
Minaret
TSOUDERON
VERWIS
NIKIFOROU-FOKA
To Airport, Chalepa & Akrotiri

PATR. GERASSIMOU
METAXAKI
CHALIDON
BALANTINOU
Folklore Museum
SKRIDLOF

Schiavo Bastion
MITR. KIRILOU
SKALIDI

Market
HADZIMICHALI GIANNARI
Post Office
EL VENIZELOU
Stadium
KORAI

KISSAMOU
KALISPERIDO
Plateía 1866
KRIARI
Plateía Kotsambari
Plateía 1897
Telephone
DIMOKRATIAS
TZANAKAKI

KIDONIAS
KORONEO
ZIMURAKAKIDO
KORAKA
PLASTIR
VOLOUDAKIDON
Public Gardens
Zoo

To Samaria Gorge, Kastelli-Kissamou & Omalos
SMIRNIS
KONSTANTINOUPOLEOS
Bus Station
K. SFAKIANAKI
POL
Tourist Police
RAISAKAKI
KONSTANTINOUPOLEOS
PERIDOU
APOKORONOU
BONIAL
SFAKION
KORNAROU

SOLOMOU
SFAKIANAKI
Historical Museum

To Souda, Rethymnon & Herakleon

---

week, at 7.45pm), also in the market square, ✆ 45 911 or 45 912. The nightly Piraeus–Chaniá ferry pulls in around 6am and is met by early-bird local buses. Every Tuesday morning, Poseidon Lines call into Soúda on route to Cyprus and Israel. The **bus** station is at Kidonías, just west of central Plateía 1866, where whiffs of faded grandeur mingle with those from the plugged up toilets; black bordered death notices posted outside merge imperceptibly with ads for campsites. Buses travel at least once a day to all the larger villages of the *nomós* and there are hourly departures for

Herákleon and Réthymnon. For information call ✆ 93 306. Rent a **mountain bike** at Trekking Plan, on Karoli and Dimitrou Streets, open 6.30–9pm, or ring Vangelis, ✆ (093) 417 040.

Chaniá ✆ *(0821–)* **Tourist Information**

EOT: 40 Kriári St, ✆ 26 426, open Mon–Fri, 8.30am–2pm.
Tourist police: 44 Karaiskáki St, ✆ 24 477 or 51 111.

Chaniá ✆ *(0821–)* **Festivals**

Chaniá commemorates the anniversary of the Battle of Crete during the Chaniá Festival, which runs from the **middle to the end of May**; for information, call ✆ 87 098. **24 June**, St John's Day. On **15 August** Chaniá hosts the Pan Cretan Festival.

Into Old Chaniá

The vortex of daily life in Chaniá is its cruciform covered market, or **Agora** (1911), where locals come to shop for food and wonder about the sanity of all those Germans videoing slabs of meat and cheese. It effectively divides the old town from the new; the back stairs of the market and a left turn leads to **Odós Skrídlof**, a narrow lane jam-packed for as long as anyone remembers with shops selling leather goods, long a traditional craft in Chaniá, although many of the bootmakers have changed over to sandals, bags and belts for the tourists.

Skrídlof gives on to **Odós Chalídon**, Chaniá's main tourist and jewellery-shop-lined funnel to the sea. Midway down is the **Archaeology Museum** (*see* p.91), and up the steps in the adjacent courtyard of the Catholic church, there is a sweet little **Folklore Museum** full of traditional weavings and needlework run by two ladies. Across the street, the sad-looking building with all the baby bubble domes is the old Turkish bath. This is next to a large square holding the **Trimartyr,** Chaniá's cathedral, which should be more interesting. In the 1850s, a soap factory belonging to Mustafa Nily Pasha stood here; as a gesture of reconciliation he donated it to the local Christians, along with a large sum of money, to erect a church.

Topanás

Chalídon flows into the crescent of the **outer port**, lined with handsome Venetian buildings. The neighbourhood on the west side of the port, Topanás, has been classified a landmark, where façades may not be altered although the interiors have nearly all been converted to bars, pensions and restaurants. The **Fírkas tower** at the far west end of the port saw the official raising of the Greek flag over Crete in November 1913 in the presence of King Constantine and Prime Minister

Venizélos, godfather of the union, and the erection of a marble plaque that reads 'Turkish Rule in Crete 1669–1913. 264 years, 7 months and 7 days of Tribulation.' Long used as a prison, the tower now contains a summer theatre and the **Naval Museum** (*open 10–4, closed Sun; adm*). Crete, naturally, is the main focus; among the photos, don't miss those showing another ruler, Prince George, who landed at this very spot on 9 December 1898, to become High Commissioner of autonomous Crete, an electrifying moment Kazantzákis describes in *Report to Greco*: 'The Cretans sang and danced in the taverns, they drank, they played the rebec, but still they did not find relief. Unable to fit any longer inside their bodies, they grasped knives and stabbed themselves in the arms and thighs so that blood would flow and they would be unburdened.' There are models of Venetian galleys and fortifications, and mock-ups of key Greek naval victories throughout history, all described in nationalistic, hysterical English translations. The first floor has an evocative collection of photos and memorabilia from the Battle of Crete.

Behind the tower, simple little **San Salvatore** belonged to a Franciscan monastery and, like most of Chaniá's churches, was used by the Turks as a mosque. Near here begins Topanás' main street, Theotokopoúlou, the most picturesque in the city, lined with Venetian houses remodelled by the Turks. On Theofánou Street (off Zambéliou) the **Renieri Gate** bears a Venetian coat-of-arms, dated 1608, and the curious inscription '*Mula tulit Fecitus et studarit dulces pater, sudavit et alseit semper requies serena*'. Further south stood the old ghetto, the Ovraiki, although the dilapidated synagogue on Kondiláki Street recently burned. In fact, it has been said that the only physical sign of Crete's Jewish population, already reduced through immigration from 1600 under the Venetians to 400 on the eve of the Second World War, is two lists of Jews compiled by Chaniá's rabbi and now in the Historical Archives (*see* below). The Germans used the list to round them up, along with other undesirable Greeks and Italians, and put them all on a ship, the *Danaë*, that set sail on 7 June 1944 and was never seen again.

At the top of Kondiláki, along Portoú Lane, you can see the last bastion of the **Venetian walls**. In 1538, just after Barbarossa left his usual calling card of death and desolation in Réthymnon, the Venetians hired their fortifications wizard Michele Sammichele to surround Chaniá with walls and surround the walls with a moat more than 45m wide and 9m deep. As it turned out, these precautions did little to keep out the Turks in 1645, when they captured Chaniá in two months.

Kastélli

The east end of the harbour has Chaniá's two most photographed landmarks: a graceful Venetian **lighthouse** in golden stone restored under the Egyptians, and the **Mosque of the Janissaries** (1645), crowned with its distinctive ostrich and chicken egg domes. Here the Christian-born slave troops of the Ottoman Empire worshipped, although little did it improve their character; not only did they terrorize the Greeks, but in 1690 they murdered the Pasha of Chaniá and fed his body to the dogs. In 1812, even the Sublime Porte had had enough and sent Hadji Osman Pasha, 'the Throttler', into Crete to hang the lot of them, an act that so impressed the locals that the rumours flew that 'the Throttler' must be a crypto-Christian.

Behind the mosque lies the Kastélli quarter, spread across a low hill above the inner harbour. This was the acropolis of ancient Kydonia, and **excavations** by a Greek-Swedish team along Kaneváro Street revealed a complex of Middle Minoan building, most with second storeys, flagstoned floors and grand entrances on to narrow streets. The presence of nearly 100 Linear B tablets suggest the proximity of a palace; a large deposit of Linear A tablets was found in a dig on Katre Street nearby. The name 'Kastélli' derives from the first, inner fortress built here by the Venetians, which sheltered their palazzi; according to the 1252 'Concession of Chaniá' these first Venetian noble colonists were obliged to rebuild the city in return for their privileges. Although Kastélli took the brunt of the Luftwaffe bombs, you can still pick out the odd Venetian architectural detail, especially along Kaneváro (the old Corso) and Lithínon Streets; the latter has the courtyard of what was once the palace of the Venetian Rector and, later, the Pasha. On the top of Ag. Markoú you can see the ruined walls and windows of the old cathedral, S. Maria degli Miracoli. Below, overlooking the inner harbour, rise the vaults (1600) of the **Venetian Arsenali**, though only seven of the original 17 shipyards survive.

Splántza

Just east of Kastélli is Splántza, or the Turkish quarter. Some interesting churches are concentrated here, such as the recently discovered underground **Ag. Iríni**, dating from the 15th century, in Roúgia Square (Odós Kallinikou Sarpani). South in Vourdouba Street, near an enormous plane tree, **Ag. Nikólaos** was a Dominican church built in the early 14th century and converted by the Turks into an Imperial mosque to shelter a magical healing sword, which the Imam would hold up while leading the Friday prayers. Note the *tugra*, or Sultan's emblem, on the entrance and the minaret (and campanile). If it's open, pop in to see the coffered ceiling and the sword. Close by, on Daskaloyánni Street, is **San Rocco** (1630), covered with weeds although back in its day charged with protecting Chaniá from the plague. The little **mosque of Ahmet Aga** and its minaret still stands in Hadzimichali Daliani street, while to the east 16th-century **Ag. Anargyri**, in Koumi street, was long the town's 'cathedral', the only church in Chaniá allowed to hold Orthodox services throughout the Venetian and Turkish occupations. Another section of Sammichele's wall survives along Minos Street, and on what remains of the Koum Kapissi (or Sabbionari) bastion, the date 1590 and a Lion of St Mark. Just outside of the wall, the **Koum Kapi quarter** was first settled by Bedouins, who immigrated here during Crete's Egyptian interlude (1831–40) and then in the 1870s, when extra hands were required to construct the new capital.

The Archaeology Museum

Open Tues–Sun, 8.30–3; adm; free Sundays.

The 14th-century Gothic church of San Francesco at 21 Odós Chalídon doesn't look like much from the outside, but it's had a hard life. Used as a mosque (the stump of a minaret and a pretty fountain survive), its cells and refectory converted beyond all recognition into shops, and bombed during the war, it has been beautifully restored for its new role as Chaniá's **Archaeology Museum**, a sumptuous collection of treasures found in western Crete. The finds from Minoan Kydonia are intriguing, and as usual raise more questions than they answer, especially the celebrated clay sealing in high relief (*c.* 1450 BC) that shows the commanding figure of a young Minoan proudly holding a staff, standing high over the sea that breaks against the gates of a city—Kydonia itself, perhaps—the roofs crowned with horns of consecration. One guess is that it shows the chief Minoan male deity, Poteidan (Poseidon), master of the sea, earth, bulls and earthquakes; another is that the curious sea rock under the god is really a tidal wave or *tsunami*, perhaps the very one that is believed to have clobbered Crete when Santoríni flipped its lid around 1450 BC.

Other cases contain Minoan jewels, vases and ceramics imported from Cyprus by the ancient Kydonians; most of the polychrome clay sarcophagi, or *larnaxes*, come from the cemetery of Arméni near Réthymnon. From the Classical period are statues and ex-votos from the shrine of Diktean Artemis, and a finely moulded 4th-century BC terracotta Tanagra statuette, still bearing the tracing of her gilt and paint (in ancient times, these figurines were as popular and as forged as Cartier watches are now). A 3rd century AD house in Chaniá yielded the series of beautiful mosaic floors based on the legend of Dionysos. Lastly, in the middle of the nave, note the cases with Linear A and Linear B tablets. Kydonia is the only town in Western Crete where both writings were discovered.

Translating the Minoans

 The great fires that ravaged the Minoan palaces around 1450 BC had the side-effect of baking the clay tablets on which the Minoans scratched their mysterious script. Three types of writing have been found: the earliest, unfathomable 'pictographic' script of the Phaistós disc (*see* p.164), Linear A, used between the 18th and ´5th centuries, and Linear B, current after 1450 BC. Relatively few examples of Linear A have been found, and nearly all of those were at the major temple sites in Eastern Crete. On the other hand, thousands of Linear B tablets were uncovered, both in Crete (some 3000 tablets at Knossós alone) and on mainland Greece.

Ancient scripts fired Arthur Evans's imagination more than anything: 19th-century accidental finds of Linear B writing are what propelled him to Crete in the first place (*see* p.175). By the time he died in 1941, he could claim to be the discoverer of Europe's first civilization, although he never accomplished what he had set out to do: translate the Minoans. A few ideograms (man, horse, spear) could be easily picked out, but there were many more signs that didn't look like anything at all.

Before the war, Evans unknowingly planted the seed that would lead to a breakthrough when he gave a lecture on the Minoans in Athens. He fired the imagination of one listener in particular, an English teenager named Michael Ventris. Ventris grew up to be an architect, but his hobby was the Minoan script; the British cracking of Hitler's secret code was one inspiration. But how could anyone hope to decipher the writing of a long-lost language? In 1952 an idea occurred to Ventris that had escaped all the scholars. Perhaps, after all, it wasn't a long-lost language. Perhaps the widespread Linear B, at least, was Greek, and the symbols were phonetic, each representing a syllable. Together with John Chadwick, an expert in ancient forms of Greek, Ventris set to and found enough instances where the system worked for scoffers to start paying attention. Although problems still remain, nearly everyone now admits that Ventris (who died in a car accident not long after his discovery) was on the right track. And, after all the fuss, what did the Minoans and their Mycenaean peers have to say? 'Five jars of honey, 300 pigs, 120 cows for As-as-wa'—i.e. inventories of goods. Imagine if modern civilization were obliterated and only our shopping lists survived.

Nevertheless, the deciphering of Linear B has opened a whole range of tantalizing new questions: on cultural exchanges between the Minoans and Mycenaeans, on the origins of the earliest known names of gods and places, on the functions and government of the palaces. Symbols borrowed from the older Linear A (believed by Chadwick and others to be in the native, non-Greek language of the Minoans) have led to tentative translations; scholars think it could be related to ancient southwest Anatolian languages, perhaps Hittite. Examples are so rare and brief that linguists will just have to sit tight and wait for archaeologists to come up with some longer and more connected texts. It is known that the Minoans used ink. A volume of poetry by their Shakespeare would be especially nice.

Chaniá's Newer Quarters and Beaches

From the covered market, Odós Tzanakáki leads southeast to the private gardens of Reouf Pasha, now the cool shady **Public Gardens** with a small zoo (your chance to see a *kri-kri*) and outdoor cinema, often showing films in English. A villa just to the south houses the **Historical Archives of Crete** (*open weekdays 9–1, closed weekends*), 20 Sfakianáki Street, containing Greece's second largest collection of archival material, dating from the Venetian occupation to the liberation of Crete in 1944, although most of it will be lost on you if you don't read Greek. In Platía Venizélos stands the house (and statue) of Venizélos, the government palace built for Prince George (now the court-house) and a Russian Orthodox church donated by the mother of a former governor. Further east, by the sea, is the fancy **Chalepa** quarter, dotted with 19th-century neoclassical mansions, many built by consulates during Crete's years of autonomy.

The town beach, **Néa Chorá**, is a 15-minute walk west from the harbour, beyond the Fírkas tower. Although sandy, shallow and safe for children, it's not especially attractive. The beaches improve the further west you go; municipal buses from Plateía 1866 go as far as lovely sandy **Oasis beach** and **Kalamáki**. The whole is well developed with good swimming and windsurfing, cafés and tavernas. There are other, less crowded beaches along the way, but prepare for a long walk.

Shopping

Chaniá certainly has no lack of shops, and where it used to specialize in making hand-carved chairs (still available here and there, but daunting to cart home), jewellery now rules the roost. Among the many shops selling handmade necklaces, bracelets and earrings based on traditional Greek designs are **Antoniou**, 22 Kondiláki, **Metamorphosis**, 50 Theokotópolou, **Mare**, 7 Chalídon Street, **Imeros**, 6 Zambéliou, and **Agora**, 92 Chalídon Street. Leather rules on Odós Skridlóf, and there are several traditional knifemakers along Sífaka, among them **Apostolos Pachtikos** at No.14, who began in 1946 at the age of 13 and still makes traditional Cretan knives, tempered on a tiny forge and anvil at the rear of the shop; in addition to knives, Apostolos offer mountain goat horns and battered Nazi helmets. **Top Hanas**, 3 Angélou in the Old Town has traditional Cretan weavings and blankets. Lefteris Klidaras' **The Herb Centre** in the indoor market has not only a wide range of spices but an excellent selection of Cretan wines. For books or papers in English, the big international shop in Plateía Sindrivani has the biggest choice; for books, new or old, tapes, and CDs, try **Apogio**, 80 Hatzimicháli Giannári. **Diamantopoulou**, at 51 Odós Potié, has an enormous selection of chess and backgammon sets.

Chaniá ⊕ (0821–)   **Where to Stay**

Chaniá's hotels have more character than any others in Crete, although be aware that some of the most picturesque places installed around the Venetian port can be noisy at night. The **Association Rent Rooms & Apartments**, 12 Isódion Street, ⊕ 43 601, ◉ 46 277, has a list of inexpensive quality lodgings, complete with a map to help you find them.

The fanciest hotels in Chaniá are out east in the Chalepa quarter, some in neoclassical mansions left over from the city's glory days as Crete's capital. The German consulate occupied the **Villa Andromeda**, 150 El. Venizélou, ✆ 45 263, ✉ 45 265 (*lux*), now divided into 8 air-conditioned suites; a lush garden, Turkish bath and swimming pool are some of the amenities. The nearby **Chalepa**, 164 El. Venizélou, ✆ 53 544, ✉ 43 335, (*B*), housed their British counterparts, and now offers 45 fully air-conditioned rooms in a quiet garden. Neoclassical **Pandora**, 29 Lithínon, ✆ 43 589, ✉ 55 213 (*A*), has comfortable, traditionally furnished apartments available by the day, with 2 to 5 beds. *Open year-round.* **Bozzali Studios**, Gavaládon (a quiet lane off Sífaka), ✆ 50 824, offers 15 A-class rooms in a lovingly restored house. *Open Mar–Nov.* The **Contessa**, 15 Theofánous, ✆ 98 566 (*A*), has the intimate air of an old-fashioned guesthouse, furnished in traditional style. The owners speak little English, but make up for it by being extremely helpful; book well in advance. A similar warning prevails for the desirable **Palazzo**, Theotokopoúlou, ✆ 43 255 (*A*), with 11 delicious traditional rooms, most with balcony, and for the nearby **El Greco**, 49 Theotokopoúlou, ✆ 90 432, ✉ 95 566 (*B*), a pretty place draped in creeper, on Chaniá's prettiest street. In a 17th-century townhouse, **Casa Delfino**, 9 Theofánous, ✆ 93 098, ✉ 96 500 (*A*), has comfortable air-conditioned suites overlooking an inner courtyard and pool, with mini-bars and satellite TV. *Open all year.* If you want to be alone, the **Xenia**, Theotokopoúlou, ✆ 91 238, ✉ 72 238 (*B*), has 80 modern rooms overlooking the sea around the corner from the Fírkas tower.

moderate

Among the small hotels located in refurbished Venetian houses, **Nostos**, Zambelíou 46, ✆ 54 833 (*B*), on a quiet flowery lane, has many rooms with views, and **Pension Thereza**, 8 Angélou, ✆ 40 118, has been lovingly restored and has magnificent views from the rooftop terrace and rooms. **Vranas Suites**, 23–25 Ag. Déka, ✆ 58 618 or 43 788, have been recently done up in an attractive, traditional style on a quiet side street near the old port. **Pension Kastélli**, 39 Kaneváro Street, ✆ 57 057, in Kastélli, has rooms with kitchen facilities priced near the bottom of this category, as does the serene **Pension Monastiri**, set in the ruined cloister of a Venetian church at 18 Ag. Markoú, ✆ 54 776; some rooms have views.

inexpensive

Chaniá has a vast selection of pensions and inexpensive rooms, and most are located within a few blocks of the Venetian or inner harbour. Some of the nicer are: **Esta**, in a charming pink house (no phone) and **Konaki**,

52 240, both on Kondiláki Street; **Meltemi**, 2 Angélou, *©* 40 192 and **Maria**, 4 Angélou, *©* 51 052, both near the Naval Museum, where some rooms have lovely views across the port to the White Mountains; try also **Venus**, 42 Sarpáki, a quiet street in the Turkish quarter, in a lovingly restored house. **Rent Rooms 47** on Kandanoléou, a cul-de-sac in Kastélli, *©* 53 243, is another place set back from the main night scooter routes.

Chaniá's **youth hostel**, at 33 Drakonianoú, *©* 53 565, is decent and exceptionally quiet because it's almost out of the city limits. To get there, take the Ag. Ioánnes bus, leaving every 15 minutes from in front of the market (no card necessary). There are two campsites near Chaniá, though again you'll need a bus to reach them: **Camping Ag. Marína**, *©* 48 555, 8km west of the town and open throughout the season (buses leave from the main bus station), and the more basic **Camping Chaniá** at Ag. Apóstoli, 5km west of town, *©* 31 686 (city bus from Platéia 1866). Both are within easy walking distance of fine beaches.

Chaniá © (0821–) **Eating Out**

It's hard not to find a restaurant in Chaniá—the harbour is one great crescent of tavernas and pizzerias. **Dino's**, overlooking the inner harbour on Aktí Enóseos and Sarpidóna, is a long-time reliable favourite (*4–5000dr*); **Aeriko**, not far away on Aktí Miaoúli, is also good and considerably cheaper, with some seafood on the menu and chicken on a spit. **Tholos**, 36 Ag. Déka, serves excellent food in the picturesque ruins of a Venetian town house (*around 3500dr*). **Monastiri**, behind the Mosque of the Janissaries, serves fresh fish, traditional Cretan dishes and barrelled wine in the same price range; if you need a change, try the Thai and Korean food at the **Golden Wok** next door. More and more places are offering Cretan specialities every year, among them **Xani**, 26 Kondiláki, *©* 75 795, with live music most evenings, and **Ela**, 47 Kondiláki, built amid the ruins of Chaniá synagogue. The **Emerald Bistro**, a friendly Irish restaurant just off the harbour-front at 17 Kondiláki, serves comfort foods—steaks, prawn cocktails, baked potatoes and, naturally, Irish coffee (*2000dr*). Middle Eastern and Anatolian specialities, sometimes accompanied by live Arabic music, happen at **The Well of the Turk**, in Rougiá Square, *©* 54 547 (*3500dr*). **Taverna Apovrado**, Isódon Street, *©* 58 151, serves a number of Chaniot specialities, including the local wine and country sausages. In the courtyard of a Venetian building dating from 1290, **Taverna Alana**, 19 Zambelíou, features well-prepared, moderately priced Greek dishes (try the stuffed cuttlefish) and live Greek music. If it's pizza or pasta you crave, get a table on the terrace of **Kariatos** behind the Arsenáli. Spring for a taxi to Néa

Chóra for excellent seafood at excellent prices at **Akrogiali**. In the evening Chaniots like to head 7km east, up to Korakiés on the Akrotíri peninsula to **Nikterida**, ✆ 64 215, one of the best tavernas in Crete, open since 1938, with views over Soúda Bay and music and dancing on Saturday nights when reservations are essential (*closed Sun; around 3500dr a person*).

Bars and Nightlife

Chaniá is delightful after dark, just for strolling and watching the passing pageant. Of the many bars on the outer port, **Remezzo**, at the mosque end, commands the best seats, although you pay for the privilege; **Valentino** and **Santé** (named after the famous Greek cigarettes) are more traditional *kafeneíons* where young Cretans hang out and play *távli*. The inner harbour is also inner fashion-wise, especially the bars along and around Sarpidóna: **Neorion** and **Dio Lux** are trendy places on Sarpidóna, the latter with 25 kinds of tea; also have a look at Chaniá post-modern design at **Trilogy**, 16a Radamánthous, by the northeast bastion, and the **Pili Tis** up on top of the same. The pretty inner courtyard of **Ideon Andron**, 26 Chálidon, is a mellow place playing classical or jazz records. **I Mouraria tou Pouni Mourgali,** 20 Sífaka, offers over 80 kinds of beer from around Europe, or, for a more distinctly Cretan experience, try **Tsikoudadiko**, 31 Zambelioú for *rakí* and excellent *mezédes*. **Fortetza**, isolated out by the lighthouse, is new on the scene, a music bar with its own shuttle boat.

Chaniá is good for a wide variety of music. The hole-in-the-wall **Kriti**, formerly the Lyraki, at 22 Kallergón is something of a local institution, where from 9pm on you can hear Cretan music for the price of a *rakí*, accompanied by *mezé* and more often than not by impromptu dancing. **Skala**, nearby at 12 Kallergón, ✆ 53 995, features live *rembétika*—Greek blues. **Café Avekoloto**, in the old harbour, frequently offers blues (western-style) and other live music; similar fare and jazz happens at **Fedra**, 7 Isóderon, ✆ 40 789. Traditional Greece dance shows are performed in the **Fírkas tower** on summer evenings.

Dancing fools make their way to **Anagennisis**, a lively disco in restored Venetian storerooms at Chalídon and Skalídi, ✆ 72 768, or **Blue Note**, 6 Sourmeli by the outer harbour, an 'American Bar' in an old Venetian building with a 26ft-high ceiling. Alternatively, head to Agia, 7km southwest of Chaniá, to bop under the palms at **Tutti Frutti**, ✆ 32 561, with a big swimming pool to cool off in if things get too hot; it sometimes hosts big-name Greek performers, as does **Chaniá by Night**, a giant venue along the road to Herákleon.

West of Chaniá

Not a single one of the countless beach hotels along this sandy stretch of coast and fertile plain existed when the strange rain of white parachutes fell on 20 May 1941. 'Out of the sky the winged devils of Hitler were falling everywhere,' wrote George Psychoundákis in *The Cretan Runner*. Few signs of the battle remain, although 2km west of Chaniá stands the monument of the diving eagle, known locally as the **Kakó Poulí**, or 'Bad Bird', the German memorial to the 2nd Parachute Regiment. The biggest battle took place one kilometre to the south, in Galatás, where Greek soldiers and civilians (armed with rusty old hunting guns and stones) and New Zealanders battled the parachutists.

Getting Around

By bus: there are buses every 15 minutes from Chaniá bus station to all the coastal resorts as far as the Maleme Beach hotel; roughly every hour they continue to Kastélli-Kíssamou. There are also early-morning connections from all the resorts to Omalós for the Gorge of Samariá.

Festivals

Ag. Marína, **17 July**. Kolimbári, **15 August** and **29 August** pilgrimage to the chapel of St John the Hermit. Tavronítis, **14 September**.

Beaches West of Chaniá

Just beyond the reach of Chaniá's city bus lines, the rooms and restaurants of **Káto Stálos** merge with **Ag. Marína**, an old town with a smattering of old Venetian and Turkish houses, and a long, partially shaded beach and lots of hotels, tavernas and watersports facilities. It looks out over the islet of **Ag. Theódori**, a refuge for the wild Cretan ibex, the *kri kri*; excursion boats make the trip from Chaniá. The vast gaping mouth of its cave originally belonged to a sea monster, bearing down on Ag. Marína with an appetite as big as all Crete before Zeus spotted the threat to his home island and petrified the monster with a thunderbolt.

Just west of Ag. Marína, **Plataniás** has two faces as well: an old village above and a built-up resort town by the sandy beach and a cane forest, planted to protect the orange groves from the wind. The Battle of Crete began further west at **Máleme**, where Chaniá airport was at the time. There's a large German war cemetery as a grim reminder, near the Creta Chandris/Maleme Beach hotel and, down a nearby lane, a monumental **Post-Palatial Minoan** tomb with a well-preserved *dromos* entrance, discovered by accident in 1966. Beyond, the resort and farming village of **Tavronítis** marks the crossroads for Paleochóra.

Cape Spáda

At the foot of rugged Cape Spáda, just before the road to Kastélli splits into old and new, **Kolimbári** (ΚΟΛΥΜΒΑΡΙ) has a beach of large smooth pebbles, a good spot for a swim and a meal. The village centre has a bust of Timoléon Vássos, commander of 1500 Greek volunteers, who in 1897 landed in Kolimbári and declared (again prematurely) Crete's union with Greece, although the revolt he ignited led directly to the island's autonomy the following year.

A short walk just north of the village is the most important monastery in western Crete. **Moní Gonías**, or Odigítrias (*open 8–12.30 and 4–7*), was founded in 1618 by several groups of monks and hermits in the area, who decided to club together and found a central, organized religious house, which they built in the form of a fortress high over a little sandy cove (or *gonías*, in Greek). The patriotic monks were often besieged by the Turks; a cannon ball shot in 1866 is still embedded in the seaward wall. The church contains a fine gilt iconostasis carved with dragons, a venerable *Last Judgement* painted on wood and a beautifully drawn St Nicholas, although the juju seems to be concentrated in an icon of the Virgin, covered with votive *tamata*, jewellery and a digital watch. The small museum holds some excellent icons from the 16th and 17th centuries: note especially the *Genesis* (1662) and a *Crucifixion* of 1637.

Next to the monastery is the Orthodox academy, with a memorial to the cadets killed in the Battle of Crete. Beyond, the road veers dizzingly up and up the coast of Cape Spáda to **Afráta**, the last village accessible by car, where you can visit the cave **Ellenóspilios**, its 90m-long corridors lined with stalactites and stalagmites. From Afráta you can either pick your way down to rocky coves for a swim in the crystal-clear water, or follow the unpaved treeless track to the north on foot or with a four-wheel-drive (here and there still using the old Roman road) or, easiest of all, take a caique ride from Chaniá to **Diktyna**, in ancient times the most holy shrine in Western Crete. Its little port, **Meniás**, is rocky but the sea is green and transparent, and seaside caves offer shelter from the sun. Diktyna's celebrated shrine to Artemis probably dates back to the Minoans, and continued to have a popular following up to the end of the Roman Empire; the Diktean mountains in eastern Crete were named after her. There are enough remains of her unexcavated shrine to make it worth a scramble.

Inland from the shrine of Artemis are the Venetian-era ruins of the Monastery of Ag. Geórgios and a frescoed church. Yet another monastery, **Ag. Ioánnis Giónas**, overlooks the bay of Kíssamos, and every 29 August attracts crowds of pilgrims (especially if their name is John), who make the three-hour walk from Rodopós, have a bite, and walk back. The nearest sandy beaches are at **Plakálona**, just to the west of the Spáda peninsula, where some of the densest olive groves in Crete provide a silvery backdrop.

Inland from Kolimbári

The farming villages south of Kolimbári can boast of some interesting churches, among them **Marathokéfala,** 2km south; just beyond the church a short path leads back to a grove of plane trees and the cave frequented around the turn of the last millennium by one of Crete's favourite saints, John the Stranger (Ag. Ioánnis Xénos); his is the small chapel near the entrance, and he left some divine magic with one of the stalactites inside. Nearby **Spiliá** has a 12th-century church of the Panagía with 14th-century wall paintings; others from the same period, on the *Life of St Stephen*, are further south in **Drakóna**'s 9th-century Ag. Stéfanos. But most interesting and oldest of all is a golden stone church in **Episkopí**, known as the **Rotunda**, dedicated to Michael the Archangel. Seat of a bishop in early Christian times, the Rotunda has the only concentric stepped dome in Crete. Inside are sections of its original mosaic floor, along with a stone baptismal font. At least five layers of frescoes cover the walls. Lastly, the church in **Delianá** southwest of Episkopí has interesting though damaged medieval paintings of the Last Judgement, where Heaven's elect swan around in Byzantine court dress. **Voukoliés** further south has a famous flea market every Saturday.

℘ *(0821–)*   ***Where to Stay and Eating Out***

Káto Galatás

Panorama, ℘ 31 700, ✉ 31 708 (*A; lux*). Built in modern Mediterranean style; all rooms have air conditioning and balconies with sea views. There are 2 swimming pools if the 50m walk to the sea is too strenuous.

Ag. Marína

Santa Marina, on the beach, ℘ 68 460, ✉ 99 221 (*B; mod*), is set in a lovely garden with a pool, and often comes up with a room when the season is in full swing. Near the beach, **Alexia,** ℘ 68 110 (*B pension; mod*) is small and attractive, with a pool and fridges in every room. **Angelika,** ℘ 68 642, has rooms with kitchens; **Villa Margarita,** ℘ 68 581, doesn't and costs even less (*both inexpensive*). Just east in Káto Stalós, and up the hill away from the noise of the main road, **Alector's Rooms,** ℘ 68 755, occupy a garden villa, immaculately run by the delightful Cretan-Californian Helen Zachariou (*moderate–inexpensive*); take the lane up from **Stavrodromi (Mari Pentari) Restaurant and Pizzeria,** ℘ 68 104, where the fried squid is delicious.

Plataniás

Geraniotis, by the beach, ℘ 68 681 (*B; exp*) is one of the more attractive of Plataniás' many hotels, set in lush green lawns. *Open April–Oct.*

Kronos Apartments, ℰ 68 630 (C; mod) is a well-kept, moderate-size complex of 53 units, with a pool near the sea. In 1961, a 15th-century water mill on the west end of Plataniás was converted into the **Taverna Mylos** (or Keratas), ℰ 68 578, a lovely place under the tall trees (2500dr). Up in Áno Plataniás, **Haroupia**, ℰ 68 603, not only enjoys lovely sunset views from its creeper covered terrace, but has delicious Cretan food. Two big discos gear up after midnight: **Portocali**, near the bridge, with Crete's biggest laser show, and **Mylos**, this one in a former flour mill from 1800.

Máleme

The **Crete Chandris** (or **Maleme Beach**), ℰ 62 221, ✆ 62 406 (A; lux), built as part of the luxurious Chandris chain and shaped like a giant trident to give each of its 414 rooms a sea view, is still one of the classiest along the coast. *Open April–Oct.* The fancy-pants **Creta Paradise**, in nearby Geráni, ℰ 61 315, ✆ 61 134 (A; lux) opened in 1992 and is even slicker and glossier, if half the size of the Chandris.

Kolimbári

The quiet, pastel complex of the **Aphea Village**, 300m above the village, ℰ 23 344 (B; exp–mod) has 30 furnished apartments, a pool and bar; **Arion**, ℰ 22 440, (B; exp–mod) is smack on the sea, with a pool and watersports. **Dimitra** (E; inexp) ℰ 22 244, has decent rooms, open all year; for a room, enquire at the Lefkas taverna, with its long shady terrace at the main crossroads. By the sea, **Paleo Arkontiko** has good fresh fish. The large grill houses along the main road do a roaring trade with the locals.

Way Out West

West of the Spáda peninsula lies the ancient province of Kíssamos, dominated by a beautiful coastal plain densely planted with olives and vineyards and knobbly hills just behind, planted with the same: the difference between its lush greenery and the arid hills of the far east couldn't be more striking. As relatively few visitors make it out this far, the unruly west coast offers not only some of Crete's loveliest beaches, but a chance to find a lonesome strand of your very own. The chief town and port here is Kastélli (ΚΑΣΤΕΛΛΙ) or officially, Kastélli-Kíssamou, a dusty, workaday wine town charmingly devoid of any tourist attraction whatsoever.

Getting Around

Kastélli's port (2km from the centre—take a taxi) is linked by Míras **ferries** to ports in the Peloponnese: three times a week to Kalamáta, once to Gýthion, twice to Monemvassía and Neápolis; there are two weekly sailings to Piraeus and three to Kythira and Antikythira, tickets from Horeftákis Tours in Kastélli, ℰ (0822)

23 888 or Omalós Tours, Plateía 1866, Chaniá, ✆ (0821) 97 119. **Buses from Kastélli:** three a week (Mon, Wed, Fri) to Polyrénia, two a day to Phalassarná, five to Chóra Sfakíon, six to Paleochóra, two to Omalós and one morning bus to Chrysoskalítissa, Topólia and Elafonísi. The Elafonísi Boat, ✆ (0823) 41 755, connects the islet of Elafonísi to Paliochóra every afternoon in the summer. Note, too, there is a daily direct bus to Elafonísi from Chaniá at 8.30, returning at 4pm.

Festivals

Kastélli: **30 May**, wine festival in **early August**, and **29 August** (Ag. Ioannes). Phalassarná: **26 July**. Monastery Chrysoskalítissa: a huge festival every **14–15 August**. Élos: Chestnut festival, first Sunday after **20 October**.

Kastélli-Kíssamou

Set at the bottom of a deep, rectangular gulf, Kastélli's long beach (pebbly below town and sandy just to the west) brings in the kind of tourists who shun the fleshpots. Its double-barrelled name, which hasn't really caught on among the Cretans, recalls its predecessor Kissamos, the port of Dorian Polyrenia (*see* below). Excavations of the ancient city behind the modern health centre have unearthed a lovely mosaic floor from the 2nd century AD; the **archaeology museum**, with other finds from ancient Kissamos, is currently being rearranged in the Venetian commandery.

Ancient Kissamos' temple and theatre were dismantled by the Venetians in 1550 and refashioned as a castle—hence Kastélli. This castle has a melodramatic history: when the Cretan Kaptános Kantanoléo captured it from the Venetians, the Venetians pretended to recognize Kantanoléo's authority and offered a highborn Venetian girl as his son's bride. At the wedding, in Alikianós, the Cretans were given drugged wine, and the Venetians slit their throats and retook Kastélli's fort.

A scenic drive 8km south of Kastélli, **Polyrénia** (ΠΟΛΥΡΡΗΝΙΑ) is set on a natural balcony and is as old-fashioned as a Cretan village can get; if your first contact with Greece predates the 1970s, the little footpaths and whitewashed rocks, the mingled smells of home cooking and coffee with potted flowers, jasmine, basil and donkeys will give you a serious dose of nostalgia.

But Polyrénia is even older than it looks at first, even older than the Roman tower (itself a collage of older bits and bobs) that stands at the village entrance. Founded in the 8th century BC by colonists from the Peloponnese, Polyrenia ('many flocks') had the usual Dorian arrangement: the main centre high up and easily defensible, overlooking the sea and port, Kissamos. It's a stiff climb up through the back gardens to the acropolis, with 360° views, an evocative tumble of overgrown, inscrutable walls and houses scattered over the tawny terraces and natural rock formations. Although the city survived the Romans (Polyrenia's attitude to the legions was that if you can't lick them, join them), it fell prey to the Saracens in the 9th century. The most tangible memory of Polyrenia's prosperity is the massive base of a 4th-century temple and altar of beautifully dressed stone, supporting the church of the 99 Holy Fathers. Down in the village, ask directions to 'Hadrian's aqueduct', a reservoir hewn out of the living rock, a present from the emperor.

✆ *(0822–)*   ***Where to Stay and Eating Out***

Kastélli

Kastélli's finest hotel, **Playies**, is isolated along the Polyrénia road, ✆ 23 404 (*A; exp*); each room has a large balcony overlooking the bay or pool. **Holiday Bay**, by the sea, ✆ 23 488 (*B pension; mod*) is modern and comfortable. **Castle Hotel**, Plateía Kastélliou, ✆ 22 140 (*C; mod*) a decent fairly modern place, and rooms have private bath. **Gallini Beach**, ✆ 23 288 (*inexp*) has quiet rooms at the far end of the beach. There are two campsites along the sea east of Kastélli: the new **Nopigia**, ✆ 31 111, with a large swimming pool, and **Mythimna**, at Drepánia, ✆ 31 444; both have lots of shade. *Both open April–Oct.* Set back in a garden by the beach, **Taverna Plaka** is a favourite for lunch. On the main seafront, which livens up in the evening, **Papadakis** serves up the day's catch while **Alatopiperi**, 'Salt and Pepper', is a pleasant little place with cooking as uncomplicated as its name. The freshest fish are grilled at **Stimadoris**, out by the fishing port. For Cretan dishes, try **Agrimi** in the centre of town.

Polyrénia

In Grigorianá, on the road up to Polyrénia, there are two pleasant tavernas: the isolated **Kastro**, with rooms to rent, and **Perivoli** set in a pretty graden. At Polyrénia itself, the **Taverna Odysseas** has average food, but the big view over the olive terraces is wonderful.

The West Coast

Phalassarná and Gramvoúsa

Crete's west coast is wild and dramatic, starkly outlined by mountains plunging sheer into the sea. They give way to a fertile coastal plain coated in plastic tomato tunnels, at **Phalassarná** (ΦΑΛΑΣΑΡΝΑ), 15km from Kastélli on a new paved road. Endowed with beautiful sandy beaches and coves, among the finest in Crete, Phalassarná has more tavernas and rooms to rent every year. North of the beach at

Koutrí stood **ancient Phalassarná**, founded in the 6th century (although its name is pre-Hellenic). Long Polyrénia's most bitter rival, it was an important sea-faring town, and minted coins with a trident and FA on one side and a lady with earrings on the other. You can measure how much this western end of Crete has risen—Phalassarná's ancient port, with it's mighty defence towers, is now 200m from the sea. Bits of the ancient city lie scattered around the stranded port while, further up, archaeologists have recently unearthed a bathhouse (now under a shelter). Most curious of all is a **stone throne** believed to date from Hellenistic times; some scholars guess it was dedicated to the sea god Poseidon.

From Kastélli you can hire a caique to sail around the top of wild, barren, uninhabited **Cape Voúxa** to the sheltered harbour of the triangular islet of **Ágria,** better known by the name of its mighty Venetian fortress, **Gramvoúsa**. Like Néa Soúda and Spinalonga to the east, it held out until the 18th century, when the Venetians gave up their last hope of ever reconquering Crete. In 1821, during the Greek War of Independence, Greek refugees from the devastated islands of Psará and Kássos managed to capture the fort. Forced to make a living in troubled times, they took to pirating so successfully that independent Greece's first Prime Minister, Capodístria, had personally to intervene to prevent a diplomatic row, and the Great Powers oversaw the island's return to the Turks. Although more than half ruined, the Venetians' Renaissance church is more or less intact and the huge reservoirs, unused for over a century, are full to the brim. Last but not least, there's a gorgeous, sandy beach nearby on Cape Voúxa. A path leads there from **Kaliviani**, at the foot of the peninsula, but it's a hot three or four hours' trek.

Down to Elafonísi

South of Phalassarná, the partially paved but easy coastal road takes in some spectacular scenery over the sea; try to do it in the morning to avoid the glare. In sprawling **Plátanos** a proto-Geometric tomb was unearthed during the road construction, while down in **Sfinári** there's a pebble beach, some tavernas and simple places to stay. Further south, the road rides a corniche high over the sea to **Kámbos**, a small village which won't detain you long, although you may be tempted by the 3km track leading down through a ravine to the wild sandy beach of **Livádia**.

The road becomes increasingly rough as it winds south to the Libyan Sea and the sheer rock pedestal of the windswept, bleached **convent of Chrysoskalítissa**, 'Our Lady of the Golden Stair' (*open 7am–sunset*). The story goes that only persons without sin, or, according to some, non-liars can see which of the 90 steps is made of gold; a rather more prosaic version says that the Patriarch in Constantinople ordered the monks to sell off the golden step in the 15th century to pay off his debts. Tour buses from Chaniá have besieged the last nun who lives there.

The prime attraction in this remote corner of Crete, however, lies another 5km southwest, the islet of **Elafonísi** (ΕΛΑΦΟΝΗΣΙ). It's a magnificent place to while away a day, set in a shallow, almost tropical lagoon that comes in a spectrum of turquoise, blue and violet, rimmed by pinkish white sand; the water is only 2ft deep so you can wade to Elafonísi and beyond to beaches with a few waves. A little less virgin every year, Elafonísi is set to be impregnated with a resort venture financed by Cretan and German concerns, headed by ex-Prime Minister Mitsotákis.

Inland: Chestnut Villages

Rather than backtrack along the coast, consider returning to Kastélli from Chrysoskalítissa/Elafonísi via Crete's chestnut country, its lush, dramatic, mountainous beauty reminiscent of Corsica. Fertile and well watered, its nine villages, the *Enneachoria*, live off the chestnut and agriculture; in July they host some of the best weddings in Crete. Some are worth a stop year-round: driving up from Elafonísi, you can pay your respects to the 14th-century frescoed church of Michaíl Archangelos and the older, twin-sailed Ag. Geórgios in **Váthi**. **Kefáli** has magnificent sea views from its porch and even better frescoes in its church, **Metamórphosis tou Sotírou** (1320), located just down a track at the end of the village; note the English graffiti on the walls from 1553. Nearby **Perivólia** is a charming green oasis, home of a private **ethnographic museum**. Delightful **Élos**, the largest and highest of the nine villages, is set in a forest of ancient plane and chestnut trees—a perfect antidote to the sunbaked sands of Elafonísi. It has a small hotel if you want to linger; one temptation is the chestnut cake baked in late October and served at Élos' chestnut festival. Six km beyond, the road forks towards Strovlés and Paleóchora (*see* below).

The main road to the north descends leisurely to Koutsoumatádos and skirts the dramatic 1500m **Topólia** (or Kousoumátados) **ravine**, excellent walking territory. A sign on the road points the way up a steep stair cut in the rock for the massive stalactite cave of **Ag. Sofía**, a holy place since Neolithic and Minoan times, still sheltering a little troglodyte church. **Topólia**, at the end of the ravine, is a handsome village with a frescoed church (Ag. Paraskeví).

ⓒ (0822–)   ***Where to Stay and Eating Out***

Phalassarná

New buildings with flats or rooms have sprouted up higgledy piggledy like toadstools. **SunSet Rooms and Studios**, ⓒ 41 204, is right on the beach, with a good taverna. **Falassarna Beach Apartments** have fine views over the sea, as does **Adam Rooms** and **Petalida**. **Aqua Marine**, ⓒ 41 414, and **Stathis**, ⓒ 41 480, have inexpensive rooms to rent near the beach; if they're full try

Anastasia, ✆ 41 480, set further back. There are simple Greek favourites served at **Panorama**, which also has rooms to rent, or for a splurge, try the fancy new **Plakures**, serving Greek and Cretan specialities.

Élos

The little hotel here is **Ai Dikios**, ✆ 61 275, (*D; inexp*), and there are rooms to rent as well.

The Southwest: Paleochóra and the Sélino

The White Mountains only permit a few north–south roads to breach their rocky fastness. Those to the southwest run into the Eparchy of Sélino, where the growing but still very attractive resort town of Paleochóra is the central attraction, along with a score of decorated medieval churches that have escaped the ravages of time, especially around Kándanos. Most of the churches are locked, but asking in the nearest *kafeneíon* mornings or late afternoons usually produces an open sesame.

Getting Around

Paleochóra is served by five **buses** a day from Chaniá; a 6am bus goes to Omalós for the Gorge of Samariá. Every Tuesday and Thursday, small **boats** leave Paleochóra for Gávdos; on Friday and Sunday a larger boat sails from Paleochóra to Soúgia, Ag. Roúmeli and Gávdos. Other boats leave Paleochóra for Chóra Sfakíon, Loutró, Soúgia, Pachiá Ámmos beach, and the island of Elafónisos; **port police** ✆ (0823) 41 214.

Two **buses** run daily between Chaniá and Soúgia; Soúgia is also linked daily by **boat** to Ag. Roúmeli when the Gorge of Samariá is open.

Festivals

Paleochóra: Musical August, **1–10 August**. Soúgia: **8 September**.

Along the Main Road from Chaniá to Paleochóra

Of the three roads from the north that wriggle down to the Sélino, the main one from Tavronítis gets the most takers. It's not the most dramatic, but still more than likely to distress anyone subject to travel sickness. There are hosts of Byzantine churches en route, beginning in **Flória**, where the 15th-century frescoes in Ag. Patéras are well worth a look. Further south, **Kándanos** means 'the city of victory' and claims the highest rainfall in Crete. Although inhabited since Roman times, nothing here is over 50 years old; in the Battle of Crete the townsmen, women and children, armed with whatever weapons they could find, resisted the Nazi advance with such stubborn ferocity that the rest were forced to retreat and return with reinforcements the next day, shooting everyone they could find and burning the village to the ground. Among the memorials is the original sign erected by Germans: 'Here stood Kándanos, destroyed in retribution for the murder of 25 German soldiers.' Excavations have recently revealed a building believed to be a Roman *praetorium*.

From Kándanos, take the left turn on the Soúgia road for **Anisaráki**. There are five Byzantine churches within the next three or four kilometres. **Taxiárchos Michaíl**, near Koufalotó, was frescoed in 1327 by one of the best artists working in Western Crete, Ioánnis Pagoménos ('Frozen John'). Anisaráki itself has three 14th-century churches: the Venetian-Byzantine **Panagía**, with well-preserved paintings, **Ag. Ioánnes**, and **Ag. Paraskeví**, the latter with more frescoes. The paintings and iconostasis in a fourth church in Anisaráki, **Ag. Anna**, date from the 1460s; the dedication is intact, and among the pictures is a fine one of St Anne nursing the baby Virgin and St George on horseback. Just south of Kándanos, in Plemanianá, **Ag. Geórgios** has frescoes of the *Last Judgement* from 1410. In **Kakodíki** to the southwest, a hundred springs with soft mineral waters are known for curing kidney stones; here two small churches house frescoes, **Taxiárchos Michaíl** (1387) and **Ag. Isódoros** (1420), both near the modern church Ag. Triáda. Further south, a sign (actually, thanks to local hunters, it looks more like a sieve) points out the road to **Kádros**, where a late 14th-century church of the **Panagía** has more frescoes.

Paleochóra

The Venetians called it Castello Selino, the Bride of the Libyan Sea. The Greeks call it simply the Old Town, or **Paleochóra** (ΠΑΛΑΙΟΧΩΡΑ). If no longer nuptially fresh, Paleochóra still attracts thousands of suitors, an incongruous but jovial mixture of charter flight tourists and hippies, who consider it home away from home and keep the supermarkets well-stocked with yoghurt and muesli. It also has the rare advantage of straddling two beaches—one wide, sandy, and lined with tamarisks, the other stony—which are never wind-smacked at the same time, allowing you to pick up your towel and move according to the weather, unless you want to enjoy the superb windsurfing the sandy beach provides.

On the tip of the peninsula, the Venetians built Paleochóra's **Castello Selino** in 1279, more to police the ornery Greeks than protect their new territory. When tested in 1539 by Khair Eddin Barbarossa, Castello Selino failed to measure up, and was captured and demolished by the pillaging Turks, leaving only empty walls to defend the poppies that fill it every April. If you need to get away from it all, there are beaches all along the road to the west, although the presence of greenhouses keep them off the postcards. But the water around pebbly **Ag. Kyriáki** at the end of the track is exceptionally crystal-clear.

Inland from Paleochóra: Ánidri and Azogyrés

If you're spending any time at all in Paleochóra, delve into the interior and its pretty, unspoiled mountain villages. **Ánidri** to the northeast is one of the prettiest and is home to Ag. Geórgios, built in the 1300s and frescoed by Ioánnis Pagoménos in 1323. In the same direction, but on the winding road through cypress forests towards Teménia and Soúgia (*see* below), **Azogyrés** has several claims to fame: the pleasures of its deep green surroundings and gurgling stream, a fascinating one room **historical museum** (*open Sat and Sun 9–2*) and, down the shady path at the bottom of the village, one of Crete's rare **evergreen plane trees**, an enormous specimen growing next to the 19th-century chapel of the Ag. Páteres, built into the cliff. The guardian of the museum has the key to the chapel; the highlight is the iconstasis, carved by a naïve local sculptor. Two km above Azogyrés, the **cave of Souré** (bring a flashlight) is said to have been the temporary home for the same 99 Agii Páteres, or Holy Fathers, who came out of Egypt after the Byzantine reconquest of Crete. The entrance, marked by a cross, is a short walk up from the road. An iron stair leads steeply down to the little chapel; instead of hermits (actually, it's hard to see how 99 of them ever fit in) the cave shelters at least 99 pigeons.

☎ (0823–) **Where to Stay**

Paleochóra

Enough people come to Paleochóra that the town has its own tourist office, on El. Venizélos (*open Mon–Fri 10–1 and 5–8*), helpful for finding accomodation if you arrive without a booking. **Elman**, at the end of the sandy beach, ☎ 41 412 (*B; exp*) is the biggest and most modern choice, with rooms and apartments (*open all year*), but for something really classy reserve a beautifully furnished studio or apartment from English-speaking **Efthisis Sfinarolakis**, ☎ 41 594 or 41 596 (*exp*).

Polydoros, on the main street between the beaches, ☎ 41 068 (*C; mod*) is an old favourite and serves good breakfasts. By the sandy beach, **Pension Ari**, ☎ 41 502 (*B; mod*) is a good bet. *Open all year*. Little **Pension Lissos**, near the bus station, ☎ 41 266 (*C; mod*), the oldest lodgings in town, often has a place if everything else is full.

Paleochóra has a fair selection of pensions and rooms in the 4000dr range, among them **Ostria**, in the middle of the sandy beach, ☎ 41 055, and **Oasis**, ☎ 41 328. For a bit more, **Kalypso**, in the centre, ☎ 41 429, offers rooms with kitchens in an old stone house. There's a campsite with shade by the pebble beach, ☎ 41 120.

Near the pebble beach, **Portofino** is for a serious Italian splurge, serving pasta dishes such as tagliatelle with smoked salmon (*around 5000dr for a full meal, much less for pizza*). **Kyma**, nearby, has a wide choice of seafood and typical taverna food (*2500dr*). **Pizzeria Niki**, in the centre, makes good, fresh and cheap pies with some seating outside. A few steps from the sandy beach, vegetarians can forgo their usual Greek salad and cheese pie at **The Third Eye**, © 41 055, for spicy Asian and Mexican specialities; carnivores can also choose from barbecued meats. **Elite**, right on the sandy beach, serves up tasty Greek food in the 3–4000dr range and has Cretan music and dancing every Saturday night.

Entertainment and Nightlife

In Paleochóra, the open-air **Cine Attikon** features a different, subtitled film every day of the week in the summer. The **Music Pub**, up by the castle, offers lovely views to go with its drinks and snacks, or linger by the beach at the trendy **Jetée Cocktail Bar**, just beyond the Elman hotel.

Europe at its Southernmost: Gávdos

If you really suffer from *mal de civilisation*, catch one of the small ferries from Paleochóra or Chóra Sfakíon that sail 50km over rough seas to the triangular maquis-matted islet of Gávdos, at 35°10' the southernmost point in Europe. The current population is around 55—down from 8000 in its heyday in the 1200s. Gávdos was known as Clauda in ancient times, and it puts in a fairly limp claim to have been the home of the fair Calypso, although its very limited tourist amenities can be seductive for anyone seeking the Greek island of decades ago. Travel agents in Paleochóra seem determined to make sure that it becomes less lonely all the time, and can arrange a room for you if you're not prepared for the possibility of camping out. Beware that it can get hot down there, and that the sea can easily leave you stranded for longer than you intended to stay. Outside June–September ferries are so irregular you'll have to stick right around Paleochóra or Chóra Sfakíon and wait for one to appear.

Karavé, the port of Gávdos, is as dinky as can be, cupped in barren hills. Most of the rooms for rent are here. Water is scarce, all electricity is supplied by generators, and nearly all the food, with the exception of honey, wine and fish has to be imported from the big island. Although minibuses usually meet the ferry, renting a moped or bike to take with you isn't at all a bad idea; none is available on Gávdos. In the centre of the island **Kastí**, the capital, has the post office, a few rooms, basic shops, an empty prison, the school (with one pupil) and the not terribly over-whelming ruins of Clauda. Most of the houses are empty in the other settlements: **Ámbelos** near the island's highest point (381m) has a path down to the little north coast beach **Potámos**; from **Vatsianá** a rather longer path leads down to **Tripití** or 'Three Holes' where a trice-pierced rock marks the southernmost point of Europe. There are good beaches, especially sandy **Sarakiníkos** with a few rooms and tav-ernas (a 40min walk north of Karavé), and **Kórfos**, reached by one of Gávdos' few roads to the south, with a taverna and rooms.

The Road from Chaniá to Soúgia

It's an hour's caique ride from Paleochóra to Soúgia, but if you're coming from Chaniá, the new route branching off at Alikianós (*see* p.110–11) will get you there quicker. It ascends the west edge of the Omalós plateau to **Ag. Iríni**, a pleasant vil-lage immersed in trees at the top of a beautiful walkable 8km gorge, although it was a lot greener before the forest fire in 1994. From Ag. Iríni, the road then descends into the Selíno, passing **Rodováni**, a village just west of ancient **Elyros**, one of the largest and most pugnacious Dorian settlements on Crete. According to legend, Elyros was founded by two sons of Apollo, Philakides and Philandros, and it exported bows, arrows and bronze and had risen to the level of a bishopric when the Saracens destroyed it in the 9th century. The English traveller Robert Pashley was the first to pinpoint its location, in 1834. Walls and the acropolis lie scattered on the hill, waiting to interest some archaeologist. The church of the Panagía was planted on top of an ancient temple, re-using its mosaic floor.

Four km west is **Teménia**, a muscat-producing village with a photogenic old stone church of the Sotír, and, on its outskirts, the double cyclopean walls of ancient **Irtakina**. Its name is pre-Hellenic, it minted coins with bees, deer, dophins and eight pointed stars, and in 170 BC it signed a treaty with Pergamon. But that's about all anyone knows. Further along, **Moní** has another church, Ag. Nikólaos, finely frescoed by the indefatigable Ioánnis Pagómeno.

The paved road south of Rodováni ends up at **Soúgia** (ΣΟΥΓΙΑ), a higgledy pig-gledy wannabe resort endowed with a long pebbly beach that never gets too crowded. The port of Doric Elyros, its ancient name, Syia, means 'pig town' for the porkers it raised, back long ago when the region was covered with oak forests; to this day the nude beach is known rather unflatteringly as the 'Bay of Pigs'. The ruins that stand are a modest blast from Syia's Roman past: walls, vaulted tombs, an aqueduct and baths; the port itself vanished with the rising of Western Crete. Prettiest of all, however, is the 6th-century mosaic floor, re-used in the foundations of the modern church. **Ag. Antónios** (1382) has frescoes, and a cave near Soúgia, **Spyliara**, is one of a multitude in the Mediterranean that claims to have belonged to the Cyclops Polyphemos.

From Soúgia you can sail in 20min or make a very pretty hour-and-a-half walk to **Lissós**, the tiny port of ancient Yrtakina, set in a green landscape. In ancient times, Lissós enjoyed a certain renown for its medicinal springs, and it attracted enough trade at its Doric Asklepeion, or healing sanctuary, to afford to mint gold coins. The Asklepeion was built in the 3rd century BC, and has a fine pebble mosaic floor with geometric forms and animals. The pit here once held snakes, a sacred symbol of immortality and of the renewal of life through death; gliding in and out of holes in the earth, they seemed to have an uncanny contact with the underworld, and were often seen around tombs (eating the mice that ate the grave offerings). You can see their descendants in any modern doctor's office, twisting around the caduceus. The population of Lissós these days is exactly one: the caretaker, who watches over the theatre, baths, houses and two old Christian basilicas with more mosaic floors, rebuilt in the 1200s by the chapels of Ag. Kyriáki and the Panagía.

Soúgia ☎ (0823–)   **Where to Stay and Eating Out**

Soúgia

Santa Irene, ☎ 51 342, ✉ 90 047, is a small and friendly complex of apartments and rooms, with a breakfast bar. **Lotos**, ☎ 51 142, is similar *(both mod)*. **Pikilassos**, ☎ 51 1242 (*B; mod*) has the 9 fanciest beds in the village and a pelican living next to its taverna. There is a fair choice of inexpensive rooms to rent, such as **Lissos**, ☎ 51 244, **Koumakakis**, ☎ 51 298, and even cheaper, **Maria Marinaki**, ☎ 51 338 and **George Ellinakis**, ☎ 51 339. Popular **Liviko** on the waterfront serves up the usual taverna treats. After dinner, make your way to **Fortuna Bar** for 60s rock, Latin, African and jazz.

Citrus Villages South of Chaniá

If you're itching for a leisurely bike ride on relatively flat ground, the Keríti valley south of Chaniá may be your ticket. The best oranges in Crete grow here and, as the locals will tell you, Cretan oranges are the best in the world; the entire valley has an estimated million trees. During the Battle of Crete it was nicknamed Prison Valley for the big white prison near **Alikianós**, just off the main Chaniá–Omalós road. It has a bloodstained past. A memorial honours the Greeks who kept on fighting here, cut off and unaware that the Allies elsewhere were in retreat; their ignorance enabled a majority of British and ANZAC troops to be safely evacuated from the Libyan coast. During the Occupation prisoners were executed in a killing ground near the crossroads. The infamous wedding massacre of Kantanoléo's Cretans took place at Alikianós' ruined Venetian tower of Da Molino (*see* p.101); although its historical truth can't be confirmed, the medieval Venetians certainly played similar dirty tricks on other *signori* with attitude problems in Verona and Padua. Next to the tower, the little church of Ag. Geórgios (1243) has exceptional frescoes, painted in 1430 by Pávlos Provatás. In nearby **Kouphós**, the early Byzantine church of Ag. Kyr-Yánnis is decorated with more superb frescoes, added throughout the centuries.

Fournés, on the Chaniá road, alone claims more than 120,000 shimmering orange trees and makes wine so delicious, the villagers say, that they can't bear to sell it. After Fournés the road to Omalós begins to rise rapidly to **Lákki**, another picturesque village immersed in greenery, set like a horseshoe into mountain terraces with a pair of rooms and tavernas. Alternatively, take the 5km detour southeast of Fournés for **Mesklá**, a lovely little village set in lush green countryside, where one glossy orange grove succeeds another. The little church of the Panagía (next to the big modern church) has traces of mosaics from a temple of Aphrodite, left by the ancient city of Rizinia; another church, Sótiros, has frescoes from 1303 by Theódoros and Michaíl Véneris. Above Mesklá, a rough four-wheel-drive road leads up to **Zoúrva**, a whitewashed village with amazing views, then circles around into the dramatic 18km **Thérisson gorge**, famous in Cretan history for the 1905 Revolution of Therisso, led by Venizélos in response to the reactionary policies of Prince George. The Thérisson gorge–Chaniá road is easy and paved; near the entrance of the gorge you can stop by the large sleepy village of **Mourniés**, birthplace of Venizélos, Greek Prime Minister most of the time between 1910 and 1932.

The Gorge of Samariá

The single most spectacular stretch of Crete is squeezed into the 18km Gorge of Samariá (ΦΑΡΑΓΓΙ ΣΑΜΑΡΙΑΣ), the longest in Europe and the last refuge of many species of the island's unique fauna and flora, especially rare chasm-loving plants known as *chasmopphytes*. Once considered a rather adventurous excursion, the walk is now offered by every tour operator; the Gorge has been spruced up as a National Park and, in short, forget any private communion with Mother Nature before you even start out. The walk takes most people between five and eight hours going down from Omalós south to Ag. Roúmeli on the Libyan Sea, and twice as long if you're Arnold Schwarzenegger or just plain crazy and walk up.

Getting Around

Buses leave Chaniá for Omalós at 6.15, 7.30, 8.30 and at 1.30; from Kastélli-Kíssamou at 5, 6, and 7; Réthymnon at 6.15 and 7; others leave early from Plataniás, Ag. Marína, Tavronítis, Chandrís, Kolimbári and Georgioúpoli. Organized **tour buses** leave almost as early (you can, however, get a slight jump on the crowds or at least more sleep by staying overnight at Omalós). Once through to Ag. Roúmeli, **boats** run all afternoon to Chóra Sfakíon,

Soúgia and Paleochóra, where you can pick up a late afternoon bus back to the north coast. Consider paying the bit extra for a tour bus, especially in the summer, to make sure you have a seat on the return journey; your tired dogs could turn rabid if you make them stand up for two hours on a bus after doing Samariá.

Practicalities

The gorge is open officially from 1 May–31 Oct from 6am–4pm, when the water is low enough to ensure safe fording of the streams, and when the staff of the National Forest Service patrols the area (it's for their services that you're asked to pay admission). Although last admission to the gorge is at 3pm, almost everyone starts much earlier, to avoid the midday heat, and to make the excursion a single day's round-trip outing. It is absolutely essential to wear good walking shoes and socks; a hat and a bite to eat are only slightly less vital, and binoculars a decided bonus for flower and bird observations. Dressing appropriately is difficult: it's usually chilly at Omalós and sizzling at Ag. Rouméli.The fresh streams along the gorge provide good drinking water at regular intervals. Beware, however, that early in the year the stream that runs through the centre of Samariá can be high and quite dangerous—drownings in flash floods have happened. Several mules and a helicopter landing pad are on hand for emergency exits; tickets (1000dr) are date-stamped and must be turned in at the lower gate, to make sure no one is lost in the park or tries to camp out. If you haven't the energy to make the whole trek, you can at least sample Samariá by descending only a mile or so into the gorge down the big wooden stair (the rub is you have to walk back up again). A less strenuous (and less rewarding) alternative, proposed by tourist agencies as 'the lazy way', is walking an hour or so up from Ag. Roúmeli to the Sideróportes.

For Gorge information and walking conditions call © (0821) 67 140.

Omalós and Around

Just getting there is part of the fun. If you're on one of the early buses, dawn usually cracks in time for you to look over the most vertiginous section of the road as it climbs 1200m to the pass before descending to the **Omalós Plateau**, 25 sq km and itself no shorty at 1080m. In winter, snows from the fairy circle of White Mountain peaks flood this uncanny plateau so often that the one village, **Omalós** (ΟΜΑΛΟΣ) is uninhabitable. But, like a bathroom sink, this plateau basin has a drain—a cave system called Tzanis, which funnels the water through 3km of galleries before regurgitating it up in resurgent mountain streams. The mouth of Tzanis regularly floods up, exactly like Greek plumbing when too many tourists have ignored the little signs about flushing down paper; the rumbling of its subterranean bubbling makes the earth shake and when the trapped air finally reaches the surface it sounds like dynamite.

The **Tourist Pavilion** for the Gorge of Samariá is a few kilometres south of Omalós. Some of the most spectacular views are from the pavilion, hanging over the edge of the chasm, overlooking the sheer limestone face of mighty 2083m **Mount Gýnglios**, a favourite resort of Zeus when the gods on Olympos got on his nerves. If you come prepared and have a bit of mountain experience under your belt, you can go up from here rather than down: a 90-minute trail from the pavilion leads up to the Greek Mountain Club's **Kallergi Shelter**, ✆ (0821) 54 560 (book in high season); among one of the easier ascents is up to Zeus' Gýnglios hideaway, through a natural rock arch and past the coldest, clearest spring on Crete.

Walking Down the Gorge

In early morning the pavilion fills to the brim as coaches pull in from across half Crete. The first of the up to 2000 people a day begin to trickle down the **Xylóskalo**, a zigzag stone path with a wooden railing, a fairly gentle descent into the Gorge, with scenic lookouts along the way. The name Samariá derives from Ossa Maria, a chapel (1379) and abandoned village halfway down the gorge, now used as the guardians' station and picnic ground. There are several other abandoned chapels along the way, traditional stone *mitáto* huts (used by shepherds as shelter or for cheese-making), and, near the end, the famous **Sideróportes** ('the iron gates'), the oft-photographed section of the gorge where the sheer rock walls rise almost 300m on either side of a passage only 3m wide; you almost feel as if you can touch both walls.

Not a few people return from Samariá having only seen their own feet and the back of the person in front, the path down is that rough. Planning to stay in Ag. Roúmeli may be the answer; it will allow you more leisure to enjoy the unique beauty of the gorge and rare cliff-hanging flowers and herbs that infuse Samariá with an intoxicating fragrance in the summer. Although the Gorge is in the White Mountains National Park, the last refuge of the *kri-kri*, the long-horned Cretan ibex, no one ever sees one any more; the few that have survived the 1993 epidemic of killer ticks, or *korpromantakes*, are shy of the hordes. Birds of prey (rare Griffon vultures, very rare Lammergeiers, buzzards and eagles) are bolder, and often circle high overhead.

Ag. Roúmeli, Past and Present

At the southern end of the Gorge waits **Ag. Roúmeli** (ΑΓ. ΡΟΥΜΕΛΙ), as isolated as any village in Crete and more or less abandoned after a torrent in 1954 swept much of it away. Recently, some of the empty houses have been recycled as stalls selling Greece's most expensive cold drinks, which may be pretty hard to pass up. When tourists began to walk through Samariá in the 1960s, a new Ag. Roúmeli obligingly rose out of the cement mixer like a phoenix (although ugly duckling might be a more apt description), only in a new spot on the coast, another blistering 2km away. This last torturous haul, however, helps to make Ag. Roúmeli looks as inviting as an oasis straight out of Hollywood, with its cool blue sea, fridges stuffed with drinks and snack bars.

Modern Ag. Roúmeli stands on the site of ancient Tarra, where Apollo hid from the wrath of Zeus after slaying Python at Delphi. While sojourning here he fell so passionately in love with a local nymph that he forgot to make the sun rise and got into an even bigger jam with his dad. A sanctuary of Tarranean Apollo marked the spot, and on top of its foundations the Venetians built a church, **Panagías**. From Ag. Roúmeli, caiques take 1½ hours either to Paleochóra (*see* p.106) or to Chóra Sfakíon (pp.125–6); Soúgia, another alternative (p.109), has fewer to Chaniá. If you linger in Ag. Roúmeli, the beach to aim for is **Ag. Pávlos**, a 90-minute walk away, with fresh springs and a lyrical little 10th-century stone church as a landmark.

Where to Stay and Eating Out

Omalós ✆ (0821–)

Neos Omalos, ✆ 67 269, 📧 67 190 (*C; mod*) is recently built, with 18 centrally heated rooms, bar and restaurant. *Open year-round.* **To Exari**, ✆ 67 180, (*C; mod*) is a bit larger and almost as nice; **Drakoulaki**, ✆ 67 269, has simple, inexpensive rooms. There's a mountain shelter up at **Kallergis** (1657m) reached by road from just in front of the Xylóskalo.

Ag. Roúmeli ✆ (0825–)

Ag. Roúmeli has plenty of rooms, but thanks to the popularity of the Gorge and the transport costs, prices are over the odds. There are several restaurant-pension combos, such as **Aghia Roúmeli**, ✆ 91 241, 📧 91 232 (*B; exp*). *Open Mar–Oct.* For something inexpensive, try **Tara** taverna and rooms, ✆ 91 231 or **Lefka Ori**, ✆ 91 219.

East of Chaniá: Akrotíri

Akrotíri (ΑΚΡΩΤΗΡΙ), the most bulbous and busiest of the three headlands that thrust out of Crete's northwest coast, wraps around to shelter the island's safest port at Soúda from northerly winds. Its strategic position has assured it plenty of history, and now that Crete is safe from immenent invasion the steep access road (Eleftheríou Venizélou) from Chaniá's Chalepa quarter is often chock-a-block with locals heading out to Akrotíri's beaches, restaurants, nightclubs and seaside villas.

Outside these suburban tenticles, Akrotíri is a moody place, dusty and junky with military zones towards the airport, lonely and wild by its famous monasteries.

First stop on Akrotíri should be little **Profítis Ilías** church (4.5km from Chaniá), perhaps better known today as Crete's chief **memorial to Venizélos**, its favourite homegrown statesman. Both Elefthérios Venizélos (1864–1936) and son Sophoklís (1896–1964) asked to be buried here to enjoy superb posthumous views over Chaniá, but they had patriotic reasons as well: in the rebellion of 1897, the monastery of the church was briefly the Revolutionary Military Camp of Akrotíri, located just within the 6km exclusion zone around Chaniá established by the Great Powers, there to police the volitile Greeks and Turks rather like the UN currently in Bosnia. To rout out the Greeks, the English, French, Italian and Russian navies bombarded it. In response the Cretans raised the Greek flag. The admirals were so impressed by the sheer audacity of the Cretans, who stood there, holding up the flag with their bare hands even after it was shot off its pole, that they stopped bombing and applauded. Later in the day, a Russian shell destroyed the monastery that encompassed the church, but the Prophet Elijah, not one to turn the other cheek, got his revenge by blowing up the Russian ship the next day. News of the bombardment—that the Great Powers were bombing the Christian Greeks—caused a great stir in Europe and led the Allies to offer Crete its autonomy.

If it's Easter Day afternoon, head just east for the spotless convent of the **Prodrómos** at **Kourakiés**, where the bishop of Chaniá reads the 'Vespers of Love' in a score of languages to the crowd in the flower-bedecked courtyard. Although abandoned after several raping and murdering rampages by Chaniá's Janissaries, the nuns returned in the late 1800s; the wife of the then English ambassador taught them embroidery and lacework as a means of supporting themselves, a tradition the 20 nuns continue to this day. To the north is Akrotíri's first sandy seaside playground, **Kalathás** (ΚΑΛΑΘΑΣ) and its nearby, quieter beach of **Torsanás**, rimmed with villas. **Stavrós** (ΣΤΑΥΡΟΣ), further north, is the end of the trail for buses from Chaniá and owes its growing popularity for longer stays to a lovely circular bay with shallow water. The beach scenes in *Zorba the Greek* were filmed here; the steep slope to the sea was the site of Zorba's half-assed cableway that collapsed like a row of dominoes under the first plummeting tree trunks.

Akrotíri's Monasteries: Ag. Triáda and Gouvernétou

East of Stavrós, Akrotíri has two venerable, faded but still barely active monasteries that well repay a visit. A number of roads across the headland eventually converge on the immaculate monastic olive groves and tree-lined avenue that announce the peach-coloured walls of **Moní Ag. Triáda** (or Tzagaróliou) (*open officially 7.30–2 and 5–7, although beware many afternoons the gate doesn't re-open at all*). The cruciform church has an austere, colonnaded Venetian façade, and in the narthex an inscription in Greek and Latin tells how Ag. Triáda was refounded in 1634 by

Jeremiah Zangarola, a Venetian who became an Orthodox monk. A little museum contains a 17th-century *Last Judgement* among later icons and hoary manuscripts. Ag. Triáda ran the ecclesiastical school of Crete until 1974, and there's talk of renewing the tradition. For now, the five monks and their cats seem content to contemplate eternity from under the tangerine trees in the courtyard.

The second and even older monastery, fortified **Moní Gouvernétou** (or Gdernetto, as the Venetians called it) stands on a remote plateau, 5km above Ag. Triáda along a narrow road that just squeezes through the wild rocky terrain with no room for on-coming traffic. Gouvernétou (*open 7.30–12 and 3–7*) played a major role in reconciling the Cretans and Venetians at the end of the 16th century; the grotesque sandstone heads of the portal, blasted by the sun and wind are curious Venetian fancies far from home. The church, impregnated with old incense, has a few icons and frescoes.

Have a flashlight and water on hand to visit the two intriguing holy places that Gouvernétou supplanted. A shadeless but easy path from the car park leads in 10 minutes to the ruined walls and arches of a monastery-hermitage outside a cave known as **Arkoudiótissa** ('Bear') for its striking bruin-shaped stalagmite worshipped since pre-Minoan times in the cult of Artemis, the Mistress of the Wild Animals. The stone bear leans over a cistern of water, filled by dripping stalactites; the low ceiling is blackened with centuries, read millennia, of candle-smoke. A walled-off corner in the cave contains a small 16th-century chapel dedicated to Panagía Arkoudiótissa, 'Our Lady of the Bear', who shares the same feast day as Artemis once did: 2 February, Candlemas.

From here the path continues down, down, down, another rough and steep 20 minutes or so, past hermits' huts and a sea rock shaped like a boat (a petrified pirate ship, they say, although coincidentally Candlemas also marked the beginning of the navigation season in the Mediterranean). The path ends with 150 steps carved in the rock, which leaves you by the dark, complex **cave of St John the Hermit** (or the Stranger) who sailed to Crete from Egypt on his mantle, founded a score of monasteries and retired here, becoming so stooped from his poor diet of roots and vegetables that a hunter shot him, mistaking him for an animal. The saint managed to crawl back to his cave, where the hunter tracked him down and found him bleeding to death (7 October 1042—the anniversery still brings crowds of pilgrims here). In this supremely inhospitable wild ravine, St John founded the **Katholikón**, its striking church and buildings gouged into the living rock of the precipice, straddled by a lofty stone bridge. Anchorites lived here until pirates in the 17th century made it too hot. Across the bridge, the path continues down to a rocky, often deserted, but delightful swimming nook, especially enjoyable when you contemplate the killer walk back up.

Kalathás

Sunrise, on the hillside overlooking Torsanás beach, © 64 214 (*mod*), has pleasant rooms in a pretty location.

Stavrós

Rea, 800 yards from the sea, © 64 189, (*B; exp*). Built in 1992, this air-conditioned complex offers a wide range of activities, from a basketball court for your teenager, tennis, swimming pool, fitness room, and babysitting. **Zorba's Studio Flats**, by the beach, © 52 525, ✆ 42 616 (*exp–mod*), are furnished with a traditional touch and perfect for a family holiday, with tennis, garden, seaside taverna and a playground; the adjacent but isolated **Blue Beach** villa and apartments complex © 64 161, ✆ 64 140 is even a tad nicer, with a restaurant, bar and sea sports (*open Apr–Oct*). **Kavos Beach**, © 68 623 (*inexp*) are among the nicest rooms to rent. **Mama's** is the favourite seaside taverna, or try the **Stavros** restaurant-pizzeria on the Chorafáki road.

Soúda and Around

Chaniá trickles scrubbily all along the road to **Soúda** (ΣΟΥΔΑ), the main port for western Crete, tucked into the magnificent sheltered bay (you can also drive down there from Akrotíri, through a fenced off military zone). Thanks to the military, Soúda will never win a beauty contest, in spite of its setting; its largest features include an active Greek naval base behind yellow walls and a recently abandoned NATO base, for years the source of a hundred local gripes. But NATO was hardly the first to appreciate Soúda Bay. The Venetians fortified the bay's islet, **Néa Soúda**, and when they and the Greeks who took refuge there finally surrendered in 1715 (50 years after the Turkish conquest of Crete) it was only by way of a treaty, in spite of frequent attacks and a gruesome pyramid of 5000 Christian heads the Turks piled around the walls.

Signs in Soúda point the way to the immaculate lawns and flowers of the seaside **Commonwealth War Cemetery**, where 1497 English, New Zealand and Australian troops who perished in the Battle of Crete are buried, the majority of them too young to vote or lying anonymous under tombstones inscribed 'A soldier of the 1939–1945 War Known unto God'. The silence is in marked contrast to the Greek families frolicking a few yards away on the beach. Two km west of Soúda towards Chaniá, a road forks south for the 16th-century walled **Moní Chryssopigí** (*open 8–12 and 3.30–6*), founded by Ioánnis Chartophylakas, a doctor ennobled by the Venetians for his tireless work in a devastating epidemic that broke out in Crete in

1595. The church, but especially the museum, contains an exceptional collection of icons from the 15th century on, and a superb, intricate cross decorated with golden filigree and precious stones. Confiscated by the Germans in 1941, the monastery was repopulated in 1977 by nuns, who restore icons and books and operate on Crete's most prestigious icon-painting workshops (*open by appointment only*).

Ancient Aptera

The Turks had an excellent if rather frustrating view of the defiant islet of Néa Soúda and the entire Bay of Soúda from their fortress of **Idzeddin,** just east of Soúda on the precipitous promontory of Cape Kalámi. Now Chaniá's prison, Idzeddin was built by the Turkish governor in the 19th century, when the Cretans seemed to be revolting every other week, and he named it for the son of Sultan Abdul-Azis I. The stone was cannibalized from the ancient city of **Aptera**, high on a plateau 8.5km east of Soúda, above **Megála Choráphia** (the site is up the steep road from the Taverna Aptera, *open Tues–Sun 8.30–3*). Dedicated to Artemis, Aptera was founded in the 11th century BC and remained one of the chief cities in western Crete until shattered by an earthquake in AD 700. Its mighty walls once squirmed 4km over the steep slopes and have been compared to the great polygonal defences of Mycenaean Tiryns, and you can pick your way through the weeds and fences to see a Classical temple foundation, the theatre, and the skeleton of Roman basilica. The Monastery of St John sits atop two magnificent if crumbling Roman cisterns the size of cathedrals. The city's curious name (*aptera* or 'featherless') came from a singing contest held between the Muses and the Sirens. The Sirens were sore losers, and tore out their feathers and plunged into the sea, where they turned into the islets far below in Soúda Bay; there are tremendous views down on them and on to the heads of the cons in Idzeddin prison from the stylish Turkish fortress on the edge of the Aptera site.

Aptera's modern heir, Megála Choráphia, has a surprising number of English holiday homes, while, to the south, the village of **Stílos** saw the ANZAC forces' last stand in the Battle of Crete, a rearguard action that permitted most of the allies to escape to the south coast and on to boats bound for Egypt. To this day, a special relationship survives with New Zealand, where many Chaniots emigrated after the war. Stílos today is a quiet place, with lazy coffeehouses under massive plane trees, although they heat up with Cretan song and dance on summer weekends. North of the village, real explorers can walk down to the **gorge of Diktimo** (signposted from the road) or visit the massive, half ruined Byzantine church of **Panagía Zerviotissa**.

From Stílos it's a 5km hairpin drive up to the village of **Samonás**, where archaeologists are unearthing a Late Minoan settlement. But the main reason for the difficult drive is the 11th-century **church of Ag. Nikólaos**, with its ravishing 13th-century frescoes by an unknown hand, located just above Samonás in Kyriakosélia.

Come in the morning or late afternoon and ask the café owner in Samonás to ring the family that has the key. Lastly, you can backtrack north of Stílos to pick up the road west to **Maláxa**, an ancient mining centre. Ruins of two Byzantine churches, Ag. Saránta and Ag. Eleoúsa, remain, but the most spectacular sight is the ravine to the south, 400m deep and riddled with caves.

Around Cape Drápanon

Once east of Aptera, the highway (with most of the buses) dives inland to avoid rugged Cape Drápanon, missing much of the area's finest scenery; vineyards and olive groves and cypresses draped on rolling hills, and rocky fringes of fragrant maquis by the sea. A pair of resort towns dot the somewhat exposed north coast of Drápanon: **Kalýves** has a long beach under the Apokoróna fortress, built by the Genoese when they tried to pinch Crete from the Venetians; it made a suitable enough impression to give the name Apokoróna to this entire area. Further east, **Almirída** is smaller and more attractive, with a curved sandy beach flying the Blue Flag of environmental correctness, a few tiny boats tucked into a tiny harbour, good fish tavernas and usually excellent windsurfing. A fenced off area at the entrance to Almirída shelters the floor of a 13th-century basilica.

From Almirída, it's 4km to the old village of **Gavalochóri**, well worth a stop for its **Museum of Folklore** (*open mornings only, 10–1; adm*), where exhibits of village life in days of yore have inspired a women's agrotourism co-operative to renew the local silk and lace industry, in hibernation since the departure of the Turks. In late July or early August the museum organizes old-fashioned Cretan evenings and other events. East of Almirída, the road begins to swing in from the rocky coast and continues up to picturesque **Pláka** and the more straggly **Kókkino Chóra**, the latter used for most of the village scenes in the film *Zorba the Greek*.

Zorba: Thirty Years Later

In the summer Kókkino Chóra seems too bright to fit the bill; come back in the winter for the brooding, overcast atmosphere that kept the black and white movie from looking anything like a tourism poster. They say that the Cretans themselves only got to know Kazantzákis' novel after watching the film, and were rather shocked to see how conditions in the 1920s were portrayed. A recent visit to the *kafeneíon* in Kókkino Chóra (where the rainy scene with the goat took place) revealed most of the local talent recruited for the film sitting in the dappled shadows, playing cards, or rather slapping them the way Greeks do. Out of the six, only one had all his arms, legs and eyes intact; it seemed indiscreet to ask what had happened to them all. There used to be stills and autographed photos of the stars on the walls, but the *kafeneíon* owner (who played the role of the priest) said he took them down a couple of years ago, 'But I still have a video around somewhere.' 'The best bit was slitting Irene Papas' throat, just down there in the square. Like this he did it.' Another man acted it out, pretending to twist a woman's long hair around his arm to pull her head back for the knife. 'The movie was nothing though, compared to that tunnel those German bastards made us dig, big enough for 30 cannons. You can still see it, up that mountain. Now that's a wonder.' 'Yes,' said another. 'But young people don't want to know about those things any more.' They all shook their heads, and slapped their cards so hard that the sound shot down the empty lanes.

Small beaches, mostly for local consumption, lie tucked under Pláka and Kókkino Chóra, but the best thing to do is circle around the cape, through **Drápanos** and **Kefalás**, sleepy villages reeking of past grandeur, old stone villas, towers and gateways. The largest village, **Vámos** (ΒΑΜΟΣ) seems quite urban in comparison, its main street dark with the shade of trees, a God-send on an August day. If you're headed towards Georgioúpolis from here, put off lunch until you reach **Exópoli**, where the tavernas enjoy a breathtaking view down to the sea.

© *(0825–)*   **Where to Stay and Eating Out**

Megála Choráfia/Stílos

Megála Choráfia's blue and white **Taverna Aptera**, just under the archaeological site, is a good bet, but for more shade try **To Fangari**, in the centre of Stílos; nearby, live Cretan music, dance and barbecues happen most summer weekends at the **Kritiko Kentro tou Moustakia**, © 41 190.

Kalýves/Almirída

In Kalýves, the seaside **Kalives Beach**, © 28 221 (*B; exp*), is the pick of the hotels; the travel agencies have lists of rooms and studios. Most accommodation in Almyrída comes in the form of apartments such as the well-tended seaside **Villa Armonia**, © 31 081, and in two rather stylish hotels, the **Almyrida Beach**, 500m from the sea, © 31 651 (*B, exp–mod*) with a pool, and the new **Dimitra Hotel** (*exp*), set back 100m from the water. The seaside restaurants are all good: most of the locals turn up at **Chrysoula Thema** under the tamarisks, where lovely waitresses serve a full swordfish meal with barrelled wine for 2800dr. The British prefer **Dimitri's** for good fresh fish, and for something different stop by **The Enchanted Owl**, whose English owners make a point of serving dishes (Mexican, Indian or Italian) not offered by their Greek neighbours.

Vrýssis, Georgioúpolis and Lake Kournás

Just south of the highway from Vámos, **Vrýses** (ΒΡΥΣΕΣ) is one of the most important crossroads in western Crete, the major bus interchange between Chaniá and Réthymnon and the route south to Chóra Sfakíon). It's a pleasant place, with lofty plane trees, restaurant and café terraces all along the torrential Almirós river, dotted with busts of heroic, moustachioed Cretans. One of the oldest cypress trees in Crete is by a ruined Venetian house in **Fres**, just west.

The road from Vrýssis more or less follows the Amirós river as it flows down to the genteel resort of **Georgioúpolis** (ΓΕΩΡΓΙΟΥΠΟΛΗ), tucked in the crook of Cape Drápanon and shaded by scores of old eucalyptus trees. Named in honour of Prince George, the High Commissioner of autonomous Crete, it has a long, sandy (if sometimes rough and windy) beach, part of the intermittent strand that extends along the Gulf of Almirós to Réthymnon. Although only a minute's walk from the coastal highway and a favourite area for hotel builders, Georgioúpolis hasn't been completely swamped in cement; perhaps the best advertisement of all are the many people who return year after year. The only drawback: the strong undercurrents that can make swimming hazardous outside the area sheltered by the breakwater. Daily excursion boats sail to Maráthi beach, and, for something different, the **Yellow Boat Company**, ✆ 61 472 by the chapel jetty, hires out paddle boats to explore the Almirós, home of turtles and birds: kingfishers are a common sight.

Lake Kournás, and a Plunge into the Hinterlands

Inland from Georgioúpolis, the narrow (and surprisingly busy) old Chaniá–Réthymnon road heads into the barren hills. These form a striking amphitheatre around Crete's only freshwater lake, **Kournás**, deep and eerie and full of eels. A path encircles the shore, or a place on the shore hires out boats for a closer look; in ancient times it was known as Korissia, and there is a story of a lost city dedicated to Athena in its environs, but not a trace has been found so far. From Kournás the road continues east through numerous small villages to Réthymnon, but if you're not in a rush consider the lovely detour south (turn at Episkopí) to Asigonía and Miriokéfala, on the fringes of *nomós* Réthymnon. The road forks just beyond **Argiroúpolis**, a handsome hill town overlooking the sea. In ancient times this was the Doric city of Lappa, destroyed in 67 BC by the Romans. In the subsequent war between Octavian and Mark Antony, Lappa supported Octavian, who gave it the right and money to rebuild once he became Emperor Augustus. To the southeast of the village you can still see ruins of the baths and aqueduct; a canopy protects a geometric mosaic in the upper part of the village. Note the Venetian doorway with the inscription OMNIA MUNDI FUMUS ET UMBRA ('All things in this world are smoke and shadow').

Just down the Asigonía road you'll find the **Myli** or Watermills, a cool, green oasis where Réthymnon's drinking water comes spilling through the little troglodyte chapel of Ag. Dýnami and down a stepped waterfall. A grove of giant plane trees and the clutch of outdoor tavernas make this a favourite stop for Greeks, who love places like this; for many this is the closest they ever get to the calendar scenes of Alpine lakes and forests they like to hang on their walls. From here the road rises through a narrow gorge under inhospitable mountains, where the boulders are softened by plane trees, oleanders, and often by tendrils of mist. Cut off from the Cretan mainstream, a nest of daredevil courage, the mountain village of **Asigonía** today seems a bit introspective as it goes about its business, especially now that there isn't an enemy at hand for its brave *pallikari* to fight. The busts of old heroes look over the square, but so far there hasn't been one erected to native son George Psychoundákis, whose tireless, danger-filled treks over the mountains delivering messages from one intelligence outpost to another (as described in his fascinating *The Cretan Runner*) was crucial for the Resistance.

A deteriorating road from Asigonía loops around the tight mountain valley to the remote hamlet of Kallikrátis, before switching back as a track to **Myriokéfala**; by car you're far better off backtracking to the crossroads near Argiroúpolis. What puts Myriokéfala on the map is its venerable monastic church, **Panagía Antifonitria** (Our Lady Who Replies): not long after the reconquest of Crete in AD 960, St John the Stranger came upon an ancient Greek building at Myriokéfala and was immediately struck blind. For a week he prayed, and on the seventh day a voice bade him look east and found a church to the Virgin where he first saw light. Although the villagers have demolished the monastery and maladroitly restored the exterior of the church, the very early frescoes in the interior have a naïve, cartoonish charm, witness to the local artists' attempts to get back in touch with Byzantine tradition.

Snails Bourbouristi

 If you're as fond of snails as the Cretans are, try one of the island's traditional recipes. Take 1½ kg of snails and boil them for half an hour. Rinse and clean well with cold water, and let them dry on a towel. When dry, sprinkle them well with salt, drench in flour and fry in hot olive oil, mouths facing down, for three minutes. Add a good helping of rosemary, stir, and cook for two more minutes. Pour a glass of dry white wine over the snails and serve.

Where to Stay and Eating Out

Vrýssis ℂ (0825–)

Rooms here are on the very modest side, as in the little hotel **Orfeas**, ℂ 61 218 (*C; inexp*). Pretty tavernas line the river: **Spiridakis** serves light lunches and grilled meats. **Two Brothers,** on the main street, is a reasonably priced taverna-pizzeria. **Dionysus** offers some tasty Cretan dishes.

Georgioúpolis ✆ (0825–)

Come prepared: it's not unusual to see hotels in verdant Georgioúpolis advertizing their mosquito nets. **Mare Monte**, ✆ and @ 61 390 (*A; lux*) stands out as one of the west coast's most luxurious hotels. **Pilot Beach**, ✆ 22 313 (*A; exp*) is a stylish complex with a pool, a good family bet spread out in a number of different buildings. By the river, **Sofia Apartments**, ✆ 61 325, are attractively built in a more traditional style. **Mina**, at Kávros (the next beach east), ✆ 61 257 (*C; mod*) is a pleasant, medium-sized hotel. **Almyros**, ✆ 61 349 (*E; inexp*) is 100m from the sea. *Open all year*. **Zorba's Rooms**, over a taverna, ✆ 61 381, are close to the sea. **Villa Mouria**, ✆ 61 342, and **Voula**, ✆ 61 259, have even cheaper rooms.

Georgioúpolis has no lack of places cooking up 'chicken kari', but it also has more *ouzeries* offering *mezédes* than the typical resort. **Poseidon**, back off the hurly-burly of the main road, is a good bet for fish; **Georgis** is similar and does the best charcoal-grilled meats in town. **Taverna Apolithos**, just up from the beach, has a wide choice of starters and pasta, followed by Greek or international courses. Bars encompass the main square and offer civilized, conversational drinking, while the **Time**, on the other bank of the river, runs free shuttle buses from the main square out to its noisy domain with disco light shows after midnight; on Thursday night, a live bouzouki show takes over.

Kournás ✆ (0825–)

Up by Lake Kournás, **Taverna/Rent rooms Panorama** overlooks both the lake and the sea far below. **Omorphi Limni**, ✆ 96 221, has rooms on the lake and serves delicious plates of spit roasted meat with pitta bread.

Argiroúpolis ✆ (0831–)

There are two simple 'rooms' places here, both enjoying wide views over the mountains: **Lappa Apartments** (ring Dimitris, ✆ 81 204) and **Zografaki**, ✆ 81 269. The best place to dine around the Myli on the Asigonía road is **Paleo Myli**, down the steep lane in an old mill, serving good Greek and Cretan specialities at prices only slightly over the odds.

South to Sfakiá

Sfakiá, long isolated under the White Mountains in the southeast corner of the *nomós* of Chaniá, was the cradle of the island's most daring and most mousta-chioed desperados, who clobbered each other in blood feuds but in times of need became Crete's bravest freedom fighters. Now connected to civilization by a good (and dramatically beautiful) road, the Sfakiots have put their daggers away, and prey no more than any other Cretan on invading foreigners. Although most tourists see the chief town, Chóra Sfakíon, only as the place where they catch the bus after the boat ride after the Gorge of Samariá, you may want to linger on this sun-bleached coast, dotted with beaches, other gorges and places to explore, but perhaps most congenial for being incredibly lazy.

Getting Around

Chóra Sfakíon is linked by **bus** to Chaniá four times a day, and once to Kastélli-Kíssamou, Kolimbári, Tavronítis, Chandrís, Plataniás, Stílos, Stavrós, Omalós, Georgioúpolis, Réthymnon and Plakiás, and there is one bus a day from Chaniá to Anópolis, Frangokástello and Skalotí. The **boat** service between Chóra Sfakíon, Loutró and Ag. Roúmeli, at the mouth of the Gorge of Samariá, is frequent, with one or two boats a day continuing west of Ag. Roúmeli to Soúgia and Paleochóra. Morning **excursion boats** link Chóra Sfakíon to Sweetwater Beach; two boats a week sail to the island of Gávdos (*see* pp.108–9). The **port police** have schedules, © (0825) 91 292.

Festivals

Chóra Sfakíon: **last Sunday in May**. Frangokástello: **15 September**; Asigoniá: **23 August** at the church of Ag. Geórgios; Alíkampos: **15 August**.

South from Vrýssis to Chóra Sfakíon

The twisting but good mountain road to Sfakiá begins at Vrýssis (*see* above). After 5km, a left turn leads up (1.5km) to the village of **Alíkampos**, where the church of the Panagía contains well-preserved frescoes (1315) by Ioánnis Pagoménos. The main road ascends the Krapí valley (prettier than it sounds) to the edge of the **Langos tou Katre,** the 2km ravine nicknamed the Thermopylae of Sfakiá. This was a favourite spot for a furious Cretan ambush, one that spelt doom to 400 Turkish soldiers after the capture of Frangokástello (*see* below), and then again in 1866 to an army of Turks fleeing south after the explosion of Arkádi.

The road and ravine give on to the striking mountain plateau of **Askýfou**, where the grey ruins of the fortress of Koulés drape a long shadow over fields of wheat and potatoes, and where a monument on the edge of the main village, **Amoudári**, commemorates Sfakiá's uprising in 1770. Further south, another by-road to the left leads to **Ásfendos**, a seldom-visited mountain village built along a roaring brook; not far beyond the Ásfendos crossroads, the blue Libyan sea sparkles into view, seemingly miles below as the road noodles through the steep, wooded **Ímbros Gorge** before zigzagging sharply down the last barren mountain crusts to Chóra Sfakíon. It's also a pretty walk down the stream bed. The path begins by the last *kafeneíon* in Ímbros and takes about three hours in all. In June an astonishing quantity of butterflies adds to its charms, but, unless you arrange with a friend or taxi to pick you up at the village of **Koumitádes**, it's a long hour or so down the tree-less coastal piedmont from the gorge's mouth to Chóra Sfakíon.

You could linger to visit two important churches. In Koumitádes, hunt up the key to the village church of **Ag. Geórgios**, with good frescoes by Ioánnis Pagoménos from 1314, with the patrons' inscription intact. Just east of Koumitádes, **Moní Thymiani** is a Cretan shrine: in May 1821, when revolution was in the air across Greece, the chieftains of Crete gathered here and vowed to take up arms. The monks blessed their rifles; typically, out of the 1200 guns the Cretans could muster, 800 belonged to the Sfakiots. By September the Turks had come to pay a visit of their own, pillaging and putting the monastery to the sack; today only the whitewashed church stands, with some old carvings on its belfry.

Chóra Sfakíon

When spring takes hold of earth again, and when the summer comes,
Then I will take my rifle, my silver-mounted pistols,
I will go down to Omalos, the highway of Mousouri,
I will make the mothers childless, and motherless the sons.

an old song from Sfakiá

Legendary for its ferocity, a viper's nest of feuds, vendettas and hot-blooded revolutionaries, **Chóra Sfakíon** (ΧΩΡΑ ΣΦΑΚΙΩΝ) today is hardly distinguishable from Crete's other coastal villages given over to the needs of tourists. At one time, however, it was the capital of its own province, one that, with few resources of its own, turned to taking everyone else's: smuggling, sheep rustling and piracy brought home the bacon for centuries. To police the locals, the Venetians constructed the fortress at Frangokástello just to the east in 1317, then, after the revolt of 1570, they added the now ruined castle on the pine-clad hill over Chóra. Chóra Sfakíon once had a hundred churches, they say, not so much for piety's sake but to enable the Sfakiots to gather at seemingly harmless *panegýria* every two or three days to plot the next moves of a revolt. Only a couple survived the fires and bombardments in the 19th century. The tradition of resistance continued after the Battle of Crete, when the locals helped the rearguard New Zealand and Australian soldiers to flee to North Africa; a monument by the sea commemorates the mass evacuation, while a memorial along the road just above town honours all the locals summarily executed by the Germans for their role in the same.

The big war, however, was only an intermission in a deadly private war between two Sfakiot families and all their relatives known as the 'Omalós feud' or the 'Vendetta of the Century', which took some 90 lives in vendettas until 1960. Not long after that, according to a friend, a German tourist went to a small village near Chóra Sfakíon and met a farmer in a field: 'Don't you remember me?' asked the

German. 'I was here in the war.' 'Oh, were you now?' the farmer said. 'Wait here, please.' He went inside, got his rifle, and shot him in the head. The locals quietly buried the German, and no one was any the wiser.

Anópolis and the Gorge of Arádena

If you like the idea of tripping down a ravine to the Libyan sea and the Gorge of Samariá is too crowded, the Gorge of Arádena is probably your most awe-inspiring alternative. It's shorter but almost as dramatically beautiful as Samariá, and is never, never crowded. On the other hand, if you aren't perfectly fit, if you suffer from vertigo, if you don't have reliable climbing shoes or if you don't have a nimble buddy, don't even think about it: there are death-defying sections that require a firm hand on the rope ladder. If you're game, the easiest way to do it is to catch the single, afternoon bus from Chaniá or Chóra Sfakíon up to **Anópolis** (ΑΝΩΠΟΛΗ), a pleasant, rustic village on a plateau offering a handful of rooms and a couple of places to eat. In the centre, a statue honours Daskaloyánnis ('Teacher John'), a native of Anópolis and the first Cretan to organize a revolt against the Turks.

Daskaloyánnis

 Because of the rugged terrain and even more rugged inhabitants, the Ottomans were content to leave Sfakiá alone in exchange for the payment of a heavy poll tax, collected by a local representative and sent off to Mecca. In the 1760s this representative was Daskaloyánnis, a wealthy, well-educated ship owner. During his travels he met emissaries of Catherine the Great who, keen to divert the attention of the Ottomans from their own schemes, convinced him that Russia would aid Crete if it rebelled against the Turks. In 1770, after two years of planning, Daskaloyánnis and 2000 well-armed Sfakiots drove off the Ottoman tax collector and began to terrorize the Turks living north of the White Mountains. At first things went fairly smoothly, to the extent that Daskaloyánnis even minted coins of free Crete in a cave above Chóra Sfakíon. However, when the promised Russian fleet failed to materialize, the Turkish response was swift: 15,000 men were sent down to Sfakiá. Women and children had already been sent to Kýthera, leaving Daskaloyánnis and his troops holed up in mountain strongholds, to watch in despair as the Turks systematically destroyed their villages. In March 1771, Daskaloyánnis gave himself up, hoping to spare Sfakiá from the worst; he was brought to Chaniá where the pasha ordered him to be flailed alive.

From Anópolis, follow the road 4km west to the new bridge (1986) that spans the dizzying gorge, making the once arduous journey up and down the steep rockface to **Arádena** a snap. Ironically, the bridge arrived too late for Arádena, now a near-ghost town after a particularly bloody Sfakiot feud caused everyone to leave (but the bridge does allow the road to continue west to another village, **Ag. Ioánnis**, with a taverna and frescoed church). Arádena has a famous Byzantine church, the **Astratigos**, dedicated to Archangel Michael in his role as heaven's *generalissimo*, sporting a dome that looks like a tiled toupée. Of all the saints on the Orthodox calendar, Michael is the most remorseless; one of his duties is collecting and weighing souls. Not even a Sfakiot would dare to shuck and jive in his terrible presence, and whenever one was suspected of rustling flocks, he would be brought here to be quizzed. The church is built of stones from the ancient autonomous city of Aradin, which gave its name to the gorge.

If you're walking down the **Gorge of Arádena**, the partly stepped track down is about ½km inland from the bridge and descends in a zigzag down the rockface to the stream bed, closed in by the tremendous walls. The path is well marked with red dots and brings you down in under four hours to charming sandy **Mármara Beach**: the sea is inviting but beware that there's nothing to drink. In the summer, however, you can catch an afternoon boat to Loutró; otherwise, it's about an hour's hike along the coast by way of **Líkkos**, a sleepy back of nowhere with rooms and tavernas and a stony beach.

Loutró and Around

Linked to the rest of the world only by boat (several a day sail to Ag. Roúmeli to the west and Chóra Sfakión to the east), **Loutró** may well be the civilized, quiet getaway-from-it-all spot you've been looking for. Although Loutró's bay is sheltered and perfectly transparent, it doesn't have much of a beach, a failing not too dismal as there are a number of coves a short walk or canoe ride away. Besides the regular boat trips to the aforementioned Mármara Beach, others will take you to the isolated strand of Glykó Neró, or **Sweetwater Beach**, cut off on one side by sheer cliffs and,. on the other by deep blue sea. True to its name, small springs provide fresh water, and there's a taverna when you need something more substantial. Other boat services to Sweetwater run out of Chóra Sfakíon, so beware: it can get busy.

The main port around here in Roman times was Finikas (modern **Fínix**) a short walk to the west, where the ship carrying St Paul as its prisoner put in to wait out a storm. It has a rocky beach and on the headland, a lonely Venetian outpost, supplied by an elaborate cistern filled with water. The environs of Loutró and Fínix are pitted with caves. **Drakoláki cave** is noteworthy—an underground labyrinth with a bottomless lake that requires both a torch and Ariadne's ball of string to explore.

The Ghosts of Frangokástello

The oldest fortress in Sfakiá is austere, crenellated Ag. Nikítas, better known as **Frangokástello** (ΦΡΑΓΚΟΚΑΣΤΕΛΛΟ). Once splendidly isolated on its long fine sandy beach 14km east of Chóra Sfakíon, the castle is now joined by a straggle of concrete buildings, housing accommodation places and tavernas. Built in 1317 by the Venetians (anyone from western Europe was called a 'Frank' by the Cretans, hence its name), it knew its most dramatic moment in 1828, during the Greek War of Independence, when an Epirot insurgent, Hatzimichális Daliánis, took and held Frangokástello with 650 Cretans. Soon 8000 Turkish troops arrived to force them out, and all the Greeks inside were slain, including Daliánis. But the Turks' victory had a price: bands of Cretans who had remained outside the fort captured the mountain passes and wreaked havoc on the Turkish army when it marched north.

The Massacre of Frangokástello has given rise to one of the most authenticated of the million or so Greek ghost stories that exist. On 17 May, the anniversary of the massacre (or, some say, during the last ten days of May), the phantoms of the Cretan dead, known as the *Drosoulités*, the 'dew shades', rise up at dawn fully armed and on horseback from the cemetery of the nearby church of Ag. Charolámbos and proceed silently towards the now empty shell of the fortress, before disappearing into the sea. The whole phenomenon lasts only ten minutes. Thousands of people have seen them, but many more thousands haven't; the morning must be perfectly clear. Meteorologists pooh-pooh the ghosts—mere heat mirages from the Libyan desert, they say. On other days of the year, Frangokástello is a rather sleepy place; a good road east of here, and one bus a day, goes to Plakiás (*see* p.143).

℗ *(0825–)*   **Where to Stay and Eating Out**

Chóra Sfakíon

Vritomartis, on the road north of the village, ℗ 91 222 (*B; exp*), is a new, self-contained holiday complex on a ledge overlooking the sea, with a pool complex, tennis courts, and frequent minibus service to Chóra Sfakíon. **Livikon**, on the quay, ℗ 91 211, is new, stylish, and comfortable, near the **Xenia**, ℗ 91 202 (*B pension; mod*), one of the oldest hotels in the village. There are also plenty of rooms. The port tavernas offer a wide selection of ready food, or **Limani**, by the port, offers a fish fry or mixed grill and salad for 3500dr. The bakery has Sfakiá's famous *myzithrópittes* (*myzíthra* cheese pies).

Frangokástello

Inexpensive rooms here include **Castello**, ℗ 92 068, **Flisvos**, ℗ 92 069 and **Pollakis**, ℗ 92 088. For fresh fish, try the shady terrace at **Artemis**.

Loutró

Porto Loutro, ℗ 91 091 (*B; exp*), is new and very comfortable, and has a number of water sports facilities. *Open April–Oct.* Another good choice, the **Blue House**, ℗ 91 127, has pleasant, moderate–inexpensive rooms (some with private baths) and good food in the restaurant.

Nomós Réthymnon

RETHYMNON

Crete's smallest province, the *nomós* of Réthymnon is also the most mountainous, wedged into between the island's highest peaks: the White Mountains to the west and Zeus' own Mount Ida, or Psilorítis, (2452m) to the east. Over the past ten years its north coast, fringed by a 12km sandy beach on either side of the delightful little city of Réthymnon, has become a popular base for exploring Crete; the Minoan sites to the east, and natural beaches to the west are all in reasonable striking distance. On the south coast there's Ag. Galíni, one of Crete's most picturesque resorts, Plakiás, low-key but growing fast, and Moní Préveli, in a lush and beautiful setting. The fortress-monastery, Arkádi, scene of the collective suicide in the name of freedom, is a popular day trip from Réthymnon, or you can venture under Psilorítis into the haunting and lovely Amári valley to find Crete at its most traditional. In the same spirit, a string of old mountain villages en route to Herákleon provide a good day's exploration, with fine views, ancient sites and three caves: Melidóni, another shrine of Cretan martyrdom, Zonianá with lovely stalactites, or the Idean Cave, sacred to the dark side of Zeus.

Réthymnon

The citizens of Réthymnon are pure at heart, modest and at the same time proud, well-read and mild-mannered; in other words, a valuable species to have upon this troubled island.

Pandelís Prevelákis, *The Tale of a Town* (1938)

Delightful Réthymnon (ΡΕΘΥΜΝΟ), Crete's third city (pop. 23,500), is the only one that 'weds the wave-washed sand', but for centuries the price it paid for its beach was the lack of a proper harbour. The Venetians dug a cute, nearly perfectly round one, but even now it keeps silting up. In some ways not having a harbour has proved a blessing, inhibiting the local economy enough to spare Réthymnon much of what passes for progress. Like Chaniá, its Venetian and Turkish architecture has earned it landmark status, but Réthymnon escaped the attentions of the Luftwaffe and is more intact. The mighty fortress peering over its shoulder and its pointy minarets lend the skyline an exotic touch; covered wooden balconies (*koultoukia*) left over from the Turkish occupation project overhead, darkening the piquant narrow streets. Its relative isolation attracted scholars who fled Constantinople, giving Réthymnon the reputation as the brain of Crete, confirmed by the construction of a new seat for the University of Crete and its faculties of the arts.

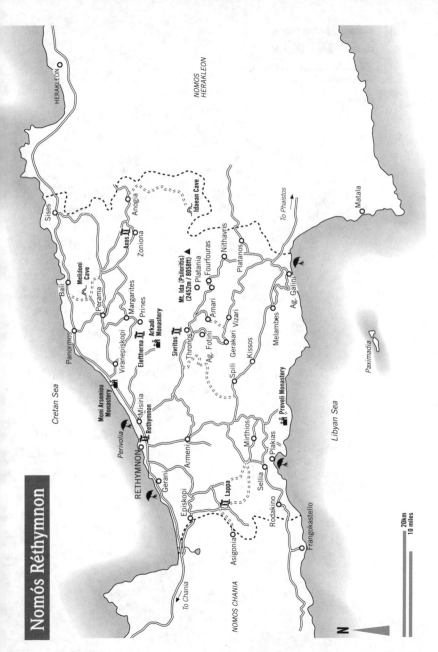

Nomós Réthymnon

Réthymnon

N

200 metres
200 yards

Old Town

Fortezza

PERIFERIAKOS

Archaeological Museum

MAKEDONIAS

Plateia Plastira

CHIMARAS

Centre of Contemporary Art

Folk Museum

SALAMINOS

ARKADIO

KATECHAKI

MINOOS

MESOLONGIOU

Rimondi Fountain

K. PALEOLOGOU

MELISINOU

A. KORAI

M. VERNARDOU

KLIDI

RADAMANTHIOS

T. Petichaki

Plateia

ARABATZOGLOU

Prefecture

POLITECHNIOU

IROON

E. VERNARDIOU

Nerandzes Mosque

P. KORONEOU

NIKIFOROU FOKA

M. NTALIANI

TSOU

P. PREVELAKI

ETHN. ANTISTASIS

AG. VARVARAS

TOMBAZI

I. DIMAKOPOULOU

Guora Gate

S. VLASTOU

Plateia Martiron

IG. GAVRIIL

Bus Station

ILIAKAKI

Municipal Gardens

P

GAVRIIL

IG.

S. DIMITRAKAKI

To Chania

KOUMOUNDOUROU

P

ZABELI

Lighthouse

Lighthouse

Lighthouse

Venetian Harbour

oggia

P

DERON

P

E. VENIZELOU

Tourist
Information

P

athedral

M. MOUSSOUROU

E. VIVILAKI

ARKADIOU

Telephones

Kara Musa Pasa
Mosque

Plateia
Iroon

GERAKARI

P. KOUNDOURIOTOU

G. CHORTATZI

P

DIMOKRATIAS

MOATSOU

I. KONDILAKI

Bus
Station

N. KAZANTZAKI

ZIMVRAKAKI

To
Herakleon

ost
ffice

OU

N. ANDROULIDAKI

Veli Pasa
Mosque

Post
Office

Réthymnon © (0831–)   ***Getting There and Around***

Thanks to a long breakwater and lots of dredging, Réthymnon now has a port and a **ferry** purchased by public subscription; it sails to Piraeus at least four times a week (Réthymnon Lines, 250 Arkadíou, © 25 876 or 29 221). In season, there's a ship to Santoríni two days a week, departing at 7am and returning in the evening. The new **bus** station is by the sea on the west end of town, between Igoum Gavriil and the Periferiaki, © 22 212 or 22 659; besides serving the main villages in the *nomós*, those labelled 'El Greco/Skaleta' depart every 45min or so for the 10km stretch of hotels along the beaches east of town. Olympic Airways buses link Réthymnon to Chaniá airport twice a day, from Olympic's office at 5 Koumoundoúrou, © 27 353.

Réthymnon © (0831–)   ***Tourist Information***

NTOG, along the town beach at E. Venizélou, © 24 143, open Mon–Fri 8–2.30. **Tourist police**: Plateía Iróon, © 28 156.

Festivals

On **Wednesdays** Réthymnon hosts a big weekly market and fair off Odós Kanzantzáki. Look out for **Carnival** and **Midsummer's Day**, with bonfires. The Cretan **Wine Festival** and Handicrafts Exhibition is during the **last 10 days of July**, in the Public Gardens; there's also the Renaissance Festival for **20 days in August**, with classical music concerts, dance and theatre performances in the Venetian fortress. The explosion at Moní Arkádi is commemorated **7–9 November**.

The Old Town

'Réthymnon is certainly a very small place and I do not know what I shall do tomorrow,' fretted Edward Lear in his journal in 1864. Limerickal Ed must have been feeling poutier than usual, for, *au contraire*, Réthymnon is exceedingly pleasant to explore, at least once past the outer sprawl and into the kernel of its historic centre.

Although inhabited since Late Minoan times (its ancient name, *Rithymna*, is pre-Greek), the oldest monuments in town are Venetian, beginning with the **Guóra Gate**, just below the Plateía of the Four Martyrs. Built in 1566 by Venetian governor Jacopo Guoro, the gate is the sole survivor of the city walls erected after the sackings by Barbarossa in 1538, and by Uluch Ali in 1562 and 1571.

Before entering the gate, note one of Réthymnon's finest mosques, the 17th-century Porta Grande or **Valide Sultana**, dedicated to the Sultan's mother, but now used by the archaeology museum to store its excess amphorae (the same fate has befallen the little Kara Musa Pasa mosque, on the east end of Arkadíou). Valide Sultana's old cemetery was converted after the 1923 population exchange into the **Municipal Garden**, across busy Koundouriótou Street. Its cool, melancholy paths seem haunted by discreet slippered ghosts—except during Réthymnon's wine festival, when it overflows with jovial imbibers reviving ancient Dionysian rites.

From the Guóra Gate, Ethnikís Antistásis leads past the church of **San Francesco**, the friary where Crete's papal contribution, Alexander V, began his religious career; when elected pontiff, he paid for its elaborate Corinthian-style portal. The building now belongs to the University of Crete, which is financing its restoration. Further down the street and branching left is the quaint lion-headed **Rimondi Fountain**, built in 1629 by another Venetian governor (you can guess his name) at the junction of several streets, now jam-packed with bars; perhaps fittingly, as the fountain was designed with a trough, as a watering hole for man and beast.

The fountain has been the heart of town since Venetian times, and all the finest buildings were close by. The **Nerandzes Mosque** on Manoúli Vernárdou retains a monumental rounded portal from its days as the Venetian church of Santa Maria. With its conversion into a mosque in 1657, it was capped with three domes; today the city uses it as a concert hall. The tall, graceful rocket of a minaret was added in 1890; if it ever re-opens, climb for a good view over Réthymnon. The city's principal *hamam*, or Turkish baths, at 25 Radamánthios was built in 1670 and is still intact, but off limits. In his *Tale of a Town* Pandelis Prevelákis described its savoury bath attendant, a woman from Provence named Hortense, whom his friend Kazantzákis borrowed for his old siren Bouboulina in *Zorba the Greek*. The handsome Venetian **Loggia** (1550s), nearby on Arkadíou, was a kind of club where the nobility and landowners would meet and gamble, and where proclamations would be read; it now does duty as the public library. Just northeast of here is Réthymnon's bijou little **Venetian harbour**, lined cheek to cheek with seafood restaurants and patrolled by a small fleet of black and white swans.

The Fortezza and Archaeology Museum

In ancient times, when Cretans were bitten by rabid dogs they would resort to the temple of Artemis Roccaéa on Réthymnon's acropolis, and take a cure of dog's liver or seahorse innards. All traces of this interesting cult were obliterated in the late 16th century, when the Venetians decided that Réthymnon had been sacked once too often and forced the local peasants to build the massive **Fortezza** over the temple (*open 8am–8pm; closed Mon; adm*). It is one of the best-preserved Venetian castles in Greece, and one of the largest, with room for the entire population of Réthymnon and environs; yet in 1645, after a bitter two-month siege, the defending garrison was forced to surrender it to the Turks. The church, converted into a mosque—a strikingly austere cube with a spherical dome—is fairly well preserved, with a painted *mihrab* directing the faithful's prayers to Mecca. The rest has been left in dishevelled abandon; trees grow out of the old ramparts, from where you can look down on the town and sea.

Near the entrance to the Fortezza, the **Archaeology Museum** is housed in the former Turkish prison houses (*open 8.30–3; closed Mon; adm*), beautifully rearranged and air-conditioned to show off its ever-growing collection of finds from the *nomós*, beginning with chubby figurines and pots made before the invention of the wheel. There are fine Middle Minoan seals and pottery from Monastiráki, and hundreds of figures of worshippers with hands on their bosoms and long-horned cattle from the Minoan Peak Santuary at Vrýsinas (note the peculiar, two headed push-me pull-you cow). The lovely strainer (1700 BC) in Case 6 was used to manufacture perfumes. The most dazzling pieces hail from the Late Minoan cemetery at Arméni (*see* below): a boar-tooth helmet, bronze double axes, lovely delicate vases, fragile remains of a loop-decorated basket from 1200 BC, and *larnaxes*, including one painted with a wild goat and bull chase and a hunter holding a dog on a leash. A very late jugged-eared goddess from Pagalchóri is little more than a personified cylinder. Post-Minoan finds include discs and mirrors from the Idean Cave, pretty marble and glass jewllery boxes (*pyxides*), Graeco-Roman marble and bronze statues and an excellent coin collection from most of the ancient cities of Crete.

In the same area, at 28 Mesolongíou, the **Historical and Folk Art Museum** (*open 9–1; closed Sun*) offers a delicious collection of traditional costumes, embroidery, photos, farming implements and pottery from a bygone age—in Cretan terms that means only 30 or 40 years ago. Nearby, on Chimáras, the new **Municipal Centre of Contemporary Art** (*open 10–2 and 5–8; closed Mon*) features changing and often excellent exhibitions of Greek art from the last 200 years.

Réthymnon ✆ (0831–) **Sports and Activities**

For a bird's eye view, **Hot Air Balloon** lifts over Réthymnon are available by reservation only; ✆ 55 095 or 51 186, or (093) 252 697. If you'd love to cycle down Mt Ida or the White Mountains but not up, contact **Hellas Bike Travel**, 118 Machis Kritis, ✆ 53328 or (094) 525 056. **Paradise Dive Center**, 51 Giamboudáki, offers scuba initiation, four-day certification courses and day trips around Crete for certified divers, ✆ (093) 252 885. **The Happy Walker** offers organized treks in the most scenic areas of western Crete; stop by the Chalkiadakis tourist office, 305 Arkadíou, for information and bookings. From the Venetian harbour, the corny **Pirate Ship** makes daily excursions to Maráthi, a little fishing village in Eastern Akrotíri; its sister ship, the **Popeye,** sails to Balí, ✆ 51 643 or 71 140.

Réthymnon's narrow tourist bazaar, **Odós Soúliou,** is crammed with desirable arty stuff and crafts to take home. Gold and jewellery shops line Arkadíou, and there are several onyx shops, including **Zacharías Theodorákis**, specializing in fine vases, at 3 Katecháki. For ceramics or handmade jewellery, try the little shops such as **Talisman** or **The Olive Tree** along Theodóros Arabatzóglou. For women's casual clothes, Greek designer **Parthenis** (of Athens, Mýkonos, Brussels and Los Angeles) has a shop in humble Réthymnon at 7 Salamínas. For English language papers, as well as a vast selection of guides and literature about Crete, try **International Press**, 81 El. Venizélou, ✆ 24 111.

luxury

The **Grecotel Creta Palace**, 4km east of Réthymnon, ✆ 55 181, ✉ 54 085 (*lux*), is the most lavish, a hotel and bungalow complex built in 1989, with an indoor heated pool and two outdoor ones, illuminated tennis courts and lots of sports, especially for children, who even have their own campground if you need a break. *Open Mar–Nov.* Grecotel also owns the nearly as plush **Rithymna Beach Hotel and Bungalows** in Ádele (7km), ✆ 29 491, ✉ 71 002 (*A*). On a lovely beach with similar facilities, it's very popular, filling up early in the spring and staying that way; book early.

expensive

In town, **Mythos Suites Hotel**, 12 Plateía Karaóli, ✆ 53 917 (*B*) has 10 suites furnished in a traditional style, sleeping 2–5 people in a 16th-century manor house; all are air-conditioned and there's a pool in the sunny central patio. **Palazzo Rimondi,** Xarthoúdou, ✆ 51 289 (*A*) is similar, containing 25 suites in a renovated mansion, built around a courtyard with a small pool. **Hotel Fortezza** is just under the castle walls at 16 Melissínou, ✆ 21 551, or 22 282, ✉ 20 073 (*B*); all rooms have balconies, and there's a garden courtyard and swimming pool. A new garden hotel isolated to the west, **Macaris**, 70 Stamathioudáki, ✆ 20 280, ✉ 20 284 (B) has rooms overlooking its pools and banana plants. Plush salmon-coloured **Hotel Ideon**, Plateía Plastíra, ✆ 22 346 (*B*) enjoys a fine spot overlooking the dock and has a small pool; reserve.

moderate

Leo, Váfe 2, ✆ 29 851, is a charming bed and breakfast inn, done up in traditional Cretan style. **Hotel Brascos**, at Ch. Daskaláki and Th. Moátsou,

© 23 721 (*B*) is slick and clean. *Open all year.* For peace and quiet, **Zorba** at the east end of the beach, © 28 540, is reasonably priced; rooms come with private shower and WC. **Garden House**, 82 N. Fokás (near the Fortezza), © 28 586, has small but delightful rooms in a Venetian residence, with a fountain (but book well in advance). **Seeblick**, on N. Plastíra, © 22 478, has good rooms with glassed in balconies.

inexpensive

The **youth hostel**, 41 Tombázi, © 23 943, is exceptionally nice and convenient, only a few blocks from the tourist office. You don't need a card to stay there; breakfast and cooking facilities are available. **Zania**, Pávlou Vlasátou (a block from the sea), © 28 169, has a handful of pleasant rooms, although in season the price is at the top of this range. **Hotel Achillion**, at 151 Arkadíou, © 22 581 (*E*) is less expensive, and offers a hint of former elegance and a view of the harbour from the balcony—and lots of noise at night. **Rent Rooms Eliza**, at Plastíra 12, © 22 581, is adequate enough but noisy and near the Venetian harbour. **Ralia Rooms**, at Salamnós and Athan. Niákou, © 50 163, are more atmospheric than most rooms places, with lots of wood. There are two good campsites a few kilometres east of Réthymnon: **Elizabeth**, © 28 694, and **Arkadía Camping**, © 22 361.

Réthymnon © *(0831–)*   ***Eating Out***

With its tiny fish restaurants, the Venetian harbour is the obvious place to dine in the evening, but expect to pay at least 4000dr for the privilege. Scan the menus; some places offer lobster lunches for two for 8000dr. **Mouragio-Maria**, © 26 475, run by descendants of an old Venetian family, is a good bet and serves meat dishes as well.

On the west side of the Fortezza, the Heliovasilemata, better known as the **Sunset Taverna**, has good solid Greek food and an extensive wine list (*about 4000dr for fish, 2000dr for pizza*) and a splendid view of you know what; cranes (feathered ones) often prowl the shore. Restaurants along the beach waterfront of El. Venizelou tend to be mediocre; here **Samaria**, © 24 681, despite unappetizing plastic pictures and *ordeure* on the menu (it turned out to be *hors -d'œuvres*), has the tastiest Greek cooking, with good *giovétsi* and lamb *kléftiko* (*around 2000dr*).

Plateía Petiháki has another row of touristy tavernas: **Agrimio** serves all the old favourites and pizza is the best bet here. **Alana** with its pretty courtyard in Salamínos Street (just south of the Fortezza) is a nice enough place to bring your parents, and serves a good fish-based menu for 6000dr for two. Nearby, in its own little square surrounded by greenery, **Petrino**, 14 Salamínos, has bargain menus for two, with mixed grills or *stifádo*.

Set up on different levels in a garden, **Avli**, 22 Xanthoudo, ☏ 24 356, is one of the prettiest places to eat but can get busy with groups. Just the opposite, **Antonias Zoumas**, across from the bus station, doesn't look like much but on Sunday afternoons it's packed with locals jawing through a four-hour lunch. Just under the Fortezza on Chimáras, **Taverna Castelvecchio**, ☏ 55 163 has a nice Cretan atmosphere and plenty of fish dishes, including sole in champagne.

But, as is so often the case, to find the genuine article you have to do as the Greek do and leave town: **Taverna Kombou**, 3km southwest of Réthymnon in Atsipópolou, is a favourite for its delicious Cretan food served out in a garden. On the Chaniá road, the **Kosmikos Kentro Kontaros**, ☏ 51 366, serves up excellent grilled food, good barrelled wine and live Cretan music; **Zygos**, just south of the E55 highway on the Spíli road, is similar. At either of these places there's a chance that a Cretan wedding will be in full swing, complete with sozzled warriors firing rifles into the air—but not to worry: even after a few *karafáki* of *rakí* they're still pretty good shots and seldom hit tourists.

Entertainment and Nightlife

T. N. Gounaki on Koronaíou St (near the church of the Mikrí Panagías) is a simple but fun place summed up by its own sign: 'Every day folk Cretan music with Gounakis Sons and their father gratis/free/for nothing and Cretan meal/dish/food/dinner thank you'. The slicker **Odysseus Club**, by the port at Ioul. Peticháki, specializes in bouzouki and Cretan music, again mostly for tourists. **Anadromi** is a trendy Greek bar on the corner of Melissínou and S. Xanthoudou, while for nostalgia, **Café Fortezza**, just below the Fortezza on Chimáras, has the little painted metal tables and wooden chairs all the Greeks miss now that they've mostly been replaced with plastic. **Baluardo**, on N. Plastíra, overlooks the sea and has a wide variety of titbits to go with your ouzo during Greek happy hour. Upstairs from 220 Arkadíou, **Dimman Music Bar** attracts a young crowd; the **Punch Bowl Bar** in Theod. Arabatzóglou has a cosy pub atmosphere and familiar snacks.

The outdoor **Cinema Asteria**, on Melissínou, shows a different film every night, usually in English with Greek subtitles, and there is also the **Cinema Pandelis** on the Herákleon road.

Arkádi

Four buses a day go to **Moní Arkádi** (*open daily 6am–8pm*), Crete's holy shrine of freedom and a favourite destination for a day out. Founded in the 11th century on the lonesome flanks of Psilorítis, the monastery was mostly rebuilt in the 17th century, although the lovely sun-ripened façade of the church, or *katholikon*, Crete's finest essay in Venetian mannerism, dates from 1587. During this time Arkádi was a repository of ancient Greek manuscripts, spirited out of Constantinople before its fall to the Ottomans, and the monks performed important work in copying the texts and disseminating them in Europe.

Arkádi resembles a small fort, which is one reason why Koronéos, at the head of the Revolutionary Committee of 1866, chose this remote spot for a base and a store for his powder magazine. When the Turks demanded that the abbot, Gabriel Marinákis, hand over the rebels, he refused; in response, a Turkish expeditionary force marched on Arkádi and in terror people from the surrounding villages took refuge inside the thick monastery walls. On 7 November 1866 the Turks attacked, and after a 2-day siege they breached the walls. Rather than surrender, Abbot Gabriel set fire to the powder magazines, blowing up 829 Turks and Greeks, many of them women and children. Another 35 who had hidden in the Refectory were summarily massacred by the furious Turks. The suicidal explosion caused a furore in Europe, as Swinburne and Victor Hugo took up the cause of Cretan independence. Hugo's article on Arkádi reads soberingly enough like a commentary on Bosnia in the 1990s: 'Kings, a word would save this people. A word from Europe is quickly said. Say it. What are you good for, if not that? No. We are silent, and we want everyone else to be silent. It's forbidden to speak of Crete. Which is expedient. Six or seven Great Powers conspire against a little people. What is this conspiracy? The most cowardly of all. The conspiracy of silence.'

Besides the Gunpowder Room, where the blast left a gaping hole in the roof, you can visit the **Historical Museum**, containing the holey, holy banner and portraits of the heroes of 1866, the vestments of Abbot Gabriel, bits of the iconostasis, monkish embroideries and unlabelled icons. An old windmill was made into an ossuary, displaying a stack of skulls with holes blasted through them. There's a snack bar at Arkádi, and a simple taverna on the road up at **Amnátos**; note the ornate Venetian doorway (and basketball hoop) stuck on to the side of the church. Another possible halt on the way back is **Maroúlas**, with two old Venetian towers and an ancient olive press.

The Prasanó Gorge

Just east of Réthymnon is one of Crete's prettiest gorges, the 'Green' Prasanó, formed by the torrential Plataniás river, which courteously dries up between mid-June and mid-October so you can walk down it (allow four to five hours, wear sturdy shoes and bring water). Get there by taking the early Amári bus as far as the first bend in the road after Prassés, where the track begins; walk pass the sheepfold and bear to the left. Lined with plane trees (many contorted from the force of the river in winter), dates, olives, cypresses and rhododendrons, the gorge has three sets of narrow 'gates' where the walls climb up to 150m. The track ends up by the old Herákleon–Réthymnon road near **Misiriá**, where you can swim and catch a bus back the last 5km to Réthymnon.

On the road to Prassés, the convent of **Ag. Iríni** is one of Crete's success stories; cut into the living rock like a citadel in the 14th century, it was abandoned after the revolt of 1866. Beginning in 1989, the restoration has been financed mostly by the needlework of its nimble-fingered nuns; in 1995 won a Europa Nostra award.

From Réthymnon South to the Libyan Coast

The *nómos* of Réthymnon encompasses the narrow 'neck' of Crete, and there's a good road that cuts between the mountains for the south, where Plakiás and Ag. Galíni have grown into major resorts, with Moní Préveli as the favourite day trip in between.

Plakiás has connections roughly every 2 hours with Réthymnon, as well as one **bus** a day west along the south coast as far as Chóra Sfakíon, by way of Frangokástello. Ag. Galíni has 8 buses a day from Réthymnon, as well as connections to Herákleon, Phaistós, and Mátala by way of Mýres.

Festivals

Plakiás: **23 April** and the **Friday after Easter**. Préveli: **8 May**. Spíli: **29 June** and **27 May**.

Arméni

Directly south of Réthymnon, the sprawling village of **Arméni** was named for the Armenian soldiers granted land here by Nikephóros Phokás after the reconquest of Crete from the Arabs in 961. They were hardly the first to settle here: recently an unusually large, scarcely plundered **Late Minoan III cemetery** was discovered near the crossroads with Somatás (signposted from the main road; the guardian lives in Arméni and can show you around outside of posted hours, which are *Mon–Fri 9–3*). Some 200 chamber tombs from 1350–1200 BC fill seven acres, ranging from simple rock-cut depressions to elaborate underground chambers reached by a *dromos* passage, steps or a ramp; the finds have been divided between the Réthymnon and Herákleon museums. The cemetery hints of an important Minoan town, but so far no one has found it, even though part of a paved road has been uncovered. Until then, you'll have to be content with the startling neo-Minoan house built by an archeological enthusiast in Arméni.

Seven km south of Arméni, the road forks; both branches plunge along gorges, where vultures, hawks and eagles circle high overhead. The westerly road follows the shorter **Kotsyfoú Gorge** and leaves you west of Plakiás, while the easterly route towards Préveli begins near Koxaré and cuts through the wild and steep-sided **Kourtaliótiko Gorge,** named for the sound the stones make when they tumble down in the wind. There's a place to pull over, where steps lead down to the chapel of Ag. Nikólaos and a waterfall spilling over a massive rock from five holes, made, they say, by St Nick himself, when he laid his hand on the rock.

Plakiás and Around

The Kourtaliótiko roads emerges at **Asómatos**, with rooms to rent and a restaurant bar with magnificent views down to the sea. Here the road forks for Préveli and Plakiás: if you're heading towards the latter, you'll pass through **Lefkógia**, a pleasant place wrapped in olive groves, with new 'rooms' places scattered here and there and a path down to Ammoúdi Beach. Lefkógia takes some of the overflow from **Plakiás** (ΠΛΑΚΙΑ) just beyond, framed in its brace of austere headlands. A well-kept secret 15 year ago, Plakiás has boomed, blossomed or blistered, according to your point of view, with more accommodation of every type added each year. Yet so far it's hardly overwhelming and remains a great centre for long walks and serious swimming both on its own rather exposed grey sands, or on the delicious golden sandy coves east of the headland at **Damnóni** (signposted from the main road, or half an hour's walk from Plakiás). Walking here, you'll see concrete pillboxes from the war, when this stretch of coast was an important escape route to Egypt. East of the main cove at Damnóni are two smaller but equally lovely naturist coves with rocks to dive from, while beyond them is Lefkógia's aforementioned Ammoúdi Beach. Half an hour's walk west of Plakiás, you'll find another beach, **Soúda**, with greyish sands and a lovely taverna in a palm grove. If you want to plunge inland, pick up a copy of *The Plakias Walk Map* by Lance Chilton, sold in the local shops. If you'd rather plunge down, the **Aegean Diving Centre**, on the Damnóni road, ✆ 31 021, moves down here in the summer from Athens. Late in the afternoon, head up to the old village of **Mírthios**, where the taverna terraces offer a superb sunset view over the sea.

From Plakiás and Damnóni, the Posidonia Fast Boat makes daily excursions to Préveli; there's also one bus to Préveli a day, two to Ag. Galíni, and one to Chóra Sfakíon. This latter passes by way of **Selía,** with more beautiful views from the church on the end of town, and **Rodákino** ('the peach'), a village hanging over a ravine with a grey beach at the end. It was from here that the Resistance finally spirited General Kriepe off Crete to Egypt. After Rodákino it's 28km to Chóra Sfakíon, passing by the pretty beach of Kalógeros, a steep walk down from **Argoulés**.

Plakiás ✆ *(0832–)*   ***Where to Stay and Eating Out***

 Built in 1993, the cream-coloured **Damnoni Bay**, ✆ 31 991, ✆ 31 893 (*A; exp*) offers studio apartments, a pool, water sports, and a seafood restaurant, and the advantage of having a view that doesn't include the Damnoni Bay resort. On the edge of Plakiás, **Alianthos**, ✆ 31 280 (C; *mod*) is a popular neo-Minoan family hotel, with green lawns and a swimming pool near the beach. **Livikon**, next to Plakiás bus station, ✆ 31 216 (*C*), and the pretty blue and white **Lamon**, ✆ 31 318 (*B*) are good bets at the bottom of the moderate price range. **Pension Sokrates**, ✆ 31 489, has inexpensive rooms near Damnóni Beach. The **youth hostel** in Plakiás, ✆ 31 560, is set back in an olive grove, but there's one that's even nicer up with the views at Mírthios, ✆ 31 202.

For delicious Greek cooking, try **Ariadni**, ✆ 31 640, a small, simple place on one of the side streets that does rare specialities such as *monastriáko*

(pork with mushrooms, peas and prunes) and *erofilí* (lamb with artichokes and potatoes) (*around 2500dr*). By the little port, **Taverna Christos**, © 31 472, under the tamarisks does a roaring trade with the locals and has a few rooms to rent upstairs. Right on the waterfront **Sophia B** has tables set on tiers of flowers and potted plants, where you can feast on a choice of 25 different starters, a selection of pasta and meat or fish courses, irrigated with a long Cretan wine list (*around 4–5000dr*). **Sunset**, just west of central Plakiás, has reasonably priced seafood menus (*4400 or 5800 for two*) on its terrace overlooking the sea. **Gorgones** is an old favourite, with Cretan specialities. For a change, English-run **Julia's** features spicy vegetarian dishes and Indian food. Pretty **Taverna Galini**, set in the palms by Soúda Beach, often has live Cretan music in the evenings. Other entertainment after midnight is concentrated in the local dance spots: the modern, upmarket **Hexagon** in the centre or the air-conditioned **Blue Note** (often with live music) or **Meltemi**.

Moní Préveli

> *This is the Paradise of Crete and one of the best chosen*
> *places to retire from the cares and responsibilities of life.*

Captain Spratt, *Travels and Researches in Crete*

Moní Préveli, 7km east of Lefkógia, is the beauty spot, main monument, and chief resistance centre on the central Libyan coast. On the way, the road passes palm groves along the river Megálo Pótamos, just before a bridge of 1850 and the abandoned lower half of the monastery, known as **Káto Préveli**. Founded in 1594 and dedicated to St John the Baptist, the monastery's monks here were in charge of agriculture, and you can walk through their old cells and storage rooms; only the church survives intact. In the early 19th century, a few decades after Daskaloyánnis' aborted revolt in nearby Sfakía (*see* p.126), Abbot Melchisedek Tsouderos began to collect arms and supplies for a new revolt. The Turks got wind of it, and in 1821, shortly before the War of Independence broke out on mainland Greece, they came to destroy the monastery. Rather than resist, Abbot Melchisedek welcomed the Turks with open arms and got them so drunk they fell asleep, so the monks were able to flee with their lives, but when the Turks woke up they sacked the monastery in rage.

The 'Back' monastery, **Píso Préveli**, is 3km down, beautifully situated high on the coast overlooking exotic green vegetation (*open 8–1 and 3–7; adm*). The original Byzantine church was demolished by the monks in the 1830s, after the Turks kept refusing them permission to make repairs. They did, however, preserve the furnishings for the new church: the intricate gilt iconostasis, with 17th-century icons, and a miraculous piece of the True Cross that both the Turks and Germans tried to steal, without success; the story goes that the Germans tried to send it off in three different planes, only to find that their engines mysteriously died each time until they returned the precious titbit to the monks. Note the famous Byzantine palindrome ΝΙΨΟΝΑΝΟΜΗΜΑΤΑ ΜΗΜΟΝΑΝΟΨΙΝ ('Cleanse your sins, not only your face') on the fountain in the monastery's lower courtyard.

Throughout Crete's revolts in the 19th century, Píso Préveli took in refugees who had abandoned their villages, and sheltered them until boats ferried them to independent Greece. In 1941, the monks performed a similar good deed in sheltering hundreds of Allied troops from the Nazis until they could be picked up by submarine and taken to Egypt; in gratitude the British gave Préveli two silver candlesticks and a marble plaque, now lovingly cared for by the last monk. From the monastery it's a steep, dangerous walk and scramble down to the lovely sands at the mouth of the Kourtaliótiko gorge, known as **Palm Beach** for its grove of date palms. Although the invaders it faces these days, mostly on boat excursions from Plakiás or Ag. Galíni, are far more peaceful, there are far too many of them for the nearly nonexistent facilities, and by July the area is littered with rubbish and worse. Up the gorge, the stream forms delightful pools, just the right size for one or two people to lie in on a summer's day, but by the end of the season it usually stinks.

Spíli and Ag. Galíni

The main road south towards Ag. Galíni continues past the Plakiás turn off, passing by way of **Mixoroúma**, an age-old basket-weaving hamlet, and **Spíli** (ΣΠΗΛΙ), a charming farming village immersed in greenery. Spíli's old houses and churches have more character than most; the village centrepiece is a long fountain, where water splashes from a row of 17 Venetian lion-heads. If too many tour buses heave into sight, you can escape on numerous rural lanes through the olives. Further along the road are turn-offs over the coastal Sidérotas ('Iron') mountains for beaches: at Akoúmia a road (quite rough towards the end) leads down in 10km for pristine **Ag. Paraskeví** beach, while further east at Néa Kría Vrísi you can turn south for Saktoúria and lovely **Ag. Pávlos**, a sheltered sandy beach that's left the pristine category, thanks to a new yoga holiday centre and a few places to stay.

The roads to the south ends up at **Ag. Galíni** (ΑΓΙΑ ΓΑΛΗΝΗ), an old fishing village under an impressive backdrop of mountains that's the most photogenic resort on the south coast, its jumble of houses spilling prettily down the hill, peering over the shoulders of its neighbours to look down at the sea. Although the beach is too puny for the number of bodies that try to squeeze on it, a variety of boat excursions sail in search of others, at Moní Préveli, Mátala, **Ag. Geórgios** (shingly with three tavernas, 15 minutes from Ag. Galíni) and Ag. Pávlos (50 minutes) and to the pebble-beached islets to the southwest, called **Paximáthia** for their resemblance to the crunchy twice-baked bread sold in Greek bakeries. At Ag. Galíni port, posters display plans for a Daedalus-Icarus garden with a maze that awaits funding to get off the ground.

Cretan Yoghurt and Meatball Soup

Soups don't often appear on Cretan menus, although at home they are served quite regularly. Most are as simple as this one. In a bowl, knead together 1lb of minced lamb, 1 grated onion, 1 beaten egg, 2tbsp finely chopped fresh mint, and salt to taste. Make into meatballs about half an inch in diameter. Bring 750ml of beef stock to boil and put in 2tbsp of short rice, then carefully drop in the meatballs; cover and cook for about 40min, until the meatballs are cooked through. Then take the soup off the flame and remove the meatballs, keeping them in a warm place. Next, blend together 1lb natural yoghurt, 1 egg yolk and 2tbsp water. Add to the beef stock, stirring constantly at a low heat to keep it from boiling (and curdling). Once it's hot, add the meatballs and cook for another minute or so. Sprinkle each bowl with a bit of fresh mint and a dash of cayenne pepper. Serves four.

Where to Stay and Eating Out

Spíli ✆ (0832–)

Green Hotel, ✆ 22 225 (*C; mod*), bedecked with flowers and plants, is a delightful refuge when the coasts are unbearably hot and crowded; book early in the summer. Other, smaller choices include **Kefalovrisi**, ✆ 22 057, and the phoneless **Neon** (*both inexp*). You can also find rooms to rent, as well as good food, at the **Yparxo** taverna on the main road; **Giannis** does tasty grills.

Ag. Pávlos ✆ (0831–)

Ag. Pavlos, ✆ 22 845 (*E; inexp*) is one of a handful of places to sleep; with a phone, so at least you can ring ahead.

Ag. Galíni ✆ (0832–)

Although it is stacked with all sorts of accommodation, don't arrive in Ag. Galíni without a reservation in the summer, when package companies block-book nearly every hotel. **Galíni Mare**, ✆ 91 358 (*C; mod*), has good views and facilities; **Areti**, at the top of town, ✆ 91 240 (*D; mod*), is your best chance if everything else is full up.

Hotel Minos, ✆ 91 218 (*D; mod*) has a good view. **Aktaeon**, Kountouriótou, ✆ 91 208 (*E; inexp*), with private baths and good views over the town offers good value. Other inexpensive places not on any package company's list are **Argiro's Studios and Rooms**, ✆ 91 470; there's also **Rent Rooms Acropol** (*inexp*)—the rooms aren't much but the setting, on the top of the cliff, is superb.

Near the bus station, **Manos**, ✆ 91 394, has among the cheapest rooms in town, some with private bath.

Some of the best cooks in Crete work in Ag. Galíni's scores of restaurants. Looming over the waterfront, **Madame Ordanz**, up on the second floor and lined with photographs of old Ag. Galíni, serves well-prepared French and Greek dishes with a glamorous touch (*around 4000dr*).

The popular **Ariston taverna** serves good *stifádo*, moussaka, and an excellent aubergine salad—(*3000dr for a full meal*); **El Greco** next door is just as good. One of Ag. Galíni's favourites is **Onar**, with excellent Cretan food cooked by Mother. **La Strada** in the centre has a real pizza oven, and serves it up to jazz music.

Stelios, a bar on the main street, dishes out warm fragrant *loukoumádes* (fritters in honey and cinnamon) every Wednesday and Saturday evening. After midnight, you can work off the calories dancing at **Legend** or **Zorbas**. If you love jazz, you'll love the excellent **Jazz n Jazz Bar**; if you don't, you won't.

Amári: The Western Slopes of Mount Ida

Wedged between the western slopes of Mount Ida and the Kédros ridge, the ancient province of Amári is well known for its fighting spirit and resistance in the last war, but also for its lush charms, cherry orchards, olive groves and frescoed Byzantine churches. These valleys that time forgot are prime walking or touring territory, and a good place to look for wildflowers. Bring a picnic.

From Réthymnon the main road leads south into the valley by way of Prasiés. **Apóstoli**, the first village, has grand views over the Amári valley and a little frescoed church, Ag. Nikólaos, dating from the 1300s; **Ag. Fotiní** just beyond marks the crossroads of the east and west valleys. Nearly all the **west valley** villages were torched by the retreating Germans, although they have been rebuilt pretty much as they were. **Méronas** is worth a stop for its church of the Panagía with a Venetian Gothic doorway, crowned with the arms of the Kallergis, one of the most prominent Byzantine families on Crete. Inside (the key's across the road) are lovely early 14th-century frescoes that show the new, more naturalistic artistic trends from Constantinople. **Gerakári**, famous for its cherries, is the starting point for a stunning drive over the Kédros Mountains to Spíli (*see* p.145), while just south the 14th-century church of **Ag. Ioánnis** has austere, almost abstract frescoes. A similar old church, Moní Kalodena, above **Áno Méros,** collapsed in 1993, but the lush setting, overlooking Mount Ida, is still gorgeous.

However, if you have to choose one or the other, the **east valley** is far lovelier, a proper Cretan Brigadoon. From Ag. Fotiní, follow the sign left for **Thrónos,** the sleepy heir of a Minoan village and ancient Sybrito, a city destroyed by the Saracens in 824. The setting, especially Sybrito's acropolis, is superb, even if the physical remains are underwhelming. In the centre of the village, the mosaic carpet of a large three-aisled basilica overflows from under the much smaller, simple little church of the Panagía, containing exceptional frescoes (late 13th and early 15th century). Just south, medieval **Moní Asómati** has a pretty Venetian church and a fountain with cool, fresh water; in 1931 it was converted into an agricultural college, but now even the future farmers have gone. Another kilometre leads to the bijou little pink-tile-domed church of **Ag. Paraskeví**, where 13th-century murals decorate the tomb of Byzantine noble George Choratzis.

Back on the main route (an important road in Minoan times that linked Phaistós to the north coast), the University of Crete is excavating a Minoan Proto-Palatial villa, a 5min walk from **Monastiráki**. After Chaniá and Réthymnon, Monastiráki is the most important site yet discovered in western Crete (and still off limits to visitors): it had abundant workshops and 50 storage rooms, where the *pithoi* still contained grape pips, either from wine or raisins. The villa burned in 1700 BC, the same time as Knossós and Phaistós. **Amári**, one-time capital of the province, is one of the lovcliest villages in Crete, surrounded by enchanting views, especially from the height of the Venetian tower. The church of **Ag. Ánna**, isolated in a field outside the village, has the oldest dated frescoes in Crete, from 1225. Heading south from Amári, there's a ruined 7th-century basilica made from Roman columns and reliefs, in Elliniká, 2km west of **Vizári**. Lastly, **Apodoúlou**, on the road to Ag. Galíni, has another Minoan villa and *tholos* tombs, and frescoes from the late 14th century in the church of Ag. Geórgios.

Réthymnon to Herákleon: The Coastal Route

Between Réthymnon and Herákleon you have a choice of routes: the scenic, fast, coast-skirting E75 highway, with a few small resorts squeezed under the mountains; or the old, winding roads through a score of villages over the northern slopes of Mount Ida. The first road passes Réthymnon's beach sprawl, and then, just before the coastal mountains block access to the sea, arrives at **Pánormos** (ΠΑΝΟΡΜΟΣ), with a small sandy beach at the mouth of the Milópotamos river. Pánormos is a pretty place, guarded by a fortress built by the Genoese in 1206; the ruins of a sizeable 5th-century basilica suggest it was once a lot more important than it is now, although some rather unfortunate new building is trying to recapture that ancient rapture.

Further east, **Balí** (ΜΠΑΛΙ), in part thanks to the exotic cachet of its name, has been transformed from a quiet steep-stepped fishing village overlooking a trio of lovely coves to a jam-packed resort. However, if you're passing, the cove behind its port, known as **Paradise Beach,** is well worth a swim (if you don't mind lots of company) and lunch. On the hill over town, the lovely 17th-century **Monastery of Balí** is currently being restored; the Renaissance façade of the church and fountain are especially worth a look.

A Detour Inland: the Melidóni Cave

East of Báli the highway is rather dull, but an 8km detour up and over the mountains just to the south of Balí will take you to the **Melidóni Cave** (bring non-slip shoes; torches are on loan in the little chapel by the car park). The access road cuts diagonally up the mountain flank, where the cave awaits just above the car park, its small mouth belying a vast and gloomy, unsettling gullet. The ceiling, ragged with stalactites, hangs 300m overhead. The Minoans worshipped here, and just to the right of the entrance is a 3rd-century BC inscription to Hermes Talaios, who shared offerings here with Zeus Talaios and Talos (*see* p.50).

In 1824, when the Turks were doing their best to cut short Crete's participation in the Greek War of Independence, 324 women and children and 30 revolutionaries took refuge in the cave. When the Turks discovered their hideaway, the Greeks refused to surrender; the Turks tried to suffocate them by blocking up the entrance with stones, and when that failed they built a fire and, in one of the worst atrocities of the war, asphyxiated them all in the smoke. With its crumbling altar and broken ossuary it still seems haunted. Curiously, the water that drips in the cave dries up between September and February—Crete's rainy season. Have a drink with Markos and Brenda Kyrmizakis at the bar by the cave; they've just re-immigrated from Alabama to the old farming village of **Pérama**, just below Melidóni.

The **Old Road** between Pérama to Herákleon is pure rural Crete. In some villages just south of the road you may see fields dotted with large round piles of logs, smouldering away like overheated igloos; charcoal-burning is alive and well and has scarcely changed since the Middle Ages.

Fódele and El Greco

Continuing east, **Fódele** (ΦΟΔΕΛΕ) lies between the Old and New Roads through solid orange groves. According to one tradition this sleepy village with its pretty Byzantine church of the Panagía (1383) was the birthplace of Doménikos Theotokópoulos, better known as El Greco, a tradition apparently confirmed by a plaque erected in his honour by the University of Toledo in 1934. Recently the **'House of El Greco'** has been restored, and a display about the master and copies of his works should be set up by 1996.

When Saints Burst into Flames

Instead of making people pray, you make them admire.
Beauty inserts itself as an obstacle between our souls and God.

Grand Inquistor Cardinal Guevra, to El Greco

Born in 1541 (apologies to Fódele, but the archives say in Herákleon), Doménikos Theotokópoulos' youth on Crete is obscure. It is known that his first training was as an icon painter, perhaps studying alongside Michael Damaskinos, his contemporary. Only a single painting by a young El Greco survives in Crete, in Herákleon's Historical Museum (*see* p.172); a Cretan document from 1566 refers to him as 'master painter'. Soon after this date, however, he was in Titian's workshop in Venice, although the elongated, linear, mystical style of another Venetian, Tintoretto, proved the greatest influence on the young painter. By 1570 he was in Rome, coming into contact with the works of Michelangelo and the great Central Italian Mannerists (Pontormo, Rosso Fiorentino), whose strange, startling colours, unrealistic perspectives and exaggerated, often tortured poses were to be a major influence on his art.

Like a true Cretan, Theotokópoulos had a proud and passionate nature. During his stay in Rome, when Pius V was casting about for an artist to paint clothes on the figures of Michelangelo's *Last Judgement*, the Cretan suggested that the Pope would be better off destroying the fresco all together, because he could paint a better one that was chaste to boot. 'Michangelo is a good man, but he didn't know how to paint,' he said. The Romans were so astounded by his audacity that they ran him out of town.

Fortunately, he had a place to go. In Rome, he had met Diego de Castilla, Dean of Canons of Toledo Cathedral, who gave him his first major commission: the High Altar of Toledo's Santo Domingo de Antiguo (1577; now in the Art Institute of Chicago). It was with this great altarpiece in Toledo that he perfected his unique, uncanny, high personal style shot full of tension, his intense, vibrant lightning colours that seem to flicker on the canvas, his nervous line and figures that rise up like flames, all perceptions heightened to a fervent rapture and honed to the spiritual essential of truth. One of the tragedies of Spanish art is that El Greco never found favour with the religious, art-loving Philip II, who panicked at the unveiling of the *Martyrdom of San Maurizio* that El Greco painted for his Escorial chapel in 1587. The painter refused all hints that supplication or an offer to soften the colours might win him the king's approval, and in a huff took his brushes off to the holy city of Toledo, where he spent his last 37 years with his common-law wife, Jeromina de las Cuevas. Incapable of doing anything halfway, he lived as extravagantly as a lord, buying a 24-room palace in Toledo's abandoned Jewish quarter, employing a lutanist and guitarist to accompany his every meal. Although he never seemed to lack for commissions from the Church or for private portraits (usually of clergymen), after his death all his worldly possessions fitted into a single trunk.

The poet Hortensio Paravicino told him: 'You make snow itself burst into flame. You have overstepped nature, and the soul remains undecided in its wonder which of the two, God's creatures or yours, deserves to live.' Although he never returned to his native island, El Greco never forgot his origins, but always signed his paintings with his Greek name in Greek letters, often followed by KRES, or CRETAN.

Towards Herákleon: Ag. Pelagía and Palaiókastro

East of Fódele, the highway continues to the junction for the attractive, upmarket resort of **Ag. Pelagía** (ΑΓ. ΠΕΛΑΓΙΑ), strewn like chunks of coconut over the headland that marks the outer gate of the Bay of Herákleon. The steep 3km road descends to the quiet coves and protected sandy beach, endowed with luxury hotels. Nearly every possible water sport is on offer, and the ranks of customers to use them are swelled thanks to buses several times a day from the Hotel Astoria in Heráklion's Plateía Eleftherías. Remnants of a Minoan harbour town called Kytaiton were found on the edge of a cliff, on the west side of the bay. Five kilometres further east on the highway, keep your eyes peeled for the striking seaside Venetian fort of **Palaiókastro** and, wedged below, a modern village with a few restaurants, one of Herákleon's choice suburban addresses.

Where to Stay and Eating Out

Pánormos ℗ (0834–)

For luxury on a small scale **Villa Kynthia**, ℗ 51 102, 🖷 51 148 (*A; exp*) has a handful of air-conditioned rooms with the works and a swimming pool, centrally heated and open all year. **Panormos Beach**, ℗ 51 321 (*C; mod*) is a larger, typical beach hotel; **Lucy's**, ℗ 51 212, has pleasant, inexpensive rooms.

Balí ℗ (0834–)

Most of these places are really only worth trying in the off-season, but Balí is much nicer then anyway. Most luxurious, **Bali Paradise**, ℗ 94 253, 🖷 94 255 (*A; exp*) offers rooms in the hotel or bungalows, and a pool and sea sports. **Bali Beach**, ℗ 94 310 (*B; exp*) was one of the first hotels here and is still one of the nicest. For something cheaper, try **Blue Horizon** by the first beach; **Taverna Wave and Rent Rooms** is a pleasant place to stay with lots of shade. **Stavros** on the edge of town offers platters of good grilled meats and local wine; the **Delfina** serves up traditional Greek taverna treats. **On the Rocks Dancing Bar** cranks up for a bop after midnight.

Ag. Pelagía ✆ (081–)

The large hotel and bungalow complex of **Capsis Beach Resort**, ✆ 811 316 or 811 212, 📠 811 076 (*A; lux*) has just about every luxury you can imagine, plus three beaches, several swimming pools, a water sports school and an ultra-modern 'New Minoan' conference centre with 1200 seats. In a similar vein, **Peninsula**, ✆ 811 313 or 811 335, 📠 811 291(*A; lux*) is perched on the rocks, with a lovely terrace overlooking the beach, and has a long list of leisure activities, from a playground and paddling pool for your offspring to sea sports, tennis, a 'do-it-yourself hardressing salon' and disco. The smaller and newer **Alexander House**, ✆ 811 303, 📠 811 381 (*A; exp*) has comfortable air-conditioned rooms with satellite TV and mini bars and balconies overlooking the pool and sea, and a good Chinese restaurant. **Panorama**, ✆ 811 002, 📠 811 273 (*B; exp*) is a comfortable, large resort hotel with a pool, water sports and tennis. **Amazon**, ✆ 811 169 (*D; mod*) is one of the nicer, less expensive choices near the sea. Eating out in Ag. Pelagía isn't cheap, but it's good: **Muragio**, ✆ 811 070 on the waterfront has delicious fish; **Valentino**, ✆ 811 106 has similar, and pizzas made in a real Italian *forno*.

Réthymnon to Herákleon: The Inland Route

A choice of roads skirts the north flanks of Psilorítis, and to see everything there is to see will involve some backtracking. From Réthymnon, the easiest route inland is to follow the coast as far as Stavroménos, where you can pick up the road for **Viranepiskopí**, with two churches of interest: a 10th-century basilica near a sanctuary of Artemis, and a 16th-century Venetian church. The old highway goes from here to Pérama and the Melidóni Cave (*see* above), but a prettier road detours higher up, 7km south, to colourful **Margarítes**, home of a thriving pottery industry (your chance to pick up your own 6ft Minoan-style *pithos*) and two churches of interest, 14th-century **Ag. Demétrius** with frescoes, and **Ag. Ioánnis** with a stone iconostasis and 12th-century frescoes.

Another 4km south, modern **Eléftherna** (ΕΛΕΥΘΕΡΝΑ) is just below the ancient city of Eleutherna. Founded by the Dorians in the 8th century BC, it survived into Byzantine times and along the way produced Diogenes the Physicist, a pupil of the Pre-Socratic philosopher Anaximenes of Miletus. Like most Dorian cities, the setting (on natural tiers, between two tributaries of the Milopótamos river) and views are spectacular; any foe that came near had to pass the once mighty walls and a formidable tower, rebuilt in Hellenistic times. According to historian Dio Cassius, Metellus Creticus was only able to capture Eleutherna for Rome after the tower was soaked in vinegar (!). Near here you can see a section of the aqueduct carved in the stone, leading to the two massive Roman cisterns capable of holding 10,000 cubic metres of water. At the bottom of the glade there's a well preserved bridge, with Mycenaean-style corbelled stone arches. In 1985, the University of Crete resumed excavations here, concentrating on the remains of a score of funeral pyres and their offerings from the Protogeometric to the Archaic period. The most beautiful treasures found to date are four small ivory heads of exquisite workmanship. One dead notable in the 8th century BC was given not only the usual animal sacrifices, food and valuables, but a human sacrifice to take along to the Underworld: the archaeologists found the remains of a man trussed up hand and foot; somehow, even after 2700 years, the coroners could tell his throat had been cut.

Axós

Even higher and more precipitous, **Axós**, 30km east along the mountain road, was founded around 1100 BC by Minoans seeking refuge from the Dorian invaders (it's believed to be the 'E-CO-SO' on a Linear B inscription from Knossós). Axós was the only town on the island to have a king of its own into the 7th century BC, and it continued to thrive well into the Byzantine period, when it counted 46 churches; today 11 survive, of which Ag. Iríni with frescoes is the most important. The far scattered remains of ancient Axos reveal a huge town (whatever did they live on? you may well ask). A sign in the village points the way up the ridge to the acropolis, scattered on terraces under its 8th-century BC acropolis walls and ruins of an Archaic sanctuary. Arrange to go up with Antonia Koutantou, © (0834) 61 311, who runs one of the weaving shops and has the key to the churches.

On the road to the east of Axós, a splendid panorama opens up all the hill towns of the Milopótamo. Just below the next one, **Zonianá**, you can visit (as of spring 1996) the **cave of Sendóni**, piercing a spur of Mount Ida and containing one of Crete's most striking collections of stalactites, cave draperies and petrified waves. The formations were discovered by a little girl, who according to the locals was lured away by the fairies, or nereids; after an eight-day search she was found dead at the far end of the cave with a beatific smile on her face. Apparently she wasn't the only one lured away; during the recent preparation of the cave for visitors, skeletons of a man and woman were found.

Anógia and the Idean Cave

The next village east is **Anógia** (ΑΝΩΓΕΙΑ), where many of the inhabitants of ancient Axos moved in the Middle Ages, and where hints of their ancient dialect survived until recently. A stalwart resistance centre, it was burned by both the Turks and the Germans, the latter in reprisal for hiding the kidnapped General Kriepe, when all the men in the village were rounded up and shot. Today rebuilt in an upper, modern town and lower, more traditional-looking town (albeit all in concrete) Anógia is not without charm. Under the plane trees in the lower town, shops display bright examples of local weavings, although don't expect to find anything approaching the quality of the intricate work you see in the museums or antique shops; brace yourself for a mugging by a score of little old ladies (including a few surviving widows of the martyrs) touting their wares. In the upper part of town, the assymetrical square around the church, jammed full of potted plants and flowers and *kafeneíons*, is a favourite hangout.

Just east of Anógia begins the paved, 26km road to the **Idaean Cave** (IΔAIO ANTPO), 1540m. As far back as the Archaic period, the Idean Cave took over the Diktean Cave's thunder, so to speak, in claiming to be the birthplace of Zeus. Ancient even to the ancients, the Idaean cult preserved remnants of Minoan religion into Classical times, presided over by Idaean Dactyls or 'finger men'. According to his ancient biographer, Pythagoras was initiated by the Idaean Dactyls into the Orphic mysteries of midnight Zagreus (i.e. Zeus fused with the mystic role of Dionysos), a cult that was believed to be the origin of his mystical theories on numbers and vegetarianism; in the Herákleon museum Minoan seals bear the five-pointed star symbol he would adopt as his own. A clue to what they got up to in the cave is preserved in a fragment of Euripides' lost play, *The Cretans,* in the confession of Cretan mystics in the palace of Minos:

> *My days have run, the servant I,*
> *Initiate, of Idaean Jove;*
> *Where midnight Zagreus roves, I rove;*
> *I have endured his thunder-cry;*
> *Fulfilled his red and bleeding feasts;*
> *Held the Great Mother's mountain flame;*
> *I am Set Free and named by name*
> *A Bacchus of the Mailed Priests.*

Since 1982 Ioánnis and Éfi Sakellarákis' excavations have produced several roomfuls of votive offerings dating from 3000 BC to the 5th century AD; at the time of writing, the cave is still off limits, although it may reopen soon—enquire in Anógia. A ski resort has opened near by, and there's a marked track from the cave to the summit of **Psilorítis**, Crete's highest peak (2456m), about 7 hours' round trip if you're a reasonably experienced, well-equipped hiker. Beware that snow falls as late as June and storms are indeed an unforgettable experience on the summit. A guide is helpful to find the most direct route to the summit, marked by a shelter and the chapel Tímios Stavrós (where an Irish girl robbed young Níkos Kazantzákis of his virginity, at least according to his *Report to Greco*). If you have very warm sleeping bags, water and food, consider spending the night.

From Anógia, the road continues east to **Goniés**, a village set in an amphitheatre under Mount Ida at the entrance to the Malevízi, the grape-growing region that gave its name to Malmsey, a favourite red wine in medieval Venice and England. The road continues in a valley to **Sklavokámbos**, where a Minoan villa went up in flames so intense that its limestone walls were baked as if in a kiln; its ruins are behind a fence right next to the road.

The Minoan Villas of Týlisos

Open daily, 8.45–3; adm; park in the village and walk up or subject your-self to the embroidery ladies who run the 'Free Parking' next door. There are four buses a day from Herákleon.

Much more remains to be seen further east at **Týlisos** (ΤΥΛΙΣΟΣ), a village in a lovely setting, surrounded by mountains and swathed in olives and vineyards, where three large Minoan villas (A, B and C) were unearthed in the early days of Minoan archaeology, between 1902 and 1913. Built in the prosperous New Palace period and destroyed *c.* 1450 BC, the villas stood two or perhaps even three storeys

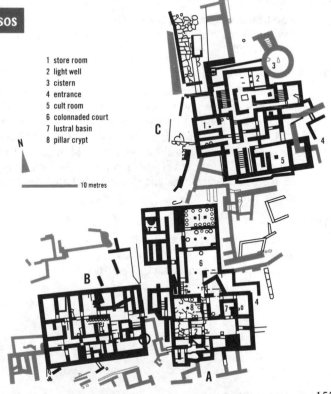

Týlisos

1 store room
2 light well
3 cistern
4 entrance
5 cult room
6 colonnaded court
7 lustral basin
8 pillar crypt

N

10 metres

high. They contained small apartments and extensive storage facilities; palatial elements such as light-wells, lustral basins, colonnaded courts and cult shrines are produced here in miniature. The typical Minoan love of twisting little corridors is further complicated here by the fact that the Dorians founded a town re-using many of the walls. Rectangular Villa B, nearest the entrance, is the oldest and least preserved; Villas A and C are extremely well built of finely dressed stone: door jambs, walls (some still standing up to 6ft high), stairs, pillars, and the drainage system survive. Water was pumped in from 2km away by aqueduct; Villa C was rebuilt in the Post-Palace period, when its round cistern was added.

The presence of these elaborate, beautifully set villas in Týlisos and Sklavokámbos seems to suggest that the Minoan nobility liked to take a few weeks off in the country, but the fact that they stand along the road from Knossós to the sacred Idean Cave may be the key to their purpose.

Where to Stay and Eating Out

Axós © (0834–)

Hotel Etearxos, in Axós, is a simple place with 30 beds; **Taverna Axós** is good for lunch and hosts the occasional 'Greek Night'.

Anógia © (0834–)

There are two places to stay, both in the upper town, and both enjoying fine views: the small, white, clean and bright **Aristea**, © 31 459, and the similar **Aris**; if these are full try the rooms atop the Mitato Taverna. Anógia prides itself on its lamb and excellent *raki*. **Taverna Ta Skalomata** is near the top of the town and the crossroads to Idean cave; **Taverna Areti**, along the main road, serves lamb and pork dishes and simple lunches. In Sísarcha, between Anógia and Goniés, **Michalis' Taverna** has simple rooms.

Týlisos © (081–)

Besides a few private rooms and a couple tavernas, there's the **Hotel Arolithos**, © 821 050 (*A; exp*), a few km west, set in an 'authentic Cretan village' under a large neon sign. *Open April–Oct.*

TRIADA MONASTERY

Nomós Herákleon

'Crete has always been a theatre for strange and splendid events,' wrote Patrick Leigh Fermor, and many of them have happened in the broad Cretan heartland of the *nomós* of Herákleon, where Ariadne danced in the Labyrinth and Europe was given a name and its first civilization. This cradle between the Psilorítis range to the west and the Diktean Mountains to the east was the core of Minoan Crete: Knossós, Mália, Phaistós, Archánes and Ag. Triáda and countless smaller sites are here, and the magnificent works of art they yielded, now in the Herákleon museum, have become one of the glories of Greece.

Besides the finest Cretan art and culture, the province also contains much of the dark side of what the last 30 years have wrought, where you often hear people say that what the Venetians, Turks and Germans couldn't conquer money has undone without a fight. Herákleon has done its best to turn itself into an ugly cement toadstool. The beach resorts along the lovely north coast, jerry-built in the first flush of mass tourism, are like a scar that won't heal, illustrating a 20th-century paradox on the island that invented paradox: prosperity makes everything worse.

Herákleon (HPAKLEIO)

Hustling, bustling Herákleon (also Iraklion among other spellings) is Crete's capital and Greece's fourth largest city, with a population of 120,000—the kind of place that most people go on holiday to escape. As Crete's main transport hub, however, it's hard to avoid: Herákleon boasts the island's two top attractions: a museum containing the world's greatest collection of Minoan artefacts and the grand palace of Knossós in its suburbs.

Herákleon has gone through as many name changes as Elizabeth Taylor. It began modestly as Katsamba, the smaller of Knossós' two ports, and took on its current name in the classical period. In the 800s the Saracens saw the potential of the site, and built their chief town and pirates' base here, naming it Kandak ('the moats') for the trench they dug around its walls. By the time it was reconquered by Nikephóros Phokás, Kandak was the leading slave market in the Mediterranean. The Venetians made Kandak into Candia, or Candy, and kept it as the capital of Crete; the mighty walls they built around it so impressed the Cretans that they called it Megálo Kástro, the 'Big Castle'. The Turks kept it their seat of government until 1850 when they transferred it to Chaniá. When Crete became autonomous, the classical name, Herákleon, was revived and it took back its role as capital in 1971.

Nomós Herákleon

To Ag. Nikolaos

NOMOS LASSITHI

Afendis ▲ (2141m)

Tzermiadon
Krasi
Mochos
Stalis
Malia
II Limen Chersonisou
II Chersonisou
Gouves

Ano Viannos

Kato Vigla
Moni Arvi
To Ierapetra

Kastri
Lytos
Kastelli
Xidas
Arkalochori
Kastelliana
Priansos II
Philippi
Tsoutsouros

Chani Kokini
Gournes
Karteros
Poros
Myrtia
Voni
Thrapsano

Dia

II Annisos
HERAKLEON ╬ II
Knossos II
Archanes
Profitis Ilias
Vathypetro II
Charakas
Pygos
Moni Koudoma

Skavidaras
Rogdia
II Tylissos
Ag. Myronas
Krousonas
Raftos II
Ag. Varvara
Prinias

Fodele
Gonies
Skalavikambos II
Anogia

Ag. Deka
Gortyn II
Zaros
Moni Vrondisiou
Ag. Triada II Phaistos II
Vori
Kamares
Moni Koudoma
Lebena II
Lendas

To Rethymnon

Mt. Ida (Psiloritis) ▲ (2452m / 8058ft)

Kamares Cave
Kamares
Myres
Platanos
Matala
Kali Limenes

Kamilario
Tymbaki
Pitsidia
Kommo II
Ag. Galini

20km
10 miles

N ▲

159

By air: Herákleon's airport, 4km east of the city in Amnísos, © 245 644, is linked to the city by public bus (no.1), beginning at Pórta Chaníon and passing through the centre of town; Olympic bus connects to all Olympic flights from Plateía Eleftherías. For Olympic information, call © 223 400 or 229 191.

By sea: travel and shipping agents line the main street Odós 25 Avgoustou, down at the Venetian harbour. Herákleon has connections by ferry every night to Piraeus on Minoan Lines (© 244 603) and ANEK (© 289 545), and to Haifa and Cyprus once a week. Port authority: © 244 912.

By road: Herákleon has a number of bus stations. For Knossós and destinations east of Herákleon (including Ierápetra and the Lassíthi Plateau) depart from the port station outside the walls, just east of the Venetian port, © 282 631; on the busy Herákleon–Ag. Nikólaos route you may get a ride on KTEL's new double deckers. The station for points west—Réthymnon and Chaniá—is across the street, © 221 765. From just outside the Pórta Chaníon on the west side of the city, buses head southwest to Ag. Galíni, Górtyn, Phaistós, Mátala, Týlisos, Anógia and Milapótamos, © 383 073 From outside the Evans Gate (Plateía

Herákleon

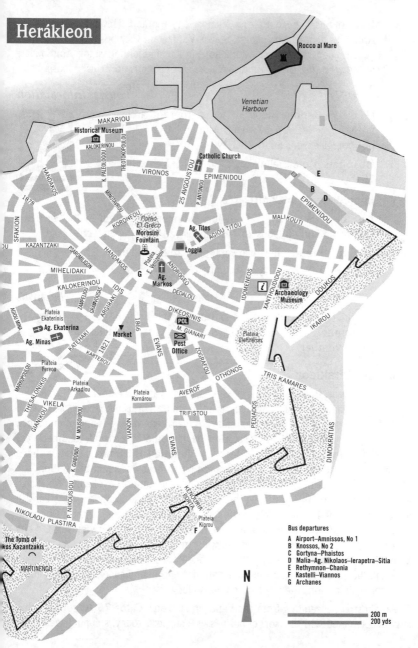

Rocco al Mare

Venetian Harbour

MAKARIOU

Historical Museum

KALOKERINOU

K. PALEOLOGOU

THEOTOKOPOULOU

Catholic Church

VIRONOS

EPIMENIDOU

25 AVGOUSTOU

P. ANTONIOU

E

B D

EPIMENIDOU

MALI KOUTI

1878

HANDAKOS

SFAKION

KAZANTZAKI

PSAROMILIGGON

MINOTAVROU

KORONEOU

Forko El Gréco
Morosini
Fountain

Ag. Titos

AGIOU TITOU

Loggia

ANDROGEO

Plateia
F. Venizelou

Ag.
Markos

DEDALOU

G

IDOMENEOS

KANTHOUDIDOU

DOUKOS

i

Archaeology
Museum

IKAROU

MIHELIDAKI

KALOKERINOU

HANDAKOS

IDIS

ZAPPELOU

GRAMVOUSAS

ARGIRAKI

1866

DIKEOSINIS

POL

M. GIANARI

Post
Office

Plateia
Ekaterinis

Ag. Ekaterina

MINW

AGIOU MINA

KATEHAKI

1821

KARTEROU

Market

EVANS

ZOGRAFOU

Plateia
Eleftherias

Ag. Minas

Plateia
Fereou

TRIS KAMARES

OTHONOS

MAKRIKPOULOU

THESSALONIKIS

GIANIKOU

Plateia
Arkadiou

M. MOUSOUROU

Plateia
Kornárou

AVEROF

PEDIADOS

DIMOKRATIAS

VIKELA

VIANON

TRIFISTOU

K. GIABOUDI

EVANS

P. NIKOUSIOU

NIKOLAOU PLASTIRA

KENOURIA PORTA

Plateia
Kiprou

F

The Tomb of
kos Kazantzakis

MARTINENGO

N

Bus departures

A Airport–Amnissos, No 1
B Knossos, No 2
C Gortyna–Phaistos
D Malia–Ag. Nikolaos–Ierapetra–Sitia
E Rethymnon–Chania
F Kastelli–Viannos
G Archanes

200 m
200 yds

161

Kíprou) buses head to Áno Viános, Mýrtos and Thrapsanó. Buses for Archánes depart from central Plateía Venizélou. City buses for the nearest beaches depart from the Astoria hotel in Plateía Eleftherías; for Ammoudári to the west (no. 6); for Amnisós to the east take bus no.7, just opposite.

© *(081–)* **Tourist Information**

NTOG: 1 Xanthoudídou St, across from the archaeology museum, © 22 24 87; open Mon–Fri 8–2.30. **Tourist police**: Dikeosínis St, © 28 31 90.

Hospitals: Panelisteimiako, © 26 91 11; Venizélou, © 23 75 02.

Immediate Help Centre: © 222 22.

Left Luggage: There's a left luggage open until 8pm in the East Bus Station, and on 48 Odós 25 Avgoustou, © 281 750, open 7am–11pm.

OTE telephones: El Greco Park, open 24 hours a day.

Post office: Plateía Daskaloyiánnis, © 282 276.

Festivals

Herákleon flower festival **2–6 June**; grape festival **11–19 September**; and a huge *panegýri* for the patron Ag. Minás on **11 November**.

Venetian Herákleon

When Crete won its autonomy in 1898, Arthur Evans (*see* pp.175–6), already locally a hero for his news reports in Britain on Turkish atrocities, was instrumental in persuading the Cretans to safeguard their Venetian walls and monuments, and it's a good thing he did because Herákleon would be a visual, landmark-less mess without them. The old front door, the **Venetian Harbour**, although now a couple of hundred yards west of the modern ferry docks and main bus station, still offers the best introduction to the city, where two monuments evoke the Venetians' ability to supply Herákleon during the 21-year siege by the vastly superior Turkish forces. Out on the harbour mole, the over-restored 16th-century fortress **Rocco al Mare** is guarded by a fierce lion of St Mark and enjoys splendid views of the city (*open 8–6, Sun 8–3; adm*). Considerably less impressive, the looming arches of the **Venetian Arsenali**, or shipyards, have been partially obscured by the street, although they are a reminder that Venetian seamanship and superior facilities at sea were the main reasons the city held out for so long.

The main street ascending from the Venetian Harbour, **Odós 25 Avgoustou**, has always been lined with the sort of businesses it supports today: shipping agents, car rental shops and banks. Halfway up, handsomely set back in its own square, the Byzantine church of **Ag. Títos** owes its stately cubic form to the Turks, who used it as a mosque and reconstructed it after various earthquakes. The chapel to the left of the narthex houses the island's most precious relic, the head of St Titus, a favourite disciple of St Paul, who converted the island to Christianity and died in Górtyn c. AD 96. When forced to give up Crete, the Venetians made off with Titus' skull and only returned it when the Pope forced them to, in 1966.

It takes a bit of imagination to reconstruct, but the Venetians designed what is now **Plateía Venizélou**, at top of 25 Avgoustou, as a miniature Piazza San Marco. Herákleon's City Hall occupies the lovely **Venetian Loggia** (1628), built as a meeting place for the Venetian and Cretan nobility and completely reconstructed after taking a direct hit in the Battle of Crete. The inner exedra is decorated all over with fine Renaissance reliefs of weapons and frowning bookworm lions (the damaged originals are in the Historical Museum). **San Marco** (Ag. Márkos), the first Venetian church on Crete (1239), was twice rebuilt after earthquakes, stripped of its lofty campanile and converted into a mosque by the Turks, and since restored for use as a concert hall and exhibition centre. Water dribbles (usually) from the mouths of the lions of the **Morosini Fountain**, commissioned in 1626 by governor Francesco Morosini, who brought water in from Mount Júktas to replace the old wells and cisterns. Although minus its figure of Neptune, the sculptural decoration of sea nymphs and mermen riding sea monsters, dolphins and bulls is some of the finest Venetian work on Crete; the 14th-century lions were filched from an older fountain.

South of Plateía Venizélou, the city's busy **outdoor market** runs along Odós 1866, a permanent display of Crete's extraordinary fecundity. Several stalls sell dried Cretan wedding cakes—golden wreaths decorated with scrolls and rosettes. Similar forays into the Baroque may be seen at the south end of the market in Plateía Kornárou, in the carvings adorning the **Bembo Fountain** (1588) which was put together by the Venetians from ancient fragments, including a headless Roman statue brought in from Ierápetra; the Turks added the charming kiosk-fountain, or **Koúbes**, now converted into a café, and the Cretans added the modern sculptures of Erotókritos and Arethoúsa, the hero and heroine of their national epic poem.

The Archaeology Museum

Open 8am–7pm, Mon 12.30–7; adm exp; free Sun. To avoid the endless tour groups, arrive early; note that if you get overwhelmed you can go out for a drink or lunch and come back with your date-stamped ticket.

A few blocks east of Plateía Venizélou, Herákleon's largest square, the great hemicycle of **Plateía Eleftherías**, is dotted with monuments to great Cretans with equally great moustaches, where evening strollers meet in the many cafés, sweet shops and pizzerias. On the north side of Plateía Eleftherías is the **Archaeology Museum**, an ungainly, somewhat airless coffer that holds nearly all the treasures of Minoan civilization. Thanks to Cretan archaeologist Joseph Hadzidákis, a law was passed in the early days of Crete's autonomy which stated that every important antiquity found on the island belongs to the museum. The result is dazzling, delightful and entirely too much to digest in one visit.

The collection is arranged in chronological order. In **Room I**, containing Neolithic (from 5000 BC) and Pre-Palatial periods (2600–2000 BC), the fine craftsmanship that would characterize Minoan civilization proper is already apparent in the delicate golden leaf pendants, the polished stone ritual vessels, the boldly shaped, irregularly fired red and black Vasilikí pottery and carved sealstones (note especially the unique 16-sided hieroglyphic seal found in Archánes, in Case 11). The future Minoan obsession with bulls is revealed in three tiny noodly clay men clinging to the head of a bull; early Cycladic idols and Egyptian seals discovered in the tombs of Mesara point to a precocious trade network. **Rooms II** and

Kamares ware from Phaistós, MMIIb

III are devoted to the Old Palace period (2000–1700 BC), when the Minoans made their first polychromatic Kamares ware, vases that follow the rules of Art Nouveau: each work individually crafted, marrying form and decoration, using stylized motifs from the natural world. The extraordinary virtuosity of Minoan potters 3500 years ago is especially expressed in their 'eggshell ware' cups, named for their delicate thin walls. One case displays the Knossós Town Mosaic: faïence plaques, each shaped and painted like a miniature Minoan house.

Kamares ware jug, MMIIb

Phaistós in particular flourished in the Old Palace period. The Kamares vases found in the palace reach a dizzying peak of decorative richness, studded with flowers in relief and dripping scalloped edgings. The mysterious clay **Phaistós Disc** (c. 1700 BC), displayed in the centre of Room III, is the world's first example of moveable type: 45 different symbols are stamped on both sides in a spiral. The theory that the disc is a forgery has been disproved by seals and other items discovered to have similar pictures and/or phonetic ideograms. At least a dozen translations have been attempted, but none has been taken seriously.

The vast majority of finds date from the Minoans' Golden Age, the New Palace period (1700–1450 BC), divided more or less geographically in **Rooms IV–IX**. Potters turned to even freer, more naturalistic designs, divided into the floral and marine styles. Stone carving became ever more rarefied as the Minoans sought the hardest and rarest marbles, porphyrys and semi-precious stones to carve into vases and rhytons (ritual pouring vessels), magnificently cut and polished to bring out their swirling grains. **Room IV** contains many of their masterpieces: a magnificent naturalistic bull's head rhyton carved in black steatite, with eyes of rock crystal and jasper (and modern gilt wooden horns) found in the Little Palace at Knossós, the leopard axe from Mália, and from the main palace at Knossós the bare-breasted snake goddess statuettes; the draughtsboard in ivory, rock crystal, blue glass paste and gold and silver leaf, complete with four gaming pieces; and the ivory bull leaper, the first known statue of a freely moving human figure, the muscles and tendons exquisitely carved, especially in the hand. Fragments of two other figures suggest that the bull leaper was part of a composition, not unlike the one shown in the Toreador fresco.

Room V contains finds from Knossós that just pre-date its destruction in 1450 BC, when the Linear A and Linear B clay tablets in Case 69 were accidently baked in the general conflagration. Note the model of a Minoan palace *c.* 1600 BC. **Room VI** contains finds from the cemeteries at Knossós, Archánes and Phaistós (New Palace and Post-Palace periods, 1450–1300 BC). Miniature sculptures offer clues about Minoan funerary practices, banquets and dances; an ivory *pyxis* (jewellery box) shows a band of men hunting a bull. Goldwork reached its height in this period, especially the elliptical rings and the Isopata ring, showing four ladies ecstatically dancing. Another in a similar style is believed to show tree-worship. The Mycenaeans influenced a number of works in this room (note the ivory plaques, decorated with warriors' heads) and are generally made to answer for the weapons that suddenly make an appearance—the boar tusk and bronze helmets and 'gold-nailed swords' as described by Homer; the pot of carefully arranged horse bones is a sacrifice from the Mycenaean/Minoan royal tomb at Archánes.

Items found in the luxurious country villas of central Crete fill **Room VII**. The show-stoppers here are the gold jewellery, particularly the exquisite pendant of two bees depositing a drop of honey in a comb from Mália, and the three black steatite vessels from Ag. Triáda, decorated in beautifully executed low reliefs that offer insights into Minoan life. The Harvesters' Vase shows a band of men with winnowing rods, accompanied by what looks like a priest and band of singers. On the 'Cup of the Chieftain' a young man with a sword over his shoulder reports to a long-haired chieftain clad in boots, loincloth and a necklace; a rhyton has four zones depicting lively athletic scenes: boxing, wrestling, and bull sports.

The New Palace period contents of **Room VIII** come from Zákros, the only large palace yet discovered that escaped the ancient plunderers. The floral and marine pottery is especially good, and the stone vases superb, most notably a little rock crystal amphora with a handle of crystal beads (incredibly, it was in over 300 pieces when found) and a green stone rhyton showing a scene of a Minoan peak sanctuary, with wild goats springing all around and birds presumably appearing as an epiphany of the goddess. **Room IX** has items from ordinary Minoan houses of the New Palace period. The collection of lovely and mysterious seals is exceptional; no

two are alike, although many repeat the same motifs, in natural or religious scenes. The Minoans probably used the seals to secure private property (such as the contents of a vase) and correspondence, and their engravers achieved an astounding technique; suspicions that they had to use lenses to execute such tiny work was confirmed when one made of rock crystal was found in Knossós.

After the Golden Age, the Post-Palace period artefacts in **Room X** (1450–1100 BC) show a gradual decline in inspiration, a coarsening, and ever-heavier Mycenaean artistic influences. Pottery decoration becomes increasingly limited to strict bands of ordered patterns. Figures lose their typical Minoan grace and *joie de vivre*; the clay statuettes of the goddess are stiff and stylized, their flouncy skirts reduced to smooth bells, their breasts reduced to nubs, their arms invariably lifted, as if imploring the fickle heavens. One goddess has opium poppies sprouting from her hat; many of the Minoans' religious cults and artistic imagination may well have involved the use of opium and alcohol (it may also explain their apparent lack of aggression typical of other 'cradles of civilization'). A terracotta group of women uncannily seem to perform a modern Cretan dance.

That the Dorian invasion was an ancient Dark Age is evident in the Sub-Minoan and Early Geometric periods of **Room XI** (1100–900 BC); the quality of the work is poor all around, generally limited to simple, abstract linear decoration, whether made by tenacious pockets of unconquered Minoans or by the invaders; note especially votive offerings from the cave of Inatos, dedicated to Eileithyia, the protectress of childbirth, and a rhyton in the form of an ox-drawn chariot. The pieces in **Room XII** show an improvement in life and art on Crete in the Mature Geometric and Orientalizing periods (900–650 BC). Familiar Greek gods make an appearance: Zeus holding an eagle and three thunderbolts on a pot lid, Hermes with sheep and goats on a bronze votive plaque. Huge Geometric vases are decorated with polychromatic patterns; Orientalizing pottery, as the name suggests, shows the strong eastern influences that dominated Greek civilization in the 8th–7th centuries. Griffons, sphinxes and lions are favourite motifs. One vase, in Case 163, shows a unique pair of lovers, naturally presumed to be Theseus and Ariadne. Bronze offerings found in the Idaean cave are especially interesting, one a boat showing a couple travelling. Some fine gold work has survived, as well as a terracotta model of a tree covered with doves.

At the foot of the stairs, **Room XIII** contains Minoan *larnaxes*, or terracotta sarcophagi. Minoans were laid out in a foetal position, so they are quite small; in the Old Palace days they were made of wood, and the changeover to clay suggests the Minoans were over-exploiting their forests. The belief that living Minoans used their *larnaxes* for bathtubs before they died seems absurd but common, perhaps because it supports Evans' designation of the Queen's bathroom at Knossós.

Yet another art the Minoans excelled at was fresco, displayed upstairs in **Rooms XIV–XVI**. Almost as fascinating as the paintings themselves is the work that went into their reconstruction by the Swiss father-and-son team hired by Evans.

A Fresh Look at the Frescoes

 What should rightfully be the biggest controversy over artistic restoration in history has not really happened yet. Look closely at the frescoes. On most, you will notice a stark difference between what you think are the frescoes, and certain dark crumbly bits that seem to deface the figures. Most people are amazed to discover that the crumbly bits are in fact all that survives of the originals, and the rest—90% in some cases—is entirely the work of Arthur Evans's restorers, notably Edmund Gillérion. The famous *La Parisienne* is one of the very few frescoes where the face was entirely intact.

Some archaeologists have derided their work as completely fanciful, a little too close to the Art Nouveau styles popular in Evans's time. This is blatantly unfair, but perhaps typical of the urge among many scientific-minded types to deny the existence of what they cannot explain. In fact, the restorers did a masterful job, and on the whole an honest one. But many of their interpretations can still be questioned, as in the 'fresco of women' from the East Wing at Knossós, to cite one among many, where the faces, the poses, and most of the decorative detail is simply invented, inferred from other works. With these frescoes, the subject matter just happens to be one of the greatest artistic achievements of all time—and maybe there should be a bit of controversy, if some doubt exists about the way they are presented to us. One might complain, for example, that the precise draughtsmanship of the restorers distorts the feeling of the originals, done in looser, more casual brushstrokes. The problem with conducting such a controversy is a matter of divided interests. Professional archaeologists tend to have little if any artistic understanding, but they know the details of how such frescoes are reassembled, how surfaces and pigments react over time, and so on. Art historians have been slow to take on this very important subject, perhaps for fear of stepping on the archaeologists' toes. Maybe the two should get together; the Knossós restorations as they are make lovely and familiar images, but it may be time to take a closer look.

In painting the Cretans followed Egyptian conventions in colour: women are white, men are red, monkeys are blue, a revelation that led to the re-restoration of *The Saffron Gatherers*, one of the oldest frescoes, originally restored as a boy and now reconstructed as a monkey picking crocuses after a similar subject was found on Santoríni. The first room contains the larger frescoes from the palace of Knossós, such as the nearly completely intact *Cup-Bearer* from the *Procession* fresco, which originally lined the Corridor of the Procession and great Propylon and is believed to have had 350 figures altogether. Here too are *The Dolphins*, *The Prince of the Lilies*, *The Shields*, also the charming *Partridges* found in the 'Caravanserai', near Knossós, and the *Lilies* from Amnísos. The 'miniature frescoes' in the other two rooms include the celebrated *Parisienne*, as she was dubbed by her founders in 1903, with her eye-paint, lipstick and 'sacral knot' jauntily tied at the back; others, full of tiny figures, show a ceremonial dance and a tripartite shrine ritual. Then take a good look at the most famous fresco of all, *The Bull Leapers* (or Toreadors).

The Bull in the Calendar

> *...there too is Knossos, a mighty city, where Minos was king for nine years, a familiar of mighty Zeus.*
>
> *Odyssey*, book XIX

The so-called 'Toreador Fresco', found at Knossós, has become one of the most compelling icons of the lost world of ancient Crete. The slender, sensual bare-breasted maidens who seem to be controlling the action are painted in white, the moon's colour, as in all Cretan frescoes, while the athlete vaulting through the bull's horns appears, like all males, in red, the colour of the sun. Mythology and archaeology begin to agree, and the roots of the story of Theseus, Ariadne and the Minotaur seem tantalizingly close at hand.

Take time to look at the decorative border—four striped bands and a row of multicoloured lunettes. Neither Arthur Evans nor any archaeologist since noticed anything unusual about it. A professor of English in Maine named Charles F. Herberger (*The Thread of Ariadne*, Philosophical Library, New York, 1972) was the first to discover that this border is in fact a complex ritual calendar, the key to the myth of Theseus in the Labyrinth and to much else. The pairs of stripes on the tracks, alternately dark and light, for day and night, count on average 29 through each cycle of the five-coloured lunettes, representing the phases of the moon—this is the number of days in a lunar month. By counting all the stripes on the four tracks, Herberger found that each track gives roughly the number of days in a year; the whole, when doubled, totals exactly the number of days in an eight-year cycle of 99 lunar months, a period in which the solar and lunar years coincide—the marriage of sun and moon.

To decipher the calendar, you can't simply count in circuits around the border; there are regular diagonal jumps to a new row, giving the course of the eight-year cycle the form of a rectangle with an 'x' in it. The box with the 'x' is intriguing, a motif in the art of the Cretans and other ancient peoples as far afield as the Urartians of eastern Anatolia. A Cretan seal shows a bull apparently diving into a crossed rectangle of this sort, while a human figure vaults through his horns. Similar in form is the most common and most enigmatic of all Cretan symbols, the double axe or *labrys*. The form is echoed further in a number of signet-rings that show the x-shaped cross between the horns of a bull, or between what appear to be a pair of crescent moons.

The home of the *labrys*, the axe that cuts two ways, is the labyrinth. Arthur Evans believed the enormous, rambling palace of Knossós itself to be the labyrinth, a pile so confusing that even a Greek hero would have needed Ariadne's golden thread to find his way through it. In the childhood of archaeology, men could read myths so literally as to think there was a tangible labyrinth, and perhaps even a Minotaur. Now, it seems more likely that the labyrinth was the calendar itself, the twisting path that a Minos, a generic name for Cretan priest-kings, representing the sun, followed in his eight-year reign before his inevitable rendezvous with the great goddess. This meeting may originally have meant his death (in a bull mask perhaps) and replacement by another Theseus. Later it would have been simply a ceremony of remarriage to the priestess that stood in the transcendent goddess's place, celebrated by the bull-vaulting ritual. It has been claimed that the occasion was also accompanied by popular dancing, following the shape of the labyrinth, where the dancers proceeded in a line holding a cord—Ariadne's thread. Homer said 'nine years', and other sources give nine years as the period after which the Athenians had to send their captives to Crete to be devoured by the Minotaur—it's a common ancient confusion, really meaning 'until the ninth', in the way the French still call the interval of a week *huit jours*. Whatever this climax of the Cretan cycle was, it occurred with astronomical precision according to the calendar, and followed a rich, many-layered symbolism difficult for us scoffing moderns ever to comprehend.

That the Cretans had such a complex calendar should be no surprise—for a people that managed modern plumbing and three-storey apartment blocks, and still found time to rule the seas of the eastern Mediterranean. The real attraction lies not simply in the intricacies of the calendar (the nasty Mesopotamians and many other peoples had equally interesting calendars) but more particularly in the scene in the middle, where the diagonals cross and where the ancient science translates into celebration, into dance. Cretan art speaks to everyone, with a colour, beauty and immediacy never before seen in art, and all too lacking in our own time. No other art of antiquity displays such an irresistible grace and joy, qualities which must have come from a profound appreciation of the beauties and rhythms of nature—the rhythms captured and framed in the ancient calendar.

The Ag. Triáda Sarcophagus

Occupying pride of place in the centre of the upstairs, the Ag. Triáda sarcophagus is the only one in stone ever found on Crete, but what really sets it apart is its layer of plaster painted so elaborately that the sarcophagus probably originally held the remains of a VIP before it was re-used in an insignificant tomb in Ag. Triáda. The subject is a Minoan ritual: on one side a bull is sacrificed, the blood pouring from its neck caught in a vase. A woman makes an offering on an altar, next to a sacred tree with a bird in its branches, the epiphany of the goddess. A man plays a flute as three other women enter in a procession. On the other long side of the sarcophagus, two women on the left are bearing buckets, perhaps of bull's blood, which are emptied into a larger pot between pillars topped by birds and double axes. They are accompanied by a man in female dress, playing a lyre. On the right three men are bearing animals and a model boat, which they offer to an armless, legless figure, either a dead man, wrapped up like a mummy, or an idol or *xoanan*, as worshipped at Archánes. On the narrow sides of the sarcophagus, pairs of women ride in chariots pulled by griffons and a horse.

Priestesses, and man with red face dressed as priestess, bringing offerings to a shrine of the double axes. Ag. Triáda, 14th century BC.

Near the sarcophagus is a fine wooden model of Knossós, and the entrance to the Giamalakis collection (**Room XVII**) containing unique items from all the previous periods, from a finely worked Neolithic goddess, unusually seated in the lotus position, to a model of a round shrine from the Proto-Geometric era. Two figures on the roof peer down through a light-well at the goddess (with uplifted arms), revealed through a detachable door.

Downstairs, products of ancient Crete's last great breath of artistic inspiration, the bold, severe and powerfully moulded 'Daedalic style' from the Archaic period (700–650 BC), are contained in **Rooms XVIII** and **XIX**. Amongst the terracotta votives from Górtyn, note the figure of Athena, with a face like an African mask and a helmet that looks like a fish hook. There is a striking frieze of warriors from a temple at Rizenia (modern Priniás) and lavish votive bronze shields and cymbals, discovered in the Idaean Cave, one showing Zeus holding a lion over his head while the Kouretes bang their shields. The bronze figures of Apollo, Artemis and Leto from the Temple of Apollo at Dreros are other key works in the 'Daedalic style'; the bronze goddesses, mother and daughter, here are reduced to anthropomorphic pillars, their once graceful dancing arms now glued to their sides, their once outlandish hats, jewellery and flounced topless skirts reduced to something approaching a nun's habit. They could be a salt and pepper set. Yet the real anticlimax is reserved for **Room XX**, the Classical Greek and Graeco-Roman periods (5th century BC–4th century AD), when Crete, one of the cradles of the 'Greek miracle', was reduced to an insignificant backwater.

Other Museums

The newest museum in town, the **Battle of Crete and Resistance Museum**, is just behind the archaeology museum on the corner of Doukós Bófor and Hatjidáki Streets (*open most mornings*), with a collection of weapons, photos and uniforms; across the street note the uprooted stacks of Turkish tombstones.

Across town, at 7 Kalokairinoú (near the Xenia Hotel and the ruined Venetian church of St Peter, currently being excavated), you'll find the **Historical Museum of Crete** (*open Mon–Fri, 9.30–4.30, Sat 9.30–2.30, closed Sun and holidays; adm*). Housed in the neoclassical mansion of its founder, Andréas Kalokairinós, this excellent collection picks up the thread where the archaeology museum leaves off, beginning with artefacts from Early Christian times. In the basement you'll find some delightful 18th-century Turkish frescoes of imaginary towns, pretty odds and ends salvaged from Venetian churches, a 12th-century marble well carved with hunting scenes, Venetian and Turkish tombs, coats-of arms, the original carvings from the Loggia, and a delightful Venetian wall fountain made of tiny jutting ships' prows. The ground floor offers a post-Byzantine Almanac of 1690, ships' figureheads, sultans' firmans, portraits of Cretan revolutionaries and their 'Freedom or

Death' flag, a large coin collection, icons and religious items, and excellent 14th-century wall paintings in a chapel setting, from Kardoulianó Pediádos, showing the influences of the naturalistic Macedonian school. Next door, in a little room all to itself, hangs the *Imaginary View of Mount Sinai and the Monastery of St Catherine* (*c.* 1576) by Doménikos Theotokópoulos (El Greco), his only known painting on Crete. It is also one of his few landscapes—in 16th-century Italy and Spain, where he spent the rest of his life, landscapes weren't very marketable—and is still very post-Byzantine and iconographic in style, although the mountains in particular fore-shadow a bit of the magic of his famous *View of Toledo*. On the first floor are photographs of Cretan *kapetános*, each bristling with bigger moustaches and more weapons in his bandolier than the last, a striking contrast with the reconstructed libraries of famous Herákleoniots who lived by the pen, Níkos Kazantzákis and Emmanuél Tsouderós, once prime minister of Greece. Other rooms contain a sumptuous array of traditional arts, in particular the intricate red embroideries and weavings that make up the most noteworthy artistic achievement in Ottoman Crete; some 700 traditional patterns have been counted in all.

The Cathedral and Byzantine Museum

West of Plateía Venizélou, and just south of Kalokerinoú, the overblown cathedral dedicated to Herákleon's patron **Ag. Miná** (1895) dwarfs its convivial little prede-cessor. The interior, capable of holding 5000 parishioners, complete with a special women's section, is pure Byzantine revival, illuminated by an insanely over-decorated chandelier, the domes and vaults frescoed throughout with stern and sad saints and a ferocious Pantocrator; the clock from Smyrna has Arabic numerals, not often seen in a Greek church. Old Ag. Miná has a beautiful gilt iconostasis with fine icons; that of Ag. Minas on his white horse, covered with *tamata*, has long been the protector of Herákleon (Orthodox martyrology claims that Minas was a 3rd century Egyptian soldier, but you can't help wondering if his name had something to do with this special devotion in the old port of Knossós).

Around back, the sun-bleached **Ag. Ekaterína** (1555) was in its day an important school linked to the Monastery of St Catherine in the Sinai. One subject taught here was icon-painting (El Greco studied here before leaving for Venice) and today the church, appropriately, holds a noteworthy **Museum of Byzantine Icons** (*open Mon–Sat 9.30–1; also Tues, Thurs and Fri, 5–7; adm*). The pride of the museum are six icons by Mikális Damaskinós, the 16th-century contemporary of El Greco who also went to Venice but returned to Crete to adorn his motherland with Renaissance-inspired icons; the use of a gold background and Greek letters are the only Byzantine elements in his delightful *Adoration of the Magi*; in his *Last Supper*, Damaskinós set a Byzantine Jesus in a setting copied from an Italian engraving—a rather bizarre effect further hampered by the fact that Christ seems to be holding a hamburger.

The Venetian Walls and the Tomb of Kazantzákis

Michele Sammicheli, the greatest military architect of the 16th century, designed Candia's walls so well that it took the Turks 21 years, from 1648 to 1669, to breach them. From the beginning the Venetians tried to rally Europe to the cause of defending Candia as the last Christian outpost in the east, but only got occasional, ineffectual aid from the French. Stalemate characterized the first 18 years of the siege; the Sultan found it so frustrating that he banned the mention of Candia in his presence. In 1667, both sides, keen to end the siege, sent in their most brilliant generals, the Venetian Francesco Morosini (uncle of the Francesco Morosini who blew the top off the Parthenon) and the Turk Köprülü. The arrival of the latter outside the walls of Herákleon with 40,000 fresh troops finally nudged the Europeans and the Holy Roman Emperor to action, but they arrived only to quarrel, and their fresh troops and supplies were all too little, too late. Seeing that his men could only hold out a few more days, Morosini carefully negotiated the city's surrender on 5 September, and with 20 days of safe conduct sailed away with nearly all the Christian inhabitants (many ended up on the Ionian Islands) and the city's archives, a result bought with the lives of 30,000 Christians and 137,000 Turks.

Brilliantly restored, Sammicheli's massive walls surrounding the historic centre are nearly as vexing to get on top of today as they were for the besieging Turks— 4000m in their total length, in places 14m thick, with 12 fort-like bastions. Tunnels have been pierced through the old gates, although the **Chaniá Gate** at the end of Kalokairinoú preserves much of its original appearance. From Plastirá Street, a side street leads up to the Martinengo Bastion and the simple **tomb of Níkos Kazantzákis**. Herákleon's great writer, who died in 1957, chose his own epitaph: 'I believe in nothing, I hope for nothing, I am free.' Sometimes you'll see offerings of fruit, which he requested just before he died; the pious have erected a simple wooden cross. In the distance you can see Mount Júktas (*see* below).

Knossós (ΚΝΩΣΟΣ)

Every 10 minutes a city bus (no.2) departs from Herákleon's main bus station for Knossós with a stop in Plateía Venizélou. The site is open daily except for important holidays, 8–7 (8–5 in winter); adm exp. To avoid the crowds, arrive as the gate opens, or come late in the day. The free car park fills up fast, but private ones have opened up along the road.

The weird dream image has come down through the ages: Knossós, the House of the Double Axe, the Labyrinth of King Minos. The audacious bull dances, its secret mysteries and Jungian archetypes evoke a deep, mythopœic resonance that few places in Europe can equal. Thanks in good part to Arthur Evans' imaginative if controversial reconstructions, brightly painted in primary colours and rising up two storeys against the hill-girded plain, Knossós has become the second most visited place in Greece after the Acropolis, with nearly a million admissions a year. These days Evans' concrete reconstructions are themselves historical monuments, and most of the work you'll see on the site is reconstructions of reconstructions. The tall cypresses and views of the dry jagged limestone hills and olive groves to the east, and vineyards to the south make Knossós something of a garden ruin.

History

The first Neolithic houses on the hill next to the river Kairatos, a stream perhaps navigable until Classical times, date from the 7th millennium BC, or perhaps earlier; few Neolithic sites in Europe lay so deeply embedded in the earth. In the 3rd millennium, an important Early Minoan or Pre-Palace settlement was built over the Neolithic houses, and *c.* 1950 BC the first palace (or temple) on Crete was erected on top. It collapsed in the earthquake of 1700. A new, even grander palace, the Labyrinth, was built on its ruins. 'Labyrinth' seems to derive from *labrys*, or 'Double Axe', a potent symbol that suggests the killing of both the victim and slayer; you'll seem them etched in the pillars and walls throughout Knossós. For the next three centuries or so new buildings went up all over the outskirts of Knossós; vast cemeteries, stretching all the way to Herákleon's modern cemetery of Ag. Konstantínos, attest to a considerable population. In 1450 BC (give or take a century or two) Knossós was again destroyed by a cataclysmic fire but, unlike the other Minoan palaces, it was repaired once more, probably by Mycenaeans, and survived at least until 1380 BC. After a final destruction, the site of the Labyrinth was never built on again; it was considered evil, cursed in some way. Evans noted at the beginnings of his excavations that the guardians he hired to watch the site heard ghosts moaning in the night.

In the Geometric era, a community near Knossós adopted its name. By the 3rd century BC this new Knossós became one of the leading cities of Crete, although following a war with Lyttos it lost its supremacy to Górtyn. The Romans built a large city in the area that survived until the early Byzantine period. For a while there was even a bishop of Knossós. Meanwhile the ruined palace was slowly buried, but not forgotten; unlike Troy and Mycenae, the site was always known. Cretans would go there to gather what they called *galopetres*—'milkstones'—Minoan sealstones, which nursing mothers prized as amulets to increase their milk.

The Labyrinth lay quietly under the dust of centuries until the great German entrepreneur and self-made archaeologist Heinrich Schliemann's excavations of Troy and Mycenae electrified the world. In 1878, in the general enthusiasm, a merchant from Herákleon, appropriately named Mínos Kalokairinós, dug the first trenches into the palace of his namesake, at once finding walls, enormous *pithoi* and the first Linear B tablet. Schliemann himself heard the news and in 1882, when he met a young

Reconstruction of the State Apartments on the west side of the Central Court. On the right is the entrance to the Throne Room; next to it is the stepped porch leading up to the Central Hall; and next to this (with the crenellated roof) is the principal shrine of the palace.

English Classics scholar named Arthur Evans, he confided his plans to excavate Knossós one day. Five years later Schliemann arrived on Crete and negotiated the purchase of the Knossós site, but the Turkish owners were impossible to deal with and asked for too much money. He left in despair, and in 1890 he died.

The field thus cleared, Evans, by then curator of the Ashmolean Museum in Oxford, arrived in Crete in 1894. A keen student of early forms of writing, he was particularly fascinated by the mysterious alphabetic and pictographic signs on Cretan seal stones, and on the Linear B tablet shown him by Mínos Kalokairinós. With dogged persistence, he spent the next five years purchasing the property with the help of Cretan archaeologist Joseph Hadzadákis, while sending home reports of Turkish oppression. The purchase of Knossós coincided happily with Cretan independence, and in 23 March 1900 Evans received permission to begin excavations in concert with the British School at Athens. Of the workmen hired, Evans insisted that half be Greek and half Turk as a symbol of co-operation for the newly independent Crete. Within the first three weeks the throne room had been excavated, along with fresco fragments and the first Linear A tablets, apparently belonging to a civilization that predated the Mycenaeans, which Evans labelled 'Minoan' for ever after.

When his father and uncle died in 1908, Evans used his considerable inheritance to embark on a project he had dreamed of from the beginning, to 'reconstitute' part of

Minos' palace. Scholars tend to dispute the wisdom and accuracy of these reconstructions, sniffing at them as if they were an archaeological Disneyland; they disagree perhaps even more on the purposes and names Evans assigned the different rooms of the palace, along with his interpretation of the Minoans as peaceful flower-loving sophisticates. Evans' queen's bathroom, for instance, is another man's basin where dead bodies were pickled before mummification. At the end of the day, no single conjecture seems to cover all the physical evidence, all the myths; the true meaning and use of Knossós may only lie in an epiphany of the imagination. The Cretans of 4000 years ago saw a different world through different eyes.

The Site

Despite the controversy, Evans' reconstructions result from guesses as good as anyone else's and succeed in his goal of making Knossós come alive for the casual visitor, evoking the grandeur of a 1500-room Minoan palace of *c.* 1700 BC that none of the unreconstructed sites can match; a visit here first will make Phaistós and Mália easier to understand. Detailed guides are on sale, but tours go through so frequently that it's easy to tag along or overhear the explanations as you follow the maze. The first stop is the **Bust of Evans**, erected by the British School and unveiled in 1935, occasioning Evans' last visit to Knossós.

Unlike most of their ancient contemporaries, the Minoans oriented their palaces to the west, not east, and the modern entrance is still by way of the **West Court.** The three large holes were grain silos, originally protected by domes; latter residents used them for rubbish. A porch on the right from the West Court leads to the **Corridor of the Procession**, named for the fresco in the Herákleon museum, and the partially restored **Propylon**, or south entrance, with reproductions of original frescoes on the wall. A staircase from the Propylon leads to an upper floor, which Evans, inspired by Venetian palaces, called the '**Piano Nobile**'. Of all his reconstructions, this is considered the most fanciful. The **Tripartite Shrine**, with its three columns, is a typical feature of Minoan palaces, and may have been used to worship the Goddess in her three aspects of mistress of heaven, earth and the underworld.

A narrower staircase descends to the **Central Court**, measuring 60 by 30m. Originally this was closed in by tall buildings, which may have provided, among other things, safe seats to view the bull leaping (but how did they lead bulls in through the Labyrinth? How could they squeeze in all the action? It seems more likely that the Central Court would have been 'Ariadne's dancing floor'). The monumental sacral horns that decorate the cornices and altars are perhaps the most universal Minoan religious and decorative symbol. It probably had multiple levels of meaning; in one Minoan picture, there's a bull with a double axe between its horns. Knossós was thickly littered with sacral horns of all sizes (one pair, found in fragments, was originally over a metre high).

Knossós

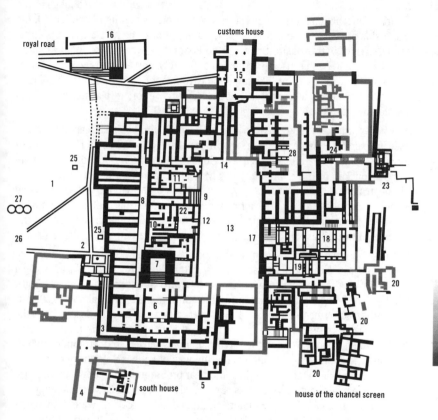

royal road

customs house

16

15

25

1

27

26

25

2

8

10

11

22

12

9

7

6

3

4

south house

5

14

28

24

23

13

17

18

19

20

20

20

house of the chancel screen

1 West Court	11 Throne Room	21 north lustral basin
2 west porch	12 Tripartite Shrine	22 temple repositories
3 Corridor of the Procession	13 Central Court	23 east bastion
4 stepped porch	14 north entrance passage	24 store rooms of giant *pithoi*
5 south entrance	15 North Pillar Hall	25 altar
6 south Propylon	16 theatre	26 bust of Arthur Evans
7 Grand Stair	17 Grand Staircase	27 storage silos
8 store room corridor	18 Hall of the Double Axes	28 Corridor of the Draughtboard
9 stair	19 Queen's Megaron	
10 pillar crypts	20 southeast house	

From here, enter the lower levels of the West Wing, site of the surprisingly tiny **Throne Room**, where Evans uncovered a scallop-edged stone throne in the same place as it stood 3800 years ago. Unfortunately, wear and tear by so many visitors has made it necessary to block off the room so that you can no longer sit where Minos—or a Minoan priestess—supposedly sat (although if you're a judge of the Court of International Justice in The Hague you may sit on its reproduction). On either side are gypsum benches and frescoes of griffons, the heraldic escorts of the goddess. The **Lustral Basin** in the Throne Room, like others throughout Knossós, may have held water used in rituals, or merely served to reflect light that descended in light wells into the rather poky rooms, or perhaps both. Evans found evidence here of what appeared to be a last-ditch effort to placate the gods as disaster swept through Knossós.

The stair south of the antechamber of the Throne Room ascends to an upper floor, used in part for storage, as in the **Room of the Tall *Pithos*** and the **Temple Repositories**, where the famous Snake Goddess statuette was found. Note the pillars that thicken near the top, unique to Minoan architecture and distinctly similar to the trunk of the 'horizontal' cypress native to the Gorge of Samariá. The Minoans may have hoped the form would make the palace more earthquake-resistant. Returning to the Central Court, note the high relief fresco copy of the '**Prince of the Lilies**' to the south, at the end of the Corridor of the Procession.

Evans, who grew up taking monarchies for granted, had no doubt that the more elaborate **East Wing** of the palace contained the 'Royal Apartments' (undergoing restoration at the time of writing). Here the **Grand Staircase** and **Central Light Well** are the Minoans' most dazzling architectural *tour de force*; almost five flights of broad gypsum steps are preserved. However, when you actually descend into the two lower floors (which were found intact) it is hard to imagine that any royal family would choose to have their living quarters buried so deep, under two or possible three other storeys, with little in the way of light and air, in spite of all the Minoans' clever architectural devices; the near proximity of the 'Royal Workshops' would have made them awfully noisy as well. The rooms did have something that modern royals couldn't live without: plumbing. The excellent water and sewer system that supplied Knossós is visible under the floor in the **Queen's Megaron** and its bathroom, complete with a fill-up bucket and flush toilet—an amenity that Versailles could scarcely manage. The King's Megaron, also known as **Hall of the Double Axes**, for the many carvings of the symbol on the walls, opens on to the **Hall of the Royal Guard**, decorated with a copy of the fresco of the large, cowhide figure-of-eight shields.

North of the royal apartments, the long **Corridor of the Draughtboard** is where the superb game-board in the Herákleon Museum was found and where you can see the clay pipes used to bring in water from the Mount Júktas aqueduct. The

Magazines of Giant *Pithoi* irresistibly bring to mind the strange old myth of Minos' young son Glaukos. While wandering in the Labyrinth, the boy climbed up into a large *pithos* of honey to steal a taste, but fell in and drowned. The anxious father eventually located his body thanks to his prophet Polyidos. In grief, Minos locked Polyidos in a room with Glaukos' body and ordered him to bring the boy back to life. As Polyidos despaired, a snake came out of a hole in the wall. He killed it, and then watched in amazement as another snake appeared with a herb in its mouth, which it rubbed against its dead friend and brought it back to life. Polyidos tried the same on Glaukos and revived the boy, but Minos, rather than reward Polyidos, ordered him to teach Glaukos the art of prophecy. Polyidos had to obey, but as he sailed away from Crete, he told the boy to spit in his mouth, so that he forgot everything he had learned.

As you leave through the north, there's a relief copy of the bull fresco, and near this the so-called **Customs House**, supported by eight pillars, which may have been used for processing imports and exports. Below is the oldest paved road in Europe, or **Royal Road**, lined with various buildings and ending abruptly at the modern road; originally it continued to the Little Palace and beyond. The road ends at the so-called **Theatre** (it looks more like a large stairway) where 500 people could sit to view religious processions or dances, as pictured in the frescoes.

Around Knossós

Some highly intriguing Minoan buildings have been and continue to be excavated outside the palace. Nearest to the palace are the reconstructed three-storey **South House**, complete with a bathroom and latrine, the **Southeast House**, and the **House of the Chancel Screen**, both believed to have been the residences of VIPs—the latter has a dais for a throne or altar. Other constructions, outside the palace grounds, require special permission to visit, such as the **Royal Villa**, with its throne and beautifully preserved Pillar Crypt, where channels and two depressions around the square pillar received libations to the god. The **Little Palace**, just across the modern Herákleon road, had three pillar crypts and was used after the Minoans as a shrine; the magnificent bull's head rhyton was found here.

To the south, a sign on the main road points the way to the **Caravanserai**, as Evans named it, believing weary travellers would pause here to wash the dust from their feet in the stone trough. The walls have a copy of the lovely partridge fresco. Further south are four pillars of the Minoan aqueduct that carried water over a stream, and south of that the unique **Royal Temple Tomb**, where the natural rock ceiling was painted blue and a stair leads up to a temple on top. One especially controversial find was Peter Warren's 1980 unearthing of the **House of the Sacrificed Children**, 100m from the Little Palace, a typical Minoan house that was found to contain a large cache of children's bones bearing the marks of knives, as if they had been carved up for supper. The Minoans, just having been found guilty of human sacrifice in the Anemospilia shrine at Archánes (*see* pp.185–6), now had cannibalism to answer for. Many historians now believe that the children had already died, and their bodies were in the process of being stripped of any last flesh before re-burial—a custom that survived in parts of Greece into the 19th century.

Lastly, you can pay your respects to the exterior of the **Villa Ariadne**, the house that Evans built for himself; it is set back in a garden just up the road to Herákleon (take the first left). After the Battle of Crete, it was selected by General Kreipe as his headquarters, and it later saw the signing of the German surrender on Crete.

Beaches around Herákleon

Herákleon is surrounded by sand, and you have the choice of backdrops for your beach idyll: a power plant, cement works, and lots of hotels and apartments at **Ammoudára** (ΑΜΜΟΥΔΑΡΑ), just west, frequently linked by bus no.6 from Hotel Astoria in Plateía Eleftherías, and to the east, the airport—from the same Hotel Astoria, bus no.1 crawls through the suburbs of Póros and Néa Alikárnassos (populated by refugees from Asia Minor) to the not exceptionally attractive city beach of Kraterós (7km) and beyond to **Amnisós** (ΑΜΝΙΣΟΣ), the first of the long string of resorts east of Herákleon. It overlooks the islet of Día, the island of Zeus, which played a role in Minoan religion: in the oldest known version of the Ariadne story she was kidnapped from Knossós, brought to Día and killed. Today the island is a sanctuary for Crete's endangered ibexes, or *kri kri,* who somehow have learned to cope with charter flights swooping overhead every five minutes.

But Amnisós has been a busy place since Neolithic times. A port of Knossós, it was from here that Idomeneus and his 90 ships sailed for Troy; here the ship of Odysseus, in the story he told Penelope, was long prevented from sailing by the north wind. The Minoans must have often encountered the same problem, and would get around it by loading and unloading at a south-facing port on Día. Minoan Amnisós had two harbours, on either side of a hard-scrabble hill topped by the ruins of a Venetian village. The east end is the fenced-off villa of 1600 BC that yielded the lovely *Fresco of the Lilies* in the Herákleon museum; on the northwest side is an Archaic sanctuary of Zeus Thenatas. In the 1930s, while excavating Amnisós' Minoan 'Harbour Master's Office', Spyridon Marinátos discovered a layer of pumice, the physical evidence he needed to support his theory that Minoan civilization had been devastated in its prime by ash flung from Santoríni's explosion.

One kilometre from Amnisós, up the road to Elia, is the atmospheric **Cave of Eileithyia**, goddess of fertility and childbirth, daughter of Zeus and Hera and mother of Eros (get the caretaker's address at the Herákleon tourist office). Few ancient divinities enjoyed Eileithyia's staying power. Her cave, which was also mentioned by Homer, attracted women far and wide from the Neolithic era to the 5th century AD. Stalagmites, resembling a mother and her children (the latter are rather hard to make out) were the main focus of worship; pregnant women would rub their bellies against a third one, resembling a pregnant belly complete with a naval. The rock-cut platform at the cave's mouth, the Square of the Altars, is named for the large cubes of living rock that may have been used in ancient ceremonies.

Herákleon ℰ (081–) — *Shopping*

The market along Odós 1866 is a good bet for edible souvenirs and spices, and all kinds of typical tourist claptrap. For Cretan and other Greek wines, the **Kava Cellar**, 3 Daedálou, ℰ 243 506, is a mine of bottles and information. Pedestrian-only Daedálou and its surroundings have most of the city's boutiques, some more touristy than others. **Cretaphone**, 6–10 Odós 1821, has a wide choice of old and new Cretan music. For books in English, **Planet International** has the widest choice on Crete, at the corner of Kydonias and Chándakos. Or try **Astrakianakis**, on Platéia El. Venizélou.

Herákleon ℰ (081–) — *Where to Stay*

Do book ahead in the summer. If you haven't and can't find a place to stay in Herákleon, try the **Hotel Managers' Union**, Idomenous and Malikoúti, ℰ 223 967, or the **Association of Room Renters**, 1 Yamaláki, ℰ 224 260.

expensive

Atlantis Hotel, near the museum at Mirabélou and Ighías, ℰ 229 103, ℮ 226 265, is an imposing A class hotel with a pool, satellite TV, roof garden and nearly everything else you could want (including a garage). The **Galaxy**, just outside the walls to the southeast at 67 Demokratías, ℰ 238 812, ℮ 211 211 (A) offers contemporary serenity and full air-conditioning; ask for a room overlooking the pool and sun terrace. **Atrion**, 9 K. Paleológou, ℰ 229 225, ℮ 223 292 (B) is relatively new, moderate-sized and air-conditioned, with a garden, patio, and underground garage. Then there are plush resort hotels on the beaches on either side of the city. To the east in Amnisós, the **Minoa Palace**, ℰ 227 802, ℮ 227 868 (A) is a big fancy beachside complex with a pool, floodlit tennis court, and a score of activities and sports for all ages. *Open April–Oct.* West in Ammoudára, **Agapi Beach**, ℰ 250 502, ℮ 250 731 (A) and the huge **Dophin Bay**, ℰ 821 276 (A) have similar resort facilities in garden settings.

moderate

Pension Ilaria, on Epimenídou, ℰ 227 103 (B) is conveniently located on a fairly quiet street near the port, and has a roof garden; **Hotel Lato**, on the same street, ℰ 228 103 (B) has modern rooms short on character, although all have balconies and some have sea views. **Hotel Daedalos**, Daedálou Street, ✆ 224 391 (*C*) is convenient for the archaeological museum and other sights in the central city, yet located on the quiet (well, traffic-free) pedestrian-only street. Paintings by local artists are in the lobby, but otherwise it's plain and modern. Less expensive, **Atlas Pension**, 6 Kandanoléontos, ✆ 288 989 (*C*) offers a touch of streamlined Art Deco on a pedestrian-only street near the centre, although the rooms don't all live up to the promise of the exterior. *Open April–Oct.*

inexpensive

Hotel Rea, 1 Kalimeráki, ✆ 223 638 (*D*) is one of the most pleasant cheap choices, near the sea and quiet. The **youth hostel** at 5 Víronos, ✆ 286 281, is well run and convenient, with usually a dorm bed to spare. **Yours Hostel**, 24 Chandáka, ✆ 280 858, in the old youth hostel building, has all sorts of accommodation available at low prices. **Lena**, ✆ 223 280 (*E*), has clean rooms on a quiet street. **Hotel Hellas**, 11 Kandanoléontos, ✆ 225 121, is pleasant, friendly and has a courtyard. **Idaeon Andron**, behind the Venetian Loggia, on 1 Perdikári, ✆ 281 795, has pleasant small rooms and a tiny courtyard. **Camping Herákleon,** 5km west of town on Ammoudára beach, ✆ 250 986 is a large A-class campsite with all modern facilities.

Herákleon ✆ *(081–)* **Eating Out**

Trendies in Herákleon have created a quiet, car-free haven for themselves in the narrow streets between Daedálou and Ag. Títou; buildings have been cleaned up and restored, and the city's most charming little restaurants, pizzerias and bars appeared on cue to fill them up. Prices are a bit over the odds, but the food is better too, in places like **Loukoulous**, on Koráli, an elegant Italian restaurant with a real pizza oven (*around 4000dr, less for pizza*) and **Giovanni** in the same street, which offers a variety of fixed-price menus for two fish, traditional Greek or vegetarian with wine (*between 5000–5500dr*). **Vizandio**, on Byzándio and Daedálou, ✆ 244 775, may look a bit touristy but has delicious Greek food. The **New Chinese Restaurant** is here as well, with garden dining on the terrace (*around 5000dr*). Not far away, the **Curry House** near Daedálou off Perdikári, ✆ 224 274, features several curry specialities daily (*around 3000dr*). The ten or so tavernas jammed along the narrow confines of Fotíou ('Dirty') Lane between Odós 1866 (the market street) and Evans Street are a favourite place to dine, all offering basic Greek cuisine and grilled meats at moderate prices (*2500–3500dr for dinner*); **Ionia** on Evans claims to be the oldest taverna in town. The attractive restaurants around the Morosini fountain are a tourist rip-off, where the waiters compete aggressively for the custom of passers-by; for a reasonable 3000dr you'll do better in the brasher, bigger environs of Plateía Eleftherías (**Doré** is one of the better bets). For a big night out, **La Tavola** in the Galaxy hotel (*see* p.181) prepares some of the finest food in Herákleon, but count on up to 5000dr a head. If you've a hankering for fish, **Ippokampos** on Sófokli Venizélou has the best, and the long-established **Ta Psaria** at the foot of 25 Avgoústou Street has the day's catch at reasonable prices and there's seating outside, overlooking the Venetian harbour. Out west in Ammoudára, **Petroussas** on the main drag serves excellent Greek food, while **Bataza** has a reputation as an authentic taverna.

Herákleon ℭ (081–)   **Entertainment and Nightlife**

When the Herákleoniots want to spend a night on the town, they usually leave it; the clubs and discos west of the city are especially popular with young boppers. If you'd rather stay in town, keep a look out for posters; Herákleon attracts numerous Greek and a few foreign groups on the concert circuit. In the summer occasional performances happen in the **Rocco al Mare** citadel on the Venetian Harbour, itself a favourite place for an evening *vólta*, or stroll. Popular bars are concentrated around Plateía Venizélou, El Greco Park and Chándakos. There's good food and even better Cretan music and dancing between the Archaeology Museum and bus station at the **Kastro**, on Doúkos Bofor. There's often live *rembétika* music at the **Taverna I Palia Argli** at the end of Theríssou, ℭ 252 600, and on Tuesday, Thursday and Friday at **Café Amalia**, 37 Idomeneos near the Archaeology Museum, ℭ 226 146. For quiet backgammon and drinks head for the **Ideion Andron**. Music bars in town include the **Finale Club**, 73 Demokratias, ℭ 236 636, or trendy **Apan** in Odós Ag. Titos. Out on the road to Knossós, **Ariadne** and **Castello** hosts big bouzoúki/Cretan music and dance evenings.

South of Knossós: Archánes and Myrtiá

One of the ancient proofs of Epimenides' paradox 'All Cretans are liars' was the fact that Zeus the immortal was born on Crete, and buried there as well, the profile of his bearded face easily discerned in the lines of Mount Júktas, visible on the main road south of Knossós. This road was a main Minoan thoroughfare, and saw some modern history as well: at the T-junction turn-off for Archánes, a band of Cretan Resistance fighters, led by Major Patrick Leigh Fermor and Captain W. Stanley Moss, dressed in Gestapo uniforms and kidnapped General Kreipe on 26 April 1944 as he was being driven from Archánes headquarters to his residence at Villa Ariadne. The General was marched up to Anógia on the slopes of Mount Ida, while the car was abandoned on Panormos beach with a note saying that it was the work of English commandos and that any civilian reprisals would be against international law. But the Germans were convinced that the General was still on Crete and launched a massive search for him (*see* Captain Moss' *Ill Met by Moonlight*).

Well-watered **Archánes** (ΑΡΧΑΝΕΣ; hourly bus departures from Herákleon) has often been called on to supply the north; the Minoan aqueduct to Knossós began here, as did the Venetian, ending in Morosini's fountain in Herákleon, as did the Egyptian, an impressive work built in the 1830s that still humps across the road south of Knossós. Besides water, Archánes has long been a major producer of wine (Archánes and Armanti) and table grapes called *rozáki*, which are trained on high wooden supports. In the centre of town, the church of the **Panagía** has a bell tower decorated with stone heads and an exceptional collection of 16th–19th-century icons amassed by the parish priest (*open mornings*). Just south of town, the lovely church of the **Asómatos** (the Bodiless One: an Orthodox attribute for St Michael) is decorated with fine frescoes donated by Michael Patsidiotis, dated 1315: *The Battle of Jericho*, *The Sacrifice of Abraham* and the *Punishment of the Damned* are especially good.

From the 15th century on, visitors would come up to Archánes, intrigued by the story of Zeus' tomb, but the first hint that there was something more than stories had to wait until the early 1900s, when a fine alabaster ladle inscribed with Linear A was found on the outskirts of town. In 1922 Evans noted the 'palatial character' of walls uncovered on a construction site and surmised the existence of a 'summer palace' in Archánes. Then, in 1964, Ioánnis and Éfi Sakellarákis began excavating what was to become, after Zákros, the biggest Minoan discovery since the war.

The **palace**, rather unfortunately for the archaeologists, is in the dead centre of the modern village, on a site inhabited continuously since 2000 BC, limiting the area they could attack with their spades. The largest visible section of the palace is between the modern buildings along Mákri Sokáki and Ierolóchiton Streets. Dating from the New Palace period (*c.* 1700–1450), some of the walls have been preserved up to 6ft in height and are very thick, to support one or more storeys; only in Knossós and Phaistós were similar coloured marbles, gypsum and other luxury materials used. It had elaborate frescoes, a drainage system and a large cistern built over a spring (a skull found here may belong to a victim of the earthquake that knocked down the palace). A 'theatrical area', with raised walkways forming the usual triangle, a small exedra and Horns of Consecration were found near the church of Ag. Nikólaos; an archive yielding Linear A tablets was unearthed along Kapetanáki Street and covered up again. Some of the finds are in the **archaeology museum** nearby (*supposedly open 8.30–2.30, closed Tues*).

The most important Minoan sites around Archánes—the necropolis at Phourní, the temple at Anemospiliá and the villa at Vathýpetro—are (again, supposedly) open Tues–Sun 8–2.30 but it doesn't hurt to ring ahead (© (081) 751 907) or confirm at the tourist office in Herákleon. In Minoan times, a paved road from the palace led to the **necropolis of Phourní**, set atop a rocky ridge, 1.5km to the southwest (a very steep walk up from the road; by car you can take the rural road up from Káto Archánes). This five-acre site has proved one of the most important prehistoric cemeteries in the whole Aegean, in use for 1250 years (2500–1250 BC). Most spectacular of all are the three *tholos* tombs, especially Tholos A, that was long used as a farmer's hut and as a hiding place in the Second World War. Debris and rocks (and a Venetian coin, apparently left by someone hunting for the grave of Zeus) filled the bottom floor, while below, tucked in a side chamber behind a false wall, lay a priestess or royal lady from the 14th century BC, buried in an ankle-length gold-trimmed garment and surrounded by her grave offerings: 140 pieces of gold and ivory jewellery, a footstool elaborately decorated with ivory and the remains of a sacrificed horse and bull, carefully carved into ritualistic bits. The *dromos* leading to the entrance is the longest on Crete. The bottom layer of the collective burials in Tholos C go back to 2500 BC and yielded a large cache of marble Cycladic figurines and jewellery in the same style as the Treasure of Priam that Schliemann found at Troy. The Mycenaean Grave enclosure with seven shaft tombs and three *stelae* is unique on Crete. Its libation pit or *bothros* had been so saturated with various liquid offerings to the dead thousands of years ago that when the Sakellarákis team dug down into it they were overwhelmed by 'the unbearable stench'.

The Bloodstained Shrine of Anemospiliá

5km southwest of Archánes, above the town dump, on the panoramic, windswept promontory of **Anemospiliá**, the Sakellarákises discovered an isolated tripartite shrine in 1979. Often depicted in Minoan art, this was the first and, so far, the only one ever found. In the middle room, the most interesting discovery was a pair of large clay feet from a *xoanon,* or idol made from wood and other perishable materials worshipped in Greece since Neolithic times; according to Pausanius, the Greeks believed they were first made by Daedalos on Crete. The eastern room was apparently used for bloodless sacrifices. The western room, however, produced one of the most startling and controversial finds in nearly a century of Minoan archaeology: it contained three bodies of people caught in the sanctuary as the massive earthquake struck c. 1700 BC. The skeleton of a 17-year-old boy was found bound on an altar, next to a dagger; the account from the Medical School of the University of Manchester (which has made a speciality out of doing coroner's reports on prehistoric stiffs) shows that the blood had been drained from his upper body, and that he had probably had his throat cut. The other skeletons belonged to a man wearing a ring of (then rare) iron, and a woman who carried sickle cell anaemia: people of fine breeding, according to Manchester, perhaps the priest and priestess. A fourth skeleton, of indeterminate sex, was caught by the falling masonry in the antechamber. A precious Kamáres ware vase was found near the body; it may have been full of the boy's blood, an offering with which the Minoans attempted to appease their furious god, possibly Poseidon, the Earth-shaker.

The gruesome findings came as a shock to the field of Minoan studies. The graceful, arty people evoked by Evans seemed too sophisticated for such barbarities, despite hints of human sacrifice in Cretan mythology—besides the tribute of Athenian youths to the Minotaur, another account tells how the Cretan sage Epimenides went to Athens to deliver the city from the curse of Kylon, which he did through human sacrifices. But such extreme acts were probably only resorted to in extraordinary situations, where the sacrifice of one is made in the hope of saving many, in this case from violent earth tremors. Even then, the practice was so disagreeable it was not done in public, but hidden behind the doors of the shrine.

Vathýpetro and Mount Júktas

Two kilometres south of Archánes, just off the main road, a short path leads through the vines to the villa complex of **Vathýpetro,** spectactularly set high on a spur facing Mount Júktas over a rolling patchwork of olives and vineyards. In plan it resembles a two-storey baby Knossós: it has a small west court and larger central court, a tripartite shrine, and a three-columned portico with a small courtyard to its east, closed off by a fancy structure found nowhere else, recessed in the centre and supported by symmetrical square plinths. First built *c.* 1580 BC, Vathýpetro was shattered, probably by an earthquake, *c.* 1550. It seems to have been rebuilt as a rural craft centre; clay loom weights and potters' wheels were found, along with the oldest known wine press in Greece. The cool cellar rooms suggest that the Minoans were already sophisticated winemakers 3500 years ago.

To this day the vintners in the area repeat a ritual that may well be as old as Vathýpetro itself: every 6 August the first fruits of the harvest are ritually offered to the deity on the summit of 811m **Mount Júktas**, in the most important *panegýri* on the local calendar. A good road just before Vathýpetro leads up to the summit and the church where it all happens, the Christian replacement for the Minoan peak sanctuary of **Psilí Korfí** just to the north. This has yielded large quantities of votive gifts and bronze double axes. A young Poseidon was one of the gods worshipped here; the mountain was an important navigational landmark.

The broad road south of Vathýpetro continues to **Ag. Vasílios** and **Moní Spiliótissa**, a convent with a frescoed church built into a dim cave, hidden in a lush grove of plane trees; the spring water bubbling out of its foundations was known for its curative properties and was piped into Herákleon by the pashas. It's a pretty walk of a few hundred yards to the simple church of Ag. Ioánnis, with frescoes dated 1291, 'in the reign of Andronicus Palaeologue' as the dedication states. Just south of here a dirt road to the west allows you to circle back to the north around the back of Mount Júktas by way of **Kanlí Kastélli**, or the Bloody Fortress, built by Niképhoros Phókas when he liberated Crete from the Saracens in 961.

Myrtiá and Níkos Kazantzákis

Alternatively, and just as scenically, you could circle back from Ag. Vasílios to Herákleon to the east, by way of Crete's most prestigious wine region, **Pezá,** and the winemaking village of **Myrtiá,** set high on a ridge over a majestic sweeping landscape of vineyards. If you're coming from Herákleon, the turn-off is just before the road to Archánes. Besides the views, the main reason to visit Myrtiá is the **Kazantzákis Museum** (*open Mar–Oct daily exc Thurs, 9–1; also Mon, Wed, Sat and Sun afternoons 4–8; Nov–Feb Sundays only 9–2; adm*), in the house where Kazantzákis' father was born; photos, documents, dioramas, and memorabilia evoke the life and travels of Crete's greatest novelist.

The Father of Zorba

Born in Herákleon in 1883, Níkos Kazantzákis was the son of Captain Michelis, a storekeeper and revolutionary, and grandson of a Saracen pirate (the old name of Myrtiá was Varvari, 'barbarians', because of the many Saracens who settled here). One of Kazantzákis' first memories was that of his father lifting him up to the gallows to kiss the feet of Cretan rebels hanged by the Turks. Although Níkos paid tribute to his father in one of his best novels, *Freedom or Death* (called *Kapetanos Michelis* in Greek), his Cretan fighting spirit expressed itself in a lifelong battle of ideas, leaving him ultimately unclassifiable; like Epimenides the Cretan Sage he relished paradox, and the Minoan double axe was the symbol on his letterhead. He seemed to fit several lifetimes into his 74 years, intellectually flirting with Nietzsche, Lenin, Bergson, Christ, St Francis, Buddha and Homer while his travels took him around the world: he served in the Greek Ministry of Education, in the Balkan Wars, and helped resettle Greek refugees from the Caucasus in 1919; in the 20s he was involved in illegal Communist activities. He translated everything from the *Iliad* to the *Petit Larousse* into modern Greek, wrote incisive travel critiques on Spain, Russia, China and England, and began the work that he considered his masterpiece, the *Odyssey,* 33,333 verses long. The public, however (as the various translations in the museum show) has always preferred his novel inspired by a Macedonian miner and skirt-chaser named George Zorbas, with whom Kazantzákis operated a lignite mine in the Mani during the First World War.

In 1930 he went on trial for atheism, and was later excommunicated from the Orthodox church. Kazantzákis spent the last ten years of his life in Antibes; perhaps like fellow Cretan Míkis Theodorákis, who lives in Paris, he found it easier to imagine and be inspired by Crete when he was far away.

During this period he wrote the *Fraticides*, *Freedom or Death*, his semi-autobiographical *Report to Greco*, and the controversial *The Last Temptation of Christ,* which made the Pope's Index when it was published in 1954, causing a furore similar to the one provoked by Martin Scorsese's film of the novel a few years ago. Kazantzákis was 74 when he was nominated one last time for the Nobel Prize for Literature (the Church actively lobbied against him, and he lost by one vote to Albert Camus) and he died shortly after, in October 1957 from hepatitis, contracted from a vaccination needle. Note the photos of his funeral in Herákleon, attended by a young Constantine Mitsotákis and George Papandréou, Socialist Prime Minister (and father of Andreas), and throngs of other dignitaries. The Church sent only one priest, at the insistence of the government —normally a hundred or so would officiate at the funeral of a great man—but forbade him to say any prayers.

If nothing else, Kazantzákis was the ultimate Cretan writer, whose writings powerfully evoked the island's fierce spirit of independence, its love of freedom, and its spiritual preoccupations, its capacity to create and kill its own gods. 'There is something in Crete like a flame,' he wrote. 'Call it a soul, something beyond death that isn't easy to define, made of pride, stubbornness, valour, disdain, and of that inexpressible, immeasurable element that makes you happy to be a Cretan.' In his best writing he re-enchants day-to-day existence, his philosophy compressed in the character of Zorba, who never loses his wonder at life and lives as if there were no tomorrow. In his *Odyssey*, his Odysseus tells of the ultimate goal, of being 'delivered from deliverance'; for Kazantzákis it isn't God who saves humanity, but humanity which must save God.

---

② (081–) **Where to Stay and Eating Out**

In Archánes, **Orestes Rent Rooms**, ② 751 619, are simple and just out of the centre; in the main square, **Myriofyto** offers light lunches under the trees; there are two other tavernas as well, and another up at Myrtía.

Southwest of Herákleon

The main road southwest of Herákleon to Górtyn, Phaistós and Mátala passes through dense vineyards, especially around Dáfnes: fine if not spectacular scenery. **Veneráto** offers the principal reason to stop, with a 2km detour to the serene convent of **Palianí**, home to 50 nuns. As an imperial Byzantine convent it was claimed by the Doge himself in 1212, reckoning himself heir of all the emperor's possessions on Crete. Besides early Christian capitals and 13th-century frescoes, the surest sign of Palianí's great age is its venerable Holy Myrtle, worshipped in a remarkable example of atavism that goes back to the Minoans. The nuns claim there's an icon of the Virgin in the heart of the tree and use a pair of ancient capitals for the consecration of bread offerings every 23 September; any myrtle twig that dares to sprout within reach is plucked by the faithful for good luck. The nuns have a shop selling their lace and embroideries. To the south, the large, straggling village of **Ag. Varvára** stands amid cherry orchards at approximately the geographical centre of the big island; a chapel dedicated to Prophet Elijah sits atop a large rock known as the '*omphalos*', or navel of Crete. The weather here can be dramatic: at Mégali Vríssi, to the east, Crete's first 'Aeolian park' or wind farm has recently been built to harness the cross-island winds with V-39 Vesta windmills, the biggest and strongest in Greece.

If you're in an exploring mood, two seldom-visited ancient sites await along the alternative road from Heráklion to Ag. Varvára. The scanty ruins of ancient **Rafkos** are just north of **Ag. Mýronas**, a large village with a 13th-century Venetian church. Further south, in the afternoon shadow of Mount Ida, **Priniás** has a pair of cave tombs and the more substantial ruins of lofty **Ryzenía** (*fl.* 1600–200 BC), 3.5km east, a city that controlled the main road between Knossós and Górtyn. On its acropolis you can see two ruined Archaic temples (origin of the striking Daedalic freize and some of the best Archaic sculpture in the Herákleon museum) and a Hellenistic fort; a Geometric-era cemetery has recently been found below.

The South Slopes of Psilorítis: Zarós to Kamáres

A lovely, windy road west of Ag. Varvára skirts the olive groves and rich orchards on the south flanks of Psilorítis. Nearly all the villages here began as Minoan farming communities, among them **Zarós** (ΖΑΡΟΣ), a famous local beauty spot and source of excellent bottled mineral water. The Romans, antiquity's most obsessive water connoisseurs, built an aqueduct from here to Górtyn so they wouldn't have to drink anything else. The **gorge of Zarós** is a good place to bring a picnic: the walk begins just outside of Zarós, at the monastery of **Ag. Nikólaos** (with a frescoed church), where a steep path leads up to the large hermits' cave of Ag. Euthymios, containing a chapel with two more wall paintings. An obvious path from here continues another 2km up to the gorge, deep and green and made easy with bridges over the tricky places, with grand views of Psilorítis on the way.

Some of the finest art in Crete was created for the two monasteries west of Zarós. The closest, **Moní Vrondísi**, was burned by the Turks in 1821 for its revolutionary activities, but it still has a pretty gate and a charming 15th-century Venetian fountain, next to a massive plane tree; its core blasted hollow by a lightning bolt. The tree now houses the small kitchen of the monastery's café. The 14th-century frescoes in its double-aisled church are only a pale shadow of the treasures Vrondísi once had—in 1800, having a premonition of its sacking, the abbot sent its finest works, the six panels by Michael Damáskinos, to Ag. Kateríni in Herákleon, where they remain to this day. These were painted during the monastery's golden age, when it was the most important artistic and intellectual centre in central Crete; now it has but two monks. Five km west, **Moní Valsamonérou** is reached by path from **Vorízia**, another village rebuilt after being obliterated by the Nazis (the guardian lives here, although he's usually at the church on weekday mornings). Once one of the most important monasteries in the area, Valsamonérou is now reduced to the little but enchanting assymetrical church dedicated to Ag. Fanoúrios, with two naves, and a third, transverse aisle added like an afterthought around the corner. The frescoes painted in the north aisle, dedicated to the Virgin, are by 14th-century master Konstantínos Ríkos, and are exceptional.

The road continues to **Kamáres** (with tavernas and rooms), the base for the 3–4-hour walk up the flank of Mount Ida to the **Kamáres cave** (1525m), an important Minoan cave sanctuary. Its gaping mouth, 20m high and 40m wide, is visible from Phaistós; pilgrims from the palace brought their offerings in the colourful pottery first discovered here—hence Kamares ware (*see* p.76)—made in Phaistós' palace workshops. The discovery of these by Italian archaeologists in 1893 were a major influence on Evans' decision to come to Crete. Experienced walkers only should attempt the steep, 5–6-hour path up to the summit of Psilorítis from the cave.

Zarós ℂ (0892–)   **Where to Stay and Eating Out**

Idi Hotel, ℂ 31 302 (*B; exp*) is one of the nicest mountain hotels on the island; its lovely views of the valley are shared by **Taverna Votomos**, ℂ 31 302, where fresh salmon and trout hold pride of place on the menu; certain evenings are given over to Cretan music and dancing.

The Mesará Plain and Górtyn

Górtyn is open daily 8–7, Sat and Sun 8.30–3; adm; if you're arriving by bus, get off at the Górtyn entrance and make your way back towards the village of Ag. Déka, with another bus stop.

Tucked under the southern flanks of Mount Ida and the eastern edges of the White Mountains, the long Mesará Plain is the breadbasket of Crete and one of its most densely populated areas since the time of the first Minoans. After the Dorian invasion, **Górtyn** (or Gortys, ΓΟΡΤΥΣ) gradually supplanted nearby Phaistós and even Knossós as the ruling city of Crete, with ports at Mátala and Lebena. Already by the time of the *Iliad* it was 'the second city of Crete'; Ptolemy Philopator of Egypt gave it a set of walls in Hellenistic times. Hannibal's brief sojourn here in 189 BC after his defeat by Rome may have given the inhabitants some insight into the Big Noise from Italy because they helped the Romans capture Crete. In reward Rome made

1	acropolis	13	baths
2	praetorium	14	amphitheatre
3	nymphaeum	15	museum
4	temple of Pythian Apollo	16	Ag. Deka
5	temple of the Egyptian gods	17	River Lethaios
6	odeon	18	mitropolis
7	basilica of Ag. Títos	19	stadium
8	agora	20	Ag. Deka village
9	theatre	21	plane tree
10	aqueduct	22	loggia & snack bar
11	little theatre	23	entrance to enclosed site
12	public fountain		

Górtyn

Górtyn the capital not only of Crete but of their province of Cyrenaica, which included much of North Africa. In AD 828 the Saracens wiped it off the map.

In its prime, Górtyn had a population of 300,000 and its ruins are scattered through a mile of olive groves—only the basilica and odeon are fenced in. The apse is all that survives of the tremendous 6th-century **Basilica of Ag. Títos**, once one of the most important in Greece but now a good roosting place for local birds. Titus, originally buried here, was one of St Paul's favourite disciples, sent to convert Górtyn and become its first bishop. Nearby, built into the walls of the elegant **Roman Odeon** (reconstructed by Trajan in AD 100), is Górtyn's prize, the **Law Code of Górtyn**, now covered by a shelter.

Human Rights, Dorian-style

The first block of engraved limestone, accidentally discovered in a mill stream in 1857, was purchased by the Louvre. It attracted a good deal of attention. At the time no one had ever seen a Greek inscription so ancient and unfathomable, and it wasn't until 1878 that this first bit, dealing with adoption, was translated, using the writing on ancient coins as a study guide. No one suspected that there was any more to it until one summer day in 1884 when Halbherr, the Italian archaeologist who would later excavate Phaistós, noticed a submerged building—the Odeon—while cooling his feet in the same mill stream, which was shallower than usual because of a drought. The rest of the inscription, covering over 600 lines divided on 12 blocks, was found soon after in a farmer's field; only the tops of blocks X and XII and a piece of block IX are missing.

The code, written in *boustrophedon*, 'as the ox ploughs'—from left to right, then right to left—is in the Dorian dialect of *c*. 500 BC. It is the longest such inscription to survive from antiquity, and because of it the civil laws of Crete on the verge of the Classical era are better known in their precise specific detail than Roman law. Significantly, the code was made for public display, and significantly, in spite of the built-in inequalities of the ancient Greek class system, which had a different set of rules for citizens, serfs (the native Minoans) and slaves, the Górtyn Code allows women property rights they've lacked in more recent laws (the Code Napoléon, for one); slaves had recourse against cruel masters, and there was a presumption of innocence until proven guilty long before it became the core of Anglo-American law.

Just up and behind the Law Code is the famous **plane tree** of Górtyn, by the Lethaios river. Although it's not immediately apparent in the summer, the plane is one of a rare Cretan evergreen species; the story goes that it has kept its leaves for modesty's sake ever since Zeus in his bull costume brought the Phoenician princess Europa into its shade and had his evil way with her, resulting in the birth of Minos, Rhadamanthys and Sarpedon (*see* p.45). Statues found during the excavations are displayed in the **Loggia**, next to a snack bar.

The rest of Górtyn is outside the enclosed area. If it's not too hot, consider climbing the **acropolis** over the other bank of the Lethaios. Currently being excavated by the Italians, it has a few remains of an 8th-century BC temple and long sacrificial altar, and some lofty Roman walls and a well-preserved defensive building of some kind, perhaps built at the expense of the city's largest **theatre**, largely chewed away in the hillside below. A few minutes' walk down to **Mitrópolis** reveals a large Early Byzantine church with a mosaic floor, cut in two by the village road.

Signs from the main road point to paths in the olive groves where you can spend an hour or two wandering, nine times out of ten without another soul in sight; the lack of labels, the ground littered with pot sherds and broken tiles, and the half-hearted fences make Górtyn especially evocative, almost as if you were intruding into a 19th-century engraving. There's a small **Temple of Isis and Serapis**, the Egyptian gods who became popular in the late Empire, and the more elaborate **Temple of Pythian Apollo**, the most important in Górtyn and often rebuilt since Archaic times; the inscription is another segment of Górtyn's law code, written in an even older dialect.

Most imposing of all is the 2nd-century AD **Praetorium**, the seat of the Roman governor charged with governing Crete and North Africa. Even after the Saracens roared through, the building continued in use as a monastery, at least until Venetian times. Part of the complex includes the fountain or **nymphaeum**, where the waters from the Zarós aqueduct flowed into the city. Further south are the massive brick ruins of the gate, an amphitheatre, stadium and cemetery, while the main path leads to the village of **Ag. Déka**, named for ten churchmen martyred here c. AD 250 on the order of Emperor Decius for their refusal to participate in a temple dedication. The block on which they were beheaded is kept in the church, and their tombs in the new chapel on the west end of the village are the subject of much Cretan devotion.

Mýres (ΜΟΙΡΕΣ), 9km to the west, is a lively workaday agricultural town that has taken over Górtyn's role as the commercial centre of the Mesará. On Saturday it hosts a big market. If you're relying on buses, count on spending time here, waiting for changes for Phaistós, Mátala, Ag. Galíni, the Amári Valley or Réthymnon.

Just outside Mýres, the **Convent of Kalyvianí** was founded by the 14th century (the date of the oldest church and its frescoes), but was abandoned when the Turks occupied the island. In 1865, an icon of the Virgin was discovered in a neglected corner of the church, then used as a stable by Turkish farmers. Believed to be miraculous, it ignited a huge controversy on Crete, where revolt already crackled in the air: the Turks were adamantly against letting Christians gather here to be cured, and the Christians insisted on standing outside the church in the hot sun until they gave in. The case eventually went to the Great Powers, who ruled in favour of the Christians. As the number of pilgrims swelled, a new church was built to house the icon, and since 1957 a new convent has filled with nuns, who run an orphanage, a retirement home, a museum of popular and religious art and a shop selling their needlecrafts. Apparently the miraculous icon is still at it. It wept in 1974, just before the Cyprus calamity, and wept again in November 1994, but no one knows why.

*The Palace of Phaistós is open daily 8am–6pm; adm exp; free Sun. Try to
arrive early or late to avoid the crowds. A tourist pavilion on the site has a
café and food, and a handful of rooms, © (0892) 91 360.*

Suzperbly situated halfway up a high hill overlooking the lush Mesará plain and
Psilorítis, **Phaistós** (ΦΑΙΣΤΟΣ) was one of the oldest cities in Crete, in Minoan
times second only to Knossós in importance. Phaistós was the fief of Minos' brother
Rhadamanthys, and it was the birthplace of Epimenides, one of the Seven Sages of

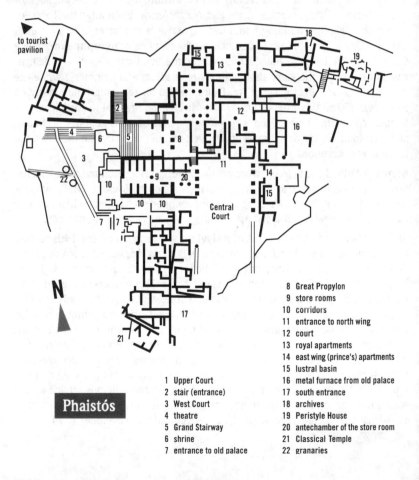

1 Upper Court	8 Great Propylon
2 stair (entrance)	9 store rooms
3 West Court	10 corridors
4 theatre	11 entrance to north wing
5 Grand Stairway	12 court
6 shrine	13 royal apartments
7 entrance to old palace	14 east wing (prince's) apartments
	15 lustral basin
	16 metal furnace from old palace
	17 south entrance
	18 archives
	19 Peristyle House
	20 antechamber of the store room
	21 Classical Temple
	22 granaries

Phaistós

ancient Greece. The first palace was constructed in the Old Palace period, around 2000 BC, and destroyed in an earthquake in 1700 BC; the second palace was built on top of the first and destroyed *c.* 1450 BC. Like Knossós but on a smaller scale, it was finely built of luxurious alabaster and gypsum, with a similar elaborate drainage system; the similarity of masons' marks suggests the two were the work of the same builders. Phaistós' workshops produced exquisite art, and yet, unlike at Knossós, no frescoes were found. Below the palace, 50,000 people lived and worked, and Minoan villages that were dependent on the palace are scattered across the Mesará. Until Hellenistic times Phaistós remained an independent little city state, warring with Górtyn, until the latter crushed it once and for all in the 3rd century BC. Excavations by the Italians, led by the flamboyant Federico Halbherr, began in 1900, just after Evans began digging at Knossós.

Archaeological purists dismayed by Evans' reconstructions at Knossós will breathe a sigh of relief at Phaistós, where only your imagination will reconstruct the original three-storey palace from the low, complicated walls and foundations; the fact that much of the second palace was confusingly built over the first means that, unless you have an especially good imagination, or opt for a guided tour, you may leave feeling singularly unenlightened. Visits begin in the northwest, in the paved **Upper Court** with its raised **Processional Way**. This carries down the steps into the **West Court**, originally part of the Old Palace—the only section the architects of the New Palace re-used after the earthquake, when the lines of the building were otherwise completely reorientated; the lower façade of the Old Palace survives just before the Grand Stairway. The West Court has the eight straight tiers known as the **theatre**, where people may have watched dances and other performances, and two circular stone-lined granaries or silos, originally protected by domed roofs.

The **Grand Stairway** was carved with special care, partly from stone and partly from the living rock; note how the steps are slightly convex, to let rainwater run off quickly. At the top, the **Great Propylon**, the main entrance to the West Wing, stands just before a light-well with three columns. Another stair descends to the **Antechamber of the Store Rooms**, where Halbherr found a huge cache of seal-stones, while beyond are the **store rooms**; one, covered with a roof, still contains its giant *pithoi*, along with a stone stool for standing on to scoop out the contents, and a built-in vessel in the floor to collect wine or oil run-offs. An important cor-ridor separated the storage areas from the main **shrine**, lined with stone benches.

From the Antechamber of the Store Rooms opens the **Central Court**, its long sides originally sheltered by porticoes; buildings on all sides would have hidden the tremendous views it enjoys today. A stepped block in the northwest corner may have been the platform used by bull dancers as a springboard for 'diving leaps'. To the southwest are a series of rooms fenced off and mingled with bits of the Old Palace and the foundations of a Classical-era temple. Landslides have swept away much of the **east wing**, but the small chamber just to the north, a bathroom, and a a gypsum-paved lustral basin with stairs earned it the name of 'Prince's Apartment'. A horseshoe-shaped **forge**, built in the Old Palace era for smelting metals, is at the end of the corridor to the north, the earliest one yet discovered in Greece.

North of the Central Court, a grand entrance with niches in the walls and another corridor leads to yet more '**royal apartments**', paved with delicate alabaster and gypsum and now fenced off to prevent wear and tear; you can barely make out the **Queen's Megaron,** furnished with alabaster benches. An open peristyle court tops the **King's Megaron**, which once must have offered a royal view to the Kamáres cave sanctuary (that dark patch between the twin summits). The famous Phaistós Disc (*see* p.164) was found to the east of here, with a cache of pottery from 1700 BC in the 'archives', in a series of mud-brick rooms from the Old Palace.

The 'Summer Villa' of Ag. Triáda

Only 3km east of Phaistós, a paved road runs to the car park just above the smaller Minoan palace of Ag. Triáda (ΑΓ. ΤΡΙΑΔΑ) (*open daily 8.30–3; adm*), named after a small Venetian church on the site. No one knows its original name, or why such a lavish little estate was built so close to Phaistós. Guesses are that a wealthy Minoan simply fell in love with the splendid setting, or it may have been a summer palace; Phaistós can turn into a frying pan in the summer, and Ag. Triáda usually has a sea breeze. In Minoan times the sea apparently came much further in and the ramp under the villa may have led down to a port. It's certainly an old site; Neolithic *tholos* tombs and dwellings were discovered under the 'palace', built around 1600 BC. This burned in the great island-wide destruction of 1450 BC. The Minoans rebuilt it, and the Mycenaeans added a *megaron* over the top and a village, dominated by an area that curiously resembles a Hellenistic agora, with a row of shops in a *stoa*. The site, excavated by the Italians off and on since 1902, yielded some of the Minoans' finest art, including frescoes and cult objects, the Harvesters' Vase and the famous sarcophagus of Ag. Triáda, all now in the Herákleon museum.

The intimate scale and surroundings—and lack of tour groups—make Ag. Tríada the most charming of the major Minoan sites. The villa had two main wings, one orientated north–south, the other east–west. The north–south wing, overlooking the sea, was the most elaborate, with flagstoned floors, gypsum and alabaster walls and benches. One room had frescoes (the stalking cat), another had built-in closets. The drainage system was excellent, and *pithoi* still stand intact in the store rooms. At the entrance to the excavations, **Ag. Geórgios Galatás** (1302) contains good frescoes (ask the guardian for the key). The cemetery, where the Ag. Triáda sarcophagus was found, is northeast of the Late Minoan/Mycenaean town.

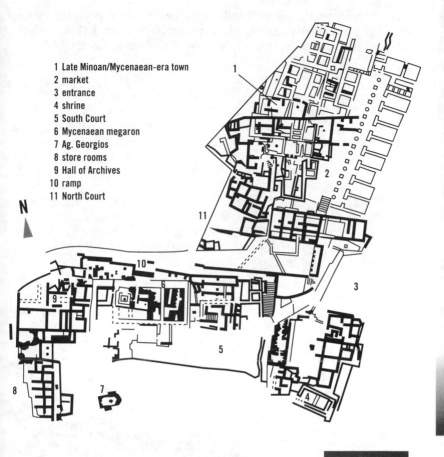

1 Late Minoan/Mycenaean-era town
2 market
3 entrance
4 shrine
5 South Court
6 Mycenaean megaron
7 Ag. Georgios
8 store rooms
9 Hall of Archives
10 ramp
11 North Court

N

Ag. Triáda

Around the South Coast

This corner offers more than the fossils of long-lost civilizations. Just to the north of Phaistós, the old village of **Vóri** on the road to Ag. Galíni (*see* p.145–7) hopes to waylay you with its superb **Museum of Cretan Ethnology** (*open 10–6; adm*), the best place on the island to learn about traditional country life in Crete—a civilization not yet lost, if in danger of extinction—with excellent detailed descriptions in English to go with the exhibitions of pottery, musical instruments, furniture, tools and costumes. Charmless **Tymbáki**, 3km west, combines tomatoes under plastic and some dogged tourism, thanks to its long ugly beach, **Kókinos Pírgos**, the 'red tower', a name that predates its career as the Ketchup Coast.

Mátala and Kómmo

Elsewhere, this is a wild rockbound coast, which only here and there permits tortuous roads to descend to the sea. One south of Phaistós leads to **Mátala** (ΜΑΤΑΛΑ), the lovely and once notorious beach enclosed by sandstone cliffs. The cliffs are riddled with tombs from the 1st and 2nd centuries AD, which over the years the locals enlarged into cosy little rooms. In the early 1960s, young Americans bumming around Europe on one dollar a day found that the caves made a perfect (and free) place to crash in the winter, and before long these pioneers were joined by a sizeable international hippy colony. In the killjoy 1990s, the impecunious hippies have been banished for the hard currency of package tourism. If you stay overnight, something of their spirit lingers on in Mátala's laid-back atmosphere, although aggressive grannies hawking their rugs may be your strongest memory if you just stop by.

If the town beach is a massive body jam (nearly every excursion bus to Phaistós calls in here), a path and a scramble over the rocks will take you in about 20 minutes to Mátala's excellent second beach, **Kókino Ámmos**, 'red sand', with caves (inhabited, this time); excursion boats sail south to other small beaches at Ag. Farago and Vathí. It's also important to avoid walking on the beaches on summer nights, when loggerhead turtles make their nests.

MATALA

Mátala has been a midwife of tourism for nearby **Pitsídia** along the main road, and more recently for **Kalamáki**, an embryonic cement resort down by the long beach north of Mátala. At the south end of this same beach (easiest reached by a track from Pitsídia) **Kómmo** has been excavated since 1976 by Canadian and American archaeologists, revealing substantial remains of Phaistós' port—as yet the largest Minoan port discovered on the south coast. Although not officially open for visits, you can stroll along the beach and see what's been revealed: a massive building of dressed stone, believed to have been the port warehouse, dry docks with five slips, houses (one with a wine press), and a paved road with worn wheel-ruts that probably leads to Phaistós. Near the beach stood an important sanctuary, sacred long after the Minoans: the 10th-century BC Dorians built a temple here, as did the sea-trading Phoenicians, and the Classical and Hellenistic-era Greeks.

Górtyn's Ports: Kalí Liménes and Léndas

Phaistós' rival Górtyn had several ports to the east, although the rugged coastal mountains preclude any seaside drive, or many paved roads; by public transport you'll have to go by way of Mýres to catch the one or two buses a day to Léndas. Not even those go down to **Kalí Liménes**, a steep winding drive by way of Sívas and **Moní Odgegitrías**, still defended by a tower complete with its 'killer'—the hole over the gateway for pouring boiling oil on enemies. Górtyn's main harbour, Kalí Liménes, the 'Fair Havens', is where the storm-tossed ship carrying St Paul put in on its way to be wrecked off Malta. Winters are so mild here that swallows don't migrate to Africa—the locals say they are the souls of all the anchorites who lived in these arid hills. Unlike its neighbours, however, Kalí Liménes as a port has kept pace with the times; instead of saints, the Fair Havens now host oil tankers. If you don't mind them, there are deserted beaches set under the cliffs, a few cafés and some (albeit scant) Roman ruins and Minoan *tholos* tombs as proof of its antique authenticity, just to the east at Lasaia.

Ruins of another of Górtyn's harbours, **Levín** (or Lebena) are near the ramshackle fishing village of **Léndas.** From Kalí Liménes, get there by way of the rough but passable coastal road and several small beaches, or you can descend by way of the new road south of Górtyn and Miamoú. The natural hot springs east of the village (now pumped elsewhere) led to the construction in the 4th century BC of a large Asklepeion, a sanctuary of the god of healing; there are some mosaics, bits of a temple, and a pool where until a few decades ago patients would wallow in the therapeutic waters. Nearly all the wallowing in Léndas these days happens 3km west at **Yerókambos**, a magnificent long sandy beach where clothes are an option few take up; a few tavernas here rent rooms.

Although Mátala closes shop at the end of October (to the extent that no one would care if you discreetly moved into a cave), by Easter it's nearly impossible to find a room, as many Greeks flock down for their first official swim of the year. The **Valley Village**, ✆ 42 776 (*B; exp*), on the edge of the village (and out of earshot of most of the bars), has a swimming pool, Greek dancing shows and barbecue nights. *Open April–Oct.* The **Zafira Hotel**, ✆ 42 112 (*D; mod*), is handy for town and beach, and reasonably priced, although completely booked by operators in season. *Open all year.*

The **Coral** pension, just outside Mátala, ✆ 42 375 (*E; inexp*), has an area for children to play. **Pension Sofia**, ✆ 42 134 (*E; inexp*) and **Pension Nikos**, ✆ 42 375 (*inexp*) with a little garden, are among the pleasant choices on a whole lane of rooms to rent.

Mátala Camping, ✆ 42 720, just behind the beach, offers cool camping in the shade with low prices. There are also cheap beds in the neighbouring villages of Kalamáki and Pitsídia, and **Camping Kommos**, ✆ 42 596, with a pool.

In Mátala people tend to drink more than eat; **Giorgio's Bar**, at the end, serves cocktails to go with Mátala's famous sunsets. **Syrtaki** has centre spot in the row of seaside tavernas and serves all the Greek favourites (with barrelled wine) at reasonable prices. Right on the beach, **Zeus Beach Taverna** offers moussaka, stuffed tomatoes and other dishes made by mama, and you can feed your extra bread to the ducks (*around 2500dr*). For an Italian or vegetarian meal, try **Bodikos**, ✆ 42 438 in nearby Pitsídia.

Across the South: East of Górtyn to the Diktean Mountains

The region along the scenic new main road east of Górtyn towards Ierápetra has no major attractions, no picture-postcard beaches, no Minoan palaces, and next to no tourists. **Pýrgos** is the largest of the farming villages along the road, with a rough track (you need a jeep to do it) that goes down to **Moní Koudoumá**. This was built in a lovely, remote pine-clad cove in 1870 by two saintly Cretan monks, although old churches and abandoned monasteries scattered along the sea towards the east show they were hardly the first to settle here. There are simple cells if you want to spend the night. **Phílippi**, 8km east on the main road, is dominated by the Byzantine fortress **Castel Belvede,** renovated by the Genoese during their brief tenure of the island. It gave its name, Kastélliana, to the clutch of surrounding hamlets and their rather overcrowded beach, **Tsoútsouros**. At Mártha the road joins the north–south road from Herákleon, north of Áno Viánnos (*see* p.202).

Southeast of Herákleon: Villages under the Diktean Mountains

Some attractive Cretan villages high in the western foothills of Mount Díkti are linked by a good road south of Chersónisos. The majority of tourists don't get further than **Karouzaná**, which is a designated 'traditional village' for the coach parties. But, hidden away just south before Kastélli, signs for 'Paradise Tavern– Byzantine Church', point the way to the village of **Ag. Pandeleímonos**, a fascinating old place under huge plane trees by a spring, built over a temple to Asklepeios (the taverna owners will summon the caretakers). Originally erected in AD 450, it was said to have 101 doors, but after being ravaged by the Saracens it was rebuilt on a more modest scale *c*. 1100, using the stones of old tombs, columns and reliefs. Note the bell made out of a German shell, cut in two. Inside, the nave with very faded frescoes is supported by marble columns from ancient Lyttos, including a peculiarly striking one made of nothing but Corinthian capitals, stacked this way and that.

Kastélli is the largest village of the Pediáda region, named after its long-gone Venetian castle. A short detour just to the west to **Sklaverochóri** has its reward in the 15th-century church **Eisódia tis Theotókou** (Presentation of the Virgin), decorated with excellent frescoes, the forerunners of the Cretan school: a fairy-tale scene with St George and the princess, the allegories of the river gods in the Baptism, and on the north wall a Catholic intruder: St Francis holding a rosary.

Four km east of Kastélli, ancient **Lyttos** (modern Xidás) was a fierce rival of Knossós after the Doric invasion and remained sufficiently powerful and wealthy to mint its own coins until 220 BC, when Knossós, allied with Górtyn, captured and demolished it. In spite of aid sent from Sparta, Lyttos never really recovered. As the Minoans hog the funds on Crete, Lyttos is just beginning to be investigated, but you can see Hellenistic walls, a theatre and remains of other buildings, including a frescoed church, built on the early Christian basilica of Ag. Geórgios.

Thanks to the fine local clay, families of potters in **Thrapsanó** (8km west) have made both small bowls and large *pithoi* for centuries. The technique for making the great jars, on wheels set in the ground, hasn't changed for centuries. **Arkalochóri**, to the south, is the scene every Saturday of a large produce and animal fair. In 1932, Marinátos and Pláton excavated the village's sacred cave and brought forth some exceptionally meaty Minoan ritual weapons: gold axes, the longest prehistoric Greek bronze sword ever found, and bronze axes, one engraved in Linear A, the other with symbols similar to those on the Phaistós Disc—which put paid to notions that the disc was a forgery. The road rises at Panagía for **Embaros**, where Cretan dittany, the island's miracle herb, has been cultivated in recent years.

A Litany to Dittany

Oregano is a Greek word meaning 'mountain joy', and no variety warms the heart of a Cretan like *Origanum ditamnus*, a fragrant, small perennial plant of the *Labiatae* family with distinctive thick hairy leaves, which likes to grow in dangerous rock crevices; over the centuries this precious herb, now used as a flavouring in herbal liqueurs, has been behind more than one death as its gatherers took one too many risks to pluck it. For Cretan dittany was attributed uncanny powers by the ancients; when Aeneas was wounded in the Trojan war, Venus rushed over to Mount Ida to gather dittany for his cure. Aristotle wrote how the wild goats on Ida, wounded by hunters, could heal themselves by munching on a patch of the stuff. Until recently, it was used to induce and ease labour pains, or taken in early pregnancies to abort. Dioscorides was the first to mention the tonic effect of Cretan dittany; another Greek name for it, *érotas*, refers to its powers as an aphrodisiac and impotence cure-all. The Cretans recommend tossing dittany leaves in a hot bath if you're feeling low; look for it in shops selling Cretan herbs and spices.

Áno Viánnos and the Coast

Beyond Mártha (where you can pick up the road west to Górtyn, *see* above), **Áno Viánnos** (ΑΝΩ ΒΙΑΝΝΟΣ) hangs on the southwest flanks of Mount Díkti. Inhabited since early Minoan times, it founded a colony on the Rhône, along the chief route to the tin mines of the British Isles, which still bears its Cretan name: Vienne. In more recent times the village was a citadel of resistance against the Turks (who in reprisals flattened it twice, in 1822 and 1866) and the Germans, who executed 820 people in the area. On the acropolis of Áno Viánnos are the ruins of a Venetian castle and Turkish tower; in the Pláka area are little white Ag. Pelagía (1360) and 14th-century Ag. Geórgios, both with frescoes. The latter is near the incredible plane tree by one of the *kafeneíons*, believed to be the oldest in Greece after the granddaddy of them all, Hippocrates' Plane Tree on Kos.

Two km west, near Káto Viánnos, a good road to the coast descends by way of the pretty village of **Chóndros** to **Keratókambos**, an attractive fishing village that was especially well defended: this was the beach where the Saracens first invaded Crete in 823, and to make sure it wouldn't happen again the Venetians built a fort by the sea and another one a kilometre to the east known as **Kastrí**. All the locals come down here to swim, and there's a handful of tavernas and rooms. A rough-and-tumble road links Keratókambos to **Árvi** (ΑΡΒΗ), although the paved road down from Amirás east of Áno Viánnos is much easier; at the Amirás crossroads there's a massive monument to the 600 Cretans killed by the Germans here on 14 September 1943. Set in the cliffs, Árvi is enclosed in in its own toasty little world, at the head of a valley of banana plantations. It has a pebble beach, good for a swim early or late in the year, and a picturesque monastery built on several tiers that originally supported a temple of Zeus. Other beaches are tucked away along a track to the east, especially at Akrotíri Sidonía.

Lastly, if you continue east on the main road, you'll find a sign pointing north for **Áno Sími**, a tiny hamlet, from where a narrow dirt track (better on foot than in your rental car) leads a few kilometres up the mountain and into a plane tree forest, where three terraces and an outdoor altar of a temple dedicated to Aphrodite and Hermes remained open for business between 1600 BC and AD 300. Beyond, the road descends through striking porphyry-coloured badlands where nothing grows, towards the oasis of Mýrtos, in Lassíthi (*see* p.246).

Where to Stay and Eating Out

Kastélli ✆ (0891–)

> **Irida**, ✆ 32 023, a pretty café-restaurant in a neoclassical house and garden, makes a good lunch stop; in the evening **Taverna To Steki**, just north, often has music.

Árvi ✆ (0895–)

> **Ariadne**, ✆ 71 300 (*C; mod*), is the biggest hotel here, but there are a number of rooms places too.

East of Herákleon to Mália

West of Herákleon and Amnisós (*see* p.180), Europa, once raped on the island by Cretan Zeus in the form of a bull, gets her revenge on Crete. Here greedy developers—the 'long-trousered men', as the mountaineers call them—raped the lovely coastline, building most flagrantly and myopically to pander to the yearning of Europa in her package-tour aspect to soak up ultraviolet rays and cheap drink. Here you can safely cocoon yourself in compounds full of embarrassing sunburnt people of your own nationality, tribes who gather together dressed in Heavy Metal T-shirts to watch the football scores and TV re-runs from home. But what goes around comes around. The Dorians, those pioneer cultural polluters who swamped these shores back in 1100 BC with heavy metal swords, were probably just as silly and tipped even worse. Even more depressing than the god-awfulness of the architecture are the rusting rods curling out of the flat roofs, promising more layers of the same, and the concrete skeletons of future monstrosities, usually crumbling away in a field of litter and weeds—some would-be Cesare Ritz's grubby field of dreams.

Even if a cup of REAL ENGLIHS (sic) TEA isn't yours, you may find a reason or two to put on the brakes in this holiday la-la land, beginning at Vathianó Kambó to see **Nírou Cháni** by the hotel Demetra, a well-preserved Minoan villa known as the House of the High Priest, where a trove of 40 tripods and enormous double axes was found. Square-shaped, it has two paved courts and stone benches, perhaps used in ceremonies (*closed at the time of writing for excavations*). In **Goúves** village (not the coastal extension) signs point the way to Skotinó village, and beyond to the enormous **cave of Skotinó**, set in a hollow on a plateau; the path begins by a white chapel. The cave has several chambers, the first a stunning 50m-high ball-room lit by sun pouring through the mouth of the cave, with a stalagmite mass in the centre. A huge amount of Minoan cult activity took place in the smaller, dimmer, low-ceilinged chambers at the back, around curious rock formations (one looks like the bearded head of Zeus) and natural rock altars; it has even been suggested that the cave, not Knossós, was the real labyrinth of the double axe.

Further east, past the turn-off at Lagada for the Plain of Lassíthi (*see* p.212), **Chersónisos** (ΧΕΡΣΟΝΗΣΟΣ), or more properly Limén Chersonísou, is a synthetic tourist ghetto from end to end, complete with a synthetic Cretan village on one end for a safe, pre-chewed dose of local culture when the charms of the Hard Rock Café and a score of clones begin to pale. What can you say about a town that has its own Finnish doctor? In more innocent times, Chersónisos was the port of ancient Lyttos and had a famous temple to Britomartis Artemis. Little remains of these ancient glories: a reconstructed Roman fountain by the beach, bits of harbour installations, and a Roman aqueduct (inland at Xerokámares, along the road to Lassíthi). On the west side of town, overlooking the harbour, are the ruins of a 5th-century basilica with three aisles, believed to be the seat of one of Crete's first bishoprics; a second basilica, from the next century, can be seen on the east end of town near the church of Ag. Nikólaos. Inland, on the same road as Old Chersónisos (packed with tavernas for organized 'Greek Nights'), **Aqua Splash Water Park** is the newest attraction for the kids (*open Apr–Oct, © (0897) 24 950*).

Mália

East of Chersónisos, in the centre of a wide sandy bay, modern Mália (ΜΑΛΙΑ) has taken over as the busiest, noisiest, rowdiest, most party-driven tentacle of the holiday sprawl east of Herákleon: at night the bars lining the beach road thump and grind away with more decibels than sense. There is an older, wiser village of Mália, inland, and oldest of all, the **Minoan Palace of Mália** (*open 8am–7pm, till 3 out of season, closed Mon; adm; free on Sun*), near a lovely, quiet stretch of beach 3km to the east (any bus to Ag. Nikólaos will drop you near). Traditionally the fief of Minos' brother Sarpedon, Mália controlled the fertile coastal plain under the Lassíthi mountains (now given over to banana plantations under plastic). Its history

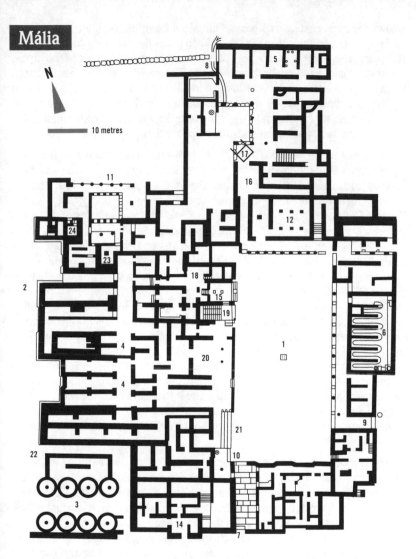

Mália

N

10 metres

1 Central Court	9 southeast entrance	16 Pillar Room
2 West Court	10 kernos altar	17 oblique room
3 storage silos	11 royal apartments	18 treasury
4 store rooms	12 Pillar Hall	19 Grand Stairway
5 northeast store rooms	13 lustral basin	20 Pillar Crypt
6 eastern store rooms	14 shrine	21 possible theatre
7 south entrance	15 loggia (opening on to	22 entrance
8 north entrance	central court)	23 Archive Room

follows the same pattern as Knossós: inhabited from the Neolithic era, the first palace was built on the site in 1900 BC. When it was devastated by the earthquake 200 years later, another palace was built over the first, then ruined in the mysterious catastrophe traditionally dated 1450 BC. Compared to Knossós and Phaistós, Mália is 'provincial', built from local stone rather than alabaster, marble and gypsum, and apparently it had no frescoes. On the other hand, the lack of later constructions makes it easy to understand the plan. Excavations were begun in 1915 by Cretan archaeologist Joseph Hadzidákis and continued by the French School.

The entrance to the palace is by way of the **West Court**, crossed by the usual raised flagstones of the Processional Walkway. Eight large round 'silos', originally covered with vaulted beehive domes, are on the south end of this, and are believed to have stored grain (similar ones have been found in Egypt). The **Central Court**, re-used from the Old Palace, had porticoed galleries on the north and east ends; in the middle are supports of a hollow altar, or sacrificial pit. A Grand Stairway led up into the important **west wing**, where finds suggest the rooms had some kind of ritual role: the raised and carefully paved **Loggia**, where religious ceremonies may have been performed, is near a large round mysterious stone stuck in the ground. The **treasury**, behind it, yielded a beautiful ceremonial sword with a rock crystal pommel and a stone axe shaped like a pouncing panther. South of this, in the **Pillar Crypt**, a variety of potent masons' marks (double axes, stars and tridents) are carved in the heavy square pillars. The four broad steps here are thought to have been used as a theatre, while in the southwest corner is the unique limestone *kernos*, a round wheel of an altar with a deeper hollow in the centre and 34 smaller hollows around the circumference. Its similarity to the *kernos* used in Classical times is striking, and it may have been the Minoans who originated the rite of *panspermia*, or the symbolic offering of the first fruits from each harvest to the deity. Near here, the **south entrance** was the most elaborate door into the palace.

A long portico, once supported by square stone pillars alternating with round wooden columns, ran along the east side of the Central Court. Mália had no lack of store rooms, and the narrow ones that take up most of the east wing (now protected by a roof) are equipped with drainage channels dating from the first palace. North of the centre, the **Pillar Hall** is the largest and most important in the palace; the chamber directly above it, reached by the surviving stair, may have been for banquets. Behind it is another pillar room, and the mysterious **oblique room**, its different orientation suggesting some kind of astronomical or lunar observation; it may also be a later intrusion of some kind, built in the palace ruins. A suite of so-called **royal apartments**, with a stepped, sunken lustral basin, are in the northwest corner. A large number of Linear A tablets were found in the **Archive Room**, with the base of a single pillar. Outside the north entrance is an open area which might have been used for bull leaping. A paved road leads north to the so-called **Hypostyle Crypt**, under a barrel-vaulted shelter; no one has the foggiest idea what went on here.

If Mália seems somewhat poor next to Knossós and Phaistós, the large Minoan estates found in the outskirts were sumptuous, especially the one to the northeast of the palace, where the only fresco at Mália has been found. In the cemetery by the sea, the **Chrysolakkos tomb** was probably the family vault of Mália's rulers; although looted over the centuries (significantly, its name means 'gold pit'), the French found the magnificent twin bee pendant of Mália inside. Stylistic similarities suggest that the golden Aegina Treasure in the British Museum was pillaged from here in antiquity. To the west, there's a mysterious 60-room building complex (Quarter M) with light-wells.

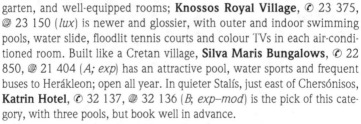

℗ *(0897–)*   ***Where to Stay and Eating Out***

Chersónisos

Don't expect to find any cheap rooms here, or even a hotel in season, although the tourist office on Giaboúdaki Street will do its best to help. Aegean-style **Creta Maris Hotel and Bungalow complex**, ℗ 22 115, ℗ 22 130 (*lux*) is the most luxurious, with lots of sports, six bars, free kindergarten, and well-equipped rooms; **Knossos Royal Village**, ℗ 23 375, ℗ 23 150 (*lux*) is newer and glossier, with outer and indoor swimming pools, water slide, floodlit tennis courts and colour TVs in each air-conditioned room. Built like a Cretan village, **Silva Maris Bungalows**, ℗ 22 850, ℗ 21 404 (*A; exp*) has an attractive pool, water sports and frequent buses to Herákleon; open all year. In quieter Stalís, just east of Chersónisos, **Katrin Hotel**, ℗ 32 137, ℗ 32 136 (*B; exp–mod*) is the pick of this category, with three pools, but book well in advance.

Less costly choices include the quiet **Selena**, 13 Maragáki, ℗ 22 412 (*mod*) with kitchenettes, or in the inexpensive category, the well-run **Youth Hostel**, El. Venizélou, ℗ 23 674 and **Caravan Camping**, with shade, ℗ 22 025. **Artemís**, ℗ 32 131, by the beach in Stalís, serves Greek and Cretan specialities; in Chersónisos try **Kavouri**, at Archéou Théatro, with better than usual Greek food at slightly higher than usual prices. After dinner, everyone gathers in the bars and clubs around El. Venizélou.

Mália

Ikaros Village, ✆ 31 267 (*A; exp*) is a large hotel complex, designed as a traditional Cretan village (most of the big hotels lack any design whatsoever); pool, tennis and sea sports are among the offerings. *Open April–Oct.* Towards the Minoan palace, **Mália Park**, ✆ 31 460, ✉ 31 460 (*A; exp*) has air-conditioned bungalows, watersports and a mountain bike centre. **Alexander Beach**, ✆ 32 124, ✉ 31 038 (*B; exp*) is a recently built complex a stone's throw from the beach, and has a heated pool if the water's a mite chilly, as well as tennis and other sports.

In Mália proper, there are a large number of small, cheaper hotels: **Elen**, ✆ 31 545 (*C; mod*), a kilometre from the beach, is typical and favoured by British tour operators) while **Ermioni**, ✆ 31 093 (*E; inexp*) is one of the cheapest hotels in town. The **youth hostel** just east of town, ✆ 31 555, is new, very nice, but fills up fast.

The best place to eat in Mália is in the old village, south of the main road, where tavernas serve barrelled wine and good food at fair prices: try **Yannis** and **Kalimera** or of the others around the main square, all far from the cacophony and brawls along the beach road.

SPINALONGA

Nomós Lassíthi

The name of Crete's easternmost *nomós*, Lassíthi (ΛΑΣIΘI) comes from the Greek mispronunciation of the Venetian La Sitía, one of its chief towns. Lassíthi doesn't have the towering peaks that characterize the rest of Crete (although Mt Díkti, on its western fringes, isn't exactly a peewee at 2142m) but it manages to be the most varied county on the island, framed on the west end by its famous plateau hanging in the clouds, too cold for olives but planted with apple orchards and wheat and irrigated by white-sailed windmills, while the east coast ends at Vaï with a luxuriant palm-lined tropical beach. Ag. Nikólaos, set in the magnificent Gulf of Mirabélo, is the most cosmopolitan and blatantly touristy of Crete's four capitals; with most of the island's luxury hotels in the environs it's not the place to come in search of traditional Crete, although, as always, you don't have to venture too far from the coast to find it.

Lassíthi was densely populated in Minoan times: if the unplundered palace of Zákros is the most spectacular find, town sites such as Gourniá, Paleokástro, Vasilikí, Fournoú Korifí and Móchlos have proved equally important in providing clues about day-to-day life in Minoan times. Sitía is one of Crete's most pleasant provincial towns, and if Ierápetra, down on the hot, plastic-coated southeast coast, is perhaps the least pleasant, it has plenty of beaches and a tropical islet to escape to. Kritsá near Ag. Nikólaos has the island's best frescoes and the most impressive Dorian remains, at Lato. Lassíthians tend to be gentler than other Cretans, and claim to be the best lovers on the island; other Cretans grant the *nomós* only its superlative potatoes and pigs.

The Plateau of Lassíthi and the Birthplace of Zeus

A steady trail of tour buses make the widening ascent to the spectacular Plateau of Lassíthi, one of the high points of Crete, both in altitude and atmosphere, although you may want to spend a night or two there after the tour groups have gone, to get a feel for the place. For it is unique: a green carpet hemmed in on all sides by the Díktean Mountains, snowcapped into April and irrigated in summer by white-sailed windmills designed by Venetian engineers in 1564; the hundreds that still turn make a splendid sight. The uncanny cave where baby Zeus first saw the light of day is the plateau's chief attraction, while Karphí, the remarkable windblasted pinnacle where a small band of Minoans took refuge, is equally uncanny, harder to get to, and far less visited.

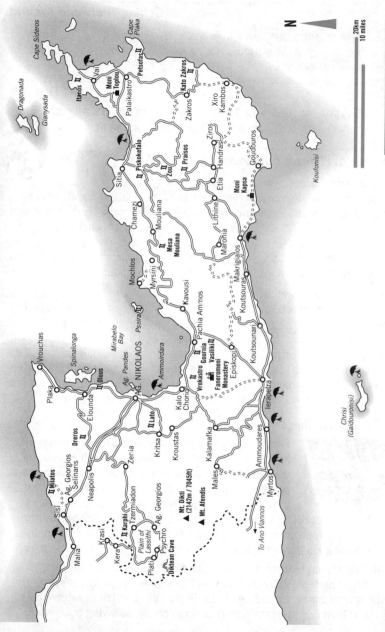

Nomós Lassíthi

Three or four public **buses** from Mália, Herákleon and Ag. Nikólaos wind their way up to the plateau, catching most of the villages and ending up at the Diktean Cave.

23 April: Ag. Geórgios; **15 August**: Mochós; **29–31 August**: Psychró, 3-day-long *panegýri*;. **8 September**: Panagía Kardiótissa.

The Lassíthi Plateau: Approaches from the West

With your own transport you have a choice of scenic routes. The main one from Chersónisos (*see* p.204) passes a series of old villages; just above one of these, **Potamiés**, the lovely cruciform church of the Panagía (in the abandoned Moní Gouverniótissa) has excellent early 14th-century frescoes, including a powerful Pantocrator who stares holes into sinners (pick up the key at the Potamiés *kafeneíon*). Frescoes from the same century decorate the church of Ag. Antónios at **Avdoú**, a pretty village dotted with small Byzantine churches.

If, on the other hand, you the take the road just east of Chersónisos at Stalís, the ascent is far more abrupt. After 8.5km of birds' eye views over the sea, **Mochós** comes as a pleasant antidote to the coastal cacophony. There are a few places to eat in the main square (Anonimo has good *myzíthra* cheese pies with honey) and some rooms, mostly occupied by Swedish tourists, who know Mochós through their assassinated prime minister Olof Palme; his simple, long-time summer residence, Villa Palme, is now something of a local shrine. South of Mochós, the Stalís and Chersónisos roads meet near **Krási**, a village famous for its curative spring.

The Healthiest Shade

Perhaps the best advertisement for the properties of Krási's water is its famous plane tree, which has thrived on it for the past 2000 years, give or take a few centuries. This superb specimen measures some 80ft in circumference and requires 16 people to encompass its girth, although before the embankment was built around the square they say it took 30 people to embrace it; in the 19th century, a café with three tables did business inside the hollow of its trunk.

For all Greeks, but perhaps most of all for old Cretan tree-worshippers, planes are considered sacred; as they will only grow by springs, they are synonymous with water, and hence life itself. No village worth its salt would be without at least one in its main square; occasionally, a flowing tap is even embedded in the trunk. According to Hippocrates, the 4th-century BC father of medicine, their shade is the most wholesome (just the opposite of the dire, enervating shade of the fig); the fact that generations of Greeks have spent much of their lives gossiping in *kafeneíons* under the rain and sun-shielding canopies of plane trees has given rise to the expression: *cheréte mou ton plátano*, 'Greet the plane tree for me,' or in other words, 'Go tell it to the marines.' As proof of Crete's holy status it has the only 29 known evergreen plane trees in the world, most famously at the island's Roman capital Górtyn (*see* pp.190–92), which proudly engraved the tree on its coins.

The Virgin in Chains

Very near Krási, in the village of **Kerá,** the much rebuilt **Convent of Kardiótissa** may not look like much from the outside, but it holds a special place in Cretan hearts. Probably founded in the 1100s, it was mentioned by the 15th-century Florentine monk Christophoro Buondelmonti, who visited Crete and wrote of the long list of miracles attributed to its icon of the Virgin. In 1498, an Italian merchant and reader of Buondelmonti purloined the miraculous icon, and, although he had to jettison his whole cargo of wine on the way home as divine punishment, he made it to Rome with the icon and donated it to the church of San Matteo, where it attracted considerable cult status as the Madonna della Perpetuo Soccorso; in 1866 it was moved to Sant'Alfonso in Rome where you can see it to this day.

For the Cretans this is all water under the bridge: they insist that the copy of the icon in the church is the real McCoy, and that it was twice carried off by the Turks to Constantinople but made its way back to the monastery on its own; the third time the Turks chained it to a column, but it flew back to Crete with the column and chain attached. The uprooted column is still in the courtyard, while the chain, hanging on the iconostasis, has the reputation of relieving pain if wrapped around the body. In 1982 the icon was stolen yet again by a gang of delinquents who tried to sell it, but by some new miracle it was found a few days later on top of a mountain near Herákleon. The Cretans were so relieved that they ceremoniously walked it back the whole 50km to the church. During the course of restoration on the handsome stone church, beautiful 14th-century frescoes were discovered; there's a fine portrait of the Byzantine lady who paid for the art, wearing a cloak with a two headed eagle medallion. Further along you can see the forbidding grey slag-like head of Mount Karphí.

The Villages of the Plateau

Beyond the stone windmills—those with sails are still used for grinding wheat—the road finally reaches the pass at the Seli Ampelou Taverna and Grill, then descends into the Lassíthi plateau. Down below, the round emerald plain presents at its best a kind of epiphany; Werner Herzog used it as such, hypnotically, in his film *Signs of Life*. A fertile chequerboard of fields divided by drainage ditches, in a bowl of barren mountains, the plateau was farmed by the Minoans, and later by the Dorians of Lytto, but it was such a fierce nest of resistance that in 1293 the Venetians forced everyone out, demolished the villages and churches, set up a guard around the passes and persecuted anyone who drew near. Only in 1543, when the Venetians were in a far more reconciliatory mood, were Greek refugees from the Turkish-occupied Peloponnese permitted to resettle the plateau. To help re-establish the orchards, the Venetians built 10,000 white-sailed irrigation windmills. In the 1970s they were still a remarkable sight, but, sad to say, since then most have been mothballed in favour of the more reliable petrol pump.

Eighteen villages dot the circumference of the pleateau, not only to preserve the best land for farming but to keep their toes dry; the plateau can get boggy from melted snow. Largest of these villages is **Tzermiádon** (ΤΖΕΡΜΙΑΔΟ) with a population of 1500, located near a sacred cave and peak sanctuary. A sign points to the path up to the first, the **Trápeza Cave**, in use since 5000 BC. Long before the first Minoan temples were built, Cretans left ivory votive offerings in the mysterious penumbra behind its narrow opening; the Middle Minoans used it for burials. Archaeologists scoff at attempts to change the name to the Cave of Kronos, to compete with the Diktean Cave trade (bring a light, or take one of the local guides).

If you've got your walking shoes and a bottle of water, another more strenuous path (or dirt road part of the way, marked 'Tinios Stavros') from Tzermiádon leads up in an hour to the Níssimos plateau and beyond to **Karphí** (ΚΑΡΦΙ), the 'nail', which is a fairly accurate description of the mountain, a weird place that held the loftiest of all Minoan peak sanctuaries (1158m). Excavated by the affable, one-eyed giant John Pendlebury between 1937 and 1939—his last project before he was killed, fighting alongside the locals in the Battle of Crete—Karphí became the refuge of some 3000 Minoans, or Eteocretans ('True Cretans'), during the Dorian invasion in 1100 BC. For a hundred years they tried to keep the fires of Minoan civilization burning, before the cold bleakness and harsh winters apparently got to be too much. In this mighty setting, Pendlebury found some 150 small houses, a temple, chieftain's house or megaron, with a porch and hearthroom, a tower and barracks, and a shrine that contained five of the very last Minoan clay idols of the goddess (*c.* 1050 BC, now in the Herákleon museum), weird and distorted and a metre tall, with a straight cylinder skirt, detachable feet and long neck, like Alice when she was mistaken for a serpent.

If you're on foot, there are tractor paths through the fields, but by car you'll have to follow the paved road. Clockwise from Tzermiádon, **Ag. Konstantínos** has the most souvenir shops on the plateau, while just above it the 13th-century **Moní Kroustallénia** enjoys a lovely panoramic spot. It has some interesting reliefs and a tragic tale: in 1823, during a baptism ceremony, Egyptian allies of the Turks broke into the monastery, murdered the men and carried off the women and children. One little boy taken to Cairo was raised as a Muslim and became Ismail Feric Pasha, a minister of war, while his brother in Crete, Antónios Kambánis, became a financier of the 1866 Revolt. One of the worst enemies the Cretans fought was none other than Ismail, who led an army up to Lassíthi and actually burned the monastery and his own village. This still wasn't enough to convince the Turks in power that Ismail was not a crypto-Christian, and a year later he was poisoned. In **Ag. Geórgios**, the next village, a 200-year-old farmhouse contains a little **Folk Museum** (*open June–Aug 10–4*) complete with everything a Cretan mountain family needed to get by, including a wine-press that doubled as a bed; it also has a fascinating collection of photos of Níkos Kazantzákis.

Psychró and the Diktean Cave

> *Hail, son of Kronos,*
> *Welcome, greatest Kouros,*
> *Mighty of brightness,*
> *Here now present, leading your spirits,*
> *Come for the year to Dikte*
> *And rejoice in this ode,*
> *Which we strike on the strings, as we*
> *Blend it with the sound of pipes, as we*
> *Chant our song, standing round*
> *this your well-walled altar.*

> *Hymn of the Kouretes to Diktean Zeus*

Psychró (ΨΥΧΡΟ), on the southwest end of the plateau, is the base for visiting the **Diktean Cave**, the birthplace of Zeus (*open 8–5; adm*). From the car park (*300dr*) it's a one-kilometre ascent up a rocky, stepped path; sure-footed donkeys are available at the site, while local guides at the entrance have lanterns in case you haven't brought a torch of your own, although it's wise to set a price from the start. Rubber-soled shoes are equally important; the descent into the gaping maw of the cave is difficult and slippery (tour group leaders naughtily fail to warn their elderly clients, creating massive single-file jam-ups at the entrance).

If you get there early, before the groups, the cave is a haunting, other-worldly place well worthy of myth. Only rediscovered in the 1880s, it contained cult items from Middle Minoan up to Archaic times; its role as the birthplace and hiding place of Zeus from his cannibal father Cronos predates the Idaean cave's claims and was confirmed by the discovery in Paleókastro of the *Hymn of the Kouretes* (the young men who danced and banged their shields to drown out the baby's cries). Down in its damp, shadowy bowels the guides point out formations that, if you squint just so, resemble the baby god, his cradle, his mantle and the place where the nannygoat Amaltheia nursed him; to help conceal the birth, Rhea, his mother, spurted her own breast milk into the heavens, creating the Milky Way. A strong tradition has it that Minos came up here to receive the law of Zeus every nine years, and that Epimenides the Sage lived here as a hermit, having strange visions.

In nearby Ag. Charalámbos, Kóstis Dávaras, the Ephor of Antiquities, has recently excavated the **Gerondomoúri Cave**, which was used by generation upon generation of ancient Cretans as a charnel house—one of the island's most important anthropological finds. A comparative study of Minoan bones and skulls with those of over a thousand modern Cretans show that the islanders have physically changed very little, so when you see one of those wasp-waisted teenagers with thick curls, large black eyes and a profile like the *La Parisienne* fresco, you aren't hallucinating. The cigarette invariably dangling from her lips somehow adds to the effect.

The Road from Lassíthi to Neápolis

The road from the plateau to Neápolis and Ag. Nikólaos is full of twists and turns with dramatic views around each bend and the minatory little roadside chapels marking each fatal accident. Bus drivers sometimes stop for a coffee break in **Zénia,** where, according to legend, a young woman who had hair down to her knees caught the eye of a Turkish captain, who threatened to destroy the village if she would not marry him. During the wedding feast she poured him more wine than he could hold, then took him to bed and lopped off his head. Running to the church, she cut off her famous hair and took the clothes of a soldier and the name Captain Manólis, and, before she was killed, pickled several more Turkish ears (as American Indians used to collect scalps, the Cretans and Turks pickled the ears of their adversaries). Her hair and knife are said still to be on display in the church.

© *(0844–)*   *Where to Stay and Eating Out*

Tzermiádon and Ag. Geórgios

Kourites, © 22 194 (*B; mod*) is the smartest place to stay on the plateau, with 13 comfortable rooms. **Krikri**, © 22 170 (*E; inexp*) is just as small and has a restaurant. *Both open all year*. **Kronias** does good food as well; try the new potatoes in season. In Ag. Geórgios, try the **Rhea**, © 31 209 or **Dias**, © 31 207 (*both E; inexp*); the latter has good food, too.

Psychró

In Psychró, there are quite a few rooms to supplement the **Zeus**, ℭ 31 284 (*D; inexp*) and the **Dikteon Andron**, ℭ 31 504 (*E; inexp*). *Both open all year.* The tourist restaurant above the souvenir shop in the Diktean Cave car park has good pizzas and ready food (*around 2000dr*).

Between Mál" and Ag. Nikólaos

After Málía, the New Road cuts inland, avoiding the rugged Cape Ag. Ioánnis. This is good news for the last two resorts, Sísi and Milátos, which are free of the grind of heavy traffic that bedevils the coast to the west. Laid-back **Sísi** (ΣΙΣΙ) is like a chunk of southern California, with its modern pastel architecture, sandy beaches, and cute little port—a turquoise crique under the cliffs, lined with a palm garden and a cascade of tavernas, bars and pubs for homesich Brits serving beans on toast.

Just east, **Paralía Milátou** (ΠΑΡΑΛΙΑ ΜΙΛΑΤΟΥ) offers a striking, unprettified contrast to swish Sísi: a bit faded and very low-key, with a handful of fishing boats and a long pebble beach graced with a few sunbeds and fish tavernas. A few disappointing bits of stone on the east end of the beach recall ancient Milatos, one of the most important cities of Homeric Crete. Myth has it that the three brothers Minos, Rhadamanthys and Sarpedon once competed for the affections of a beautiful boy. When the boy chose Sarpedon, his brothers were such poor sports about it that Sarpedon left Crete for Asia Minor, taking with him not only the boy but the inhabitants of Milatos, where they founded the great city of Miletus. 'When Minos was in his prime, his very name terrified great nations: but now he was weak and very much afraid of Miletus, the son of Deione and Apollo, for the latter was young and strong,' Ovid wrote in the *Metamorphoses,* summing up the decline of Crete and rise of Ionia in the 8th and 7th century BC. Up the hill, the dusty old village of Milátos proper still has a dusty, forsaken air.

It has a more recent reason to look forlorn. In 1823, during the War of Independence, the large stalactite **Cave of Milátos** (on the edge of a wild, rocky ravine, 6km from the beach, then a 10-minute walk from the narrow parking area) served as a refuge for two weeks for 3600 people. The Turks under General Hassan besieged them, and after two battles the refugees surrendered; Hassan had promised them safe conduct, but instead massacred all the men and children and enslaved the women. Under the bulbous rock at the entrance, the cave has a low, smoke-blackened ceiling supported by slender stalactites. One large chamber has a chapel, or *heroön*, containing a glass reliquary full of bones.

The main coastal highway passes over a ravine where the Cretans tend to pull over and light a candle to the miraculous icon in **Ag. Geórgios Selinári**, St George of the Moon; the story goes that a monk found the icon, but was refused permission from the pasha to build a church for it, so he did it secretly, by moonlight. Another, now abandoned monastery dedicated to George, **Ag. Geórgios Vrachasiótis**, is south of Vrachási (pick up the key from the priest in Vrachási) and contains a carved wooden iconostasis, a marvel of Cretan folk art. A relief of the saint killing the dragon accompanies the 16th-century dedicatory inscription on the belltower. South of Milátos and just north of the highway, **Latsída**'s churches of Ag. Paraskeví and the Panagía both have 14th- and 15th-century frescoes.

✆ *(0841–)*   ***Where to Stay and Eating Out***

Sísi

The new resort on the block is the vast, luxurious **Kalimera Kriti Hotel and Village Resort**, on the east end of Sísi, ✆ 71 134, ✉ 71 598 with two private beaches, outdoor and indoor pools, tennis courts and rooms with everything you could possibly want. On the far west edge of Sísi, the stylish **Hellenic Palace**, ✆ 71 568, ✉ 71 502 (*A; exp*) is modern and comfortable, near the local riding centre. More reasonable, smaller choices with kitchenettes include **Zygos Apts**, ✆ 71 279 (*C; mod*) and **Antzela Apts**, ✆ 71 121(*C; mod*). The **Elite** restaurant, run by George Sevadalis, has an excellent reputation; **Mediterraneo** has good fresh fish.

Paralía Milátou

There are a dozen places that rent rooms in the village, but most people stop by just for seafood. **Taverna Mary Elen** gives you a a free carafe of local wine with every fish you order, or try **Sirenes**, serving the day's catch. In the centre, **Zephyros** will regale you with home-made wine and *rakí.*

Neápolis and Ancient Dreros

Immersed in greenery and almond groves, prosperous **Neápolis** (ΝΕΑΠΟΛΙΣ) is the largest town on the Herákleon–Ag. Nikólaos road. In its former incarnation as a village named Karés it witnessed the birth of Pétros Fílagros in 1340. Raised by Catholics, he became a professor of theology and was elected Pope Alexander V in 1409, one of several popes-for-a-year during the Great Schism. Karés predeceased him, however, when the Venetians destroyed it in 1347 after a revolt. The rebuilt village grew into the 'new town', Neápolis, the provincial capital before Ag. Nikólaos. It has a leafy central square, with a small **museum** (*open Tues–Sun 10–1 and 6–9; adm*) housing traditional crafts and a few finds from Dreros.

Once the important city in these parts, **Dreros** lies up a narrow winding road north of Neápolis (cross under the New Road and follow signs for Kouroúnes); above the tiny parking area, a rough path leads up through the maquis and rocks that look like Licorice Allsorts to a saddle between two peaks. Excavated in the early 1900s, there's a jumble of walls, a cistern, an Archaic agora and, under a protective shelter, a 7th-century BC Geometric temple to Apollo Delphinios; the latter yielded the oldest hammered bronze statues ever found in Greece (in the Herákleon museum) and Eteocretan inscriptions—Minoan words in Greek letters. Pilgrims used to trudge up the long stair from the gorge to pay homage. Now Dreros is a lonely, wild place, with views down to the sea, both to the east and west.

The whole Akra Ag. Ioánnis (St John's Cape) north of Dreros is lonely, crisscrossed by a network of winding roads linking forgotten farming hamlets. The most scenic of these routes is the main one, zigzagging up from Nikithaniós to Kastélli and over to Eloúnda (*see* below). If you have the time or inclination, there are some good icons to see in the parish church of **Doriés**, near the vaulted stables of an abandoned monastery, and, north of that, the handsome agricultural complex of **Moní Aretíou**, founded by a Venetian nobleman and currently undergoing restoration.

Ag. Nikólaos

When Ag. Nikólaos (ΑΓ. ΝΙΚΟΛΑΟΣ) was selected capital of *nomós* Lassíthi in 1905 only 95 people lived in the little village, built as an amphitheatre overlooking a round lake, the sea, and breathtaking Mirabélo Bay. It didn't even have a proper port; ships had to call at Pachiá Ámmos to the east. A new port in 1965 attracted the first yachties and jet setters, charmed by 'Agios' as the locals call it. What has happened since is not exactly hard to guess, although, if this is your first visit, exaggerate, perhaps mathematically cube, what you imagine mass tourism has wrought on this town named after Santa Claus. The resident population has multiplied by 100. The British contingency who swarm there have dubbed it Agnik, a name with all the charm of an industrial by-product, and a few years back it was the first place on Crete to cross over the courtesy threshold. Signs were erected, pleading: 'During your stay in Ag. Nikólaos you become a fellow sitizen (*sic*). Please respect our local mores and customs. Do not disrupt the town's tranquillity and keep the environment clean. Thank you. The Mayor.' They must have worked: the rowdies now concentrate at Chersónisos and Mália, leaving Agnik older, wiser and nicer.

Ag. Nikólaos ✆ (0841–)   ***Getting Around***

The Olympic Airways office is at Plastíra 20, ✆ 22 033. Ag. Nikólaos **port** (✆ 22 312) has three ferries a week to Piraeus and Sitía, and one ferry a week to Kássos, Kárpathos, Rhodes, Santoríni, Síkinos, Folégrandros and Mílos. The **bus station** (✆ 22 234) is near the rocky beach of Ámmos at the end of Sof. Venizélou. Beaches within easy bus range are Eloúnda (*see* below) and Kaló Chorió (on the road to Sitía). Other buses go to Herákleon, the Lassíthi plateau, Kritsá, Sitía, Ierápetra, and other points in the *nomós.*

Tourist office: Between the lake and the sea, 20 Aktí S. Koundoúrou, ℗ 22 357. **Tourist police** and Lost Property, 34 Kontogiáni, ℗ 26 900.

Festivals

New Year and **Easter**: festivities, including the burning of an effigy of Judas on a platform in the middle of the harbour. **29 May**: Ag. Triáda; **27 June–3 July**: nautical week, with fireworks on the last day; **6 December**: Ag. Nikólaos.

Around Town

Ag. Nikólaos stands on the ruins of Lato Pros Kamara, the port of ancient Lato, and the town still concentrates much of its rather mercenary soul around the port, overlooking the islet of **Ag. Pándes**. The chapel of the same name draws pilgrims on 20 June, but at other times you need to go with a cruise party to visit the *kri-kri* goats, the islet's sole inhabitants, who will probably hide anyway. The other tourist vortex is round **Lake Voulisméni**; although its Greek name means 'bottomless', it has been measured at 210ft/64m. Believed to be the mouth of an underground river, Voulisméni was often stagnant, until 1867 when the local pasha connected it to the sea. From the cliffs there's a fine view of the many fish that call it home, some over 2ft long and well fattened by bread from the restaurants, only to appear now and then on their menus. Behind the tourist office, there's a small but choice **Ethnographic Museum** (*open 8–2 and 6–8*), with a collection of old icons, costumes, embroideries, instruments (including a *toumboúrlo,* a drum that used to accompany the *lýra*) and stamps from independent Crete. Aktí S. Koundoúrou follows the waterfront, past rocky places where you can swim. There is a beach at the very end and the little stone church that gave the town its name, **Ag. Nikólaos**, with rare 9th-century Geometric frescoes from the Iconoclastic period (pick up the key at the Minos Palace Hotel).

The excellent **Archaeology Museum** up the hill at 68 K. Paleológou (*open 8.45–3, closed Mon; adm*) displays artefacts discovered in Eastern Crete; among the highlights are Neolithic obsidian blades ('still razor-sharp!') and fish hooks, Middle Minoan vases from a shipwreck near Pseíra islet, a unique Neolithic phallus-shaped idol from Zákros, and the peculiar Early Minoan pinhead 'Goddess of Myrtos' who could pass for a chicken, her long pipe arms wrapped around a pitcher. There is lovely gold jewellery from Móchlos, a clay staff imprinted with Linear A on four sides and a stone vase in the form of a triton shell, engraved with two demons making a libation (both from Mália) and a delicate Late Minoan gold pin, decorated with a bramble design and Linear A inscription. A rare Late Minoan infant burial in a *tholos* tomb found near Sitía is displayed exactly as it was found.

To Elounda,
Spinalonga

ERYTH. STAVROU

Archaeological
Museum

To Herakleon,
Sitia, Ierapetra

MILATOU

K. KORITSAS

PRIGIPOSGEORGIOU

PERIKLEOUS

DAVAKI

KANTANOLEONTOS

AKTI S KOUNDOUROU

ETHNIKIS ANTISTASEOS

K. PALEOLOGOU

DOM. THEOTOKOPOULOU

KORNAROU

I. KAZANTZAKI

D. SOLOMOU

NIK. PLASTIRA

TITOU

Lake
Voulismeni

Ethnographic
Museum

KATEHAKI

KORAKA

Youth
Hostel

KONDILAKI

Tourist
Information

Bank

OMIROU

28 OCTOVRIOU

R. KOUNDOUROU

AKTI JOSIF KOUNDOUROU

LASTHENI

PASIFAIS

MILOU

SAROLIDI

AKTI THEMISTOKLEOUS

Post
Office

Olympic
Airways

NIK. PLASTIRA

ARKADIOU

GARIL

DASKALOGIANNI

DIMOKRATIAS

FILELLINON

Plateia
Eleftheriou
Venizelou

25 MARTIOU

M. SFAKIANAKI

EVANS

TSELEPI

ARIADNIS

Kato Plateia

TELNINAS

AKTI PANGALOU

POLITECHNIOU

NIK. FOKA

ALEXOM

K. SFAKIANAKI

OTE

V. MERARCHIAS

S. VENIZELOU

Agii Triada
Cathedral

Church of
our Lady

Prefecture

MIRABELLOU

SOLONOS

MANOUSOGIAN

KONTOGIANI

HIMARAS

To Kritsa,
Ierapetra,
Sitia

TAVLA

I. KOZIRI

Plateia
Atlandithos

AKTI NEARCHOU

Bus Terminus

To Stadium,
Municipal Beach,
Almyros Beach

Marina

Spinalonga

Rhodes

Ferries
Arrival/
Departure

Harbour

N

100 metres
100 yards

Ag. Nikoláos

221

There's a Daedalic bust from the 7th century BC that looks like Christopher Columbus and a unique lamp from Olous with 70 nozzles. In the last room, a 1st century AD skull still has a fine set of teeth, a gold burial wreath embedded in the bone of its brow, and a silver coin from Polyrenia, to pay Charon, the ferryman of the Underworld. A plate of knucklebones found near the head of a woman may have been used for divination.

Many tourists are surprised to discover that Agnik was asleep when God was handing out beaches: there's little sand at shingly **Kitroplateía**, sheltered and safe for children, named for the cypress wood once exported from here. The pocket sand beach of **Ammoúdi** is at the end of Aktí S. Koundoúrou, while at the other end of town, near the bus station, **Ámmos** is a clean piece of sand, but not a terribly atmospheric one. To the south, on the other side of the stadium, is the crowded, clean **municipal beach** (*entrance fee*); from there, a walking path leads past little, sandy **Gargardóros** beach and beyond that to the bamboo-curtained naturalist beach **Almyrós**.

Shopping

Don't confuse the three streets named after the Koundoúrou family. Mixed in with the more blatant tourist-oriented stores flogging embarrassing T-shirts, Ag. Nikólaos has some excellent Cretan boutiques, such as **Maria Patsaki**, at 2 K. Sfakianáki, with embroideries, clothes, fabrics and antiques, or **Syllogi**, on Aktí S. Koundoúrou, with a display old paintings, antiques, silver and other fine crafts. **Sofia**, 33 R. Koundoúrou, has a good selection of Cretan crafts, jewellery and weavings. **Kerazoza**, 42 R. Koundoúrou, has puppets, toys and postcards from the 1950s. Gold and jewellery shops are clustered around I. Koundoúrou, overlooking the port. **Anna Karteri**, 5 R. Koundoúrou, has a wide range of titles in English and books about Crete.

Ag. Nikólaos ✆ (0841–)   **Where to Stay**

luxury

Ag. Nikólaos' reputation as a posy tourist hotspot owes much to the posh hotels in the area, such as the **St Nicholas Bay**, spread over a narrow peninsula 2km from Ag. Nikólaos, ✆ 25 041, ✉ 24 556, a 130-bungalow complex which has a private sandy beach, three adult pools, and every other comfort, including an art gallery. *Open Mar–Nov.* **Minos Beach,** on the secluded garden-covered promontory of Ammoúdi, ✆ 22 345, ✉ 22 548, has 132 sumptuous bungalows. Although built back practically in the Minoan era by Agnik standands (1962) it is still one of the best; some bungalows are directly on the sea. The complex includes a good restaurant and three bars, and a patch of private beach.

expensive

Villa Olga, 3 Pitarokili, ✆ 23 382, 🖾 24 655, offers central furnished apartments, with a small pool. **Moskonas**, by Almyrós Beach, ✆ 22 605, has apartments sleeping up to 5 people; **Melas**, 26 Aktí Koundoúrou, ✆ 28 734, also has stylish apartments, sleeping 2–5; book in the winter through Ioánna Melás, 47 Amarilládos St, 15452 Athens, ✆ (1) 647 0133.

moderate

Panorama on Aktí Koundoúrou, ✆ 28 890 (*C*) has a good view over the harbour, and all rooms come with bath. **Miramare Apts** sleep up to five over Kitroplateía Beach, available through Knossos Travel, ✆ 22 146, 🖾 28 114. A row of pleasant guesthouses—**Adonis,** ✆ 51 525 (C), **Perla,** ✆ 23 379 (C) and **Linda,** ✆ 22 130 (B)—lurk just off the centre of Aktí S. Koundoúrou. Near the bottom of this category, the noisy **New York**, near the bus station at 21 Kontogiáni St, ✆ 28 577 is known for having rooms when the other hotels are all booked up with package tours.

inexpensive

The tourist office lists over 1000 rooms to rent in Ag. Nikólaos but just try to find one—and when you do, expect to pay over the odds. The **Green House**, 15 Modátsou, ✆ 22 025, has little wooden rooms leading out to a small courtyard, filled to overflowing with shrubs and trees, and patrolled by a small army of cats. **Loukas**, in central Plateía Eleftheríou, ✆ 23 169, offers good-value rooms with bathrooms and kitchen facilities, although summer prices verge on the moderate range.

Ag. Nikólaos ✆ *(0841–)*   **Eating Out**

Restaurants and tavernas across the spectrum compete for your dinner drachma, but there are good ones worth looking out for. **Pelagos**, on Str. Kóraka (just inland from Aktí Koundoúrou), is a trendy seafood restaurant, with a long list of tasty *mezédes* to start with (*4–5000dr*). When the Greeks want to dine on the lake, they make for the last place, **Pefko**, with delicious, reasonably priced taverna food. Although it has no view at all, **Itanos**, next to the cathedral on Str. Kíprou, ✆ 25 340, has some of the finest cooking in eastern Crete, with a wide selection of old fashioned ready dishes (the lamb and spinach in egg-lemon sauce is excellent) and good barrelled wine. Near Almyrós Beach on Odós Anapatseos, little **Portes** is a local favourite, with good Greek and Cretan specialities; further south **Taverna Gargadoros**, towards the beach of the same name, is good, too. Halfway up to the archaeology museum, on K. Paleológou, **Aovas** is small, inexpensive and good, serving Cretan dishes in a green shady courtyard far from the madding crowd.

Near Kitroplateía Beach, **Trata** on M. Sfakianáki has a roof garden where you can tuck into dishes such as fish soup, Trata chicken *kleftíko* (chicken with cream, cheese and ham) and a long list of casserole dishes. Of the tavernas along Kitroplateía, **Ofou to Io** at the far end offers a good choice of more unusual Greek and Cretan dishes: boiled kid, *tigania* pork with white sauce, *soutzoukakia*, oval meatballs with tomato and green pepper sauce, roast lamb stuffed with garlic and cheeses. Down at Ammoúdi Beach the **Dolphin** has good food served by jovial twin waiters (*2500dr*), or head out of town all together for **Synantysi**, a popular taverna along the Old Road to Herákleon. If the joys of Greek cuisine wear thin, Ag. Nikólaos has plenty of alternatives: **Il Capriccio**, 31 Aktí Koundoúrou, serves authentic Italian pizzas and pasta dishes. Near the tourist office on Kondyláki Street, **The Embassy**, © 24 775, does a wide variety of reasonably priced vegetarian, Indian, and even weight-watching dishes if you're having trouble fitting into your bikini, as well as a traditional English Sunday lunch; open until 2am. Its neighbour, the **New Dragon**, offers a better than average 4000dr Chinese menu.

Bars and Nightlife

After-dark action is not hard to find, concentrated around the lake and port, although finding anything remotely Greek is not always easy. **Café Ellinikon**, on Kapetán Kozýri, has excellent *rakí*, local wine and *mezédes* to start an evening; other good bets for a civilized drink include the quay-side **Porto** or the small bar overlooking the Marina, just up from the bus station. For music, there's the perenially popular roof terrace at **Alexandros** on K. Paleológou, and the dancing disco bars **Lipstick** and **Borabora** overlooking the main port.

A Cretan Easter Treat: *Kalichouniá*

Of all the cities of Crete, Ag. Nikólaos puts on the best show at Easter, and it's also as good a place as any to find *kalichouniá*, the island's special sweet cheese pies, traditionally baked on Thursday before Easter. Outside Crete, it's hard to find sweet *myzíthra* cheese for the creamy filling, but an unsalted or lightly salted ricotta is a decent substitute. For the pastry, mix 200ml olive oil, 50g sugar, 3 egg yolks, a pinch of salt and grated zest from a half lemon. Heat 350ml of milk and pour into a separate bowl, slowly stirring 1tsp of soda into the milk, then pour this into olive oil mix, stirring all the time. Sift 1kg of flour with 1tsp baking powder, and pour it into the mix. The dough should be soft and smooth. If it's too sticky, add a bit more flour. Cover and put to one side.

For the filling, crumble 1kg of sweet *myzíthra* (or ricotta) in a bowl, and add 2 well-beaten eggs, the grated zest of an orange and lemon, 350g sugar, and 1tsp baking powder. Blend together well. Pre-heat the oven at 150°C. Roll the pastry out as thin as possible, and use a glass to cut into circles around 8cm in diameter. Take a spoonful of filling and place in the centre of the pastry circle. Lightly brush the edges with water and fold to form a hexagon (easier said than done) leaving a small cheese 'window' in the centre. Brush the surface with beaten egg, arrange on a greased baking sheet, and bake for around 30 minutes, until the pastry turns golden brown.

Eloúnda, Olous and Spinalónga

View after view across the sublime Bay of Mirabélo and its islands unfold along the 12 kilometres from Ag. Nikólaos north to Eloúnda; below, the rocky coastline is interspersed with pocket-sized coves, draped with Crete's most glamorous hotels. Perhaps thanks to its role in the BBC series, *Who Pays the Ferryman,* **Eloúnda** (ΕΛΟΥΝΤΑ) attracts a high percentage of British tourists, many of whom never seem to drift too far from bars and restaurants in the central square overlooking the sea. Every here and there are pocket-sized shingle or sandy beaches, many good for snorkelling. On the south edge of Eloúnda, a little bridge crosses an artificial channel dug by the French in 1897, separating the promontory of Spinalónga ('Long Thorn') from mainland Crete.

Along this channel lie the sunken harbour installations of ancient **Olous**, the port of Dreros and goal of the 'sunken city' excursions from Ag. Nikólaos. It's a pretty place under the windmills, lined with grey and pink stone, a favourite haunt of cranes. The moon goddess Britomartis, inventor of the fishing net, was worshipped here, represented by a wooden cult statue (a *xoanon*) with a fishtail, made by Daedalos; one story has her turning into a fish to wiggle away from the embrace of King Minos. Fish mosaics also figure in the geometric black, white and brown mosaic floor of an Early Byzantine basilica excavated to the northwest, near the Canal Bar; one of its walls re-used a block inscribed with part of a 2nd century BC treaty in Doric dialect between Rhodes and Olous (now in the Ag. Nikólaos museum). Oxa, the mountain just behind, was an important source of whetstones.

The tiny island of **Spinalónga** (ΣΠΙΝΑΛΟΓΚΑ, not to be confused with the promontory) is a half-hour caique trip from Eloúnda, or an hour by excursion boat from Ag. Nikólaos. Venetian engineers detached it from the promontory in 1579 when they dug a canal to defend their huge round fortress, built on the ruins of the ancient fort of Olous. After the Turkish conquest, it held out like the other island forts of Nea Soúda and Gramvoúsa as a shelter for Cretan refugees and base to harry the Turks; in 1715, the Venetians gave up all hope of ever re-conquering Crete and handed the forts over to the Ottomans. The Turks settled the island with soldiers and civilians. When they were evacuated in 1904, Spinalónga became a leper colony—the last in Europe—that survived until 1957, when word filtered through to Crete that leprosy wasn't contagious. Today the poignant little streets, houses and the lepers' church are abandoned and forlorn. **Pláka**, opposite the islet, was the supply centre for the lepers and now has a tiny laid-back colony of its own, dedicated to rest and relaxation by a little pebble beach.

✆ *(0841–)*   ***Where to Stay and Eating Out***

Eloúnda

Elounda Mare, ✆ 41 512 (reservations) or 41 102, ✉ 41 307 *(lux)*, is a member of the prestigious Relais & Chateaux complex with 50 hotel rooms and 40 bunga- lows—and 35 private swimming pools on the seafront. **Eloúnda Beach**, ✆ 41 412, ✉ 41 373 (*lux*) incorporates
traditional Cretan architecture in its central hotel and bungalows, and has a sandy beach as well as its own cinema, deep-sea diving expeditions, fitness centre, heated pool and other luxuries. **Candia Park Village**, between Ag. Nikólaos and Eloúnda, ✆ 26 811, ✉ 22 367 (*A; exp*) is recently built and perfect for families, with a wide range of sporting activities from the *de rigueur* large pool to basketball, windsurfing, waterskiing and a small aqua park; all rooms are air-conditioned with kitchen facilities. **Korfos Beach**, ✆ 41 591 (*B; exp*) comes complete with a private beach. Near the Olous causeway **Olous Beach**, ✆ 41 270 (*C; mod*) is a popular place, with a pool and roof garden. Cheaper rooms are rare: try **Pension Oasis**, in a villa on the north edge of the village.

Eloúnda is well endowed with restaurants, especially around the port area. **Restaurant Vritomartis**, out on a little islet in the middle of Eloúnda's port, serves well-prepared seafood and lobster. Nearby **Kalidon** has tables out on a small pontoon, and a good selection of vegetarian dishes and a wide choice of *mezédes*. **Poulis** has reasonably priced fish, next to the **Taverna Ferryman** 'as seen on the BBC'. **Marilena**, ✆ 41 322, has a vine-covered rear garden and Greek and Cypriot dishes on the menu. On Friday nights there's live Greek music at **Café Ellas**. At least once make the scenic drive up to Pinés, where the windmills are still in working order and there's a good taverna, **O Mylos**; also outside the centre, on the Pláka road, **Taverna Despina** has a good name for fish, although it's a bit dear.

Pláka

Spinalonga Village, ✆ 41 285(*A; exp*) is the fanciest here, although there are several more basic choices, such as **KriKri** (*D; inexp*) or the simple rooms at **Stella Mare**. Taverna **Dolphin** has fresh seafood.

Above Ag. Nikólaos: Kéra Panagía and Kritsá

One excursion from Ag. Nikólaos that shouldn't be missed is the short trip up to Kritsá, with a stop a kilometre before the village for **Kéra Panagía** (*open 9–2; adm*), set back from a road in an olive grove. It looks like no other church on the island: the three naves with gable roofs cut from a cookie cutter, training long triangular buttresses, crowned by the simplest of belltowers and a drum-shaped dome, the whole coated with a hundred layers of whitewash. Within, however, the entire wall surface is alive with the colours of Crete's most celebrated fresco cycle, one that well illustrates the evolution of Byzantine art before the Turks, when Byzantine art stopped evolving altogether.

The central aisle, dedicated to the life of the Virgin, dates from the 12th century; it seems that in the mid-13th century the first paintings were destroyed and replaced with new ones in the severe, so-called 'archaicizing linear style', characterized by a rhythmic use of lines (especially in draperies) and in the flat perpectives. Note especially *The Nativity*, *Herod's Banquet* and *Last Supper*, and the patriarchs sit under the pine trees, clutching to their bosoms platters holding the souls of the Just, while, under a damaged *Crucifixion*, in the *Harrowing of Hell* the damned are meekly resigned to their interesting punishments. The four ribs dividing the structure of the dome prevented the painting of the usual figure of the Pantocrator, or Christ in Majesty. Instead, you'll find scenes from the Gospel: Candlemas, Baptism, the raising of Lazarus, and entry into Jerusalem, with four angels overhead and prophets and evangelists below. Further down, SS. George and Dimitrios appear as military saints in full gear, while on the northwest pillar look for *St Francis*, with his slightly crossed eyes and Catholic tonsure. It's rare that a western saint earns a place among the Orthodox, but Francis, introduced to Crete by the Venetians, made a considerable impression among the common people.

The two side aisles were later additions, painted in the more naturalistic, Palaeologan style coming out of Constantinople in the early 14th century. The south aisle is devoted to St Anne, an unusual choice in Byzantine art. Even more unusual, many of the scenes are based on apocryphal gospels, perhaps by special request of the donors, whose names are inscribed near the door. A large portrait of Anne, Christ's grandmother, fills the apse, while the frescoes on the walls and in the barrel vaults are characterized by large figures against dark, uncluttered back-grounds, typical of the Macedonian school: the *House of Joachim*, the *Birth of the Virgin*, *Joseph's Sorrow* (for his fiancée's unexpected pregnancy), the *Water of Testing* (Mary is given a pitcher of water to drink by a rabbi to test her purity before marriage), and the *Virgin as the Closed Gate*.

The apse of the north, or St Anthony, belongs to Christ Pantocrator, while the *Last Judgement*, crowded with figures, covers most of the nearby vaults: female allegories of the earth and sea render up their dead to be weighed for better or worse on the big scales, while the Virgin pleads for mercy. Amid the saints on the walls are scenes from the Life of St Anthony, and at the end of the row don't miss the portraits of the donors, George Mazezanes (with his white bonnet), his wife, and their small daughter, rare pictures of medieval Cretans.

In 1956, director Jules Dassin chose the lovely white village of **Kritsá** (ΚΡΙΤΣΑ) as the location for his film *He Who Must Die* starring Melina Mercouri, and ever since the tourist boom in Ag. Nikólaos its role has been as something of a film set, the traditional Cretan village swamped by tourists from the capital, who are in turn swamped by villagers selling them tablecloths, rugs and lace, some rather more hand-made than others. Kritsá is famous for throwing real roll-out-the-barrel Cretan weddings, and although there are far too many foreigners around now to get a casual invite as in the past, in August weddings are re-enacted with food, drink and dancing for fee-paying 'guests'. There are more churches with good 14th-century frescoes to see: Ag. Konstantínos, Ag. Geórgios and the cemetery church, Ag. Ioánnis, just up the Kroústas road.

Ancient Lato

A scenic 3km walk (the path begins near the crossroads) or drive north of Kritsá leads up to the extensive remains of Dorian **Lato**, or more properly, Lato Etera *(open 8.30–5, closed Mon)*, its ruins splendidly curling down the saddle between the hills, with eagle-eye views over the sea. Named for the Minoan goddess Leto (Lato in Dorian Greek), the city was founded in the 7th century BC; it flourished through the Classical era and gave birth to Nearchus, Alexander the Great's admiral and explorer, before it was eventually abandoned in favour of its port, Lato Kamara (modern Ag. Nikólaos). One of the most intriguing things about Lato is the Minoan influence on the Dorian design: the double gateway, the street of 80 steps lined with small houses and workshops (one was a dyeworks), and the architecture of its agora, with its columnless sanctuary and cistern in the centre. A Doric portico with benches lined the west side, its end converted into a round threshing floor after the French excavated the site in the early 1900s.

The wide steps continuing up from the agora to a peristyle court and the *Prytaneion*, where the sacred fire burned day and night, date from the 8th century BC and are believed to have been inspired by Minoan 'theatres'; spectators could sit and watch events down in the agora below. Monumental towers stood on either side of a narrower stair, leading up to the altar and sacred hearth itself. On the second hill stands the beautifully built, column-less city temple (probably dedicated to Leto), an isolated altar, and a primitive theatre capable of seating a few hundred people. Here especially you don't have to wander far to realize that Lato was large and has only been partially excavated; walls stick out helter-skelter everywhere.

A few buses from Kritsá continue up to **Kroústas** (ΚΡΟΥΣΤΑΣ), which is just as pretty but has been spared the tourist hordes. It has some Byzantine frescoed churches and a huge festival on 25 June, the feast of St John, celebrated with bonfires and dances. A rough road continues to flower-bedecked **Prína**, affording magnificent views and the chance to circle back to Ag. Nikólaos by way of Kaló Chorió (*see* below).

East of Ag. Nikólaos: The Gulf of Mirabélo

The stunningly beautiful coastline that lends Ag. Nikólaos its panache owes its name to the Genoese fortress of Mirabélo, 'Beautiful View', demolished by the Turks. Where sheer precipices aren't crowding the sea, the land around the Gulf of Mirabélo is immensely fertile, and has been densely populated for some 5000 years; archaeological zoning of the area has kept Agnikish development here to a minimum, although frequent buses run between the capital and the popular sandy beach of **Kaló Chório** (ΚΑΛΟ ΧΩΡΙΟ), 12km from Ag. Nikólaos. From Kaló Chorió a path leads to up to **Vrókastro**, a Late Minoan peak sanctuary used as a refuge settlement during the Doric invasion; a Geometric-era fort stands on the hill.

The main road east continues past the up-and-coming resort of **Istro** to the turn-off for the 12th-century **Moní Faneroménis**, a dizzying climb up the hill but worth while for the absolutely stupendous views over the Mirabélo gulf. The monastery is built like a fortress into the cliff, sheltering a cave where a miraculous icon of the Virgin was found by a shepherd, guided by a light. It was a nest of resistance against the Venetians and Turks and had a secret Greek school; today two monks live there, one of whom will show you the beautifully frescoed cave-church.

© *(0841–)*   ***Where to Stay and Eating Out***

Kaló Chório

Fancy white and built into the hillside under the road, **Istron Bay**, © 61 303, ✆ 61 383 (*lux*) has everything a lazy holiday requires, from a special children's pool and game rooms to seawater pool, jewellery shop, and private beach and beach bar. *Open April–Oct.* **Elpida**, © 61 403 (*C; mod*) is on the west side of the beach, 500 yards from the sea, but with a restaurant and pool. *Open April–Oct.*

Gourniá: 'The Pompeii of Minoan Crete'

East of Ístro, the road passes directly below the striking hillside site of **Gourniá** (*open Tues–Sun, 8.30–3*), the best-preserved Minoan town on Crete. It was excavated between 1901 and 1904 by American Harriet Boyd, who was not only the first woman to lead a major dig but did so under circumstances hard to imagine today: a Classics scholar just out of university, she was in Athens when the news of the first big finds in Crete began to pour in. Caught up in the excitement, down she sailed to Crete, where she met Arthur Evans; the next year, she hired a Cretan foreman and his mother, and the three travelled about eastern Crete on donkeys, looking for a likely place to dig. After a few weeks they had the luck to stumble on the most complete Minoan town of them all.

Gourniá reached its peak in the Late Minoan period, around 1550 BC, and was never rebuilt after a massive fire c. 1225 BC. Narrow, stone-paved lanes meander up and down, densely packed with workshops, store rooms and what seem like very small houses, although originally most had a storey or two on top, made of mud brick. Tools found in several of these has led to the identification of a carpenter's and smith's workshop. At the highest point, a small 'palace' with store rooms is built around the obligatory rectangular court; there's an L-shaped arrangement of steps, a mini-version of the theatrical areas in the palaces, near a stone slab that may have been used for sacrifices. Just north, the Shrine of the Minoan Snake Goddess had its little shelf for cult items, including long, tube-like snake vases. The fact that Boyd found no Linear A tablets here has led to the theory that Gourniá had only limited local authority, handling the traffic of goods across the isthmus of Crete.

From Gourniá, it's a short drive down to **Pachiá Ámmos**, a rather woebegone-looking resort village along a sandy beach that sadly seems to corner all the garbage in the Cretan sea. Perhaps by the time you arrive the much-talked-about plans for doing something about it may have improved matters. Cretans come from miles around to eat fish here, and as they usually know what they're about you may want to follow suit.

Pachiá Ámmos stands at the beginning of the Ierápetra road (*see* p.243) bisecting the isthmus of Crete, a mere 12km of land separating the Aegean from the Libyan sea. There are plans (rather more likely to happen than Pachiá Ámmos's breakwater, unfortunately) to build Ag. Nikólaos an international airport of its very own here by 1998. Besides rescue digs on the airport site, the isthmus is undergoing a close survey; as Gourniá wasn't a palace, archaeologists suspect one must be somewhere near by. After all, this was one of the regions first settled by the Minoans. In **Vasilikí**, 5km south of Pachiá Ámmos, a Pre-Palace Minoan settlement (2600–2000 BC) was discovered in 1906 that yielded the first known specimens of what has since been known as 'Vasilikí ware', the Minoans' first distinctive pottery style, boldly mottled in red and black, an effect produced by uneven firing. Excavations here have recently been taken up again in search of clues to the Minoans' origin, as Vasilikí is one of the few sites from the period that was abandoned and never rebuilt; some of the walls have retained their red-plaster decoration, but otherwise there's not a lot to see. A bit further south, however, **Episkopí** is worth a stop for a delightful blue domed Byzantine church, the see of a Catholic bishop in Venetian times.

Pachiá Ámmos to Sitía: the Cretan Riviera

Pachiá Ámmos is also the crossroads for Sitía, some 47km east down a new corniche road that rates among the most scenic on Crete, slithering along the jagged, often precipitous coast of the Gulf of Mirabélo, with the bright lights of Ag. Nikólaos twinkling far below. **Kavoúsi**, just east of Pachiá Ámmos, lies between a small but littered beach called **Thólos** and two small Late Minoan sites: a settlement and cemetery at **Vrondá**, high on a plateau in the Thriptís Mountains, and even further up, 700m above sea level, **Kástro**, located near a fresh spring, with the whole Gulf of Mirabélo spread out below. Both have received a good deal of attention lately from American archaeologists, who believe Vrondá was settled by refugees from Gourniá; when the Dorians invaded, they moved to Kástro and stayed there until the 7th century BC. Next on the corniche road, **Plátanos** has a wonderful belvedere over the gulf, and a pair of tavernas to linger over the sunset.

Móchlos

The earliest Minoan site along the gulf is **Móchlos** (ΜΟΧΛΟΣ), a charming Greek island fishing village with a pebbly beach, down, down, down from the main road. The setting is lovely: barren cliffs behind and a small islet barely a stone's throw from the shore. This was originally attached to the mainland, giving Minoan Móchlos the advantage of two harbours, one facing east and the other west. Abandoned after the disaster of 1470 BC, its cemetery of house-like tombs has helped in the understanding of trade and industry of a proto-urban Minoan town of 300 souls; Móchlos specialized in pots with lid handles shaped like reclining dogs. Recently, seven intact chamber tombs with their clay *larnaxes* were discovered cut into the cliffs facing the islet. One Late Minoan building on Móchlos is known as 'the House of the Theran Refugees' for its architectural similarities to the top-floor timbered houses at Akrotíri, on Santoríni; pot sherds from Akrotíri littered the floor *on top of* a 20cm layer of volcanic ash. Obviously life went on after the Big Bang.

Yet another Minoan settlement existed from 3000 BC—and one that likewise continued to exist after the eruption of Santoríni—on **Pseíra**, 2km offshore, where the inhabitants used the pumice that floated ashore to build up the floor of their shrine. The little town was excavated in 1907 by American Richard Seager and, judging by the rich finds, it was a prosperous little port town in its day, although now it's completely barren. Pseíra's House of the Pillar Partitions, with a bathroom equipped with a sunken tub, plughole and drains, is one of the most elegant in eastern Crete. The ruins on top belong to a Roman-era lighthouse and fortification. There are occasional excursions to Pseíra from Ag. Nikólaos, although it usually isn't too hard to talk an off-duty fisherman in Móchlos into taking you over for a small fee.

Looking for Atlantis

And wishing to lead them [the Egyptians] *on to talk about early times, he embarked on an account of the earliest events known here... And a very old priest said to him, 'Oh, Solon, Solon, you Greeks are all children; there's no such thing as an old Greek.'*

Plato, *Timaeus*

As Plato tells the story, his friend Critias had heard the story from his grandfather, who had got it from the legendary sage Solon himself. Solon in his travels had gone to Egypt, where a priest familiar with the ancient records there had told him an incredible tale 9000 years old, of the lost island of Atlantis and how it sank into the sea. Athens was involved too, and it was that city's finest hour. The Egyptian recounted the wonders of Atlantis's great civilization, and how the Atlanteans had grown haughty and degenerate in their latter days and attempted the conquest of all the peoples of the eastern Mediterranean. Athens alone stood against them, and her army won a famous victory on Atlantis—just before the earthquakes and floods, sent by the gods to punish the Atlanteans, destroyed the island and the Athenian army too in the space of a day.

Plato gives more details on all this in a companion dialogue, the unfinished *Critias*, which has been called the 'first work of science fiction'. It has certainly spawned more crank theories over the last 2500 years than any book excepting of course the Bible. And as soon as scientists started bringing the facts in about the catastrophic eruption of Santoríni *c.* 1500 BC, which seemed to have put an end to Minoan civilization, it was only natural that someone would make the logical connection between mythical Atlantis and ancient Crete.

There is no sunken continent in the Atlantic (which probably takes its name from Plato's tale), and if you're looking for Atlantis Crete will simply have to do. There are some odd hints in the *Critias*. Atlantis's capital was built as a series of concentric rings, alternately land and water, rather like a labyrinth, and at the centre stood a temple of Atlantis's founder, Poseidon, the god of the sea, along with a sanctuary inhabited by sacred bulls. A pillar stood there, over which one of the bulls was sacrificed 'alternately every fifth and sixth year'. To the Greeks that meant at the end of four- and five-year periods—the nine-year solar cycle encountered in Cretan mythology.

The story of Solon's trip to Egypt is plausible enough, and the Egyptians certainly would have had a memory of Crete in their records, something the Greeks, who had even forgotten how to write in their post-Mycenean Dark Age, did not. Classical Greeks, for all their delight in precision, never seemed to have a very good sense of time. If Solon (or Plato) had misunderstood 9000 for 900 years, then the date would be remarkably close to the time of the Santoríni eruption. How much of Atlantis came garbled from the Egyptians, and how much was simply invented by Plato, a fellow with quite a lively imagination, will probably never be entirely sorted out.

Móchlos ✆ (0834–) **Where to Stay and Eating Out**

Barbarossa Tours, ✆ 94 179, can reserve a hotel or villa for you. **Aldiana,** ✆ 94 322 (*B; exp*) precludes the need to go anywhere else, with a restaurant, sports, a pool, and nightclub. *Open April–Oct.* **Sofia,** ✆ 94 554 (*D; mod*) is pleasant and small. *Open Mar–Oct.* **Móchlos,** ✆ 94 205 (*E; inexp*) is 20 yards from the beach. *Open all year.* Even cheaper are the rooms at the edge of the village ✆ 94 428.

Sta Limenaria, ✆ 94 206, at the far edge of the beach, has good food, including vegetarian meals, and special music or theme nights that make up Móchlos' nightlife; nearly all the seaside tavernas specialize in fresh fish.

Minor Sites Between Móchlos and Sitía

East of Móchlos, the road continues to encompass huge views on route to **Myrsíni**, a Venetian village with important Minoan tombs in the vicinity. Visitors are welcome at Myrsíni's pottery and weaving workshops, and there are 14th-century frescoes to see in the church if you can hunt up the key. Further east, in **Mésa Moulianá**, two beehive tombs date from the end of the Bronze Age, while in **Éxo Moulianá**, a village famous for its red wine, Ag. Geórgios has frescoes (1426).

Just before **Chamézi** (XAMEZI), high above Sitía, there's a unique oval, Pre-Palatial house or sanctuary with a paved entrance isolated on a hilltop; one theory has it that it was a coastal lookout post, or even a mini-fortress predating Minoan rule of the waves. Chamézi is a laid-back place that can get pretty wild at *rakí*-distilling time. It has a charming **folklore museum** by the church, open by request (ask for Giánni).

An antidote to the tourist mills of Ag. Nikólaos, sunny Sitía (ΣΗΤΕΙΑ) has kept its Greek soul and natural courtesy to a greater extent than any other town on the north coast, perhaps because it has a livelihood of its own, devoted to sultanas and wine. It is more pleasant than stunningly beautiful, set in an amphitheatre and endowed with a long, sandy beach that flies the blue flag of environmental right-eousness. Sitía was once ringed by Byzantine, Genoese and Venetian walls, before earthquakes and the bombardment of Barbarossa toppled them, leaving only a restored Venetian fortress as a souvenir, to close off the western end of the port.

Sitía ☏ (0843–)   ***Getting Around***

Sitía's little **airport** is linked by regular weekly flights to Kárpathos and Kássos, and to Athens twice a week; the Olympic office is at 56 Venizélou, ☏ 22 270. **Ferries** run twice a week to Kárpathos and Kássos, Ag. Nikólaos and Pireaus, and once a week to Chálki, Sými and Rhodes (port authority, ☏ 22 310). The bus station is at the south end of the water front, ☏ 22 272, and has frequent connections to Ag. Nikólaos and Ierápetra, and less often to Vaï and Káto Zákro.

Festivals

24 June: large local festival, Piskokéfalo; summer Kornaria cultural festival; **mid-August**: a 3-day wine and sultana festival, Sitía.

Around the Town

Sitía, filled with the everyday bustle and gossip of a provincial town, the lazy charms of its beach, the pranks of its pet pelicans, and general schmoozing along the waterfront is a paradise for lazy visitors. But *la dolce vita* is nothing new here; under the fortress you can see the ruins of a Roman fish tank, where denizens of the deep were kept alive and fresh for the table. The **Archae-ology Museum**, incongruously set among the garages near the triangular square at the top of Ítanos Street (*open 8.45–3, Sun 9.30–2, closed Mon; adm*), has a small but interesting collection of finds from the eastern end of the *nomós*, Minoan *lar-naxes*, a wine press and a cache of Linear A tablets from the palace archive at Zákros, and votive offerings from the 7th century in the Daedalic style. Among the newest finds are from Pétras, on the south edge of Sitía, where a large structure from the New Palace period is currently being explored: it may well be the Se-to-i-ja inscribed in the Minoan tablets. A small **Folklore Museum** near the very top of town on G. Arkadíon and Therisoú (*open Wed 5–8, Tues, Thurs, Fri 9–1 and 5–8, Sat 9–1; adm*) has colourful examples of arts and crafts, weavings and embroideries.

Erotókritos

On Crete, Sitía is best known for Vincénzo Kornáros, the 17th-century Creto-Venetian author of the *Erotókritos*, the island's national epic. A 10,000-line romance, written in the Cretan dialect, the *Erotókritos* is still memorized and sung today to the *lýra* and *laúto*; some shepherds can rattle off thousands of verses off the top of their heads.

The story, inspired by Ariosto's *Orlando Furioso*, is set in Byzantine times and tells of the love between Erotokritos, son of a poor commoner, and Aretousa, daughter of King Heracles of Athens. After serenading the princess Aretousa incognito, Erotokritos is forced to flee Athens after slaying two of the guards the king sent to ambush him. Although Erotokritos boldly returns to win a knightly tournament, the king still refuses his marriage petition because of his humble birth, exiles him, then cuts off his daughter's long hair and throws her in prison for loving Erotokritos and refusing to marry the prince of Byzantium. Three years later, the kingdom of Athens is invaded by the Vlachs, and all seems lost until Erotokritos reappears on the scene to pummel them, unrecognized by all thanks to a magic potion that turned his skin black. The Vlachs' greatest warrior, a giant, challenges him to single combat, and when Erotokritos slays him their army withdraws. Aretousa eventually recognizes her lover in spite of his new skin colour, although he drinks another magic potion to change it back before they are happily married and he accedes to the throne of Athens.

Interspersed with all the action, Kornáros included enough philosophy to make the *Erotókritos* a rich source for *mantinade* singers or others in search of the *mot juste* for any occasion; for example, one favourite:

> *Clouds and mists in*
> *Time disperse;*
> *Great blessings in time*
> *Become a curse.*

If the town beach at Sitía is too crowded, try the sandy cove of **Ag. Fotía**, 5 km to the east. In 1971 a large Pre-Palatial Minoan cemetery was discovered near the sea (fenced in, off a path on the east end of the village). Here some 250 chamber tombs yielded a fine haul of stone vases, fish hooks and stone axes. The hill above is the site of a large Old Temple building that was mysteriously but peacefully destroyed just after its construction, and replaced with a round fortlike building—perhaps part of a coastal warning system; the oval structure at Chamézi would have been in easy signalling distance.

moderate

Denis, 60 El. Venizélou, ℰ 28 356 (*B*) is in the centre of the action, above Zorba's restaurant. **Hotel Itanos,** Plateía Venizélou, ℰ 22 146 (*C*) is a stylish hotel near the park. **Alice**, 34 Papanastassíou, ℰ 28 450 (*C*) is good value, modern and offers Cretan evenings once a week. **Crystal**, 17 Kapetán Sífi, ℰ 22 284 (*C*), 50m from the sea, has comfortable rooms.

inexpensive

Hotel Star, 37 M. Kolyváki, ℰ 22 917 (*D*) offers some peace and quiet, and convenience for ferries; ditto for **Nora**, 31 Rouseláki, ℰ 23 017 (*D*), where rooms have balconies. **Archontiko**, ℰ 28 172 (*D*) is a nice quiet little hotel on the western edge of town, by the whitewashed steps. **Venus,** near the top of town at 60 Kondiláki, ℰ 24 307, is comfortable and welcoming. The **youth hostel,** 4 Theríssou St, ℰ 22 693, is just east of town and again very pleasant and friendly, with kitchen facilities and a garden. **Flisvos**, by the bus station at 4 K. Karamalí, ℰ 22 422 (*D*) is simple, and has sea views.

Sitía is a civilized place, where *mézedes* automatically come with your drink. **Zorba's** has a wonderful location on the water, and, although the ready food can look a bit tired, the seafood, lobster and grilled meats are fresh and delicious (*3500dr*); **Remegio,** further along the port, is similar. **Mixos Taverna Ouzeri,** two streets in from the port, serves lamb baked or on the spit with barrelled wine (*3000dr*). For a good meal with a good view, **Neromilos**, 4km east, is the local favourite, located in a former watermill. There's a stylish clutch of bars near the pelicans' house: both **Skala** and **Glyfada** are popular places for an early evening or late-night drink.

Inland from Sitía: Minoan Farm Villas and the Last True Cretans

A plethora of minor archaeological sites are scattered south of Sitía. Most are Minoan country villas and farms, built *c.* 1550 at the time of a Minoan baby boom; from the Pre-Palatial to the Late Minoan period (2600–1600) Crete's population is estimated to have multiplied a hundredfold. One such villa is signposted just off the road before **Piskokéfalo**; and another, more rustic, is further south just before the village of **Zou**. Yet another is in **Achládia**, 5km west of Piskokéfalo; 2km further west there's a well-preserved Mycenaean *tholos* tomb of 1300 BC.

Along the main road south, whitewashed **Maronía** amid emerald terraces makes a good place to stop. Two km further south the road forks for Néa Praisós, just below ancient **Praisos**, the chief stronghold of the Eteocretans—the 'true Cretans' or last Minoans—who took refuge here during the Dorian invasion and survived into the 3rd century BC, in some fashion co-existing with the Dorians, running an old Minoan shrine of Diktean Zeus at Palaíkastro and keeping other ancient cults on their three acropoli. By the 2nd century, however, Praisos was competing too openly with Dorian Ierapytna (Ierápetra) and in 146 BC it was conquered and decimated. Ironically, this last Minoan town was one of the very first to be discovered, in 1884 by Federico Halbherr, who was completely mystified by the unfathomable inscriptions in Greek letters, now generally held to be in the native Minoan language of Linear A (there's a memory of it in the *Odyssey*: 'There [in Crete], one language mingles with another. In it are Achaeans, great-hearted native Eteocretans, Kydonians and Dorians in three tribes and noble Pelasgians.' The Dorian Ierapytnans did such a good job of demolishing Praisos that the scenery is really the main reason for coming: if the foundation of a temple can be traced on the first acropolis, almost nothing remains on the second hill; there's a wall and a few remains of houses, including a fine one from the 3rd century BC that managed to survive in pretty good nick.

The slightly more substantial remains of another long-gone civilization may be seen further south, off the main road, in **Etiá**, a village noted for its lovely setting. It was a major town in the Middle Ages, the fief of the Di Mezzo family, who in the 15th century built themselves a fortified *palazzo*, the most beautiful Venetian building on Crete—once three storeys high, with vaulted ceilings and intricate sculptural decorations. Destruction began when a band of Turkish administrators were besieged here by angry locals in 1828, and a later fire and earthquake finished the job. Now partially restored by the Greek Archaeological Service, the entrance hall, ground floor and fountain house offer a hint of former grandeur. **Lithínes**, back on the main road, is a charming village with the remains of a Venetian tower; the Libyan sea can just be seen below. If you're continuing south, *see* pp.243–7.

East of Sitía: The Monastery of Toploú

Open 9am–3pm and 4–6pm.

This, one of Crete's wealthiest monasteries, is really named Panagía Akroterianí, but Toploú ('cannoned' in Turkish) more aptly evokes this fortress of the faith, isolated on a plateau 3.5km from the Sitía–Palaíkastro road. The first building was a chapel dating from Nikephóros Phokás' liberation of Crete, dedicated to Ag. Isidóro (hence Cape Sideros). The monastery itself was founded in the 15th century by the Kornáros family, and rebuilt first after its destruction by the buccaneering Knights of Malta, and then after the earthquake of 1612. Square 30ft walls defend Toploú;

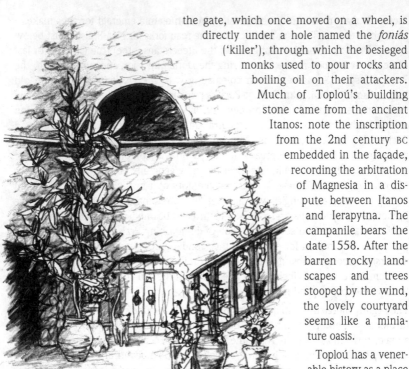

the gate, which once moved on a wheel, is directly under a hole named the *foniás* ('killer'), through which the besieged monks used to pour rocks and boiling oil on their attackers. Much of Toploú's building stone came from the ancient Itanos: note the inscription from the 2nd century BC embedded in the façade, recording the arbitration of Magnesia in a dispute between Itanos and Ierapytna. The campanile bears the date 1558. After the barren rocky landscapes and trees stooped by the wind, the lovely courtyard seems like a miniature oasis.

Toploú has a venerable history as a place of refuge, revolution and resistance, and more than once the monks have paid for their activities. At the beginning of the War of Independence in 1821, the Turks captured it and hanged twelve monks over the gate as a warning to other rebels, although as usual it only made the Cretans mad as hell, and by the end of the war Toploú was theirs again. During the Second World War, the abbot was shot by the Germans for operating a radio transmitter for the Resistance; proud artefacts from Toploú's battles are on display in the museum (*adm*), next to the monastery's icons. The finest of these is one of the masterpieces of Cretan art: the beautiful *Great is the Lord* by Ioánnis Kornáros (1770), with 61 lively, intricate scenes illustrating the Orthodox prayer of Megálos Agiasmós.

Palaíkastro, Vaï and Itanos

All roads on the east coast converge at **Palaíkastro** (ΠΑΛΑΙΚΑΣΤΡΟ), a pleasant village and an increasingly popular place to stop over, with a fine beach a kilometre below, lined with restaurants and tavernas. The first edition of Palaíkastro was down here, on route to Chiona beach, at **Roussolakos**: a large Late Minoan settlement on a plain by the sea, with streets and houses similar to Gourniá. Finds suggest this was a manufacturing town, inhabited by craft specialists. It had no palace and may have been under the jurisdiction of Zákros. In summer, excavations continue apace, but the site is fenced off and you probably won't see much unless you get friendly with an archaeologist. A rough track south of here leads to **Petsofás**, where a Minoan peak sanctuary dedicated to the goddess yielded a trove of votive offerings. From Geometric to Hellenistic times, the inhabitants moved up the hill to **Kastrí**, where in the ruins of a 4th-century BC temple to Diktean Zeus—the same one controlled by the Eteocretans of Praisos—the *Hymn of the Kouretes* (*see* pp.215–216) was found engraved on a stone, although the words hark back to a tradition much older than the temple. Two kilometres north of the village, a narrow road leads down to **Koureménos Beach**, a favourite for windsurfing.

Palaíkastro is the last bus stop before **Vaï** (ΒΑΪ), its name derived from the Cretan *váyies*, or palm, Crete's most stunningly beautiful beach, Vaï's silver sands are lined with Europe's only wild palm trees, a species unique to Crete called *Phoenix theophrastii*. As you approach, signs among the 5000 palms direct you to a banana plantation to complete the Caribbean ambience, or you can buy a bunch in the stands around Vaï's bus-gorged car park; the only way to avoid sharing this tropical paradise with thousands of body-bakers is to get there at the crack of dawn or star in the next Bounty ad filmed on the beach. There's a mediocre overpriced taverna overlooking the sands—and if you wonder why people are hopping about in the water, it's because the fish sometimes bite. Of late there's been concern for the palms' health; insufficient drainage and torrential winter rains have threatened the roots with rot. Although there were plans to make Vaï a national park, the latest word is that an English company has recently signed a contract to develop the area. Enjoy it while you can.

A number of small beaches around Vaï act as crowd overflow tanks and free campsites. The three best have a few palms of their own and lie along the path north of Vaï, 1.5km up Cape Sideros near ancient **Itanos**. Inhabited from Early Minoan times (the *u-ta-no* on the Linear B tablets), Itanos minted the first (and, artistically, many of the finest) coins on Crete. In 630 BC, according to Herodotus, the Delphic oracle commanded a murex fisherman from Itanos to found the city of Cyrene in Libya. In later times, after the razing of Praisos, the city was a fierce rival of Ierápetra for control of Palaíkastro's temple of Diktean Zeus, leading to the Arbitration of the Magnesians of 132 BC—a decision in Itanos's favour, as we know from the inscription embedded in the Toploú's wall. The Ptolemies of Egypt used Itanos as a naval station, and the city exported dyes and glass. Pirates forced its abandonment in the 8th century, and also spoiled a 15th-century attempt at resettlement; best preserved of the remains are a basilica and fine cut Hellenistic wall.

The Minoan Palace of Zákros

Open 8.30–2.30; closed Mon; adm.

From Palaíkastro, the road south cuts through a curious purple/porphyry-coloured landscape planted with olive groves and sleepy hamlets to the largish village of **Zákros** (ΖΑΚΡΟΣ). A rich Minoan villa from the New Palace era was excavated by the English archaeologist David Hogarth in 1901, complete with wall paintings, sewers, wine presses and cellars. The villa is a short walk from the head of a dramatic gorge, the stark but beautiful 'Valley of Death', named not for tourists with broken necks but for the Minoan tombs from 2600 BC cut into the cliffs along the way. On foot it's not terribly difficult, an 8km walk down to Káto Zákros if you have reasonable shoes. Softies can take the new road, chiselled into the cliffs, plied by two or three buses a day from Sitía.

For decades farmers kept digging up seals and other Minoan relics by the sea at Káto, or lower, Zákros, and it was there that Hogarth next planted his spade, uncovering 12 houses in the surrounding town before a torrential downpour forced him to abandoned the site—literally a few feet from the prize. This, the **palace of Zákros,** the fourth largest on Crete, waited patiently underground until a Greek archaeologist, Níkos Pláton, began digging where Hogarth left off in 1961. Built over an older site in the New Palace period (c. 1700 BC), the town that surrounded the palace was probably the Minoans' chief port for Egypt and points east, the base of the 'Keftiu' (as the Egyptians called them, and as the Minoans may well have called themselves) who appear in hieroglyphs on the pyramids; the importance of trade for Zákros is highlighted by the fact that the valley could never have supplied such a large settlement with enough food.

The palace collapsed in the general catastrophe of 1450 BC, followed by fire, and was never rebuilt, never plundered; Pláton found over 10,000 items here, including large quantities of unworked ivory, which may have been a local speciality. The discovery of precious cult items suggests that disaster overwhelmed the residents before they could grab their treasures: now most are in the Herákleon museum. Thanks to the slow subsidence of the east coast of Crete (or rise in Mediterranean sea-levels, according to others) the once important harbour of Zákros is now under the sea. If you come in the winter or early spring, much of the palace may well be in puddles.

The entrance to the site is by way of the original harbour road, leading into the northeast court; the covered area is a foundry predating the palace. A corridor leads into the long **Central Court**, which preserves the base of an altar. As usual, there are sanctuaries and ritual chambers in the West Wing, entered by way of a monolithic portal near the altar base. **Store rooms** of giant *pithoi* are to the northwest, while the large **Hall of Ceremonies** extends to the west, with a paved light-well in

Zákros

1 Central Court
2 Banquet Hall
3 Hall of Ceremonies
4 lustral basin
5 shrine
6 archive room of the shrine
7 shrine treasury
8–15 store rooms
16 kitchen-dining room
17 Queen's apartment
18 King's apartment
19 cistern room
20 spring
21 well
22 lustral basin
23 altar base
24 dye house
25 store rooms
26 entrance
27 main road to harbour
28 courtyard
29 workshops

N

front and two windows. Traces of frescoes were found here, as well as two fine rhytons and large bronze saws that may have fallen in from the floor above. A quantity of wine vessels and cups found in the large room to the south led the archaeologists to dub it the **Banquet Hall**. Behind this is the **shrine** and **lustral basin**, probably used for purification, and the unlooted **Shrine Treasury,** divided into eight compartments by brick walls, where Pláton found the precious rock-crystal libation vase in the Herákleon museum among scores of other stone vases. Boxes of Linear A tablets came out of the shrine's **archive**; unfortunately exposure and water dissolved the bulk of them into a mass. **Workshops** closed in the southern end of the Central Court. In the southeast corner, a **well** with worn steps was used for sacrificial offerings. At the bottom Pláton found a bowl of perfectly preserved Minoan olives; they tasted pretty good, too, according to Pláton and his team.

The east wing of the palace is tentatively identified as the **royal apartments**. The so-called **cistern room** behind the apartments is even more of an enigma: was this plaster-walled basin, 5m in diameter with a balustrade and steps leading down to the paved floor, a swimming pool, a fish pond, or used to float a sacred ship as in Egypt? Nearby, steps lead down to a '**well-fashioned spring**', as Pláton called it after Homer's description, which may have been a shrine connected with the spring that fed the cistern. On the north end, a large **kitchen** (the only one found in a palace) and **banquet hall** had fragments of original decoration; in the Sitía museum you can see the little barbecue grill discovered here.

As a protected archaeological zone, the little fishing hamlet of **Káto Zákro** seems utterly idyllic, with no new buildings or big hotels; after the daily onslaught of three or four tour groups, you can hear what the Greeks call *flísvos*, the soft whoosh of lapping waves on the shore. The pebbly beach is fine for a swim or a snorkel, but if it's remote soft white sands you have a yen for, make your way 10km south down the tortuous coastal road to **Xerókambos** (signposted off the new road). The village itself is minute, with a lazy, uncanny end-of-the-world feel: the Minoans not surprisingly had a peak sanctuary in the mountains above. There are roads that go inland from here, but they're of the kind that can chew up the suspension of a cheap rental car.

✆ *(0843–)*   ***Where to Stay and Eating Out***

Palaíkastro

Hotel Hellas, near the central square, ✆ 61 240 (*B; exp*) is the most comfortable. *Open all year.* **Marina Village**, below the village and 500m from the sea, ✆ 61 284 (*C; mod*) is a little resort complex with its own restaurant, pool and tennis courts. **Hotel Thalia**, ✆ 61 448 (*D; mod*) is on a side street, smothered in bougainvillaea. *Open April–Oct.* Many people rent rooms; a municipal tourist office on the main street can help you out.

Zákros

In the upper village, **Hotel Zákros**, ✆ 93 379 (*C; mod*) is small, a bit frayed at the edges, and open all year. In the summer there are a few rooms to let along the road to Káto Zákro, and about 50 beds scattered in the various rent-rooms near the sea that are in great demand, among them seaside **Poseidon**, ✆ 93 326, and **George**, ✆ 93 316, set a bit inland. Three small tavernas hug the shore; **Maria's**, serving fresh fish under the tamarisks, is the best, but not by much. Down in Xerókambos, try to book a room at **Liviko View**, ✆ 91 473 (*inexp*).

Ierápetra

By all rights, **Ierápetra** (ΙΕΡΑΠΕΤΡΑ, pop. 7000), as the southernmost town in Europe—a mere 370km from Africa—and main market centre for Crete's banana, pineapple and winter veg crops, should be a fascinating place instead of an irritatingly dull dodoburg with a long grey sand beach and a plastic-wrapped hinterland. The myths say it was founded by the mysterious, mist-making Telchines who named it Kamiros, the same name they gave to the city they had founded on Rhodes. When the Telchines began to foul up Crete's weather, Zeus sent them packing, and the Dorians, to keep things straight, renamed the town Ierapytna. Under Dorian tutelage the city boomed and bullied its way into occupying much of eastern Crete by Hellenistic times, and it was strong and contrary enough to hold out against the Romans after they had conquered all the rest of Crete. Piqued by their resistance, the Romans flattened it, then, to show there were no hard feelings, rebuilt it in grand style. The Byzantines made it a bishopric, but it was sacked by the Saracens and toppled by an earthquake in 1508.

Getting There

The **bus station** is on Lasthénou, © 28 237: there are fairly frequent connections to Sitía (by way of Makrigialós), Gourniá and Ag. Nikólaos, Mýrtos, Koustounári, and Ferma; on Mon and Fri only to Herákleon by way of Ano Viánnos.

Festivals

July and August: Kyrvia cultural festival, in Ierápetra; **July 27**: Ag. Panteleímon, Vianiá; **August 15**: at Kentri.

A Town and Two Islands

Dominating Ierápetra's seafront is the 13th-century Venetian **Kastélli**, a small fort later rebuilt by Sammicheli (*open 9am–9pm, although there's precious little to see inside*); it stands on the south mole of the ancient harbour, once Roman Crete's chief port for Africa, now bobbing with fishing and pleasure craft. Near here, the domed church of **Aféndi Christós** was first built in the 1300s and has a fine carved wooden iconostasis. Behind, in a warren of narrow streets, is a house where Napoleon supposedly spent the night of 26 June 1798, before sailing off to campaign in Egypt; a sign on the door begs busybody tourists to leave the archaeologists who live there in peace. There's a neglected (as usual) little **mosque** and stump of a minaret further on in the old town, and, to the west, a few Roman remains including a theatre. The most beautiful thing in Ierápetra is the Late Minoan *larnax* found in Episkopí, colourfully painted with scenes of animals and a hunt, and the second most beautiful thing is a charming Roman statue of Demeter, both residents of the **Archaeology Museum**, Plateía Dimarchéiou (at the corner of Adriánou and Koraka streets (s*upposedly open 9–3, closed Sun and Mon, adm*).

All in all, the best thing to do in Ierápetra is leave—take Thethelatákis' caique or one of several other excursions out to the golden sands of **Nisos Chrisí** (or Gaidouronísi, or 'Donkey Island'), an uninhabited islet 8 miles off in the Libyan Sea, where one of Crete's last natural cedar forests survives intact. The sea is immaculate and deposits seashells by the millions on Chrisí's shores; in season tavernas by the beach ward off any chance of starvation. In high summer you can also find excursion boats to **Koufonísi**, a remote island to the east, where the seashells were mostly of the murex variety, used to dye cloth royal purple. This resource made it a prize, and Ierápetra and Itanos fought over it endlessly; a theatre and settlement have recently been excavated, and the water is crystal-clear for snorkelling.

Ierápetra ✆ *(0842–)* **Where to Stay**

Modern **Petra Mare**, on the edge of the beach, ✆ 23 341 (*A; exp*) is the closest to town. On the so-so town beach, the brand new, pristine **Astron**, 56 M. Kothrí, ✆ 25 114 (*C; exp–mod*) is pleasant, and all rooms are air-conditioned, with sea-view balconies. **Hotel Iris**, 36 M. Kothrí, ✆ 23 136 (*D; mod*) by the water, with 12 pleasant rooms, is typical for price and comfort, as is **El Greco**, 42 M. Kothrí, ✆ 28 471 (*C; mod*). Open all year round. The **Cretan Villa**, in from the bus station at Lakérda, ✆ 28 522 (*D; inexp*) has rooms in an attractive 19th-century house. The **Ierapytna,** Plateía Ag. Ioánnou Kale, ✆ 28 530 (*D; inexp*) offers good value, while the **Coral**, Emm. Nikikatsanváki 12, ✆ 22 743 (*D; inexp*) is even cheaper, in a quiet neighbourhood not far from the castle, with balconies for each room; if it's full, try the nearby **Gorgona**, 16 Manóli Triadaphillídi, a pretty blue and white pension. **Rooms Leon**, a few steps from the beach on Grannákou (near the Astron hotel) is another good bet.

Ierápetra ✆ *(0842–)* **Eating Out**

Tavernas line the parália along Samonil and Kougoumoutzáki, on either side of the fort. The great favourite is **Napoleon**, on the waterfront, with authentic Greek and Cretan food. Fresh fish (the owner has his own caique) and varieties of snails are specialities (*around 4000dr for fish*); **Kyknos** by the sea and fortress is good too. Near the town beach, **Siciliana**, ✆ 24 185, has a real pizza oven that produces a good honest pie. The local favourite is a small no-name restaurant grill in the little square by the mosque (*2500dr for a full* *meal*). **Lambrakis**, 1km east, © 23 393, has meat and fish grills, and delicious *myzithropitákia* (Cretan cheese pies).

Along the Costa Plastica

Sardinia has its Costa Smeralda, Spain its Costa Dorada and France its Côte d'Azur, so it seems only fair that Crete should take the public relations bull by the horns and flaunt the greatest assests of its southeasternmost coast: sand and plastic, the latter to force endless fields of tomatoes to redden before their time. Ierápetra's most recent claim to fame, after all, is its recycling plant, cranked up in 1994 and capable of dealing with 1,200,000 kilos of discarded plastic a year.

West of Ierápetra, the Costa Plastica is metaphysically dull in its featureless anomie. The first place that might tempt you to put on the brakes is Gra Lygiá, to find relief in the coastal hills, where pretty villages such as **Kalamáfka** have a sense of place; the hill just above it is said to be the only spot on Crete where you can see both the Libyan and Cretan seas. The churches at **Anatolí** and the hill town of **Máles** have important icon collections garnered from the numerous abandoned monasteries of the area. If you fancy a day's trek, follow the riverbed down from Máles to Mýrtos, after taking in Máles' frescoed church, Panagía Messochorítissa (1431). En route, there's another Byzantine church, Ag. Geórgios, in a ruined village.

West of Gra Lygiá there's a beach with a plastic hinterland at **Ammoudáres**. Things were no doubt prettier back in the days when the early Minoans lived further west, at Néa Mýrtos, a site better known as **Fournoú Korifí**. In 1968 the British School excavated this Minoan proto-town of close to 100 rooms, occupied in two periods between 2600 and 2100 BC, when it was destroyed by fire and never re-inhabited. Finds at Fournoú Korifí have proved vital in reconstructing daily life in the Pre-Palatial period; located, perhaps for defensive purposes, on a dry hillside, the first conclusion is that the inhabitants must have spent a lot of time fetching water. The small quantity of precious imported goods such as metal, obsidian blades from the island of Mílos and stone vases from Mochlós suggest that such valuables were exchanged as dowries or gifts. Cereals, grape pips and olive stones and the bones of cattle, goats and sheep confirm that the essentials of the Cretan diet were already established; the oldest known potter's wheel in the Aegean was found here, from 2500 BC, with discs which were turned by the potter's hands, predating the later, spindle-turned wheels. Some rooms were decorated with coloured plaster. Studying the find-places of the storage vessels and the cooking and dining areas, it is estimated that the population ranged between 25 and 30 people in five families, supporting the theory that the nuclear family may have been the essential unit of Early Minoan times. The shrine at Fournoú Korifí is one of the oldest on Crete and yielded the long-necked terracotta Goddess of Mýrtos in the Ag. Nikólaos museum.

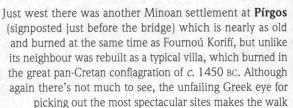

FISHERMAN

Just west there was another Minoan settlement at **Pírgos** (signposted just before the bridge) which is nearly as old and burned at the same time as Fournoú Korifí, but unlike its neighbour was rebuilt as a typical villa, which burned in the great pan-Cretan conflagration of *c.* 1450 BC. Although again there's not much to see, the unfailing Greek eye for picking out the most spectacular sites makes the walk up worthwhile. Further west, **Mýrtos** is the one place along this coast where you may well want to linger: although burned by the Germans it was rebuilt as it had been, with a good deal of charm and atmosphere thrown in—the way a Cretan fishing village is supposed to be. The beach is clean but shingly.

Where to Stay and Eating Out

There are plenty of rooms to rent along the tree-lined lanes, and one hotel, the **Myrtos**, ✆ 51 226 (*C*), with a good restaurant.

East of Ierápetra

Every year new developments sprout up along the Costa Plastica east of Ierápetra. Old houses at the abandoned village of **Koutsounári** have been restored to rent out to visitors, near the dull beach resort at **Férma**; **Ag. Fotiá**, off the main road to the east, is far more attractive, with a good beach and plenty of cheap rooms. Just east of here things improve, with a much battered and burned pine forest that is nevertheless slated to become a national park, the **Dásakis Butterfly Gorge**; true to its name, it is a favourite late spring and summer haunt for several species of butterflies as well as a wide variety of birds, including wild flamingoes.

The best beach of all is further east, at **Makrigialós**, with fine sand and shallow waters safe for young children, although it has attracted some oversized hotel development that has obliterated much of its charm. A sign from the road directs you towards yet another large Minoan villa that burned around 1450 BC.

From Makrigialós the main highway heads north to Sitía, while the rough coastal road leads to **Kaló Néro**, with more greenhouses, a pebbly beach and a 14th-century church of the Panagía with faded frescoes. This is all that survives of the original possessions of **Moní Kápsa** before it was destroyed by pirates. In the mid-19th century it was rebuilt over the road at the end of a wild ravine, its white walls part of the austere cliff draped with cascades of prickly pears. The man responsible for all this was known as Gerontogiánnis ('Old John'), a charismatic anchorite who never learned to read and never had any official statues in the Orthodox church, but who remains locally legendary (and locally canonized) for his defiance of the Turks, faith-healing, and the occasional posthumous miracle. You can pay your respects to his relics in the church, or in the nearby cave where he was wont to retire. There's a good road and an excellent beach, a few tavernas and acres more dingy plastic further east, at **Goúdouros.**

Where to Stay and Eating Out

Lyktos Beach Hotel, ☏ (0842) 61 480, ✉ 61 318 (*A; lux*) is the queen of the resort hotels here, 7km east of Ierápetra, on a lovely beach, offering seven floodlit tennis courts, watersports, gymnasium, sauna, jacuzzi, basketball and volleyball courts, children's pool, three restaurants, nightclub and piano bar. 'Let yourself be pampered' is their slogan. All rooms are air-conditioned and have their own balcony or terrace. **Sunwing** much further away at Makrigialós, ☏ (0843) 51 621 (*A; lux*) is in a similar vein; **Messodokia,** ☏ (0843) 51 433 (*D; mod–inexp*) at Makrigialós is one of the few reasonably priced choices. **Koutsounári Camping** is the coast's one organized campsite, ☏ (0842) 61 213. In Férma, **Elena Taverna,** ☏ (0842) 61 244, serves good food in a lovely garden setting overlooking the sea. Further east, **Taverna Achlia** in the village of the same name is a simple place with a deep shady terrace.

The Cretan Police Blotter

This is the end, and if you've come this far you deserve to know what's really going on in Crete. A look through the newspapers reveals the usual Greek island woes: an appalling accident rate on the roads, several robberies a week (jewellery stores, hotels and bars seem to be the most vulnerable), round-ups of illegal workers (mostly Russian and Romanian bar hostesses), forest fires (usually arson) and the occasional rape case, although these are still very rare by Western standards. A surprising number of Cretans go to prison for following in the footsteps of the Minoans— growing opium and hashish. Germans get caught practising black magic or smuggling antiquities; one, found to have 300 Minoan artefacts in his house, claimed 'they came from the town dump'. A Cretan behind on his car payments tried to rob a bank with a rubber hand grenade. Five British tourists a year fall out of windows. *Rakí* is put in the baby's formula instead of water. Every Easter, over-enthusiastic celebrants of Christ's resurrection from the dead blow themselves up with fireworks and dynamite. Tons of illegal *rakí* are seized every autumn. In December it's raids on illegal gambling dens; Cretans just can't help wagering a few million drachmas just before the New Year to test their luck.

As is always the case in Greece, however, the worst problems on Crete are caused by other Cretans. In Ammoudáres, a mayor refused to attend an important feast day because the priest supported his rival in the last elections. Hotheads, especially in the western half of the island, have a tendency to resort to their *karlofíli* (from 'Carlo e Figli', the Italian rifle manufacturers) in disputes, especially over land: 'Shoot-out at the OK Kafenéion' scream the headlines. Although economy depends to a large degree on tourism, Cretans seem to have a knack for peak-season strikes at the airport and archaeological sites; at least once a month it seems a group of tourists is laid low with dodgy *taramosalata*, cheese or *souvlakia*; there are complaints about hotel rip-offs. One recent article in the weekly *Kriti News* was headlined 'Traders 'tie' Tourists to Port', an unseemly, petty stunt staged by 70 shopkeepers in Réthymnon, who set fire to the tyres around the dockside to keep tourists and their money leaving on a day trip to Santoríni. 'Surely action should be taken,' the paper fumed, and then sighed, 'Although a plea of insanity would automatically be accepted and the case dismissed.'

CYPRESS TREE

The Flora and Fauna of Crete

Crete, small as it is, has nearly a continent's worth of different environments, habitats and micro-climates. Some rare native Cretan animals survive, if just barely: Cretan horses (*Kritikos ihnilatis*), the Cretan spiny mouse, Cretan bees (*Kritiki melissa*) and perhaps most famous of all, the long horned wild goat (or ibex), locally known as the *kri-kri*. A favourite motif in Minoan art, it now survives mainly on offshore island refuges and in Samariá National Park, although even there numbers have diminished dramatically in a recent tick epidemic. To find out more, contact the Cretan Native Fauna Association in Oasis Park, by the Ergotelis football ground in Herákleon, © (081) 258 459.

Birds

Spring's the best time to come for birdwatching, when the pleasure of sighting year-round residents is doubled by the many migrants returning to Europe after their winter in Africa. Crete's mountains are one of the last bastions of the enormous, unforgettable lammergeyer or bearded vultures, with the widest wing-spans in Europe (nearly 10ft) and the striking habit of dropping bones on rocks, to break them open for their marrow. Smaller vultures, eagles, buzzards and falcons are often seen, floating high over the valleys and gorges. For other birds, an especially good place to look for migrants and others (herons, warblers, marsh harriers, egrets and the occasional pelican) is along the rivers and lake near Georgioúpolis and by Moní Préveli, or near coastal islands and lagoons (Eloúnda and Elafonísi). There aren't many songbirds, but if you're lucky you'll hear the distinctive 'hoop hoop hoop' of the hoopoe, known as the king of the birds for its crown; there are several warblers in the groves, most prominently the black-capped Sardinian warbler, and, by the sea cliffs, swift crag martins and red-rumped swallows.

Snakes and Lizards

The only snakes you're likely to see on Crete are the ceramic ones, clutched by the Snake goddess in the Herákleon museum. Of the island's four species, only the grey blotchy chequerboard cat snake is poisonous, but as its venemous fangs are at the back of its mouth it can do you no harm. The most spectacular reptile is the Balkan green lizard, half a metre long and emerald-green; smaller lizards and geckos, and more elusive chameleons, are present in the woodlands and brush. Loggerhead sea turtles have established nests on the sandy beaches of Mátala, Chaniá and Réthymnon and are officially protected, but human economics and the fact that the turtles nest in July and August doesn't bode well.

Trees

Crete has millions of trees, but nearly all of them are olives or citrus. Deforestation is nothing new: the Minoans only made their *larnaxes* out of clay once timber was running low, and 15th-century writers tell of a fire in the White Mountains that burned for three years. Most Cretan trees are typical Mediterranean species, but some are worth a special mention (such as the oriental plane, *see* pp.212–13). In ancient times, forests of horizontal cypress covered Crete, the oil prized by Egyptian embalmers and the long-lasting wood by Minoan palace builders; depletion continued apace until 1414 when the Venetians enacted the first conservation measure, banning the export of Cretan cypress. These days you're far more likely to see tall, slender Italian cypresses, planted for ornament, but Chrissí Island, south of Ierápetra, has the last big stand of native trees; other impressive specimens are in the White Mountains. Vái on the east coast has Europe's only wild date palm grove, although tall Calabrian pines are the main species by the sea and coastal mountains, especially in the south; east of Ierápetra, efforts are under way to protect the last native stand that stretches from the mountains to the sea. The little evergreen maple, which grows as high as 1600m, provides the first colour in autumn, the red that made it sacred to Ares, the god of war. Red is associated with another evergreen, the kermes oak, the host of the coccus, an insect long used to extract red dye; the Greeks say Theseus used it to dye his sail when he sailed to Crete to kill the Minotaur. Rarer by far is the short, deciduous Zelkova that blooms in May and June, once used by Cretan shepherds to carve their crooks; there are only four species of Zelkova in the world, and Crete has a few of the only kind that grows in Europe.

Flowers

Yellow anemones and white arum lilies, blue campanulas and mauve cyclamens cover the hills and mountains in spring, and as summer approaches, the little white star flowers of asphodel spill over the hills...yet most tourists only see Crete as dehydrated and sunburnt as they feel at the end of an afternoon on the beach, never suspecting that wild flowers are one of the island's crowning glories.

Some 1500 different species, including 130 endemics, unique to Crete, brighten the landscape in the spring with all the intensity of 1950s Technicolor. The hot dry summers force the flowers to bloom at the same time, in general between March to June. If you come earlier you'll find the first flowers along the coast, especially in the arid east; if you come later, you can still find a fair amount of blooms by heading into the mountains, especially the Omalós and Lassíthi plateaus, the Amári valley, and the plain above Anógia. Some unusual Cretan flowers are especially fascinating: *chasmophytes* grow safe from predators and competition, in impossible niches or sucking the bare walls of the gorges. *Xerophytes* adapted to the dry, hot climate by developing fleshy, water-storing leaves. The wild orchids trick insects into their boudoirs to pollenate them, and deserve a book to themselves (and have one, *Orchids of Crete,* by Christos and Antonios Alibertis). An excellent general field guide to pack is *Flowers of Greece* by Anthony Huxley (Hogarth Press).

Early bloomers include yellow spiked Cretan mullein, the first flower of winter (but only in the west), Cretan ricotia on pebbly wastelands and the delicate Cretan tulip, green outside with white-rosy petals inside, which grows at low altitudes and blooms January–June. Mountain crocuses burst open just as the snows melt, including the superb, large white and violet striped Sieber's crocus in subalpine regions, the source of saffron, prized by the Minoans and everyone since; it requires over 100,000 flowers to make a kilo. Another valuable flower is the pink and white Cretan cistus, or rock rose, which blooms on hillsides from March to May. You can see one in the blue bird fresco from Knossós; the balsam, used for ointments, perfumes and incense in ancient times (it's called *ponikijo,* or Phoenician incense, on Linear B tablets) was harvested by plucking the sticky stuff from goats' legs and beards. You may occasionally see women gathering it in with special rubber-edged rakes.

In April–June, you can see masses of little white flowers known as mouse ears . *Anchusa caespitosa* with its long narrow leaves and dark purple flowers bloom in the White Mountains at 1200–2000m, and Cretan calaminth, which likes alpine attitudes, has tiny white-pinkish flowers in June and July. Other special flowers of April and May include Scorpion vetch or coronilla, with round white flowers hanging from the sides of the gorges; Burnet saxifrage (*pimpinella tragium*), a shrub known as Cretan ebony, with fragrant stalk cluster flowers, once used to stuff pillows; and the large white peonies, named for the Minoan god Paeon and reputed to cure madness and nightmares. Wild aromatic herbs, which come into their own in June, include the famous Cretan ditanny (*see* p.202), marjoram, thyme, lavender and Greek mountain tea made from the flower stems of *sideritis syriaca,* another Cretan endemic that grows over 1000m and is a common remedy for everything from the common cold to indigestion.

Later, up in the mountains, look for Cretan squill in white or blue varieties, or shade-loving Cretan symphandra, which has lovely pinkish-violet bell-shaped flowers and blooms in western gorges in July and August, a cousin to the almost extinct purple and white bellflower last seen on the walls of the Samariá Gorge. Typical autumn bulbs come out with the first rains: fragrant sea daffodils and sea squill, with tall spiring white spikes by the shore, and autumn crocuses and cyclamen in the meadows.

7000–6000	Arrival of first people, probably from the Middle East.
2600–2000	Early Minoan, or Pre-Palatial civilization in Crete (artistically subdivided into EMI, II, III and MMIa).
2000–1700	Middle Minoan, or Proto-Palatial (MMIb, II): Crete rules the Aegean.
1700	Earthquakes detroy the palaces.
1700–1450	Late Minoan, or Neo-Palatial (MMIII and LMI), the height of Minoan civilization.
1600–1150	Mycenaean civilization begins with invasion of the Peloponnese.
c. **1450**	Destruction of Minoan palaces.
1450–1100	Post-Palatial period, showing considerably Mycanean influence; Eteocretans keep the remnants of Minoan religion alive in the hills.
1180	Traditional date of the fall of Troy (4 July).
c. **1150**	Beginning of the ancient dark ages: Dorian invasion disrupts Mycenaean culture. Crete divided into rival city states.
1100–900	Geometric Period.
900–650	Geometric and Orientalizing Period: Dorian artists pick up a few tricks from the east. Daedalic sculpture.
650–550	Archaic Period.
550–323	Classical Age.
323–146	Hellenistic Age.
67	Romans conquer and subdue Crete, and make Gortyn the capital.

AD

c. **60**	Titus, disciple of St Paul, begins converting Crete to Christianity.
391	Paganism outlawed in Roman Empire.
330–824	First Byzantine Era.
727–843	Iconoclasm in the Eastern Church.
824	Saracen/Arab Occupation.

Chronology

961	Future Emperor Nikephóros Phokás reconquers Crete from the Saracens.
1204–12	Venetians lead Fourth Crusade conquest of Contantinople and purchase Crete from the share of Boniface of Montferrat, defeat Genoese attempts to horn in.

1261	Greeks retake Constantinople from Latins.
1271–36	Most successful island-wide revolt against the Venetians.
1332	Kallérgis revolt.
1453	Turks begin conquest of Greece.
1538	Barbarossa attacks Réthymnon.
1540–70	Venetians fortify Crete.
1541	El Greco born on Crete.
1645	Turks capture Chaniá.
1669	Venetians lose Herákleon to the Turks after a 20-year siege.
1771–74	Catherine the Great sends Russian fleet into the Aegean to harry the Sultan; Daskaloyannís leads first Cretan revolt against the Turks.
1821–27	Greek War of Independence begins: revolt in Sfakiá.
1856	Crete clobbered by an earthquake.
1866	Another major revolt: gunpowder explosion at Arkádi.
1883–1957	Cretan writer Níkos Kazantzákis.
1898	Crete given its autonomy under High Commissioner Prince George.
1905	Venizélos leads the Revolution at Thériso; Prince George abdicates.
1909	Troops of the Great Powers depart.
1912–13	During Balkan Wars Crete is officially united to Greece.
1922–23	Greece invades Turkey with catastrophic results; exchange of populations.
1941	Nazi paratroopers complete first ever invasion by air in Battle of Crete.
1945	Liberation of Crete.
1960s	First hotels built along the north coast.
1981	First-ever nominally socialist government (PASOK) elected.
1983	Greece joins the EEC.
1990	PASOK lose election to conservative New Democracy (ND).
1993	PASOK's Papandréou re-elected.

Greek holds a special place as the oldest spoken language in Europe, going back at least 4000 years. From the ancient language, Modern Greek, or Romaíka, developed into two forms: the purist or *katharévousa*, literally 'clean language', and the popular, or Demotic *demotikí,* the language of the people. But while the purist is consciously Classical, the popular is as close to its ancient origins as say, Chaucerian English is to modern English. These days few purist words are spoken but you will see the old *katharévousa* on shop signs and official forms. Even though the bakery is called the *foúrnos* the sign over the door will read ΑΡΤΟΠΟΛΕΙΟΝ, bread-seller, while the general store will be the ΠΑΝΤΟΠΟΛΕΙΟΝ, seller of all. You'll still see the pure form on wine labels as well.

At the end of the 18th century, in the wakening swell of national pride, writers felt the common language wasn't good enough; archaic forms were brought back and foreign ones replaced. Upon independence, this somewhat stilted, artificial construction called *katharévousa* became the official language of books, documents and even newspapers. The more vigorous and natural Demotic soon began to creep back; in 1901 Athens was shaken by riots and the government fell when the New Testament appeared in *demotikí*; in 1903 several students were killed in a fight with the police during a *demotikí* performance of Aeschylus. When the fury subsided, it looked as if the Demotic would win out by popular demand until the Papadópoulos government (1967–74) made it part of its puritan 'moral cleansing' of Greece to revive the purist. *Katharévousa* was the only language allowed in secondary schools and everything from textbooks to matchbook covers had to be written in the pure form. The great language debate was eventually settled in 1978 when Demotic was made the official tongue.

Greeks travel so far and wide that even in the most remote places there's usually someone who speaks English, more likely than not

Language

with an American, Australian or South African drawl. On the other hand, learning a bit of Greek can make your travels more enjoyable. Usually spoken with great velocity, Greek isn't a particularly easy language to pick up by ear. But even if you have no desire to learn Greek, it is helpful to know at least the alphabet—so that you can find your way around—and a few basic words and phrases.

Greekspeak

Sign language is an essential part of Greek life and it helps to know what it all means. Greekspeak for 'no' is usually a click of the tongue, accompanied by raised eyebrows and a tilt of the head backwards. It could be all three or a permutation. 'Yes' is usually indicated by a forward nod, head tilted to the side. If someone doesn't hear you or understand you properly they will often shake their heads from side to side quizzically and say '*Oríste?*' Hands whirl like windmills in conversations and beware the emphatic open hand brought sharply down in anger. A circular movement of the right hand usually implies something very good or in great quantities. Women walking alone might hear hissing like a demented snake emanating from pavement cafés. This will be the local Romeos or *kamákis* trying to attract your attention.

Greeks also use exclamations which sound odd but mean a lot, like *po, po, po!* an expression of disapproval or derision; *brávo* comes in handy for praise while *ópa!* is useful for whoops! look out! or watch it!; *sigá sigá* means slowly, slowly; *éla!*, come or get on with you, *kíta!* look. Other phrases you'll hear all the time but won't find in your dictionary include:

paréa	gang, close friends
pedhiá	guys, the lads
ré, bré	mate, chum, slang for friends
endáxi	OK
malákka	rude, lit. masturbator, used between men as term of endearment
kéfi	high spirits, well-being
kaïmós	the opposite, suffering, sad
lipón	well, now then
hérete	formal greeting
sto kaló	go with God, formal parting
listía	rip-off
alítis	bum, no-good person
palikári	good guy, brave, honourable
pedhí mou/korítsi mou	my boy/my girl
yasoo koúkla/os	Hi doll, hello gorgeous
etsi íne ee zoí	that's life!
ti na kánoume	what can we do!
kaló taxídhi	good trip, Bon Voyage!
kalí órexi	Bon appetit!

The Greek Alphabet (*see* also **Introduction** p.x)

Pronunciation			English Equivalent	Pronunciation			English Equivalent
A	α	*álfa*	short 'a' as in 'father'	M	μ	*mi*	m
B	β	*víta*	v	N	ν	*ni*	n
Γ	γ	*gámma*	guttural *g* or *y* sound	Ξ	ξ	*ksi*	'x' as in 'ox'
Δ	δ	*délta*	hard *th* as in 'though'	O	o	*ómicron*	'o' as in 'cot'
E	ε	*épsilon*	short 'e' as in 'bet'	Π	π	*pi*	p
Z	ζ	*zíta*	z	P	ρ	*ro*	r
H	η	*íta*	long 'e' as in 'bee'	Σ	σ	*sígma*	s
Θ	θ	*thíta*	soft *th* as in 'thin'	T	τ	*taf*	t
I	ι	*yóta*	long 'e' as in 'bee'; sometimes like 'y' in 'yet'	Υ	υ	*ípsilon*	long 'e' as in 'bee'
				Φ	φ	*fi*	f
K	κ	*káppa*	k	X	χ	*chi*	German *ch* as in 'doch'
				Ψ	ψ	*psi*	*ps* as in 'stops'
Λ	λ	*lámtha*	l	Ω	ω	*oméga*	'o' as in 'cot'

Diphthongs and Consonant Combinations

AI	αι	short 'e' as in 'bet'
EI	ει, OI οι	'i' as in 'machine'
OΥ	ου	*oo* as in 'too'
AΥ	αυ	*av* or *af*
EΥ	ευ	*ev* or *ef*
HΥ	ηυ	*iv* or *if*
ΓΓ	γγ	*ng* as in 'angry'
ΓK	γκ	hard 'g'; *ng* within word
NT	ντ	'd'; *nd* within word
MΠ	μπ	'b'; *mp* within word

Useful Phrases

Yes	*né/málista* (formal)	Ναί /Μάλιστα
No	*óchi*	Οχι
I don't know	*then xéro*	Δέν ξέρω
I don't understand... (Greek)	*then katalavéno... (elliniká)*	Δέν καταλαβαίνω... (Ελληνικά)
Does someone speak English?	*milái kanis angliká?*	Μιλάει κανείς αγγλικά?
Go away	*fíyete*	Φύγετε

Help!	voíthia!	Βοήθεια!
My friend	o fílos moo (m)	Ο φίλος μου
	ee fíli moo (f)	Η φίλη μου
Please	parakaló	Παρακαλώ
Thank you (very much)	evcharistó (pára polí)	Ευχαριστώ (πάρα πολύ)
You're welcome	parakaló	Παρακαλώ
It doesn't matter	thén pirázi	Δέν πειράζει
OK, alright	endaxi	Εντάξι
Of course	vevéos	Βεβαίος
Excuse me, sorry	signómi	Συγγνώμη
Pardon? Or, from waiters, what do you want?	oríste?	Ορίστε?
Be careful!	proséchete!	Προσέχεται!
Nothing	típota	Τίποτα
What is your name?	pos sas léne? (formal)	Πώς σάς λένε?
	pos se léne?	Πώς σέ λένε?
How are you?	ti kánete? (formal/pl)	Τί κάνεται?
	ti kanis?	Τί κάνεις?
Hello	yásas, hérete (formal/pl)	Γειάσας, Χέρεται
	yásou	Γειάσου
Goodbye	yásas, hérete (formal/pl)	Γειάσας, Χέρεται
	yásou, adío	Γειάσου, Αντίο
Good morning	kaliméra	Καλημέρα
Good evening/good night	kalispéra/kaliníchta	Καλησπέρα/Καληνύχτα
What is that?	ti íne aftó?	Τί είναι αυτό?
What?	ti?	Τί?
Who?	piós? (m), piá? (f)	Ποιός? Ποιά?
Where?	poo?	Ποιός?
When?	póte?	Πότε?
why?	yiatí?	Γιατί?
how?	pos?	Πώς?
I am	íme	Είμαι
You are (sing)	íse	Είσε
He, she, it is	íne	Είναι
We are	ímaste	Είμαστε
You are (pl)	ísaste	Είσαστε
They are	íne	Είναι
I am lost	échasa to thrómo	Εχασα το δρόμο
I am hungry	pinó	Πεινώ
I am thirsty	thipsó	Διψώ
I am tired	íme kourasménos	Είμαι κουρασμένος
I am ill	íme árostos	Είμαι άρρωστος
I am poor	íme ftochós	Είμαι φτωχός
I love you	s'agapó	Σ΄αγαπώ

good	kaló	καλό
bad	kakó	κακό
so-so	étsi kétsi	έτσι κ'έτσι
slowly	sigá sigá	σιγά σιγά
fast	grígora	γρήγορα
big	megálo	μεγάλο
small	mikró	μικρό
hot	zestó	ζεστό
cold	crío	κρίο

Shops, Services, Sightseeing

I would like…	tha íthela…	Θά ήθελα…
where is…?	poo íne…?	Πού είναι…?
how much is it?	póso káni?	Πόσο κάνει?
bakery	foúrnos	φούρνος
	artopoleion (above entrance)	Αρτοπολείον
bank	trápeza	τράπεζα
beach	paralía	παραλία
bookshop	vivliopolío	βιβλιοπολείο
butcher	kreopolío	κρεοπωλείο
church	eklisía	εκκλησία
cinema	kinimatográfos	κινηματογράφος
food	fayitó	φαγητό
hospital	nosokomío	νοσοκομείο
hotel	xenodochío	ξενοδοχείο
hot water	zestó neró	ζεστό νερό
kiosk	períptero	περίπτερο
money	leftá	λεφτά
museum	moosío	μουσείο
newspaper (foreign)	efimerítha (xéni)	εφημερίδα (ξένη)
pharmacy	farmakío	φαρμακείο
police station	astinomía	αστυνομία
policeman	astifílakas	αστιφύλακας
post office	tachithromío	ταχυδρομείο
plug, electrical	príza	πρίζα
plug, bath	tápa	τάπα
restaurant	estiatório	εστιατόριο
sea	thálassa	θάλασσα
shower	doush	ντούς
student	fititís	φοιτητής
telephone office	Oté	OTE
theatre	théatro	θέατρο
toilet	tooaléta	τουαλέττα

Time

What time is it?	*ti óra íne?*	Τί ώρα είναι
month	*mína*	μήνα
week	*evthomáda*	εβδομάδα
day	*méra*	μέρα
morning	*proí*	πρωί
afternoon	*apóyevma*	απόγευμα
evening	*vráthi*	βράδυ
yesterday	*chthés*	χθές
today	*símera*	σήμερα
tomorrow	*ávrio*	αύριο
now	*tóra*	τώρα
later	*metá*	μετά
it is early/late	*íne norís/ argá*	είναι νωρίς/αργά

Travel Directions

I want to go to ...	*thélo na páo sto (m), sti (f)...*	Θέλω νά πάω στό, στη...
How can I get to...?	*pós boró na páo sto (m), sti (f)...?*	Πώς μπορώ νά πάω στό, στη...?
Where is...?	*poo íne ...?*	Πού είναι...?
How far is it?	*póso makriá íne?*	Πόσο μακριά είναι
When will the... come?	*póte tha érthi to (n), ee (f), o (m)...?*	Πότε θά έρθη τό, ή, ό...?
When will the... leave?	*póte tha fíyí to (n), ee (f), o (m)...?*	Πότε θά φύγη τό, ή, ό...?
From where do I catch...?	*apó poo pérno...?*	Από πού πέρνω...?
How long does the trip take?	*póso keró pérni to taxíthi?*	Πόσο καιρό πέρνει τό ταξίδι?
Please show me	*parakaló thíkste moo*	Παρακαλώ δείξτε μου
the (nearest) town	*to horió (to pió kondinó)*	Το χωριό (το πιό κοντινό)
here	*ethó*	εδώ
there	*ekí*	εκεί
near	*kondá*	κοντά
far	*makriá*	μακριά
left	*aristerá*	αριστερά
right	*thexiá*	δεξιά
north	*vória*	βόρεια
south	*nótia*	νότια
east	*anatoliká*	ανατολικά
west	*thitiká*	δυτικά
corner	*goniá*	γωνιά

Driving

where can I rent ...?	*poo boró na nikiáso ...?*	Πού μποπώ νά? νοικιάσω ...?
a car	*éna aftokínito*	ένα αυτοκίνητο
a motorbike	*éna michanáki*	ένα μηχανάκι
a bicycle	*éna pothílato*	ένα ποδήλατο
where can I buy petrol?	*poo boró nagorásso venzíni?*	Πού μπορώ ν'αγοράσω βενζίνη?
where is a garage?	*poo íne éna garáz?*	Πού είναι ένα γκαράζ?
a mechanic	*énan mihanikó*	έναν μηχανικό
a map	*énan chárti*	έναν χάρτη
where is the road to...?	*poo íne o thrómos yiá...?*	Πού είναι ο δρόμο γιά...?
where does this road lead?	*poo pái aftós o thrómos?*	Πού πάει αυτός ο δρόμος?
is the road good?	*íne kalós o thrómos?*	Είναι καλός ο δρόμος?
EXIT	*éxothos*	ΕΞΟΔΟΣ
ENTRANCE	*ísothos*	ΕΙΣΟΔΟΣ
DANGER	*kínthinos*	ΚΙΝΔΥΝΟΣ
SLOW	*argá*	ΑΡΓΑ
NO PARKING	*apagorévete ee státhmevsis*	ΑΠΑΓΟΡΕΥΕΤΑΙ Η ΣΤΑΘΜΕΥΣΙΣ
KEEP OUT	*apagorévete ee ísothos*	ΑΠΑΓΟΡΕΥΕΤΑΙ Η ΕΙΣΟΔΟΣ

Numbers

one	*énas (m), mía (f), éna (n)*	ένας, μία, ένα
two	*thío*	δύο
three	*tris (m, f), tría (n)*	τρείς, τρία
four	*téseris (m, f), téssera (n)*	τέσσερεις, τέσσερα
five	*pénde*	πέντε
six	*éxi*	έξι
seven	*eptá*	επτά
eight	*októ*	οκτώ
nine	*ennéa*	εννέα
ten	*théka*	δέκα
eleven	*éntheka*	έντεκα
twelve	*thótheka*	δώδεκα
thirteen	*thekatría*	δεκατρία
fourteen	*thekatéssera*	δεκατέσσερα
twenty	*íkosi*	είκοσι
twenty-one	*íkosi éna (m, n) mía (f)*	είκοσι ένα, μία
thirty	*triánda*	τριάντα
forty	*saránda*	σαράντα

fifty	*penínda*	πενήντα
sixty	*exínda*	εξήντα
seventy	*evthomínda*	ευδομήντα
eighty	*ogthónda*	ογδόντα
ninety	*enenínda*	ενενήντα
one hundred	*ekató*	εκατό
one thousand	*chília*	χίλια

Months/Days

January	*Ianooários*	Ιανουάριος
February	*Fevrooários*	Φεβρουάριος
March	*Mártios*	Μάρτιος
April	*Aprílios*	Απρίλιος
May	*Máios*	Μάιος
June	*Ioónios*	Ιούνιος
July	*Ioólios*	Ιούλιος
August	*Avgoostos*	Αύγουστος
September	*Septémvrios*	Σεπτέμβριος
October	*Októvrios*	Οκτώβριος
November	*Noémvrios*	Νοέμβριος
December	*Thekémvrios*	Δεκέμβριος

Sunday	*Kiriakí*	Κυριακή
Monday	*Theftéra*	Δευτέρα
Tuesday	*Tríti*	Τρίτη
Wednesday	*Tetárti*	Τετάρτη
Thursday	*Pémpti*	Πέμπτη
Friday	*Paraskeví*	Παρασκευή
Saturday	*Sávato*	Σάββατο

Transport

the airport	*to arothrómio*	τό αεροδρόμιο
the aeroplane	*to aropláno*	τό αεροπλάνο
the bus station	*ee stási leoforíou*	ή στάση λεωφορείου
the bus	*to leoforío*	τό λεωφορείο
the railway station	*o stathmós too trénou*	ό σταθμός τού τραίνου
the train	*to tréno*	τό τραίνο
the port	*to limáni*	τό λιμάνι
the port authority	*to limenarchío*	τό λιμεναρχείο
the ship	*to plío, to karávi*	τό πλοίο, τό καράβι
the steamship	*to vapóri*	τό βαπόρι
the car	*to aftokínito*	τό αυτοκίνητο
a ticket	*éna isitírio*	ένα εισιτήριο

Finding your way round a Greek menu, *katálogos*, takes some doing, but there's a basic lay-out with prices before and after local tax. You begin with Orektiká, OPEK-TIKA; dishes cooked in olive oil are known as Laderá, ΛΑΔΕΡΑ; main courses are Entrádes, ΕΝΤΡΑΔΕΣ; Fish are Psária, ΨΑΡΙΑ; dishes with minced meat, Kimádhes, ΚΥΜΑΔΕΣ and things grilled or barbecued to order are either Psitá, ΨΗΤΑ or Tis Oras, ΤΗΣ ΩΡΑΣ.

Ορεκτικά (Μεζέδες)	Orektiká (Mezéthes)	Appetisers
τζατζίκι	tzatziki	yoghurt and cucumbers
ελήές	eliés	olives
ντολμάδες	dolmáthes	stuffed vine leaves
ταραμοσαλάτα	taramosalata	cod's roe dip
ποικιλια	pikilía	mixed hors d'œuvres
χόρτα	chórta	wild greens

Σούπες	Soópes	Soups
αυγολέμονο	avgolémono	egg and lemon soup
χορτόσουπα	chortósoupa	vegetable soup
ψαρόσουπα	psarósoupa	fish soup
μαγειρίτσα	magirítsa	giblets in egg and lemon

Λαδερά	Latherá	Cooked in Oil
μπαμιες	bámies	okra, ladies' fingers
γιγαντες	yígantes	butter beans in tomato sauce
μπριαμ	briám	aubergines and mixed veg
φασόλακια	fasólakia	fresh green beans
φακή	fakí	lentils
πατάτες	patátes	potatoes

Κυμάδες	Kymadhes	Minced Meat
παστίτσιο	pastítsio	mince and macaroni pie
μουσακά	moussaká	meat, aubergine with white sauce
μακαρόνια με κυμά	makarónia me kymá	spaghetti Bolognese
ντομάτες γεμιστές	tomátes yemistés	stuffed tomatoes
μελιτζάνες γεμιστές	melitzánes yemistés	stuffed aubergines/eggplants
πιπεριές γεμιστές	piperíes yemistés	stuffed peppers

Ζυμαρικά	Zimariká	Pasta and Rice
πιλάφι	piláfi	pilaf
σπαγκέτι	spagéti	spaghetti
μακαρόνια	macarónia	macaroni

Ψάρια	Psária	Fish
αστακός	astakós	lobster
καλαμαράκια	kalamarákia	little squid
αχταπόδι	achtapóthi	octopus
μπαρμπούνι	barboúni	red mullet
γαρίδες	garíthes	prawns (shrimps)
μαρίδες	maríthes	whitebait
συναγρίδα	sinagrítha	sea bream
σαρδέλλα	sardélla	sardines
μπακαλιάρος (σκορδαλιά)	bakaliáros (skorthaliá)	fried cod (with garlic sauce)
στρείδια	stríthia	oysters
λιθρίνια	lithrínia	bass

Αυγά	Avgá	Eggs
ομελέττα μέ ζαμπόν	omeléta me zambón	ham omelette
ομελέττα μέ τυρί	omeléta me tirí	cheese omelette
αυγα τηγανιτά (μπρουγέ)	avgá tiganitá (brouyé)	fried (scrambled) eggs
άυγά και ζαμβόν	avgá kai zambón	egg and bacon

Εντραδεσ	Entrádes	Main Courses
κουνέλι	kounéli	rabbit
στιφάδο	stifádo	casserole with onions
γιουβέτσι	yiouvétsi	veal in a clay bowl
συκώτι	seekóti	liver
μοσχάρι	moschári	veal
αρνάκι	arnáki	lamb
μπριζόλες χοιρινές	brizólas chirinés	pork chops
σουτζουκάκια	soutsoukákia	meat balls in tomato sauce
λουκάνικο	lukániko	sausage

Ψητά	Psitá	Grills/Roasts
κοτόπουλο	kotópoulo	chicken
αρνί	arni	lamb
χοιρινό	hirinó	pork
μοσχάρι	moshári	veal

Της Ωρας	Tis Oras	Grills to Order
μπιφτέκι	biftéki	beefsteak
σουβλάκι	souvláki	meat or fish kebabs on a skewer
κοτελέτες	kotelétes	veal chops
παιδακια	paidakia	lamb chops
κοτόπουλο ψηστό	kotópoulo psistó	roast chicken
κεφτέδες	keftéthes	meat balls

Σαλάτες	Salads and Vegetables	Salátes
ντομάτες	domátes	tomatoes
αγγούρι	angoúri	cucumber
ρώσσικη σαλάτα	róssiki saláta	Russian salad
χοριάτικη	choriátiki	salad with *Feta* cheese and olives
κολοκυθάκια	kolokithákia	courgettes/zucchini
πατάτες	patátes	potatoes
παντσάρια	pantsária	beetroot
μαρούλι	maroúli	lettuce

Τυριά · Tiriá · Cheeses

τυρόπιττα	tirópitta	cheese pie
φέτα	féta	goat's cheese
κασέρι	kasséri	hard buttery cheese
ροκφόρ	rokfór	blue cheese (roquefort)
γραβιέρα	graviéra	Greek 'Gruyère'
μυζήθρα	mizíthra	soft white cheese

Γλυκά · Glyká · Sweets

παγωτό	pagotó	ice cream
κουραμπιέδες	kourabiéthes	sugared biscuits
λουκουμάδες	loukoumáthes	hot honey fritters
χαλβά	halvá	sesame seed sweet
μπακλαβά	baklavá	nuts and honey in fillo pastry
γαλακτομπούρεκο	galaktoboúreko	custard in fillo pastry
γιαούρτι	yiaoúrti	yoghurt
ρυζόγαλο	rizógalo	rice pudding
καταΐφι	kataífi	shredded wheat with nuts and honey
μπουγάτσα	bougátsa	custard tart
αμιγδαλωτά	amigthalotá	soft almond biscuits

Φρούτα · Fróta · Fruit

αχλάδι	achláthi	pear
πορτοκάλι	portokáli	orange
μήλο	mílo	apple
ροδάκινο	rothákino	peach
πεπόνι	pepóni	melon
καρπούζι	karpoúzi	watermelon
δαμάσκινο	thamáskino	plum
σύκα	síka	figs
σταφύλια	stafília	grapes
μπανάνα	banána	banana
βερύκοκο	veríkoko	apricot

Miscellaneous

ψωμί	psomí	bread
βούτυρο	voútiro	butter
μέλι	méli	honey
μαρμελάδα	marmelátha	jam
αλάτι	aláti	salt
πιπέρι	pipéri	pepper
ζάχαρη	záchari	sugar
λάδι	láthi	oil
ξύδι	xíthi	vinegar
μουστάρδα	moostárda	mustard
λεμόνι	lemóni	lemon
πιάτο	piáto	plate
μαχαίρι	mahéri	knife
πηρούνι	piroóni	fork
κουτάλι	koutáli	spoon
λογαριασμό	logariasmó	the bill/check
στήν γειά σας!	stín yásas (formal, pl)	to your health! Cheers!
στήν γειά σου!	stín yásou (sing)	

Drinks

άσπρο κρασί	áspro krasí	wine, white
κόκκινο κρασί	kókkino krasí	wine, red
ρετσίνα	retsina	wine resinated
νερό (βραστό)	neró (vrastó)	water (boiled)
μπύρα	bíra	beer
χυμός πορτοκάλι	himós portokáli	orange juice
γάλα	gála	milk
τσάι	tsái	tea
σοκολάτα	sokoláta	chocolate
καφε	kafé	coffee
φραππε	frappé	iced coffee
παγοs	págos	ice
ποτίρι	potíri	glass

If you can't find these titles at home, the better bookshops in Crete carry many of them.

'Alder', *The Battle of the Trees* (local edition). It had to happen: crackpot explanation of how the Minoans were behind the Holy Grail and tons of other mumbo jumbo.

Beevor, Anthony, *The Battle of Crete and the Resistance* (Penguin). Most recent and concise history

Cadogan, Gerald, *Palaces of Minoan Crete* (Routledge). Good detailed guide to the sites.

Caughey, Bruce and Naomi, *Crete off the Beaten Track* (Cicerone). A good hiking guide.

Castledon, Rodney, *Minoans: Life in Bronze Age Crete* (Routledge). A good summing up of the finds, taking recent discoveries into account.

Chadwick, John, *Linear B and Related Scripts* (British Museum). The story of the translation of the Knossós tablets.

Detorakis, Theocharis E., *History of Crete* (local edition). The only book in English that covers the subject, with in-depth accounts of the island under the Venetians and Turks, by a Professor of Byzantine philology and native of Crete.

Evans, Arthur, *The Palace of Minos* (Macmillan). The four-volume classic that started it all, but impossible to find outside libraries.

Godfrey, Jonnie and Elizabeth Karslake, *Landscapes of Eastern Crete/Landscapes of Western Crete* (Sunflower). Detailed suggestions for serious and not so serious walkers; available on Crete.

Hawkes, Jacquetta, *Dawn of the Gods* (Chatto & Windus). Support for the view that priestesses, not priests, were in charge of the Minoans.

Herberger, Charles F., *The Thread of Ariadne* (Philosophical Library, New York). All about the calendar in the labyrinth; try the library.

Higgins, Reynold, *Minoan and Mycenaean Art* (Thames and Hudson). A fine pictorial survey that whets the appetite for more.

Hood, Sinclair, *The Minoans* (Thames & Hudson). A good general account and plausible theories.

Further Reading

Hopkins, Adam, *Crete, Its Past, Present and People* (Faber & Faber). Excellent introduction to the island and islanders.

Kazantzakis, Nikos. His specifically Cretan books, *Zorba the Greek* and *Freedom or Death (Captain Michalis)* (Faber & Faber) are must reading before you go or while you're there; *Report to El Greco* (Faber & Faber) is an autobiographical/ spiritual quest, with vivid scenes of Crete at the turn of the century.

Khourdakis, Aristophanes, *Wooden Mary: Folktales from the Island of Crete* (local edition). A new collection of fairytales collected from oral sources

Kondylakis, Ioannis, *Patouchas* (Efstathiadis Group). A humorous 19th-century 'anthropological' novel about a big oaf in a Cretan mountain village.

Kornaros, Vicenzo, *Erotokritos,* trans. by Theodore Stefanides (Merlin Press). Crete's (and Greece's) classic epic poem from the Renaissance.

Moss, Stanley W., *Ill Met by Moonlight* (Buchan & Enright). Thrilling account of the capture of General Kreipe by one of the leaders. Local editions available.

Nilsson, M. P., *The Minoan-Mycenaean Religion and its Survival in Greek Religion* (Gleerup). The seminal work on Minoan religion since 1949, but out of print and difficult to find, even in libraries.

Palaologu, Eleni, *Stickereien aus Webmotiven Kretas* (local edition). In German, but the only pattern-book of traditional Cretan embroidery motifs; available in better bookshops on the island.

Prevelakis, Pandelis, *Tale of a Town* (Doric). Nostalgic story of Réthymnon before the exchange of populations.

Psilakis, Nikos, *Monasteries and Byzantine Memories of Crete* (local edition). A new illustrated guided to the churches and frescoes, with sidelights on Orthodox monasticism and Cretan church history.

Psychoundakis, George, *The Cretan Runner*, trans. and introduced by Patrick Leigh Fermor (Efstatiades Group). A unique, delightful 'Dounier Rousseau' account of the Cretan resistance from the point of view of an active Cretan participant, widely available on Crete.

Willetts, R. F. *Everyday Life in Ancient Crete* (Batsford). An easy-to-read account; His *The Civilization of Ancient Crete* is more scholarly.

Wunderlich, H. G., *The Secret of Crete* (Efstatiades Group). Cranky theory that the Minoan palaces were really temples of the dead.

Numbers in *italic* indicate maps or plans.

Index

269

The Cadogan Guides Series

'Cadogan Guides have a reputation as the outstanding series for the independent traveller who doesn't want to follow the crowd...'

Daily Telegraph

'The quality of writing in this British series is exceptional... The Cadogan Guides can be counted on for interesting detail and informed recommendations.'

Going Places

'The characteristic of all these guides is a heady mix of the eminently practical, a stimulating description of the potentially already familiar, and an astonishing quantity of things we'd never thought of, let alone seen.'

The Art Quarterly

'Cadogan Guides are entertaining... They go a little deeper than most guides, and the balance of infectious enthusiasm and solid practicality should appeal to first-timers and experienced travellers alike.'

Michael Palin

'...the guidebooks that are widely acclaimed for their wit, originality and revealing insights.'

Sunday Telegraph

'...proper companions...amusingly written with fascinating snippets on history and culture.'

Woman magazine

'Perhaps the nicest thing about these Cadogan Guides is that they are very informal and relaxed. They strike a happy balance between background and sightseeing information, plus lots of helpful historical notes and amusing anecdotes.'

The Good Book Guide

The Cadogan Guides Series: Other Titles

Country Guides

THE CARIBBEAN & THE BAHAMAS
CENTRAL AMERICA
CENTRAL ASIA
ECUADOR, THE GALAPAGOS &
COLOMBIA
EGYPT
FRANCE: THE SOUTH OF FRANCE
FRANCE: SOUTHWEST FRANCE;
Dordogne, Lot & Bordeaux
GERMANY
GERMANY: BAVARIA
GUATEMALA & BELIZE
INDIA
IRELAND
IRELAND: SOUTHWEST IRELAND
ITALY
ITALY: NORTHWEST ITALY
ITALY: SOUTH ITALY
ITALY: THE BAY OF NAPLES &
THE AMALFI COAST
ITALY: LOMBARDY, Milan & the
Italian Lakes

ITALY: TUSCANY, UMBRIA & THE
MARCHES
JAPAN
MEXICO
MOROCCO
PORTUGAL
PORTUGAL: THE ALGARVE
SCOTLAND
SCOTLAND'S HIGHLANDS & ISLANDS
SOUTH AFRICA
SPAIN
SPAIN: SOUTHERN SPAIN
SYRIA & LEBANON
TUNISIA
TURKEY
TURKEY: WESTERN TURKEY

Also Available

HEALTHY TRAVEL: BUGS BITES &
BOWELS
TRAVEL BY CARGO SHIP
FIVE MINUTES OFF THE MOTORWAY

City Guides

AMSTERDAM
BERLIN
BRUSSELS, BRUGES, GHENT &
ANTWERP
FLORENCE, SIENA, PISA & LUCCA
LONDON

MOSCOW & ST PETERSBURG
NEW YORK
PARIS
PRAGUE
ROME
VENICE & THE VENETO

Island Guides

BALI
THE CARIBBEAN: N. E. CARIBBEAN
The Leeward Islands
THE CARIBBEAN: S. E. CARIBBEAN
The Windward Islands
CYPRUS

GREEK ISLANDS
GREECE: THE CYCLADES
GREECE: THE DODECANESE
GREECE: THE IONIAN ISLANDS
MALTA, COMINO & GOZO
SICILY